Richard Edmondson

Rising Up

Class Warfare in America
From the Streets
to the Airwaves

Librad Press

LIBRAD PRESS
750 LaPlaya St. #852
San Francisco, CA 94121
415-386-3135
sflr@slip.net

First published by Librad Press 2000

10 9 8 7 6 5 4 3 2 1

Rising Up: Class Warfare in America from the Streets to the Airwaves
ISBN 0-9678909-4-2

Printed in the United States of America

Cover photo by Light Touch Studios; inside photos by Martha Enzensperger,
Jan Spence, Andrea McHenry; cover design by Jackie Dove

Dedicated to all those in the struggle
to free the airwaves

Acknowledgements

I would like to thank most of all my mother and father, the late Dorothy and Geren Edmondson; my sisters, Beverly Scales, Judy Rippy, and Valerie Loftis. Beyond these individual members of my immediate family there are those who have contributed enormously—either to this book, to San Francisco Liberation Radio (SFLR), or simply to the liberation of the airwaves in general. These include: Jackie Dove, for editorial guidance on this book, maintaining the SFLR Web site, and for being the most all-around indispensable person I know; Carolyn Blackburn for copyediting; Kiilu Nyasha, for hundreds of interviews with past and present political prisoners and other soldiers in the struggle; Herb Mintz for friendship and for keeping the finances straight; Harry Ashton and his family for the hospitality of their home; Stephen Dunifer, whose technical assistance made it all possible in the first place; Jo Swanson, for being willing to put up with an obsessive/compulsive best friend and a radio station in her living room for seven years; George Perry, for friendship for an almost equal duration; my past lawyer, Luke Hiken; my present lawyer, Dennis Cunningham; Keith McHenry, for revolutionary inspiration; members of San Francisco Food Not Bombs, who shared their recollections with me; Andrea McHenry; Mbanna Kantako, for pointing the way.

Special thanks to Elsa, the greatest dog that ever lived.

Contents

Preface

In the 1980s it was fashionable, amongst those of a certain jocular mindset, to refer to Ronald Reagan as "the Teflon president"—so called, it was said, because "nothing sticks to him." Much the same could apply to the city of San Francisco and its policies toward homeless people. Seemingly, San Francisco can shoot the homeless; it can run them out of town; it can confiscate their belongings; it can even throw people in jail for giving food to the homeless—it can do all this yet none of it sticks. Like a sinner washed in the blood of the lamb, San Francisco, time after time, re-emerges, in the national media, as a city of uncommon "compassion" and "tolerance."

It's perhaps true that this city is more tolerant of certain behaviors than other parts of America. But being homeless is not one of them. Yet the corporate media continue to perpetuate this stereotype. This is not surprising. Stereotypes are the corporate media reporter's stock in trade. However, this particular stereotype—i.e. that the city of San Francisco either now or has in the past dealt compassionately with homeless people—has shown a unique propensity for longevity.

It was in August of 1988 that the city began jailing people for serving food to the homeless. However, in November of 1998—just over a decade later—the *Washington Post*, in an article on San Francisco's homelessness problem, described the city as "ever-tolerant." For those who have endured the experience of living outdoors in this city, seeing such adjectives in the major media can grow nauseating after a while. And perhaps it is just that—a certain sort of nausea—which lies at the heart of the public's anger and distrust of the press.

When the major media give voice to a would-be aphorism, such as "the economy is good," it denies the reality we all see, both homeless and housed alike, with our own eyes. Nothing makes one madder than somebody attempting to refute what one believes to be reality, especially if it's a reality which one has learned the hard way. The fact is that many, many millions of Americans live below the poverty line. What the corporate media really mean when they say the economy is good is, "It's good for *us*."

Taken to the level of the homeless person living on the streets of San Francisco (there are an estimated 10,000 – 15,000 such souls), this problem of reality denying becomes particularly vexing. Compassion? Tolerance? Just what are they trying to say? That the cops who woke me up in the middle of the night last night were figments of my dreams? To be sure, the *Washington Post* article in question, by reporter Rene Sanchez, did purport to show how even "tolerance" has its limits. Under the headline, "City of Tolerance Tires of Homeless," Sanchez wrote:

> San Francisco has become so intent on cleaning its streets of the homeless that it is targeting them with its own distinct version of the three-strikes-and-you're-out laws in vogue across the country: anyone arrested here three times in 60 days for public drunkenness must enroll in a rehabilitation program for six months or spend at least a month in jail.
>
> The crackdown, which has the blessing of Mayor Willie Brown, has just begun. As part of it, police officers are also rousting the homeless from storefronts as they sleep, attempting to drive them out of tourist areas, even confiscating the carts of those who refuse to abide by the new rules. [1]

Post reporter Sanchez certainly could not be accused of being innovative, or of breaking new journalistic ground. Reportorial exposes purportedly giving the scoop on how this or that American city has grown "tired" of the homeless, have been around almost as long as the homeless themselves. But the *real* difficulty here lies in the suggestion by Sanchez that the "crackdown" against San Francisco's poorest citizens "has just begun." The confiscation of homeless people's shopping carts—and other possessions, including clothes, shoes, sleeping bags and prescription medications—has been taking place off and on here for years. The implication that this is something "new" goes beyond merely stretching things a bit; it is a lie.

Property confiscation without due process is of course highly illegal under the U.S. Constitution. But apparently the illegality of taking homeless people's belongings without their permission is of no concern to the *Washington Post*; it isn't mentioned.

Farther down in his story, Sanchez quotes Paul Boden, of the San Francisco Coalition on Homelessness, to the effect that, "This is not the same liberal mecca it used to be." This rather innocuous sentiment, of course, fits nicely with the *Post's* premise that the "tolerant" city of San Francisco has begun to "tire" of the homeless. But again, there's more at issue here than a simple predilection for stereotypes.

Knowing Paul Boden as I do, there is little doubt in my mind that he would have informed Sanchez of the rather historical, ongoing nature of the cart seizures. Certainly he would have taken pains to avoid leaving Post Reporter Sanchez with the impression that there was anything "new" about such confiscations. My guess—and this is only a supposition, mind you—is that such an illumination simply didn't fit in with the *Posts* preconceived notion of what a story on an "ever-tolerant" city "tiring" of the homeless should say—and so it was omitted.

Had Sanchez bothered to dig a little deeper, he would have come away with a far different picture. Sanchez, however, missed a few things. In mid-October, 1998—less than two months before his piece was printed in the *Post*—a stalker, who would later lay claim to being a 2000-year-old vampire, began to slash the throats of San Francisco's homeless. Two men were so attacked in the North Beach section. Both survived, though one was critically injured. A homeless woman, however, did not fare so well, as the *San Francisco Chronicle* reported in a front-page story on November 7, 1998.

> The most recent victim was Sheila Dillahunty, who was killed early October 29 as she slept in a doorway on 18th Street. On the ground near her body was what appeared to be a message or symbol, written in the victim's blood, police said.
>
> Thirteen days earlier, two men were attacked in separate incidents early in the morning in Trenton Alley, off Washington Street. The slasher cut both their throats, and in at least one case a bloody message was left behind. Both men survived the attacks.
>
> Police say that the blood messages were characters of symbols in an unspecified Asian language. [2]

On November 10, police made an arrest in the case, taking into custody one Joshua Rudiger, a 21-year-old youth with a history of mental problems. According to the *Chronicle* report on the arrest, Rudiger "allegedly told police he is a 2000-year-old vampire who uses the blood of his victims to scrawl an Asian language character for death." Further, the paper reported, Rudiger "was arrested early yesterday after a fourth victim in the month-long string of slashing assaults was attacked in Chinatown."[3]

It was good that the police had made an arrest; no one disputed that. Yet from the start, questions were raised about how the city had handled the case. If the first attack occurred on October 16, as the *Chronicle* reported, why did the police wait until November 6 to announce publicly their belief that a serial-throat-slasher was targeting homeless people? And why then only in a two-paragraph press release issued at 4 p.m. on a Friday afternoon? Why hadn't San Francisco's "tolerant" city officials released this information sooner, thus giving those who lived on the streets the opportunity to take extra precautions?

Some of these questions were raised by Paul Boden (the same Paul Boden quoted by our oh-so-astute *Post* reporter Sanchez). Yet even the conservative *San Francisco Examiner* registered some raised eyebrows at the failure of the police to get the news out sooner. In a story appearing before Rudiger's arrest, but after the November 6 announcement, the *Examiner* reported:

> News of the attacks was relayed to the homeless and their advocacy groups not by The City, but by reporters who sought out their opinions after police sent out a two-paragraph press release minutes before 5 p.m. Friday.
>
> "We haven't heard anything from the police or the mayor's Office on Homelessness," said Paul Boden, head of the nonprofit Coalition on Homelessness. "People have got to hear about this. Word-of-mouth is a tremendous tool on the street."...
>
> Boden criticized not only the failure of police and the mayor's office to contact him and shelter providers, but for taking three weeks to establish a link.[4]

Growing a bit self-defensive at this point, police officials told the *Examiner*, and a third newspaper, the *San Francisco Independent*, that they *had* made an effort to get the word out.

"We got the information out," said Lt. David Robinson. "But we have to be cautious not to create a false mass hysteria."[5]

Yet the question remained: had there been a slasher at large preying upon tourists, say, or business executives, or perhaps (perish the thought) politicians, would the city have waited three weeks to make the news public?

Police Chief Fred Lau weighed in on the issue, announcing to the *Examiner*, "Whether you live in a home or on the street we have an obligation to provide public safety. We're not going to differentiate our delivery of police services."[6] Was the chief trying to say that the homeless who lived in the city's Tenderloin district enjoyed the same level of police protection as the wealthy residents of Pacific Heights? If so, the assertion bordered upon the ludicrous.

A slightly different view of Lau's was expressed by the *Street Sheet*—the Homeless Coalition's monthly newspaper, put out by, for, and about homeless people. The *Street Sheet* made note of the fact that throughout the slasher's spree, homeless people might have had the opportunity to find safety in numbers—had not the city deliberately continued its policy of breaking up homeless encampments.

> For six days prior to the Police Department's press release on the afternoon of Friday, November 6, they had known that the slasher was specifically targeting homeless people. Yet they chose not to tell any of our shelters, outreach programs, advocacy groups, hospitals or service providers. In fact, staff at the Mayor's Office of Homelessness said they were never given any information that homeless people might use to protect themselves. And instead of encouraging or even allowing encampments during this dangerous time, the police broke up several encampments. Even after the press release went out, neither the police nor the mayor's office on Homelessness did any targeted outreach to any homeless organizations or advocacy groups. [7]

As might be expected, the throat cuttings, in combination with the dearth of any official announcement regarding the attacks, gave rise to a fair number of rumors. The rumor mill was fed by an additional number of violent incidents, occurring at roughly the same time though not believed to have been the work of the arrested suspect.

> Because these stabbings of homeless people overlapped with the spate of stabbings in Civic Center over the Halloween weekend, paranoia was rampant. Many homeless people thought there had been seven or eight throat slashings; some thought more; yet others thought it was only one or two. Everyone knew *something* was going on, but the only source of accurate information—our government—refused to share it.
>
> Homeless people today are not considered a part of mainstream society and therefore are not seen as a

community. For police officials to tell the media about what is happening at 4 p.m. on a Friday afternoon and then go home for the weekend constitutes nothing more than covering your ass, politically and legally. It also sends a clear message to those for whom homelessness is a 24/7 reality: the pretense of our concern is far greater than its reality. [8]

And what of the police assertions that "we got the information out"? The *Street Sheet* had some interesting information to impart here as well.

After some heat came his way in a November 12 interview with the *Independent*, Deputy Chief Richard Holder felt that since a suspect had been apprehended (on the 10th) and two weeks had passed since the cops had allegedly done outreach to the community, it was safe to just flat-out lie about it. He stated, "The hospitals, homelessness organizations, and others in the community had been alerted by the department about the recent spate of attacks."

After reading this, and knowing that the Mayor's Office claimed Holder's statement was untrue, the Coalition checked with every shelter in the city. Not one had been alerted by the police. Not one outreach program had been given information to distribute, and yet everyone had witnessed people's fear and heard rumors from the street. The only outreach by the Police Department or Mayor's Office was conducted for the benefit of the TV news cameras and was done verbally by a couple of cops. [9]

Interestingly, the above-mentioned Richard Holder, deputy police chief, had, one full decade earlier, led the charge in the city's efforts to prevent the aforementioned distribution of food to the homeless. Additional activities of Holder's at that time included the circulation of internal police memos concerning his (Holder's) intelligence gathering efforts against Food Not Bombs, the group of activists who were serving the food. More about that whole business later in this book. For now, however, some rhetorical questions: What conclusions must homeless people surely be justified in drawing from all this? When authorities cite them; arrest them; force them to move on: confiscate their belongings—even take food from their mouths and fail to warn them when a killer is on the loose; what inferences might the unhoused reasonably draw regarding the *true* motives and intentions of said officials?

A certain insight into this was provided, once again, by the *Street Sheet*:

> Think about this: If three tourists had their throats slit (with one death) with the same drawings in blood found next to their bodies, would the hotel and covention bureaus have been alerted? If three business owners had been found in a similar situation, would City Hall and the police have done their jobs and informed the Chamber of Commerce and other business organizations?...
>
> The crimes followed a clear pattern, with definite evidence, and yet City Hall and the police chose not to alert the people being targeted for death. And what happened? A fourth person got his throat slit, in the same neighborhood as the first two victims...
>
> You truly seem to hate us, yet we are supposed to show respect to you and your authority. Obey the laws you keep creating to control us or get rid of us. Mostly we show the respect *you* think you deserve, but don't ever think we mean it. For this was one deadly public relations game you played that we will never forget. [10]

The above-cited article is accompanied by a front-page graphic illustration depicting a scene from hell. The drawing is replete with flames. In it, a corporate-CEO-type figure sits astride a pathetically bridled sex worker, who crawls on hands and knees as the CEO, his shoes equipped with spurs, rides her like a horse. The CEO is ordering a corporate underling—another white male—up a ladder, presumably in an effort to find an escape route from hell. The sex worker, though bent over and shamefully exploited, appears to be clasping hands with a homeless woman in a gutter, the woman's face partially hidden by a ragged scarf. Behind the CEO, an African-American prowls intently through the inferno, armed with a machine gun, as if hunting for prey. Presumably he might find the CEO a logical target at which to shoot, but he is not looking in the CEO's direction. Meanwhile, Satan, with his hands together overhead and his fingers intertwined, presides over the scene, bellowing in triumph, his mouth drawn in an O, as hell's flames leap higher engulfing the whole scene. The drawing, by artist Art Hazelwood, is entitled, "America: A Prophecy."

At first glance I thought Hazelwood's vision of the future to be a flawed one. While assuredly the rich have created the hell that is present-day America, thought I, they are far too safely ensconced in their bastions of power to ever have to worry about being dragged down into the flames themselves. Then I began to reconsider. Nothing is eternal. It seems likely that the day will come when even America's corporate ruling class—for all their seemingly invincible power—will follow the dinosaurs, the Egyptian Pharaohs, and the city of Pompeii into oblivion. The Book of Revelation, should one subscribe to the Christian Bible, promises a day of judgement in which a "mystery" governmental entity, known only as "Babylon," is destroyed in the space of "one hour."

> And the merchants of the earth shall weep and mourn
> over her, for no man buyeth their merchandise any more. [11]

The potential of the future to hold wars, revolutions, plagues, comets (said to have already struck once, killing off the unfortunate dinosaurs), desertification, shifting global weather patterns, and the like, is far too great for the rich to remain forever in their gated communities safely above it all. So upon reflection I decided that perhaps Hazelwood was right and the rich *will* be dragged down into the flames with the rest of us—though, of course, as always, the poor seem destined to suffer the most.

In regards to Rudiger's claim of being a 2000-year-old vampire, the reaction from the "punditocracy" of San Francisco corporate-owned media was one of amusement. *San Francisco Chronicle* columnists Matier and Ross served up the following:

> So the guy accused of slashing the homeless thinks he's a vampire—nothing new there.
> As Sheriff Michael Hennessey tells us, "We've had vampires before in the jail—after all, this is San Francisco, home of Anne Rice."
> Indeed, just last year, we had the case of Daniel Sterling, who repeatedly stabbed and sucked the blood of his estranged girlfriend.
> Sterling, then 28, claimed that he had bipolar disorder and became convinced that he was a vampire after watching the film "Interview With a Vampire."[12]

As to the failure of police to notify shelter providers and outreach workers of what was going on—the witty Matier and Ross had nothing to say.

At San Francisco Liberation Radio, we had always regarded ourselves as a voice for homeless people. Thus it was extremely frustrating for us being unable to report on the throat-slashings, Rudiger's arrest, and the controversy which made up the aftermath. We were unable to report on these things because they occurred in October and November of 1998; we had gone off the air in June of that year in the wake of a federal court decision which went disastrously against micro radio.

For the uninitiated, micro radio stations are low-power stations (around 100 watts or less) which broadcast without license from the Federal Communications Commission (FCC). In an earlier time, such stations were referred to as "pirate" radio stations. The FCC has considered stations of this nature highly illegal. However, the rapid proliferation of micro radio throughout the 1990s brought about considerable pressure on the FCC to change its rules.

Since 1978 the federal agency had refused to license stations of under 100 watts in power. In 1995, when it sought (and eventually obtained) a court injunction against Stephen Dunifer, one of the nation's more reknowned "pirates," the FCC seemed of a mind to stick to its guns. In addition to hauling Dunifer into court, it raided a number of stations, seizing broadcast equipment, and in some cases carrying people to jail. Public statements in praise of the FCC for its crackdown on "broadcast bandits" were issued by the National Association of Broadcasters (NAB), the Washington lobbying arm of the corporate broadcast media.

However, by 1999 the FCC, under a new chairman, William E. Kennard, had begun to change its tune slightly. In January it issued a "notice of proposed rule making" with a view toward possible legalization of micro radio in some form—and suddenly the NAB went from praising the FCC to publicly condemning it. This condemnation revealed, if nothing else, how incomparably deep ran the NAB's sense of proprietary ownership of the nation's airwaves, for Kennard's proposals were so tepid they were, if I might be permitted to employ such an oxymoron, "moderate in the extreme."

"Don't infringe upon our turf," these gang leaders of the airwaves were in essence saying. "Not even one little tiny bit."

In point of fact, there were, as is discussed more fully in the final chapter of this book, some serious flaws in Kennard's micro radio legalization scheme. In truth, so serious were these flaws that they led some in the micro radio movement—myself included—to speculate that Kennard really was not endeavoring to democratize the airwaves at all, but merely engaging in a public relations ploy. This is not intended as a criticism of Kennard per se, but rather of the system he represents.

Since the passage of the 1934 Communications Act, the airwaves have been regulated solely in the interests of the rich. The consequences of this are that the concerns of poor and working class Americans are rarely addressed on nightly news programs. However, advancing technology has made it feasible to put a low-powered radio station on the air fairly cheaply. This puts station ownership within the reach of small, grassroots community groups with limited funds.

The struggle we are witnessing today over micro radio is in every respect a class struggle. Who will win? The outcome is uncertain as of this writing. But on both sides of the battle line the stakes are regarded as high. The rich broadcasters see their profits as being jeopardized. Perhaps they are. I don't know. I can tell you without a doubt, however, that for the poor it is—just as for those homeless people who awakened to the horror of a knife blade at their throats—literally life and death that hang in the balance.

This book is the story of the struggle for homeless people's rights in San Francisco—and of how that struggle led to the founding of a micro radio station. While I deal primarily with events taking place in San Francisco, I have nonetheless endeavored at all times to keep the "big picture" in view. The injustices faced by the homeless here are by no means unique to this city. Homelessness, as has been often remarked, is a national problem. Yet it is a problem which has been virtually ignored by the corporate-owned media. It will go on being ignored until homeless, poor and working class Americans own and control their own media.

This problem of homelessness didn't start under the Teflon-like Ronald Reagan, but it was certainly under Reagan that it grew into the proportions of a national phenomenon. It was also during the Reagan years, not coincidentally, that the wealth disparity between rich and poor in America began to rise toward the unprecedented level at which it now sits.

Reagan's being dubbed "the Teflon president" was, of course, a tacit commentary to the effect that the media had failed in its role as a watchdog over government. Then, when Reagan's trademark teflonism was picked up by the Bush administration, which in turn lobbed it off to the Clinton team, there dawned the realization that *all* presidents were Teflon presidents. This realization—that the "free press" had ceased to be free—set the stage for the nationwide rise of the micro radio movement.

During the throat slashings of late 1998, we at San Francisco Liberation Radio were busily employed, not in broadcasting, but in drawing up papers to submit to the FCC. By December we were in the home stretch of this rather formidable enterprise, and on Dec. 5 we did it—formally filed an application for a license to broadcast at 75 watts at 93.7 FM in San Francisco.

As applications go, I suppose ours was legible, well printed and what not. However, it requested waivers on a certain required engineering study, as well as on the FCC's rule prohibiting the licensing of stations under 100 watts in power. Furthermore, under the FCC's current spacing regulations there was no room on the FM band for an additional 75-watt station in San Francisco—thus we were also asking for a waiver of FCC regulations governing station separation. However, given the fact that many of the rules under which the FCC was operating had been promulgated decades earlier, this was not an unreasonable request. The radio sets on the market today are of a much sharper sensitivity than those manufactured in the 1960s. The *real* question was this: Why was there so little room on the FM dial? The answer: because of six and a half decades of mismanagement of the airwaves by the FCC—six and a half decades of granting broadcast licenses *only* to the rich.

Consider the irony: here we were at the end of the 20th century. Suddenly the FCC, which has been licensing stations in this country since 1934, considers a rule change which would allow poor people to operate their own inexpensive, low-power radio stations. There's one small catch though—because all the frequencies have been given out, there's hardly any room for these theoretical new stations other than, perhaps, in rural areas of the country. In this theoretical scenario, in which broadcast frequencies are worth a king's ransom, the rich broadcasters are not going to willingly give up their vast holdings. Presumably, neither will the poor be satisfied with the proverbial crumbs for which they have always settled. The stage would thus seem to be set for a class war—fought over the airwaves, with freedom of speech as the prize.

Richard Edmondson
San Francisco, January, 2000

Chapter 1
War
And Peace

Our first broadcast was on a Saturday night at Keith McHenry's house. It was May 1, 1993. We were using a yagi antenna (named, I think, after its inventor) and a 5-watt transmitter. Nobody had told us, however, that you're supposed to mount a yagi horizontally, like a TV antenna. We had mounted it vertically. It was up there on Keith's roof, tall and proud, swaying slightly in the wind, but mounted the wrong way.

We didn't know it, but there were a lot of other things wrong with what we were doing. We were using only a light, RG-58 coaxial cable instead of the heavier, more expensive RG-8; plus, rather than operating with a regulated DC power supply (a device we had never heard of) we were supplying electricity to our transmitter through an AC to DC converter, the cheap kind, that you simply plug into your appliance on one end, and into your wall outlet on the other. I guess the thinking was that our transmitter was more or less just another home appliance, like a toaster, stereo, or electric coffeepot. And in a way it was. But like most Americans, we were dumber than doornails when it came to technology. We had spent all of our lives having corporations supply us with everything we needed. We were addicted to them.

Such an addiction is a big reason why an overthrow of the government and the present order are so unthinkable to many people. Where would we get our food if we didn't have Safeway to go to? Safeway and other corporations rule us not only through the governments they have put into power over us—most people realize that, at least instinctively, if not on a more overtly conscious level. But also through our fear of the unknown: what on Earth, we wonder apprehensively, would we ever do without them? And we wonder this, ironically, even as they are killing us with their toxic wastes and destroying our environment.

One of our main reasons for wanting to do "pirate" radio was to make these things more clear to people, and, maybe, to start people to actually thinking about the "unthinkable." And now we were ready to begin.

Oblivious to our aforementioned blunders, we were very excited. We had two boom boxes and a cassette with a pre-recorded program on it, mostly music, a little bit of revolutionary poetry, and ourselves introducing the various records and artists. Our plan was to play the cassette on one boom box, and listen to ourselves over the radio with the other. Taking up one of the boom boxes, we inserted the cassette. On top of the box was a jack marked "headphones." Into this we inserted an audio patch cord. We connected the other end to the transmitter, which was equipped to receive an RCA plug. Earlier I had scoured a nearby Radio Shack (once again relying on corporate America) for an audio cord with a mini-plug on one end and an RCA on the other.

The sheer proliferation of Radio Shacks throughout the city of San Francisco, I recall now, once prompted one pirate DJ to comment over the air one night, "We'd like to thank Radio Shack for being there for us."

In fact, the national chain does carry an assortment of items important for running a radio station, including miscellaneous cords, adapters, and connectors, coaxial cables, and power meters. What it doesn't have, of course, is the most essential item of all—an AM or FM transmitter, which makes you wonder what the name Radio Shack is all about—maybe it should be called "The Accessory Shack."

***

A thin ray of late afternoon sun fell through Keith's window and then was swallowed by the room's dimly lit interior as we made our preparations. Our transmitter consisted of a hodge-podge of little electrical parts soldered into a circuit board, which in turn had been drilled and fastened into a small, light aluminum box about the size of an open hand. The thing was small. When I first saw an FM transmitter I thought, "That's all there is?"

There just wasn't much to it, at least from the standpoint of width, height, and cubic volume. Looking inside of it, at all the tiny parts soldered to the board—not randomly, but in careful, precise relation to each other—is when I began forming a different opinion about its initially-presumed simplicity.

I was terrible at soldering and still am to this day. Like brain surgery, it's a task for the steady of hand. I tend to be the nervous type, and I was nervous then. For several months I had been working on this project, making numerous trips back and forth over the Bay Bridge, from San Francisco to Berkeley. Berkeley was where Stephen Dunifer lived and had his workshop.

I had met Dunifer in November of 1992 at the San Francisco Art Institute, where he had been giving a workshop on "pirate" radio. The workshop had been only a small part of an overall exhibition and open house at the institute put on by Paper Tiger TV, a collective of alternative video producers. Much of the exhibition focused on the corporate control of information and why the media in America were as bad as they were. No one disputed that they were bad.

One of the things you got to see as you wandered around the open house area was an actual working FM radio transmitter. It was resting on a table and being given an audio feed by a small, portable cassette player. The transmitter was pushing out about a quarter or half a watt. Sitting on a stand a few feet away was a radio. The radio was tuned in to the frequency on which the transmitter was broadcasting.

I remember staring mesmerized, amazed. The thing was working! It was actually working! And in doing so it—or whoever put it there—was committing an illegal act, which gave me a little bit more of a thrill. The display was unattended and the tape, which sounded quite innocuous—someone talking or reading in a boring tone of voice—seemed to simply be playing over and over again in a continuous loop, but it was broadcasting! A sign announced there would be a live workshop coming up on the following Saturday.

***

Continuing the preparation for our on-air debut, I looked at all the parts in the transmitter, remembering that just a few months ago I couldn't have even named what they were. I still didn't know what they did. I just knew that if you soldered them down to the right circuit board in just the right manner, following the right loading diagram, and that if the board had been etched out in just the right pattern, and if you were lucky and all your solder connections were perfect—the thing *might* work.

That was pretty much the sum total of my knowledge about radio frequency electronics in those days, and to this day I'd have to say I don't know a whole lot more than that. This book, moreover, is not intended as a technical how-to guide to get you through the process of constructing a transmitter and an antenna. There are many other books, as well as sites on the Web, which serve that purpose.

What I've tried to do in writing this book, moreover, is to tell why a group of friends in San Francisco who were involved in the struggle for homeless and poor people's rights decided to put our own radio station on the air—as well as to describe the hurdles we had to overcome in doing so and the legal entanglements it brought down upon us (the Federal

Communications Commission turned out, in some respects, to be a much more civilized foe than the San Francisco Police).

***

When I arrived at the San Francisco Art Institute that Saturday in November 1992 the place was packed. Several dozen people had crowded into a small room to attend the radio workshop. Just a few months earlier, the *Bay Guardian,* a local weekly newspaper, had published an article on pirate radio. (I use the name "pirate" radio here because in those days that's what it was called. Today the more accepted term is "micro radio.") The *Guardian* article had been accompanied by an electrical schematic of an FM transmitter. It announced the imminent start-up of a station in the city's Mission district. Supposedly this new station was going to broadcast on Sunday nights.

Nobody I knew had ever actually heard the new station, if it existed at all. But truly in those days, back in 1992, there was a sort of public awareness of the *potential* of such a wildly incredible thing happening—and certainly the mood was right.

A lot of anger still lingered in those days over the U.S. news media's coverage of the Gulf War the year previous. The famous film footage brought back to this country by former U.S. Attorney General Ramsey Clark merely confirmed what a lot of people already guessed: The U.S.-led bombing was taking a horrendous toll on the Iraqi civilian population.

Four years later, after the Oklahoma City bombing   , Keith became fond of pointing out to the listeners (by then our radio station, which we had christened "San Francisco Liberation Radio" was going pretty strong) that, as truly devastating as the bombing of the federal building had been for the people of Oklahoma City, it had only occurred in the flash of one moment and was only a small percentage of what the people of Baghdad went through around-the-clock for 42 consecutive days in 1991.

Noticeably absent from the U.S. news media's coverage of the Gulf War, of course, was any mention of Iraqi deaths. Death and war are sort of inseparable. Anybody with any sense knows that. Somewhere in Iraq, I knew, mothers were crying for lost children, and children for lost mothers and dads. But none of that was showing up on our TV screens. Where were the tears and the wails of grief that had to be rending the air all over what was once ancient Babylon, the cradle of civilization? Missing. Instead we heard Iraqi civilian casualties referred to obliquely as "collateral damage." This "collateral damage" was being kept to a minimum, we were told, due to the incredibly amazing "smartness" of our bombs.

Furthermore, our leaders assured us (and our news media subserviently reported), our bombs were only being aimed at military targets. Every time I heard that I thought of all the "military targets" all over the United States located so close as to be virtually inseparable from the civilian populations to which they lie adjacent.

I once lived for a time in Oceanside, California. Oceanside lies next to the Camp Pendelton Marine Base. The Oceanside Marina, where I used to walk my dog every morning, abuts up next to the marine base, separated from it only by a chain link fence. Camp Pendelton, theoretically, would be a "military target" for any nation wishing to go to war with the United States. I would find it difficult to conceive of a cruise missile landing on the Pendelton side of that fence without killing people in the marina next door.

Where I now live in San Francisco is less than a mile from the Presidio Army Base. The Presidio no longer is a military base, having been converted to civilian use. But in 1991, during the Gulf War, it still belonged to the Army. As literally thousands of other San Franciscans, I do (and did in 1991) frequently walk, bike, or drive through the Presidio to get from one part of the city to another.

Under the rules of war, Saddam Hussein would have been justified in launching scud missiles, say from ships off the coast of California, into the Presidio. Such an attack would surely have killed dozens, perhaps hundreds of civilians. A round-the-clock onslaught continuing for 42 consecutive days would have brought the death toll well up into the thousands or even tens of thousands. It would have killed many children, demolished the Golden Gate and Bay Bridges (both of which would have been military targets), and, assuming some "collateral damage," turned our neighborhoods to rubble and Golden Gate Park into a strip-mined moonscape.

It would have pulverized the downtown freeway system and skyline. Our sewer system likely would have exploded and our water supply would have been poisoned. Our doctors would have been overwhelmed and our emergency rooms inundated with casualties, and, because of the embargo (remember the Iraqi ships off our coast) we wouldn't have been able to renew our medical supplies when they began running out. There would be no antibiotics to fight infection and eventually doctors would have been forced to perform surgery without anesthetics. This is what George Bush did to the Iraqi people. And this is what was missing from our news coverage of the War—the human tragedy of it all. That tragedy was—had to be—occurring on a massive scale. At the time, though, all we could do was speculate—speculate that maybe it was the worst we could imagine multiplied a hundred times.

6   Rising Up

Then along came Ramsey Clark with his video. Suddenly there was no more speculation. Suddenly we knew.

In February of 1991, during the height of the allied bombing, Clark, a former attorney general of the United States, took a professional film crew, including veteran NBC cameraman Jon Alpert, into Iraq. The footage brought back from that trip was made into a video entitled "Nowhere to Hide." It documents widespread casualties of Iraqi civilians.

The story of Clark's efforts to get the film aired on network TV in the U.S. is related in his book, *The Fire This Time*. Why, you may wonder, was it even necessary for a private citizen like Clark to finance his own trip into Iraq to gather such documentation? Isn't this the function of the news media? Wasn't it a reporter's job to go where the news was happening? Not in the Gulf War, says Clark. In that war the news media, with one lone exception, checked out en masse. Quoting from Clark:

> One moment on the day before the bombing of Iraq began best illustrates how the American press covered the crisis. The deadline for Iraq to withdraw from Kuwait was hours away, and standing in line at the cashier's desk of the Al-Rashid Hotel in Baghdad were some of the most famous and highly paid personalities in the U.S. media. A very major news event was about to occur, the biggest part of which was bound to be in Baghdad and the rest of Iraq. There must have been times over the years, as they dreamed of their futures, that these reporters yearned for just such a moment: like Edward R.Murrow in London, William Shirer in Berlin, and Ernest Hemingway in Barcelona. And they were checking out. The media was not going to report what would happen in Iraq. [1]

Alone among the entire contingent of American reporters, Peter Arnett of CNN remained in Baghdad. In doing so, he was able to bring the world news of the bombing of the baby milk factory and the horror of the "collateral damage" done to the Al-Amariyah bomb shelter. Clark says Arnett "fulfilled his duty to the American people and the First Amendment." He adds, however,

> What was revealed about the media and the U.S. government by Arnett staying in Baghdad was worth more than his reporting. Almost immediately he was the center of a controversy over whether Saddam Hussein was using

him for propaganda purposes. Although virtually the entire American media was prostituted as an unpaid public relations firm for the Pentagon, the question it raised was whether Peter Arnett was aiding and abetting the enemy. The inaptly named organization Accuracy in Media sent out 100,000 post cards asking its supporters to call for Arnett to be removed from Iraq, and called his reporting a "betrayal of the (American) troops." [2]

Arnett also ran into difficulties in his efforts to report on Clark's excursion through Iraq. Says Clark,

> When I met Peter Arnett my first morning in the Al-Rashid Hotel during the bombing, he asked immediately for an interview...
>
> "They will only give us one minute," he said. Knowing I was the first American eyewitness to the destruction of Basra, he told me he would ask one quick question: "You've just returned from Basra, Mr. Clark. What did you see?" Arnett urged me to talk as fast as I could to get as much said as possible. I was describing the damage we had seen and filmed, when I heard through my ear plug, "That is one man's opinion." I assumed we were off the air and answered angrily that it was not an opinion; it was an eyewitness account. The voice was that of reporter Reed Collins from the United States. He then challenged my statement that we had seen extensive damage, all civilian. [3]

Clark's film met a similar fate as his interview with Peter Arnett; it was "never shown by the mass media in the United States." [4] It *was* shown, however, to a packed house at the Third Baptist Church in San Francisco in early March, 1991. I attended that event. Approximately 1200 people were there.

Through January and February there had been protests on the streets of San Francisco drawing thousands of people. With traffic disrupted, and even the bridges blocked at one point, the protests were too large to ignore, even by the pro-war San Francisco media. The first official acknowledgement that something truly abnormal was occurring, however, came on January 19, 1991, when the *San Francisco Chronicle* reported then-

Mayor Art Agnos'concern about the demonstrations potentially driving the city into bankruptcy.

> San Francisco's anti-war demonstrations—now costing at least $100,000 a day in police overtime pay—could devastate city finances if they drag on over several weeks, Mayor Art Agnos warned yesterday.
>
> "If this were to continue week after week we could be in a deficit position that would necessitate some kind of emergency funding from a source we don't have right now," the mayor said. [5]

Assuming perhaps that the protestors were mainly welfare recipients, Agnos warned that any future cuts in city services would have to come primarily from social services. Few, however, appeared to heed the mayor's words. On the same day Agnos' dire admonishments appeared in the *Chronicle*, an estimated 200,000 people streamed into San Francisco's Civic Center Plaza—for what was viewed as the largest demonstration in the city since the Vietnam era. Quoting from the *San Francisco Examiner's* January 20 page one story:

> Thousands of people for peace filled the streets of San Francisco Saturday, registering passionate dissent to the U.S. war with Iraq. The march and rally was the biggest war protest in The City in almost 20 years—and possibly the most disciplined. [6]

In the story, reporter Eric Brazil quoted the San Francisco Police as putting the march turnout at 40,000. To many people this figure seemed ridiculously low, and Brazil, to his credit, also included attendance estimates from march organizers, who estimated the turnout at 200,000.

Brazil's story ran down the front page for eight paragraphs, then jumped to page A-6, where it shared equal billing with a pro-war demonstration staged by some 200 people in the city of Alameda. The Alameda story, containing lyrical quotes from flag-waving participants, rested under the numerically inaccurate headline, "'Silent Majority cheers on troops." It did, in fact, acknowledge, seven paragraphs down, that there had been a larger protest against the war in San Francisco the previous day. However, by now the attendance at that protest had dwindled significantly in the minds of the *Examiner* editors, who estimated the attendance as being in the "tens of thousands." [7]

Gloria LaRiva, one of the organizers of the January 19 march in San Francisco, remembers the *Examiner's* coverage that day with a sense of dismay. She estimates the attendance at the march she helped organize to be roughly a quarter of a million.

"The march got equal coverage with a pro-war demonstration of 200 people that day," LaRiva said. "It (the rally) was so full that the BART (Bay Area Rapid Transit train system) in Berkeley stopped. The BART in Berkeley closed because it couldn't handle that many people, it was so jammed. People remember that."

***

My own most vivid memory of a Gulf War protest in San Francisco is of standing with about 5,000 other people one weekday evening at the corner of 5th and Mission Streets. The building at that intersection houses the offices of the *San Francisco Chronicle* and *Examiner*. It was a crisp, cold, late afternoon and several people in the crowd had drums, the reverberations from which had an almost military flavor. The march had wound, long and snake-like, through the downtown financial district, and as it approached 5th and Mission, with the "*Chronicle*" sign looming up ahead, people had begun to chant, "*San Francisco Chronicle*, NO MORE LIES!" The closer the crowd got to the newspaper offices the louder and more precisely in time with the drumming became the chants. Directly in front of the building the procession halted, and the sound seemed to engulf me.

I was floored. I had taken journalism in college, had served as managing editor of my college paper, and had worked for a while as a reporter after graduation. In those days I had held a lot of lofty beliefs in the sanctity of the press as a watchdog over the government and defender of the people. My heroes at one time had been Bob Woodward and Carl Bernstein, the *Washington Post* reporters who had broken the Watergate story. America thankfully had a free press. That free press, I had felt—and had been taught in school—was the only thing standing between us and government tyranny. Those were the 1970s. In those days it was inconceivable to me that I would ever witness 5,000 people standing in front of their town newspaper office screaming "No More Lies!" Equally inconceivable was that I would actually think they had a good reason for doing so.

Most of my illusions about America's "free press" had dissipated during the 1980s. How, after all, could tiny Nicaragua possibly be a threat to the United States? And certainly no thinking person, it seemed to me, could look upon the coverage given in this country to the Palestinian/Israeli conflict and not see the almost absurd imbalance and lack of fairness afforded to the Palestinian side of the question. But perhaps I still retained, that day in 1991, a remnant of some of those old feelings and ideals.

For about 15 minutes the march held up in front of the *Chronicle/Examiner* offices as shouts of "lies" continued to fill the air. During that time, a feeling of being dumbstruck washed over me. The thunder of the drums inevitably drew newspaper employees to the windows of the building. The sight was an incredible one. I watched in amazement as these employees, many of them probably reporters—some of them, no doubt journalism school graduates—stared expressionlessly down upon the angry crowd.

It's my most vivid memory of the Gulf War.

Why were so many people mad at the media? (The anger felt by that crowd certainly was not focused alone upon the San Francisco *Chronicle* and *Examiner*.) It wasn't just the feeling that April Glaspie, America's ambassador to Iraq, had tricked Saddam Hussein into invading Kuwait. It wasn't just U.S. officials professing their outrage over a country invading a weaker neighbor while remaining strangely and peculiarly silent over parallel events elsewhere, such as China's invasion of Tibet or Indonesia's occupation of East Timor. It wasn't just George Bush buying off votes at the UN, or the ugly, Vietnam-like spectacle of the most powerful nation on earth bombing a Third World country into oblivion. And it wasn't even the nauseating sight of Bush posturing as a man of peace while pressing behind the scenes for war and rejecting offers by Mikhail Gorbachov and others to negotiate a settlement that would include a peaceful Iraqi withdrawal from Kuwait. It was a feeling of outrageous betrayal.

People were mad because their "watchdog" had turned upon them and bitten them. The American media, becoming the ever-increasing tool of their multi-national corporate owners, had violated their social contract with the people of America.

***

I think it was the sense of being victims of a betrayal that drew so many people to the pirate radio workshop that day a year and a half or so after the war. Now that I think on it, there was probably also an element of having one's intelligence insulted. I mean, what kind of dupes did the corporate-owned media take us for to think they could hoodwink us so easily? Did they really expect us to believe Saddam Hussein was "worse than Hitler," and other such puerile notions as that? Or maybe it simply didn't matter to them whether everybody believed what they were saying, only as long as some did. Enough to keep things stable. And how many is that?

Probably, at some theoretical point, there indeed is a "critical mass" that can be reached wherein enough people stop believing the corporate/government line as to trigger a system meltdown, and probably, just as surely, no one knows what that magic number is. Will we reach it in time to save the earth? It's the great question of our epoch and the great horse race of our time.

I took a seat in the rear of the crowded room at the pirate radio workshop and looked around. Of those present about half were men and half women. It's fair to say that not everybody was there because they wanted to overthrow the government. Many of them, perhaps, just wanted to play their own favorite music over the air. But looking around, I saw a number of faces I recognized—some from the Rodney King protests a few months back, and others from the Gulf War demonstrations of year before. So it's fair also to say that many were there because they knew what kind of a screwed-up system we were living under and wanted to do something to change it. That was the category I fell into.

The workshop began first with a presentation by Jesse Drew of Paper Tiger TV. While sounding fairly knowledgeable, Drew nonetheless spoke mostly in generalities, and I found myself wondering whether or not he was the real brain behind all this pirate radio stuff—and whether he was the one who possessed the technical know-how to actually make a people's radio station happen. As he spoke, I thought mostly that he was not. Then Stephen Dunifer spoke, and no longer was there any doubt in my mind who had the technical smarts.

Having a conversation with Stephen Dunifer is similar to what carrying on a conversation with Einstein might have been like. You may not know what he's talking about half the time, but you know he's light years ahead of everybody else. I had heard Dunifer's name mentioned a time or two around town—it was rumored that he was doing something with pirate radio. I should have put two and two together and realized he had had some part in the *Bay Guardian* article on pirate radio which had appeared a few months earlier, but for some reason I didn't. It's a big city.

Dunifer was thin and lanky of build, with sleeves rolled to the elbows. He looked like the quintessential Berkeley radical that he in fact was. His straight brown hair was long, well below his shoulders. His beard, containing a little bit of gray, hung down several inches below his chin, and somewhere set in the middle of it all was a pair of wire-rim glasses.

Dunifer once remarked, without boasting, that he could be working in Silicon Valley, if he wanted, making a couple of hundred thousand a year. I believed him. He's the perfect example of a scientist who has refused to sell his knowledge and talents to the highest bidder. These "highest bidders", of course, invariably turn out to be either the government or corporations—which is to say, essentially, the same thing. Instead of prostituting himself to these interests, Dunifer had chosen to make a living helping people with hardly any money at all put their own radio stations on the air. It wasn't making him much of a living. In all the years I've known him, Dunifer has always been several months behind on his rent and barely able to get by. All of this would come much later, of course.

That day in 1992 there was no "micro radio movement." In those days there were hardly any micro *stations* to speak of. Much of the micro radio activity in the country at that time was centered in the state of Illinois, where Napoleon Williams and Mbanna Kantako had, using Panaxis transmitters, set up stations within 40 miles of each other. Both stations in those days operated under the handle of "Black Liberation Radio." It wasn't until April of 1993 that Free Radio Berkeley, the station Dunifer founded, would go on the air, and it wasn't until the month after that, that we would go on the air in San Francisco. At the workshop that day at the Institute, however, all the other unscientific-minded people there with me struggled mightily to make some sense of what Stephen Dunifer was saying. It wasn't easy.

Some people use big words to impress others with their vocabulary. This is not the case with Dunifer. I think he's just so steeped in the language of high-tech electronics that he forgets sometimes how to communicate with ordinary people. Of course the ability to understand someone depends in large part on what world you're from. It wasn't that everything coming out of Dunifer's mouth was a 10-syllable word, but some of the terms he used, for instance, were more likely to be understood by a hardware store owner than by the sort of inner-city-dwelling student/artist crowd that showed up that day. For instance, the word *dremmel* came up a lot. I didn't know what a dremmel was. Then there was a string of names of electronic parts. Diodes. Capacitors. Inductors. Resistors. This radio stuff was going be pretty woefully complicated, I realized.

When the workshop broke up I took a deep breath that turned into a long, frustrated sigh. I hadn't gotten much out of the workshop, and I thought the same was pretty much true for others. The suspicion was confirmed a week or so later when only a fraction of those who had been present turned up for a second workshop—at Dunifer's workspace in Berkeley. Then a third workshop, at which only a fraction of those turned out, came and went, until pretty soon, out of those who had been at the original workshop at the institute, there was pretty much only me—turning up at Dunifer's door and calling him on the phone, trying to make myself as useful as possible without being too much of a nuisance. Dunifer tends to be a bit short-tempered at times. He's also a very private person. My success in getting San Francisco Liberation Radio on the air, I realized later, came with my willingness to "inflict" myself on this man. Inflict myself I did, although not always in a bad way, I hoped.

In December, for instance, Dunifer moved from his quarters into a new live/work space. I volunteered to help. Moving day was a Saturday. We were joined by Berkeley activist Carol Denney, who had recently won a victory in a police brutality case against the city of Berkeley. We attacked the moving job methodically. For somebody who lived alone, Dunifer had an enormous amount of stuff to move.

You can learn a lot about someone by helping them move. Dunifer's life as a solitary technical wizard was laid before us in spectacular disarray. There were tools of all descriptions—both hand and power tools—and numerous metal workshop shelves loaded with books, technical manuals and other stuff, some of it already boxed up but most of it just lying around. But the predominant feature of the landscape was computers. They were everywhere. On desks, on the metal shelves—even the floor, across which you had to step with extreme care just to cross the room. Some of the computers were intact, but most of them lay with their guts spilled out. There was a sort of dysfunctional, lived-in chaos to it all, and moving Dunifer's belongings from one side of Berkeley to the other was an all day job.

At a Mexican restaurant where we stopped for lunch, Carol asked me about the Food Not Bombs Radio Network. The Food Not Bombs Radio Network was a project that Keith McHenry and I had started six months earlier. It involved the production of a monthly half hour radio program. The first program we ever produced had involved the Rodney King uprising.

The L.A. rebellion didn't just happen in L.A. After the four cops who had beaten King were acquitted, massive protests erupted in San Francisco, resulting in some window breaking and a curfew declaration by the mayor. In reporting on these events, San Francisco's media by and large quoted the cops and ignored the thousands of demonstrators who had taken to the streets. In our radio program we did the opposite—we quoted the demonstrators and ignored the cops. We also reported the impact of the curfew on San Francisco's homeless population, and how, throughout the entire rebellion, Food Not Bombs, an activist group Keith had co-founded, continued its on-the-street food serving operations despite the pressure of being under almost constant police attack.

Food Not Bombs at this time was already widely known in San Francisco for getting arrested. The jailing of its members—for serving free food to homeless people—is a social phenomenon that had been going on in this city since 1988. "A strange pageant," reporter Gary Covino called it in a piece produced for Soundprint and which aired on a few NPR stations. The piece was entitled "The Great San Francisco Food Fight."

The curious story of the treatment meted out to Food Not Bombs by the City of San Francisco, is one which I'll go into in more detail later. It's a shocking story for anybody who still believes we have a Bill of Rights in more than just name only, and it offers a telling commentary, I think, about how local, state, and national officials perceive the large numbers of homeless people now roaming American cities—and of how threatened they feel by anyone attempting to seriously organize hungry and homeless people on their own behalf.

The conscious and deliberate political repression aimed against Food Not Bombs by San Francisco officials is a big reason why we started San Francisco Liberation Radio (SFLR) and why we were having our first broadcast at Keith McHenry's house that May night in 1993.

While working on that first program for the fledgling Food Not Bombs Radio Network, I conducted a number of interviews right at the Food Not Bombs table in Civic Center Plaza. I did this while Keith and other members of the group served food. The people who kindly consented to be interviewed, many of whom had just gotten out of jail after being swept up in the police sweeps conducted during the rebellion, didn't, for the most part, know me. But they knew Food Not Bombs. And this, I believe, was a big factor in their willingness to open up to me and tell me their stories. I also discovered that a Food Not Bombs table is a great place for a journalist to go and get interviews. The abundance of bread, bagels and hot steaming soup tends to put people in a relaxed and talkative mood.

This to me was the birth of a new kind of journalism, a sort of "populist journalism." It was sometimes referred to as "new journalism" or "advocacy journalism" taken a step further. It was a people telling its *own* story.

This is what we tried to do in covering the Rodney King uprising—simply tell people's personal stories. And suddenly, before we knew it, we had a half hour radio program that was pretty terrific, we thought, and certainly newsworthy. We had covered angles of the rebellion that no one else had thought of, including those in the so-called "alternative media." which in those days in the Bay Area meant primarily KPFA and the *San Francisco Bay Guardian*.

KPFA has often done a great job of reporting human rights abuses in far away places like East Timor—while often ignoring those in its own back yard. Both KPFA and the *Guardian* had a rather poor record of covering homelessness and police brutality in the early 1990s, though in respect to the *Guardian* that has improved in the years since then. KPFA, on the other hand, has had its ups and downs under the control of the Pacifica governing board, which has purged radical programmers, hired a union-busting firm, and, in the summer of 1999, locked out the entire staff for 23 days while implementing a daily broadcast schedule of canned, pre-recorded musical programming.

Even before the lockout of '99, KPFA had long been criticized for a perceived "drift to the right" that had been the result of the Pacifica Board's influence. If KPFA, under Pacifica directorship, had been genuinely challenging the present order and living up to its promised objective as a "free speech radio station," there never would have been a need for a Free Radio Berkeley. The micro radio movement—at least that part of the movement which has evolved in Northern California—was, to a large degree, a direct result of the bitterness and disillusionment felt toward KPFA and Pacifica throughout the 1990s—a feeling stemming from a sense that the station had abandoned its mission. Revolution, one might say, starts at home, not in East Timor.

Noticeably missing from the airwaves of KPFA in large part were the voices of what Chiapas, Mexico's Zapatista rebels would refer to as "civil society," the citizen groups who were struggling for positive social change. Contrast this with Free Radio Berkeley, where Earth First!, Copwatch, the Industrial Workers of the World, and other groups all hosted their *own* weekly programs.

The *Bay Guardian* is a far different matter. With regard to police brutality, for instance, the *Guardian* over the years has by and large not flinched in reporting on individual incidents of brutality. Its main failing, however, has been in not making the connections between these incidents. A highlight of the more infamous episodes of brutality and misconduct involving the San Francisco Police Department would include the following:

- The choking assault on singer/songwriter Michelle Shocked by San Francisco police officer Bruce Maravich outside the 1984 Democratic National Convention. The moment was captured on film and later appeared on the front of Shocked's album from Mercury Records.

- The beating of United Farm Workers organizer Delores Huerta at a protest in 1988 against George Bush. Huerta suffered 4 cracked ribs and a ruptured spleen in the clubbing assault by SFPD Officer Francis Achim.
- The 1989 incident referred to as the "Castro riot," wherein police carried out arrests, beatings, and a martial-law-like "street emptying."
- The 1992 Rodney King-related mass arrests resulting in the jailing of hundreds who had committed no crime and whose charges would ultimately be dropped.
- The June 26, 1995 attack on a protest against the impending execution of Mumia Abu Jamal, Pennsylvania's famous Death Row inmate who authored the book *Live From Death Row*. In this incident a dumpster fire provoked a particularly wrathful police response. Unable to determine who had actually lit the match, the SFPD rounded up 279 people, including author Michael Parenti, and charged all of them with starting the fire. Charges of "felony arson" were later thrown out and the alleged arsonists were all released after one to three days in jail.
- Murder—from mid-1995 through early 1996 the San Francisco Police went on what probably wouldn't be too exaggerated to refer to as a "killing spree." This spree resulted in the death of Aaron Williams on June 4, 1995; followed by William Hankston on Sept. 6; Edwin Sheehan on November 1; and Mark Garcia on April 7. All were unarmed.

The above events do not take into account the beatings and arrests of Food Not Bombs members dating back to August of 1988. In not one of the above cases have criminal charges been filed against the officers involved, and only in rare circumstances have even departmental disciplinary procedures been forthcoming. In the 1995-96 "spree," Williams died a short time after being beaten and pepper-sprayed by 12 officers in front of dozens of neighborhood witnesses. Despite the savage brutality inflicted upon Williams, the San Francisco coroner's office ruled that the 35-year-old African American had died of "excited delirium" related to drug use. Another fanciful term that began appearing in the San Francisco media at this time, in an effort to explain police-custody deaths, was "sudden-in-custody-death-syndrome," apparently a new ailment just discovered by medical science.

It was incidents such as these—coupled with the willingness of the corporate-owned media to say that these victims of police murders had died because of drug use—that convinced us that poor, homeless, and low-income people in this city needed their own radio station. In every single incident of police brutality related above, the victims were poor.

An astute observer of these events might conclude that the SFPD has a clear and deliberate, albeit tacit, policy of employing violence and false arrests in order to suppress dissent and generally control the population. Yet the analysis of the *Bay Guardian* has always been that the problem lies with a few "rogue cops."

In November of 1996 the San Francisco Police Commission rendered a 2-2 split decision on the question of whether or not to discipline Marc Andaya, the ranking officer on the scene at the time Williams was killed. The split decision resulted in no discipline being imposed. This came as no surprise, as the San Francisco District Attorney's office had previously declined to press charges against Andaya. After the police commission's inaction in the case, the *Bay Guardian* offered the following remarkable editorial analysis:

> The family of Aaron Williams, like the families of so many others who've died at the hands of the few rogue cops who cause the vast majority of the problems in the San Francisco Police Department, is no longer counting on the city's ability to protect its own citizens. [8]

The statement is remarkable because of all the apparent contradictions contained within it. If, as the *Guardian* acknowledges, there are indeed "so many others" who, like Aaron Williams, have "died at the hands of" the San Francisco Police, then it would stand to reason that the problem must be more pervasive than that of a "few rogue cops." And likewise, if citizens are "no longer counting on the city's ability to protect" them, then the same must be true: there must be far more wrong here than a "few rogue cops."

On Liberation Radio we asked the question: Does the City of San Francisco have an unwritten, unspoken policy of authorizing its police department to use violence and false and illegal arrests—in extremely rare cases, even murder—for the purpose of controlling its citizenry? How else can you explain the repeated failure of the district attorney to bring charges in all these cases—or the equally repeated failure of the mayor and the Board of Supervisors (San Francisco's equivalent to a city council) to comment publicly in a forceful, substantial manner on it?

Some might be tempted to conclude that the police are "out of control." I would say it's the opposite. The police—and this is one thing we specifically wanted to point out on Liberation Radio—do exactly what they are led to believe will bring about career advancement.

Contrast the *Guardian* editorial with an opinion piece written by Abu Jamal, which was circulated on the Internet the same week. In the column, entitled "Just Doing My Job," Abu Jamal mentions a number of police murder cases across the country, including the killings of Johnny Gammage by police in Pittsburgh; Anthony Baez in New York; and an 18-year-old black youth in St. Petersburg, Florida. In each case the cop walked. Commenting on these deaths, the Death Row journalist comments:

> In case after case they (the police) are "just doing their jobs." What is their "job?"
>
> There are two ways of answering this question.
>
> 1.   Their job is what they say their job is, i.e. keep the peace, protect the weak, etc.
>
> 2.   Their job is what they actually do, i.e. create social disorder, repress the weak, and protect the interests of the status quo—be a defender of the wealthy and powerful.
>
> How else could killer cops be acquitted when they say in their defense that they are just doing their jobs—and that job is terrorizing and killing black, brown and poor youths? [9]

As Abu Jamal's column shows, the problem of police brutality is nationwide in scope; and it shows that there is far more wrong with the system than that of "a few rogue cops."

***

Despite San Francisco's large activist community, members of that community who have run for political office have often had little luck getting coverage in the "alternative" *Bay Guardian*. This was certainly the case with Gloria LaRiva.

After helping to organize the giant Gulf War protest, which drew some 200,000 people on January 19, 1991, LaRiva launched a campaign for mayor of San Francisco. Her candidacy was virtually ignored by the

Guardian. Instead the paper focused coverage on the five "major" candidates of the Democratic Party. Of these, it gave an editorial endorsement to one: former Sheriff Richard Hongisto. Hongisto ultimately lost the election, but he received a nice consolation prize from the winner, Police Chief Frank Jordan. The latter appointed Hongisto to his old job as chief of police. In its endorsement of Hongisto, the *Guardian* cited the record of incumbent Mayor Art Agnos, who had run as a liberal but had swung to the right upon taking office. Said the paper,

> The political shift Art Agnos went through, once he had attained the mayor's office, is a danger with any politician. But unlike any of the other challengers, Richard Hongisto has a long track record that makes that kind of shift unlikely. [10]

Slightly over six months after that editorial appeared, came the Rodney King Rebellion, during which Hongisto and Jordan, acting practically in tandem, declared a "state of emergency," imposed a curfew, and essentially placed certain areas of the city under martial law. The *Guardian* responded to these rather draconian acts with a story under the headline, "Hongisto: Knock it off, folks." According to the article,

> Hongisto said the protests were scaring away tourists and urged demonstrators not to continue. "Some people are mad because they didn't get to make a speech," he said. "Well, they're going to have to make it another day." [11]

Those who claimed they had been arrested while engaged in some activity other than protesting were accused by Hongisto of "lying." The chief also echoed Agnos' lament of the previous year during the Gulf War: that the protests were costing the city money. Hongisto put the price tag for the Rodney King demonstrations at $3 million.

With regard to the then-current media spectrum in San Francisco, the *Guardian*, one must keep in mind, was at the far end of the *good* side. Over the years the *Guardian* has done some excellent investigative reporting on political corruption and many other issues. The people of the Bay Area are indeed fortunate to have a weekly newspaper of the *Guardian's* caliber. But with regard to the San Francisco Police, the paper turned a blind eye to reality in 1992. For instance, nowhere in the *Hongisto* story was there any mention that, in addition to protesting the Rodney King verdict, people had also been responding to years of unredressed police abuse in San Francisco.

This was one thing which our own program—that first we did for the fledgling Food Not Bombs Radio Network—attempted to make very clear. Now that we had a radio program, what we needed was a radio station willing to play it!

To this end, we typed up letters and sent them out to every radio station in the Bay Area. We presented the program as "the voice of the streets." We offered to make the program available to any station wishing to air it, but we also asked for money to cover the cost of tapes. Not a single station replied. Not even to offer the excuse that the production quality wasn't good enough. Actually, the quality was pretty good, by the standards of that day. We had recorded the program on a Tascam 424 4-track Portastudio, the kind with the mixer and recorder built into one unit. The Tascam 424 was *not* a digital recorder, but it *was* a pretty good quality analog unit by the standards of that day. How we came by that piece of equipment is an interesting story.

***

In November of the previous year Jo Swanson and I had been coming back from a camping trip in Death Valley with my dog, Elsa. Death, indeed, is what nearly befell us all. On a state highway north of Bakersfield a man in a pickup truck pulled out in front of us. When we crashed into him we were probably doing about 55 or 60. He was driving a big, American-pick up with large wheels and a lot of heavy metal on it. We were driving a flimsy Toyota truck with a little camper thing on the back that crumpled like an aluminum can upon impact. While Jo and I were writhing on the ground in pain, waiting for the ambulance, I glanced over at his truck. There didn't seem to be a scratch on it. My truck was totaled, however. We never drove it again.

They took us to an emergency room in Bakersfield where we were x-rayed and found to be okay. Just bruised and swollen. We were lucky to be alive. Some kind people who stopped at the wreck scene followed us to the hospital in Bakersfield with Elsa in their car. It was pretty clear to everyone, including the highway patrol, (and maybe even to Elsa), that the fault had been with the other driver. His insurance company paid our hospital bills. Then when the insurance company told me how much they were reimbursing me for the loss of my truck my jaw just about dropped. It was some two thousand dollars more than I had paid for it. There was more than enough for me to buy a new truck, with plenty left over. We bought recording equipment.

So that's how the Food Not Bombs Radio Network got started—as a windfall from an insurance company. As for Jo and I—there's nothing like escaping death together to cement a relationship. We ended up moving in with each other and eventually founded SFLR together.

***

After we got no reply from Bay Area radio stations, Keith accessed a resource at the public library that contained a listing of public radio stations across the United States. We sent out a 750-piece mailing, once again under the banner of The Food Not Bombs Radio Network and describing ourselves as "the voice of the streets." This time we got one reply—from WCSB in Cleveland, Ohio, the campus station at Cleveland State University. Not only did they want to air the program, but also they sent us a $50 check to cover a one-year subscription. We were ecstatic.

Then two other really great things happened. A friend told us about Chuck Rosina, a DJ in Boston who hosted a program called "No Censorship Radio" over WMBR. We wrote to him and sent him sample tapes. He wrote back with enthusiastic praise, informing us he was airing our material on his program.

The other good thing that happened was that our program ended up on a station in the Bay Area. Ironically, it was not KPFA but KPOO, a small, low-powered station serving the African American community in San Francisco. Keith had gone over there one day to be interviewed about the police harassment of Food Not Bombs, which had been in the news. During the interview he mentioned the Food Not Bombs Radio Network. They were interested in airing our programs. Suddenly we had a "network" of three stations!

As great as the people at KPOO were, and remain to this day, we didn't feel like our half hour program, played once a month there, and at two other stations on the opposite side of the country, was really enough to get our message out regarding the attacks on Food Not Bombs or the many other things about which we wanted to speak. We needed our own radio station.

In those days a lot of very intense things were happening, most of which were unknown to the public. Every day, just about, there were new arrests of Food Not Bombs members, at either the noon or evening meal servings. Occasionally, if someone refused to hand over a soup ladle or something, the police would turn violent.

While almost never mentioning the latter, the media did sporadically report that arrests happened. The San Francisco *Examiner* had even mentioned the occurrence of one rather sorry episode in which the police had taken the Food Not Bombs' food and dumped it in the Civic Center fountain—as a crowd of hungry, homeless people looked on. The homeless people had been standing in line waiting to be served by us at the time. This kind of thing had happened before. What was surprising this time was that it had gotten reported—not, oddly enough, as a news story, but as an editorial, which had appeared in the *Examiner* on May 10, 1991:

Soup in the Civic Center

It's bizarre for The City to be throwing away food when people are going hungry in the streets. The political theatrics over whether free food can be distributed to the homeless in city parks has gotten out of hand. Some 300 people have been arrested over the last three years for feeding the hungry. All but a couple of the charges were dismissed. Recently, police officers dumped soup into the Civic Center fountain as scores of people stood in a food line.

There are several issues involved. The Health Department establishes and enforces minimum standards for food, and those standards must be observed. Mayor Agnos says The City can do better for hungry people than let them eat gruel ladled out of a bucket on the streets, but that is not always the case. Not everyone is served by the existing soup kitchens. [12]

While paying us the compliment of referring to our soup as "gruel ladled out of a bucket," it was nice, nonetheless, that the *Examiner* had finally noticed what was going on in the Civic Center. In reporting (or in this case editorializing) on such things as this, however, the media never told the real story. The real story was that the San Francisco Police had determined to rule the streets by terror and violence. And Food Not Bombs had been especially targeted, probably because there were so many homeless people in San Francisco and the city viewed us as playing with social dynamite. Maybe in a sense we were. But then so were they. But because of such repression there were Food Not Bombs members, myself included, who were genuinely afraid to take food down to Civic Center Plaza and hand it out. For the most part those fears didn't stop us from getting the food out to those who needed it. We're a pretty determined bunch.

***

From December of '92 through April of '93 I made numerous trips, usually once or twice a week, from San Francisco over to Stephen Dunifer's live/work space in Berkeley. The new place was a lot larger than the old, but soon it was every bit as cramped and filled up with stuff. Ironically, it was upstairs over a radio-TV repair shop and fittingly there was a picture of a giant radio dial on the front of the building. The downside of being located above the repair shop was that turning on the transmitter upstairs could —when used with an antenna rather than a dummy load—interfere with the shop's electronic equipment. This meant we had to wait until after the shop's 5 o'clock closing time every afternoon to test out new or newly repaired transmitters.

The workroom was ventilated with skylights, and despite the noise of a drill press and a few other power tools, it had a quiet feel most times. This was in contrast to the chaos, violence and repression that were happening in the world outside. It was in those days that I learned what a dremmel is. A dremmel is a small, motorized, hand-held instrument with a tiny, rough-edged cylindrical tip on the end. When you turn it on, the tip vibrates at high speed. If you press the tip to a metal surface it makes a scratch, and if you press harder the scratch turns into a groove. It's used for etching out design-patterns on copper-coated circuit board. Dremmels, however, were already becoming obsolete in the micro radio movement, even in those early days.

One of the first innovations Dunifer made was the conversion to pre-fabbed circuit boards. These are boards that are "pre-etched" using a chemical process. The process of etching out circuit patterns with a dremmel is slow and tedious. The new boards saved a lot of time. But the transmitters we were building had an annoying habit of testing out fine in Stephen's lab and then failing after I got them over to San Francisco. It was a problem we encountered throughout much of 1993.

Dunifer is a man who tends to waste little time with idle chatter. If you don't ask about something he assumes you know it. It was this trait that led us to launching San Francisco Liberation Radio that night in May with our antenna mounted the wrong way. It's hard to believe that I had spent the better part of six months working with Stephen without learning whether a yagi is supposed to be mounted vertically or horizontally, but it had never occurred to me to ask. I had assumed vertically.

Keith and I had built our yagi in a spare room in Keith's apartment a few days before. We had even cut the three elements precisely to the lengths specified for the 93.7 frequency. But that night we had mounted it—well, you already know—wrong. A yagi is a directional antenna, which means you aim it in the direction you want the signal to travel. That night we had mounted the antenna with the signal aimed directly down into the roof of the building. Presumably that night the signal was fine a couple of feet below the antenna. But this was not where we wanted to be received.

***

Jo and Keith helped me hook up all the myriad of cables connecting everything together. We could hear Keith's wife, Andrea, making dinner in another part of the apartment. The three of us were absorbed in our own task. There was a lot to connect. There was the power feed from the wall outlet to the transmitter; the audio feed from the boom box to the transmitter; the cable going out of the transmitter into the filter; finally we screwed the antenna cable into the other side of the filter. All the cables, wires, and boxes covered practically the whole table.

I looked over at Jo. When I had first met her I thought she was kind of cute, but even more striking, I quickly learned, was her incredible sense of humor and razor-edge wit. She was always saying funny things. We had come a long way since that day in '91 when we had almost died together on that highway near Bakersfield.

Jo and Keith went back a long way together too—even further. Both had helped to found Food Not Bombs, along with six other friends in Boston. This tiny group of eight people later grew into a world-wide movement. A lot of things can sure turn out unexpectedly in life, and I guess for those eight people this counts as one of the most unexpected of all.

Jo had worked as a pre-school teacher in Boston, and with her experience, was quickly able to land a teaching job when she moved to San Francisco in 1991. She didn't know it, but she was about to embark upon a double life as a pre-school teacher by day and a radio pirate by night. In her latter capacity she would spend many a cold night huddled over a transmitter in the hills in the dark.

We plugged in the adapter and power surged into the transmitter. Jo dropped our pre-recorded cassette into her boom box. Quickly, almost giddily, I reached for the radio and tuned in 93.7 FM. There it was! But something was wrong. There was a terrible hum in the signal. "There's a hum in the signal!" I cried, distracted, annoyed.

We spent about fifteen or twenty minutes checking connections and jiggling various wires and cables but could not make the hum go away. I was growing crestfallen. We were on the air—yes—but it sure didn't sound like anything you'd want to listen to very long. You could understand the words, but there was that irritating hum.

Okay, I thought. So we don't sound that great. But maybe we're still getting out there!

"Let's go see how far the signal travels," I suggested, to which the other two quickly agreed. Excitedly, we grabbed up the radio and raced down the stairs of the building to Clement Street. When we got on the sidewalk we paused and listened for the signal. It sounded kind of weak, but it was there! We began to walk. Quickly it began to fade. My heart began to sink. The signal should have traveled a few miles. Or, I thought bitterly, at least a mile! But when we reached the end of the block a short distance away we heard nothing but static.

We started back for the house. Jo knew I was feeling angry and despondent, and didn't say anything. We went back in and ate dinner, and I wondered all the while where I had failed. The city's homeless population was under severe attack. Food Not Bombs was under severe attack. The world was full of sorrow—and I couldn't get the stupid transmitter to work, I thought. And I blamed myself.

Chapter 2:
Food Not Bombs

The U.S. Government has been sponsoring oppression around the world for years, but it wasn't until that oppression came home and touched us personally that we were finally spurred into the act of building a radio station. This is really too bad. But typical. People tsk-tsk and shake their heads over this or that, and sometimes, commendably, even go out in the street and protest, but for the most part they don't truly begin to seriously act until racism, tyranny or injustice impact their own particular group and they themselves begin to suffer the consequences. Maybe this is just human nature, but if it is, perhaps therein lies the tragedy of the human race: We don't feel other people's pain.

Maybe a course in empathy should be required for all school children right along with math, science and language. And maybe, too, this lack of empathy is the inevitable by-product of survival-of-the-fittest capitalism and of living in a society based so thoroughly on competition rather than cooperation. Perhaps that's why the murder rate is so much higher in the U.S. than in western Europe where they still have a few social programs left.

Our own social programs have always been meager and miserly compared to those in Europe. If the U.S. didn't spend so much money trying to be the military big cheese around the world, and telling other countries what to do, there'd be funds left over for our own citizens. It would, in fact, *all* be left over for our own citizens. Of course, to empathize with something you need to know about it. Maybe it's bad for business for the American people to know too much about the suffering engendered by their government around the globe. That's where corporate control of our media comes in.

The small number of corporations who now own every major media outlet in this country simply don't tell us about things they don't want us to know about. Or, if something is too widely known to deny—such as the existence of U.S.-trained and supplied death squads in Central America—they will downplay or de-emphasize it, pass it off as a peculiar aberration or a mistake. This is the way the corporate media works. It's quite the rigged carnival game. With the coming of micro radio, can some of this suffering possibly be avoided in the future?

Why did we start doing radio in the first place? It was, mainly, because of the repression against Food Not Bombs (FNB) by the City of San Francisco. That repression started on August 15, 1988.

***

It was a Monday and it was foggy. Mondays for FNB were lunch-serving days at the east end of Golden Gate Park, near the intersection of Haight and Stanyan. Lots of homeless people who lived in the area gathered there on most days. Homeless people, like all other groups, sub-groups and divisions of humanity, think of themselves as a community. Most all communities have something that passes as a "community center." This is what Haight and Stanyan had become: a place where homeless people gathered to chat, socialize and exchange news. This had come about despite efforts on the part of the city to drive people out—using police clubs, misdemeanor citations, the judicial system, and just about every other means at its disposal.

The reasons for this failure to eradicate homeless people from the area are many, but basically they boil down to this: homelessness is a reality, and efforts to drive homeless people out of sight are tantamount to a denial of reality. A person who consistently denies reality is someone psychiatry would characterize as "delusional." The fact that we have so many delusional people in government raises some real questions about where most of the mentally ill people in our society can be found: perhaps more really and truly *are* roaming the corridors of power rather than through the streets and alleyways of our cities.

When I use the word "government" I'm speaking collectively of all levels of government, from federal down to local, which are all essentially partners in the same crime that's being perpetrated on the people of this country. So if "government" doesn't want homeless people to "take over" city parks and other areas, then it should never have created the conditions that brought about homelessness in the first place.

To blame homeless people for the inarguably worsening conditions on the streets of America is purely an indulgence in misdirected blame on the part of government. This, too, is another symptom of mental illness. It's also just a sign of a very childish, immature individual: blame everything and everybody else when all along the problem really lies with yourself. And the problems in America really *do* lie with the government, or with those *running* it. For it was government, or those running it, that deliberately embarked, in countless innumerable ways, upon a policy of driving corporate profits up and workers' wages down; it was the government that chose to pass the international "free trade" agreements which are now causing so much poverty and misery around the globe; and it was government that created many, many boondoggles of corporate welfare for the rich while slashing programs for the poor and needy to the bone.

Why do corporations get so much, while the people of this country get so little? Is it because the corporations essentially run the government—at least in practice if not in name?

It was also government that, on local levels in city after city, did away with rent controls, enriching landlords and developers, while forcing more people into the streets. The problems we face in society today are not the fault of the *people* who make up our society. *We* are not somehow deficient. No. The problems we face today are directly the responsibility of the people who hold power and run the country in their own interests.

If you want to blame someone, and you should, those are the people to blame. There should be no confusion about that. But there is. There's a great deal of it. And the reason there's so much confusion is that the tiny one percent who pull the strings and hold all the power, also control the media. The job of the media in this country, rather than report the news, is to deflect blame from the rich and powerful. The legalization of micro radio in this country, and the taking to the air of thousands of low-power stations such as our own, could potentially begin to refocus this blame, placing it squarely where it belongs.

If the government wants to end homelessness in this country, it has two choices how it can go about it. 1. It can kill the homeless, through police death squads or possibly some other means involving even greater subterfuge, or, 2. It can stop creating the conditions that bring about homelessness.

Doubtless there are many well-intentioned government officials that have pondered long and hard how to solve the homeless problem by using the latter method. Equally doubtless there are those who have considered the former solution. But regardless of how you deal with it, the blame for it, from the viewpoint of those who created this problem, must, at all costs, be deflected. This is what the government and the media work hand-in-hand at doing. It's a quid pro quo arrangement. The government does the will of the corporations, thereby creating the conditions of homelessness, while the corporations, using the smoke and mirrors of their awesome media power, deflect attention from that, essentially casting the blame upon the existence of the homeless themselves.

The question for you, as a housed person sharing a neighborhood with the unhoused, then becomes: Who do you blame for the human feces upon your sidewalk or in your park? Do you blame the homeless man who couldn't hold his bowels any longer? Or do you blame the people who created the conditions bringing about homelessness in the first place? That in a nutshell is what the media debate in this country is all about. It all boils down to feces—and who to blame for how wrong everything is. Do you blame the people who hold all the power and make all the decisions? Or do you blame those at the other end of the spectrum, who are utterly without power and who are not involved in the decision-making process in any form? Against all logic many people blame the latter. To the extent this is the case, that media debate is being won by the corporations. And it's being won through sheer volume of ownership.

I would contend that, upon walking out of your house and finding human feces on your doorstep, the first three people who should pop immediately to mind are the president of the United States, the governor of your state, and the mayor of your city, in that order. Because they are the ones most directly responsible for putting it there. The next rung down on the ladder of blame should be occupied by the corporations who put these people into their positions of power, and whose will they do. Or maybe they should all be up on the same rung together. The point is, we on the ground must find a way to pull that ladder out from under the people on top. Micro radio affords us an opportunity to at least begin to talk about doing that.

***

So that's what the corner of Haight and Stanyan had become in those days: A "community center" for the people on the bottom. Grassy, shady, and, if you looked carefully enough, somewhat feces-strewn to a degree. It was also a "high visibility" location, in terms of passing traffic. Haight and Stanyan is an extremely busy intersection. Thus it not only facilitated food distribution, being, as it was, a gathering point for people in need, but it also afforded the FNB members a nice opportunity to get their political message—food not bombs—out to the public-at-large who weren't homeless. There are other locations around San Francisco that fulfill the same twin purpose. I'm just telling you about this one because this is where the first arrests took place. And they took place precisely because the location was so public. This at first was only speculation on our part.

It later was borne out, however, when the city offered us a deal: Move to a quieter, more visually obscured location and we'll stop arresting you. Another thing that tended to be borne out by the offering of that deal was that the issue all along never was our lack of a health permit, as the city for eight years maintained.

Haight and Stanyan's homeless people differ from the homeless who frequent other areas of San Francisco in that they tend, overall, to be younger. Teenagers, young "Dead heads" and the like, all make the area their home. You see a lot of pierced lips and pierced noses that you don't see so much of in homeless people farther downtown. This is the famed Haight/Ashbury district. The Haight, with its hip shops and abundant drugs, still draws young people by the droves, much as it did in the 1960s. Some things never change.

Today's young, however, must contend with shrinking social services, a rabidly anti-homeless police force and a neighborhood "community policing" group which gets government funding to essentially function as the eyes and ears of the police. Still, life in the Haight pulses on. Typically the kids will spend several hours a day asking for spare change, then walk down Haight, cross Stanyan, and drift into the park to rest.

Yes, there are minimum wage jobs these kids could get. There in fact is a McDonald's right across Stanyan Street from the park. But imagine, those of you who've never done it, pouring 40 hours a week, a third of your life, into a tough, stoop-labor endeavor—and then imagine that endeavor not even paying you enough to put a roof over your head. But say you do it. You get your striped uniform and your pointy hat and you go to work—and that uniform is demeaning. It says all kinds of things about you. It says you don't belong to yourself any longer but to the McDonald's corporation. It says you're a minimum wage slave and a clone and a cog. It says you've given up your sense of adventure in order to meekly go along and become part of a system you hate and loathe, and you hate and loathe it because it offers you nothing but this, and it says that not only are you now the property of McDonald's, but also your shit, your piss, your very identity—your heart, your soul, all belong to McDonald's. That's what the uniform says. It's demeaning, like an organ grinder's monkey suit. And you feel embarrassed when your friends see you wearing it.

But like all Americans you're an avid media consumer, and splashed across TV screens everywhere are America's pious, self-righteous rulers telling you that the thing you should do is pick up that uniform, put it on, and go to work. Maybe you stop for a moment and think that these are the same rulers who are taking beau-coup campaign bucks from McDonald's. Or maybe you don't. The media you're such an avid consumer of don't point things like that out. They mostly just want to sell you things. At any rate you buy the propaganda line. You put on the uniform. You go to work—at McDonald's. What do you do now? The average one-bedroom apartment in San Francisco costs nine hundred or a thousand dollars a month.

What do you do now? Live at home with your parents? Maybe you don't have any parents. Or maybe your home life is an unpleasant reality. Maybe your family is the Brady Bunch from hell. Or maybe they're not the Brady Bunch from hell. Maybe they're just poor and doing not much better than you are. Or maybe your parents are stressed out from working two jobs, and maybe even though they're working two jobs their real income is still declining. Maybe they know it's declining, and they're angry about it and taking it out on the kids. Maybe they're sinking into depression—or alcoholism, an addiction they can't get any help for because there are no social programs left in America. College maybe? But the thought of all the zillions of dollars it takes to go to college nowadays is both frightening and depressing. And besides that, how many college grads are now working as waiters and waitresses? Or as cashiers at Wal-Mart?

But for the moment, anyway, you're still working at McDonald's and trying to make your rent, and you stop having a social life after work because you're too tired, and pretty soon your whole reality boils down to eating, sleeping and going to your job to work. After a while you notice your whole life has become like nothing more than the greasy smoke going up the vent over the McDonald's grill.

Let's say you're 18-years-old and these are the grim choices life offers you. Do you pursue one of these options? Or do you go live in the park for free with your friends? Which path do you think a lot of kids are going to choose? Which would you choose? These are the choices the children of the Haight have to make. America has completely and utterly failed these children, as it has failed millions of others like them across the length and breadth of this country. And, having failed them, it then sends its police forces to roust them out of the parks, doorways and bushes they call home. And so remote, out of touch and completely opiated with wealth have America's rulers become that they either don't know or don't care that this is their plight.

In America we can either join other of our fellow Americans in donning uniforms which proclaim to the world, "We have been colonized by multi-national corporations," or we can go live in a bush somewhere. This is the reality for many people in this country. The children of the Haight have at least chosen not to be colonized.

Yet still America's "leaders" remain out of touch and show no sign of climbing down out of their ivory towers any time soon. It is precisely for this reason that FNB chooses to serve food in very public, "high visibility" locations: so as to make the problems of poverty, homelessness and unequal wealth distribution in this country glaringly apparent for all, even the out-of-touch, to see.

That's why the group was at Haight and Stanyan on August 15, 1988.

***

In 1988 Ronald Reagan had been waging a seven-year long campaign to topple the Sandinista government of Nicaragua. This was the same year that George Bush, running for president, began doing his "thousand points of light" schtick and extolling the virtues of citizen "volunteerism" (as opposed to "government handouts").

Now reflect. Repressive governments often find themselves caught up in absurd contradictions, but here was a real whopper: here was the United States, a government which provides basically no social services for its citizens, funneling millions of dollars into an effort to overthrow a government which, in those days, very much so *did* provide social services, a great deal of them, for its citizens—doing all this while at the same time arresting *us*, a group of volunteers who were trying to provide food for our fellow citizens at *no* cost to the government.

At times during the eight year long repression against FNB in San Francisco, it almost seemed like the number one agenda priority of the United States government was to stop people of the world from eating.

***

FNB at that time had only been up and going for a few months, and the San Francisco group was only the second Food Not Bombs chapter ever established. It came about in 1987 when Keith McHenry, one of the original founders, and his wife, Andrea, moved to San Francisco from Boston. Up until that time, FNB had been pretty much a Boston/Cambridge thing. It had been active there since 1980.

In 1979-80, a group calling itself the Clamshell Alliance attempted to occupy a nuclear power plant in Seabrook, New Hampshire. The protests at Seabrook were pretty big and made a lot of national news. But the media, as usual, were doing their damndest to blur, obfuscate and confuse. Remember, that's their job. I often think that looking at the world through the eyes of the corporate-owned media is like looking through a lens that's constantly out of focus, and 3/4 of America is walking around dizzy and suffering a headache from looking through this blurred lens. All America really needs is a good optometrist.

Here's what really happened at Seabrook: Thousands of people came together concerned that what had only just recently taken place at Three-Mile Island, might be repeated at Seabrook. Government officials assured, and the media dutifully reported, that the Seabrook plant was safe. But how safe is "safe?" And why should people believe these statements from the government when the nuclear industry and the politicians running the government were all in bed together?

Just as much as the construction of that nuclear power plant, the government's credibility gap with its own people was equally responsible for drawing thousands of protestors to Seabrook. The local power company stood to gain millions in profits from the plant's construction. But what was in it for the people in the nearby cities and towns? These people, depicted as kooks and nuts by the media, were justifiably afraid of being exposed to cancer-causing radiation for the sake of nuclear industry profits. History has proven their concerns valid.

"Cancer clusters" now exist in many areas of the United States. Many of these clusters are located around nuclear power plants, nuclear test sites or national laboratories which engage in nuclear weapons research. In their 1990 book *Deadly Deceit*, Jay Gould and Benjamin Goldman documented increased mortality rates in surrounding counties following accidents at Three Mile Island and Savannah River nuclear plants, with infants and young adults being the most effected. Their data convinced them of the dangers of low-level radiation, heretofore thought safe, and led them to conclude that "free radical-induced biological damage may be thousands of times more efficient at low doses of radiation than at high ones." [1] The book also exposes evidence of government attempts to cover-up the data through manipulation of local mortality statistics.

Seabrook is located about an hour's drive from Boston. The eight people who later started FNB in Boston all came together either at Seabrook or as a result of what happened there. Though all from the same city—Boston—many, ironically, had not known each other prior to Seabrook. Two who had, however, were Jo Swanson and Brian Feigenbaum. Swanson remembers talking to Feigenbaum outside the plant fence when suddenly the latter was grabbed by police. Someone earlier had thrown a grappling hook over the fence that had struck a police officer. The person throwing the hook had been dressed in white and was wearing a beard. Feigenbaum was dressed in white and had a beard. Case closed as far as the police were concerned. Swanson, grabbing hold of her friend in hopes of pulling him back from the police, was knocked to the ground. Dragged away, Feigenbaum was locked up inside the plant incommunicado for six hours.

When Feigenbaum went to court, charged with throwing the grappling hook, an effort was made to pack the courtroom with people who looked like quintessential bearded protestors. To confuse matters further, C.T. Butler, a friend of Keith's, sat in front with Feigenbaum's mother while Feigenbaum sat in the rear with the spectators. After the arresting officer took the stand and mistakenly identified Butler as Feigenbaum, the judge threw the case out, and Food Not Bombs was born at a party celebrating the victory that night.

During the Seabrook protests, the government had deployed thousands of police from all over New Hampshire, Rhode Island, Connecticut and Massachusetts to guard the seven mile perimeter of the plant. These police used tear gas, water hoses, dogs and clubs to keep the protestors at bay. In doing so, they were essentially saying to the public, "We don't give two hoots in hell about your health and the fact that you might be exposed to radiation—we're only here to make sure that the nuclear power industry is allowed to continue to make profits." This is precisely the reason why the police, notwithstanding the fact that they are "only doing their jobs," are regarded with fear and suspicion in America. Author Michael Parenti has stated:

> The police sometimes protect life and limb, direct traffic, administer first aid, assist in times of community emergency and perform other services with commendable dedication and courage. But aside from this desirable social service function the police also serve a class control function, that is they must protect those who rule from those who are ruled. And they protect the interests of capital and property, big property, from those who would challenge the inequities of the system. [2]

If the police performed only the first role Parenti mentioned above, that of the social service function, they would be greeted everywhere they went with warmth and admiration, probably even hugs and kisses—not wholly unlike the way American and allied soldiers were received in Paris after liberating France from the Nazis. They would be among the most cherished members of our society. But handshakes, boisterous greetings and swooning women are generally not among the reactions that occur when police officers enter public places. This is merely another testimony to the fact that we live in an inherently unjust society, one which functions mainly in the interest of those who run it. Far from love and goodwill, the reaction many Americans have when they see a police officer is one of fear.

Why weren't the police, many at Seabrook might have wondered, arresting New Hampshire power executives for endangering the public health and foisting a nuclear plant upon an unwilling populace? After all, the townspeople of Seabrook, in a public referendum, had voted against the plant by a margin of 768-632. This vote, however, apparently meant little to the ruling politicians. They declared it "non-binding." The plant was built, and thousands of police had to be deployed to protect it from outraged citizens. Scarcely could a more vivid example be pointed to of police being used in a manner antithetical to democracy. Hardly any wonder is it then that many in America today, especially those in poor and minority communities perceive the police as an "occupation army."

Most essential of all, for any people to end its occupation by a foreign power, is a means of communication.

***

After Feigenbaum's charges were thrown out, some of the folks who had organized his legal defense—Butler, Jo Swanson, Keith McHenry and several others, and Feigenbaum himself, started a food-for-the-poor program on the streets of Boston. The first action was to set up a soup line outside the stockholder's meeting of the First National Bank of Boston. First National had financed the Seabrook Nuclear Plant.

This tiny group of anti-nuclear activists served food to the poor as the bank's stockholders walked by, some stopping to chat and a few even stuffing a dollar or two in the group's donation can. Such a reaction from the stockholders was a gratifying surprise, but even more overwhelming was the response of Boston's homeless population. By the event's conclusion, 300 people had been served hot food. "We should be doing this every day," McHenry commented as they were packing to leave. The others agreed that conditions on the streets, vis-a-vis homelessness, merited such a continuation. Food Not Bombs was born.

The year was 1980—a time in which homelessness, as I said, wasn't near the dimensions at which it exists today. Yet even then, as the Reagan administration was just coming to power, there certainly were connections that could be seen between military spending abroad and poverty and declining living standards at home.

FNB was never arrested in Boston. It was even publicly lauded by the Cambridge City Council for its work with the poor. The thought that you could be arrested for serving food to the poor never occurred to McHenry when he moved to San Francisco. And who after all would think it? Giving charity to the poor is advocated throughout the Bible. It's one of the most fundamental tenets of Christianity, a religion which America's rulers claim to embrace. Yet getting arrested is precisely the fate which awaited Keith in San Francisco—more than a hundred times.

Cops for the most part, I guess, don't understand politics and don't believe there is any such thing as political prisoners in America. When a cop runs your I.D. and discovers you've been arrested sixty, seventy, eighty or ninety times, he tends to think you must be somebody really dangerous. Thus each arrest by and large became an increasingly worse experience for Keith.

He has been hit with fists, flashlights, and batons, which caused injury and even trips to the emergency room. He has lost jobs because of arrests, his personal life has been placed under severe strain, and his wife has anguished over his fate many a night while he remained in the custody of police who hated him enough to want to kill him. That's the reality for anyone who gets right up in the faces of the powers-that-be in San Francisco (and probably most anywhere else in America) and challenges their authority in any significant way.

Chevron, The Gap, Levi-Strauss, Bank of America and Bechtel all maintain corporate headquarters in San Francisco. These five corporations, plus Pacific Gas and Electric, hold an enormous amount of political power here. The city essentially is run for them. It is their private fiefdom. The politicians who get elected, with only a few lonely, isolated exceptions, serve their wishes blindly and obediently.

Just a few miles away, as the crow flies, from the gleaming office towers of these corporate giants, however, lies the homeless "community center" at the corner of Haight and Stanyan. It's a grassy, wooded area with dirt paths and a small lake. A walk through the area takes one around and past clusters of bushes and trees, some of them with undergrowth so dense as to offer a small modicum of privacy and, in a weird way, shelter of a sort. As you wind your way along the path the clusters reveal blankets, worn out tennis shoes and other random, limp items.

It's obvious that human beings, at least a few anyway, are making their homes in these bushes. Considering that San Francisco has an estimated 10,000-15,000 homeless people, you're amazed there aren't even more blankets and all sorts of other junk lying around as well. Of course not everyone who's homeless in San Francisco sleeps here in the east end of Golden Gate Park at the corner of Haight and Stanyan. But even so it seems, despite everything the media says about how awful the homeless are, that a fair number may be making an effort to clean up after themselves when they wake up. Even animals will not defecate in their own dens, and surely the members of this class, more so than any other in society, have been treated much like animals.

Bums, drug addicts, alcoholics and criminals—these are some of the names that pandering politicians like to call homeless people. Hearing these descriptions, I'm often reminded of some of the disparaging statements made by our "founding fathers" about the Indians. These highly revered fathers, and later rulers of America, had some pretty terrible things to say about the continent's original inhabitants.

In the Declaration of Independence Thomas Jefferson refers to them as "the merciless Indian Savages, whose known rule of warfare, is an undistinguished destruction of all ages, sexes and conditions." Or take Teddy Roosevelt's historical view of the Sand Creek Massacre, in which a band of peaceful Cheyenne Indians, including women and children, were murdered by American soldiers. Roosevelt, whose likeness looks out from Mount Rushmore in the heart of the Sacred Black Hills, called this supremely ugly chapter of American history "as righteous and beneficial a deed as ever took place on the frontier." [3]

And then there's the weirdly convoluted ideology of George Washington. Washington, displaying the sort of contradictory, upside-down logic for which the nation he founded would later become famous, once referred to the Indians as "those barbarous and insolent invaders of our country." [4] It makes you think Ronald Reagan may have been right *after all* when he called the Nicaraguan contras "the moral equivalent of our founding fathers."

In some respects homeless people today are America's new Indians. Just as the cavalry used to chase, harass, and hound Indians and Indian tribes, driving them from place to place and region to region, always removing them and relocating them—so, too, do police today relentlessly pursue, harass, kick and badger homeless people, never allowing them to sleep or call one place home for very long. Much like the U.S. Army ran Sitting Bull and his people completely out of the United States and into exile in Canada for a period, so do mayors rejoice in driving homeless people out of their own cities and into neighboring ones.

But how can this be happening? Where are the constitutional protections supposedly guaranteed to all citizens of the United States, including those who are homeless? This issue was addressed in a 1992 article in the *Tulane Law Review* entitled "Towns Without Pity: A Constitutional and Historical Analysis of Official Efforts to Drive Homeless Persons from American Cities." Written by Harry Simon, the article outlined the basic problem succinctly by citing some documented examples of rights violations:

> On August 15, 1990, police officers in Santa Ana, California arrested sixty-four homeless persons in the city's civic center area...and drove them to a nearby stadium for booking and fingerprinting.

At the stadium, police officers chained the homeless to benches for up to six hours without food or water. The police used markers to write numbers on the arms of homeless arrestees. At the conclusion of the six-hour detention, the police loaded the homeless into vans, drove them to the edge of the Central Command Area of the Santa Ana Police Department, and dropped them off.

In January 1990, police officers in Miami, Florida roused seven homeless people sleeping in a local park, handcuffed them, and dumped their belongings in pile and set it ablaze. In New York City, police have repeatedly clashed with the homeless, often violently, during sweeps designed to drive them from Tompkins Square Park. The mayor of San Francisco announced last summer that homeless people would no longer be permitted to sleep or camp on any public or private land within the city. As one commentator recently noted, "cities across the nation are starting to adopt a closed-door attitude toward the displaced." [5]

Simon argues that such treatment of homeless people raises a number of serious constitutional questions. At issue here, among other things, are discrimination, equal protection, and punishment of condition or status, he says. "The enforcement of laws against homeless individuals that prohibit sleeping on public and private land may constitute effective banishment abridging the rights of the homeless to freedom of movement," writes Simon. The bonfire in the Miami, Florida incident obviously would evoke questions of unlawful search and seizure as prohibited by the fourth amendment, or deprivation of property without due process of law as guaranteed against in the Fifth Amendment. According to Simon,

> Official efforts to relegate the homeless to a kind of second class citizenship, where their property and liberty are subject to official deprivation virtually at whim, cannot be tolerated. In light of the long history of unconstitutional actions taken against the displaced poor and the relative powerlessness of homeless individuals, the courts must be ever vigilant against official attempts to expel the homeless, in whatever forms such efforts may take. [6]

People who write for law reviews tend to speak in a very cautious, guarded manner. That's the way lawyers are trained. What Simon is essentially saying here, though, is that with regard to homeless people the constitution's in danger of being tossed out the window. That was written in 1992.

Today, and probably even then too, I would have had to go Simon one better and say that it *has* been tossed out. Given the fact that police in America routinely commit human rights offenses, such as those Simon describes, and get away with them; and given the fact that few homeless people have the means to hire a lawyer, go to court, and challenge some action or offense that a cop has taken against them (a fact of which the police are all too comfortably aware); then what other conclusion can you draw?

The constitution has been suspended for homeless people in America.

And if you're going to say that, then you might as well leave off the second part and just say the constitution's been suspended. Period. Because if it's been suspended for some it's been suspended for all. How can it be in effect for some of us without being in effect for all of us?

A visitor from outer space or some other naive individual might be of the belief that the suspension of the U.S. constitution would be the top news story in America. This of course is not the case. The suspension of the constitution has never been proclaimed by the *New York Times* or the *Washington Post,* who *have* of course proclaimed a lot of other silly notions, such as, for instance, the CIA's innocence of any involvement in drug trafficking.

Although city officials deny it, San Francisco's Matrix program (discussed later on) was little more than a concerted attempt to drive homeless people into Oakland, Berkeley and San Mateo County. Although the program officially began in 1993, a lot of its policies were in effect long before that, and remained in place long after its official demise in 1996.

When homeless people, driven to the point of desperation, attempt to make a stand against these forced relocations, their isolated little revolts are quickly crushed by the police. Marcelino Corniel found this out, and paid the ultimate price in the learning.

Corniel, a 33-year-old African American homeless man, had been living in the park across the street from the White House in Washington, D.C. That park is referred to as "Lafayette Square" by the media. However, to the people who frequent the area, many of them homeless, it is known as "Peace Park—" so called because for quite a number of years a group of activists have maintained within its boundaries a "vigil" for peace, a sort of on-going 365-day-a-year protest against the U.S. government.

On the morning of December 20, 1994 Corniel, brandishing a knife, chased Officer Stephen J. O'Neill out of the park. The story of Corniel and O'Neill is the saga of two men with similar last names but far different stations in life. As the pair, Corniel, the homeless pursuer and O'Neill the pursued policeman, crossed Pennsylvania Avenue, four of O'Neill's fellow law officers drew their weapons and aimed. A moment later Corniel was gunned down on the sidewalk in front of the White House.

The U.S. Park Police, who have jurisdiction in the area, claimed the shooting was justified, saying their officers had feared for their lives. This is a standard claim made by police any time they shoot someone, and usually the media never question it. In this case, however, the shooting of Corniel was captured on videotape and aired extensively on local television. What the film showed was that Corniel had quit chasing O'Neill and was standing still when the police fired upon him. This sparked a controversy over whether police lives had really been in danger and whether officers had really needed to resort to lethal force in the situation. The police went immediately into damage control mode.

In 1992, two years before his death, Corniel had suffered burns over 75-80 percent of his body in a car crash in California. He was treated for six months in a hospital burn center. The fire had fused together two of his fingers and left him overall permanently disfigured. Apparently unable to grip the knife in his hand, Corniel had taped the weapon to his appendage prior to his confrontation with police.

While reporting on Corniel's burn scars and mentioning the fact that the knife had been "taped or strapped" to his hand, the *Washington Post*, in its report on the killing, never pressed police officials to explain how someone in his physical condition could pose such a threat.

In our own report, which we produced for both the Food Not Bombs Radio Network and San Francisco Liberation Radio, we interviewed Than Painter, of the Washington D.C. chapter of FNB, and William Thomas, one of the peace vigil participants. The two were able to offer us much insight into Corniel's last days. The homeless man was constantly in pain. Painter, who had served food to him, had particularly noted that "he had a lot of trouble holding onto things," while Thomas disclosed that he had trouble walking and that his feet bled. The two also described relations between the police and park residents as being particularly tense, with Thomas informing us that Officer O'Neill had a "custom" of "kicking people and prodding them with night sticks."

The illegal seizure of homeless people's property, a la Miami in the "Towns Without Pity" article, seems to have been operative here in Washington as well. Both Thomas and Painter told us of numerous incidents wherein blankets and other belongings had been taken by police from people in the park. The *Post* even went so far as to mention the blanket confiscations, though it did so in a backhanded sort of way, presenting the information as a possible motive for Corniel's having sought "revenge" upon the police. Never addressed was whether or not such property seizures should have been taking place at all. Clearly the property rights of homeless people are of no concern to the *Post* editors.

While the *Post* did allude to some "tension" between police and park people, the closest it came to hinting at any impropriety on the part of O'Neill was a quote from Thomas' wife, Ellen. Said Ellen Thomas of O'Neill, "He's our 1994 candidate for an officer with an attitude problem." [7] On the other hand, the newspaper went at great length into Corniel's past as a "gang member with a history for using knives to commit violence," quoting extensively from police and court records in California. These sources relied upon by the *Post* gave a picture of the man, Marcelino Corniel, much different from the one we formed by talking to Painter and Thomas.

Perhaps Corniel, as the *Post* said, really had been a gang member with a history of violence. Yet there is evidence also that he had undergone a change. Maybe this change had come about as a result of his catastrophic injuries, or maybe being around the peace activists in the park had begun to rub off on him. We'll never know. Here, though, is what Thomas told us,

> Every once in a while he (Corniel) would have a
> sign about the Ku Klux Klan or health issues—
> health issues especially—because I think that that
> was something that he was very concerned about
> because he was really suffering physically. [8]

In turning upon his tormentor, Corniel the budding political activist, gave way to Corniel the gang member.

Did Officer O'Neill deliberately provoke Corniel into an act the officer knew would result in Corniel's death? Or did he simply do what he had been accustomed to doing so many times before without thinking what the consequences might be? In some ways it doesn't matter. The net result was the same: obviously with the knife taped to his hand, Corniel was unable to obey police orders to drop it. Aiming down the barrels of their guns, the officers, in the heat of the moment, saw, or thought they saw, not a suffering, disabled human being, but a scarred monster.

Interestingly the *Post* included a very poignant quote from Corniel's 12-year-old son, who was interviewed by CNN. Says the *Post*,

> Corniel's 12-year-old son offered a different perspective in an interview with CNN yesterday, saying his dad was a "good person" who was depressed about his disfigurement and reaction to it.
>
> "When somebody was in that sort of situation they'd feel the same way if they got rejected from society," Marcelino Ronald Corniel said. "Nobody wanted to see him or even look at him." [9]

In choosing to include the quote from Corniel's son, the *Post* writers reveal a fair degree of sensitivity. But if you don't know the truth about Corniel's last days on earth, or the reality of day-to-day life in the park across the street from the White House (and you wouldn't from reading the *Post*'s coverage), then the quote loses much of its emotional impact.

Our own report on the killing of Marcelino Corniel aired in January 1995. We entitled it "Free at Last."

***

The number of people who die homeless every year is a statistic which should be kept nationally. One reason why it's so important to keep such a statistic is that the figure is almost certainly growing. In San Francisco a newspaper called the *Tenderloin Times* used to run a story every year reporting the number of people in the city who had died on the streets homeless during the previous 12 months. The paper folded in 1994, but in the nine years of its existence it never failed to publish an annual story on the homeless death toll. Here, then, based upon information from the San Francisco coroner's office, are the mortality figures the *Tenderloin Times* found and reported:

1985—16
1986—54
1987—69
1988—103
1989—110
1990—113
1991—109
1992—138
1993—101

In 1994, after the *Times* folded, the San Francisco Department of Public Health took over the task of keeping the grim statistic. Here are the figures published for the six years hence:

> 1994—117
> 1995—142
> 1996—-154
> 1997—-97
> 1998—157
> 1999—169

Do the above figures reflect something deeper—something truly terrible happening in America? Why do we appear to be a civilization coming to pieces? Why are more and more people dying every year on the streets of this country? Have we as citizens of this country done something wrong? Are *we* somehow deficient? Or have we been failed by our leaders? Who's really screwing up? We can continue to blame ourselves or each other for all the things that are going wrong in this country, or we can place the blame where it truly and justly belongs: on America's rulers.

In 1994 an interesting little book came out called *Homelessness: A Sourcebook* by Rick Fantasia and Maurice Isserman. The book is a compilation of all kinds of fascinating statistics and information about homeless people in America, including just who they are and who makes up their ranks in terms of age, sex, employment status, where they can be found, and so forth. Perhaps most interestingly of all the book provides some insight into just how strikingly these figures have changed since the 1950s. Here are a few things the authors discovered:

- A 1958 study estimated that no more than 3 percent of the skid row population in the U.S. were women. Current estimates put that figure at 25 percent, while women and children together comprise nearly 40 percent of the homeless population. [10]
- A 1990 *New York Times* poll revealed that 54 percent of all Americans say they see homeless people in their neighborhoods or on their way to work each day. In New York City the figure jumped to 82 percent. [11]
- An estimated 18 percent of homeless people now work at part time or full time jobs. [12]

- In his book *Address Unknown,* sociologist James Wright estimated that one in every seven homeless persons is under age 19, while the U.S. Conference of Mayors put the figure at one in every four. [13]

Fantasia and Isserman also cite statistics gathered by Jonathan Kozol from his acclaimed book, *Rachel and Her Children: Homeless Families in America.* One finding of Kozol's is especially sobering:

- If all the homeless children in the U.S. were gathered in one city they would represent a larger population than that of Atlanta, Denver, or St. Louis. [14]

America's "rural homeless" especially figure into Kozol's equation. The loss of a farm can not only mean the loss of a family's income, but, of course its home as well. According to Kozol:

- There were over 650,000 foreclosures of farms during the 1980s—a decade in which an average of 2000 farmers gave up farming every week. [15]
- In California and Maryland 18 percent of the homeless population resides in rural areas. [16]

Are the *Washington Post* editors who failed to question the police confiscation of homeless people's property representative of the media as a whole? If so, then the millions of people who make up America's homeless population, and whose statistics fill Fantasia's and Isserman's book, have *no* representation in the media. This underscores the enormous need for micro radio.

According to a 1996 UN Development Program report, income inequality in the U.S. is becoming comparable to that in such nations as Brazil and Guatemala. [17] Between 1975 and 1990 the wealthiest one percent of the U.S. population increased its share of national assets from 20 to 36 percent. During roughly the same time period, however, average real wages fell by 9 percent. [18] When so many are poor while a small number at the top have wealth beyond most anyone's wildest dreams, it's obvious the system is rigged bigger than a poker game with a marked deck.

So lopsided, in fact, has become wealth disparity in the U.S., according to MIT economist Lester Thurow, that we are now entering "uncharted waters for American democracy." [19] According to Thurow, the inequalities in earnings between the top 20 percent and the bottom 20 percent doubled from 1968 to 1993. [20] He adds: "No one has ever tried survival-of-the-fittest capitalism for any extended period in a modern democracy, so we don't know how far rising inequality and falling real wages can go before something snaps." [21]

These then are the defining characteristics of what has been called "the third-worldization of the United States."

***

It was 8 a.m. on Monday, August 15, 1988. The day's cooks, servers and the driver met at what used to be a Food Not Bombs house at 54 Albion St. The group began preparing the lunch that would be served at Haight and Stanyan, cooking up an enormous amount of rice and beans. There was also salad and bread. The abundant amount of food on hand had come from three San Francisco businesses: Veritable Vegetable, an organic produce warehouse, Thom's Natural Food Store, and the House of Bagels. Though perfectly edible, all the food was deemed unsellable for one reason or another. Rather than throw it out, however, the workers at these places had set it aside for FNB to pick up.

At 10:30 that morning the hot, delicious-smelling food was ladled into plastic 5-gallon buckets. The buckets were then sealed and carried out to the truck and loaded. The servers, some of whom had earlier doubled as cooks, climbed inside. The driver started the engine. The truck began to thread its way through busy San Francisco traffic. As they neared Haight and Stanyan, those inside felt their tension begin to mount.

For several weeks cops had been showing up at the Monday servings, demanding that the activity cease, and on one occasion a cop named Gardner had punched Keith. Keith had been taken to jail that day, had missed work, and had lost his job as a result. While the events leading up to the fifteenth boded ill, no one knew for sure what would happen. Arrests were certainly possible, even likely. The jitteriness was contagious. Everyone in that truck knew that when they got to the park they could be risking jail if they so much as picked up a ladle and filled up a cup with rice.

The truck lumbered through the crowded Haight/Ashbury district, turning finally onto Stanyan and pulling up at the park. Here the riders breathed a little easier. No cops in sight.

The driver halted the truck. The back was opened up. Arms reached inside. First out came the long, folding table, then buckets and buckets of food. Finally, stacks of literature. "Cook for Peace," read one flier:

The money spent by the world on weapons in one week is enough to feed all the people on Earth for a year. When millions of people go hungry each day how can we spend another dollar on war? If you feel that people need food more than bombs we want you to call us today. The next few years could profoundly change the world for generations and Food Not Bombs is working to make those changes positive for everyone. The Food Not Bombs organization is starting several projects in our area:

- Free food distribution to local people in need
- Literature tables to provide information about food, peace and justice
- Providing hot meals at demonstrations and events
- Organizing creative actions in protest of war and poverty

We invite you to work with us to provide desperately needed services and information to our community. You can make a difference.

Around a hundred or so homeless people, many of them in their teens and twenties, began lining up at the table as the servers ladled out the steaming food. A giant box of bagels had been set up at the end of the table. Folks helped themselves to pumpernickels, onions and whole wheats as they filed by. The air was foggy and cool. The green of the park and the gray of the sky met each other in a rough embrace.

Suddenly someone looked up and saw the first cops advancing quietly through the trees to the west and north. They were moving in columns and were dressed in full riot gear. Several patrol cars and police vans appeared now as well. The servers ignored the approaching police and continued serving food, firm in their belief that what they were doing was right. There was no turning back now.

Lieutenant Richard Holder barked an order into a bullhorn and a column of cops bore down and surrounded the food and the table, effectively isolating the food servers behind the table from the rest of the humanity which had gathered. Holder, who is affectionately known as "Dick Holder," owes much of his career advancement through the ranks of the San Francisco Police Department to FNB. After this initial arrest in 1988 he went on to work with the SFPD's intelligence unit. Internal police memos with Holder's name on them, later obtained by FNB through court discovery motions, indicate his extensive involvement in spying on the group.

More orders were barked through the bullhorn. Amidst vocal protests, the police arrested nine people, then loaded up a second van with the table, food, literature, and an eye-catching banner with the words FOOD NOT BOMBS on it. Nine people were taken to jail and all the group's equipment was confiscated.

While given a big thumbs down by the crowds of people who had witnessed the arrest at the scene, the police could not have hoped for a better spin from the *San Francisco Chronicle*. The next day the paper depicted the people who had witnessed the arrests as "a crowd of homeless Haight Street residents" who had "jeered" at police, who, on the other hand, were presented as having merely had genuine concerns about health and sanitation and crime.

> Police contend that the food handouts draw drug and alcohol abusers and other troublemakers to the park and result in more than a dozen complaints a day from nearby homeowners and business people.
>
> "We bent over backward to explain the city and state ordinances regarding the issue," Lieutenant Holder said yesterday. "They're in violation of the health code, the park code and the penal code."
>
> Holder proposed serving the food at nearby Hamilton Methodist Church, which serves free meals Tuesday through Friday. The church has sanitary facilities to handle the food distribution, he said.
>
> Police donated the fruits and vegetables confiscated yesterday to the church's food program.
>
> "If they're truly concerned about feeding people, there is a better place for it," Holder said. [22]

Nowhere in the story was there any indication that reporter Bill Gordon had consulted any of the homeless people on hand as to whether they regarded the food giveaway as useful. Apparently the *Chronicle* deemed the concerns of homeless people as insignificant. Also if the only concern was food sanitation, why didn't the police simply confiscate the food? Why did they have to also take approximately $150 worth of folding tables, banners and Xeroxed literature?

And why—again if the issue was food sanitation—did they take this supposedly unsanitary food over to a nearby church, where, presumably, it would only be handed out to more homeless people? Could it be that the authorities had some additional motive other than merely ending the serving of purportedly unhealthy food in the park? None of these questions were raised in the *Chronicle* article.

The next Monday the police were no-shows in their expected rendezvous with FNB. Food was served that day—peacefully and without hindrance. On August 29, however, the cops were back, once again in riot gear. This time 29 people were arrested. More confiscations took place as well. Back again also was *Chronicle* man Bill Gordon with his mostly-about-the-police style of reporting:

> "This appears to be more of a political statement than
> a program to feed the hungry," police spokesman Jerry
> Senkir said yesterday. "We can't allow them to take over
> the park."
> The program quickly drew complaints from members
> of some area property-owners associations who claim that
> the free meals attract criminals and drug users. [23]

With the property owners thus given space to claim the meals attracted "criminals and drug users," would it not have been fair and balanced journalism to allow homeless people an opportunity to also express how they felt about the food program? But again none were quoted.

The following Monday was Labor Day. This time 54 people were arrested and the police knocked to the ground and bloodied a TV camera man as they chased people out of the park and up Haight Street. By now the arrests had thrown the entire Haight/Ashbury district into an uproar, causing deep rifts and divisions between wealthy property owners and the neighborhood's less affluent residents, many of whom supported FNB. A neighborhood newspaper, *The Haight Ashbury Newspaper*, commented on these divisions, which had begun to take place almost entirely along class lines:

> It is...unacceptable behavior for the police to be used
> to arrest people who, for whatever reason, are handing out
> free food to those who need it in our neighborhood...

What was the object of this para-military police operation? A crack house raid? A hostage taking perhaps? A wino riot? An organized band of hate-crazed panhandlers rifling the bedrooms of the neighborhood?

No. The object of this dangerous buffoonery were 30 or so militant vegetarians serving beans, rice and fruit to the down and outers in Golden Gate Park. The police were there because Art Agnos ordered them to be there in order to show that he was "in control." [24]

Then-San-Francisco-Mayor Art Agnos had campaigned and gotten himself elected to the city's highest office as a genuine, bonafide, bleeding heart, died-in-the-wool liberal. There were no risks here. That generally is what plays well with San Francisco voters. Immediately upon assuming office, however, the people Agnos began cozying up to were conservative property-owners associations such as the Cole Valley Improvement Association, which had advocated that police action be taken to stop the food servings in the park. At one point the group's members had cheered—from the patio of the Stanyan Street McDonald's, no less—as FNB servers were handcuffed and thrown into paddy wagons.

While indeed striving to appear aggressively in charge of the situation, Agnos, a former social worker, also was concerned least he seem callously indifferent to the plight of the poor. As the *Chronicle* reported,

"We will look for a permanent solution" over the next several weeks, Agnos said, because the city "must develop a policy for this kind of program where people can be fed with dignity and in privacy." [25]

So Agnos was ordering the arrests of homeless-care-providers for the good of homeless people? It was an interesting position for a former social worker to take. It's interesting, too, that the mayor's concern about preserving the "dignity and privacy" of homeless people only applied to eating, and apparently did not include sparing them the "indignity" of having to sleep in public doorways.

Perhaps the most ironic quote to appear in the media during this time was issued from the mouth of Richard Hechler of the district attorney's office. A question had arisen in the media as to whether the D.A., an elected official, intended to prosecute FNB members for serving food. In liberal San Francisco, as may be expected, there was a distinct reluctance to pursue such prosecutions in the politically charged atmosphere that had evolved. D.A.

Arlo Smith, another would-be-liberal poseur, basically wanted nothing to do with the whole mess—and if the D.A. wasn't going to prosecute, then that must mean the arrests would stop, right? "The police can't just go out and arrest people if we're not going to prosecute," Hechler said. [26]

Now, I don't think Hechler intended that statement to be prophetic at the time, but that is precisely what ended up happening—for the next eight years. It became an endless cycle of arrest, jail, dismissal of charges and release, and then arrest again. Thus the arrests, and the 1-3 days each person had to spend in jail every time they were arrested, became the punishment for the "crime" of serving free food in San Francisco. This also in essence gave the police the final say on the issue of serving food to the homeless in San Francisco. The framers of the constitution, of course, never granted the police such powers in this country, but this is precisely where a whole host of sorry state and federal judges, one right after another, allowed the matter to rest for the next eight years.

The failure of the media to point these things out, or to report on the level of violence the police were sometimes employing against the people they arrested, is what led to the founding and establishment of SFLR—in supposedly the most "liberal" city in America.

***

On Thursday and Friday, September 8 and 9, negotiations took place at City Hall between FNB and the City of San Francisco. The agreement reached at the end of the first day of discussions was that the talks would continue. Meanwhile there would be no further arrests and no one would make any statements to the media. FNB agreed to these stipulations. Negotiations were set to resume at 1 p.m. the following afternoon. Unfortunately, the city couldn't keep its word even for 24 hours. At noon the next day Keith McHenry was arrested while distributing the "Cook for Peace" fliers at the corner of Haight and Stanyan. At 1 p.m., when he was supposed to be in the mayor's office, Keith was sitting handcuffed in the back of a police car. At 1:30 he was released, the officer announcing simply, "Okay, we're releasing you."

Arriving for the negotiations over an hour late, McHenry found Agnos visibly angry at having been kept waiting. McHenry responded that the mayor had broken his word about calling a halt in the arrests. The two shouted at each other for fifteen minutes. Despite this rocky beginning, what came out of that day's talks was a temporary cessation of arrests while a permit application process had begun. Under this agreement FNB was to move its food distribution site from Haight and Stanyan to the less visible

Page and Stanyan location. McHenry had been opposed to the site-change, but was pressured into accepting it by FNB members who were tired of being arrested. The concession proved valuable to the city. At the new location the group's ability to organize in the area became greatly diminished.

The permit application process seemed to drag on endlessly, which may have been the city's real objective all along. In the upcoming months FNB members spent literally hundreds of hours meeting with officials from two city departments: Recreation and Parks and the Department of Health. These city officials, some of them drawing quite handsome salaries from the taxpayers, were well paid for the time they put into these meetings. FNB members were, of course, pouring in their own hours for free.

The incessant wrangling with the bureaucracy finally led, on March 13, 1990, to the issue of a Health Department permit to serve food at Page and Stanyan. On July 19, just over four months later, that permit was effectively rendered null when Recreation and Parks adopted a new policy prohibiting the distribution of free food in city parks. All that time spent negotiating with the city had essentially been wasted. A new flier was printed:

> After two of S.F. Recreation and Parks Department's largest public meetings, Food Not Bombs received a very ambiguous permit. Food Not Bombs pointed out at the hearings that the revolution has no permit.

In the summer of 1989 FNB took the homeless population's revolution literally to the front door of City Hall. In June of that year a group of homeless people in Civic Center, responding to police harassment and property confiscations, organized a "tent city," inviting homeless people from other parts of the city to pitch tents in Civic Center Plaza—directly across Polk Street from City Hall. FNB was asked to participate as well. It did, setting up a 24-hour-a-day outdoor field kitchen which became the food support for the entire tent city. All this occurred simultaneously to events in Tianamen Square in China, which may have been a factor in the spin it was given in the media—as well as in Agnos' decision to allow it to go on as long as it did. Patterning themselves after the protestors in Tianamen Square, the occupants of Civic Center Plaza erected a statue dubbed "the Goddess of Free Food."

The Grand Dukes at the Bank of America and elsewhere throughout the financial district must have viewed with alarm this peasant uprising on their royal estate. It never ceases to amaze me how distraught and disjointed business people become at the thought of possibly losing a single tourist dollar. But even more than the tourism issue, I think, the tent city represented a direct challenge to the right of the corporate barons to run San Francisco in the manner they saw fit. Publicly Agnos vacillated, but privately the pressure had to be mounting on him to end the protest. The t-shirts probably pushed him over the edge.

Someone—a party unknown, though doubtless one of the mayor's political enemies—had a bunch of white t-shirts printed up with the words "Camp Agnos" in large, block letters. The shirts, clean and brand new, began appearing on the backs of homeless people in Civic Center. The distinctive apparel had been passed out free of charge. Many of the homeless, realizing they were being played for propaganda purposes, actually refused to wear the shirts, but the ones who did almost invariably got their pictures taken and printed in the *Chronicle* and the *Examiner*. It was all too much for Agnos. Out came the riot cops. In less time than it took the Chinese military to clear Tianamen Square, Civic Center Plaza was swept and the Goddess of Free Food torn down.

The tent city episode ushered in a new wave of food serving arrests and property confiscations. FNB met the challenge with a seemingly inexhaustible supply of vegetarian soup and bagels. It's amazing really the amount of food that gets thrown away in this country.

***

All of this took place before I happened along on the scene.

In those days I was living in my vehicle, mostly in Southern California, working here and there, while struggling to finish a novel. The thing about living in your vehicle is you frequently get harassed by the police. I don't know how many times I woke up in the middle of the night with a cop's flashlight shining through the window and my dog, Elsa, barking and going insane on the seat next to me. One minute you're sleeping peacefully, and the next minute it's pandemonium. I have to give Elsa credit; she was just protecting us. It was the cops who wouldn't leave us alone.

Think about it from a dog's point of view, though. It's night. Total darkness. You can't see a thing beyond the frost-clouded windshield. All of a sudden creeping up to the vehicle comes this weird sort of "alien presence" trailing a flashlight beam. These nocturnal visits by the cops were, in short, interrupting our sleep and driving us both a little crazy. To make things doubly bad, the officers were usually hostile, belligerent, and meaner than snakes.

I'll never forget the meanest cop I ever encountered. It was north of San Francisco up in Sonoma County. I had just gotten off after a grueling night of dishwashing at the Flamingo Hotel in Santa Rosa. I was making about $5 an hour at the time, which is nowhere near enough to put a roof over your head in California. I was, therefore, homeless. Now some homeless people don't seem to mind getting along by hitting up other folks for money. I've never been much for doing that. I've always preferred to work when I could.

I was going into the Flamingo every afternoon at four. That night we had washed dishes until about 1 a.m. When I got off I was so damn tired and worn down that I could hardly walk straight. I grabbed a shower in the employee changing room, then drove out to the Santa Rosa fairgrounds, where I had gotten away with bedding down on several occasions before. It was pitch black and there was this huge expanse of a dirt parking lot, maybe an acre or two big, and at night the place was completely deserted, with no lights.

I figured I was far enough away from anybody where I wouldn't disturb them and they wouldn't disturb me. There were these night birds out there, too, with this funny, strange sort of call. Or maybe they were bats, not birds. But at any rate it was sort of nice settling down at night and listening to them. I let Elsa out to do her business, fed her, and then the two of us settled back inside the vehicle to catch some sleep before the sun came up. I guess it was about 2 or 3 a.m. Suddenly along comes this cop.

"Hell!" I swore. I was dead tired and in no mood to be trifled with. He came speeding across the dirt parking lot, blowing up dust and aiming his spotlight beam directly on us, to which Elsa gave her customary response: pandemonium and bristling rage.

"What are you doin' here?" he drawled after walking over to my window.

"Tryin' to get some sleep," I replied—a bit testily. Well that did it. Never be testy with a cop, especially if you're a homeless person. When you're in the presence of a cop you're only allowed by be pliant and obsequious. They don't, by and large, cotton to anything but the most servile demeanor.

I was ordered out of the car in a belligerent manner and told to produce some I.D. He was a big fat stocky white cop, with a beer or maybe a donut belly, and a cop moustache, which is kind of like a Hitler moustache only slightly lengthened. In all my dealings with cops the worst-case scenario I had ever imagined is that I might someday be arrested, my vehicle would be towed and Elsa would be taken to the dog pound and put to sleep before I could get out of jail and rescue her. That's if Murphy's Law prevailed and everything that possibly could go wrong did.

Suddenly it occurred to me, however, that my imagination had been far too limited and that something much worse could happen: I could end up with a bullet in the head. This guy was a killer. I could see it in his face. He had killed before and would do it again. I could see something else in his face too: He hated my guts.

Why cops hate homeless people is a question I used to ponder and dwell upon long and hard, trying to rack my brain to figure out, sort of as if finding the answer were the key to unlocking the mysteries of the universe. What have homeless people ever done to cops that they should be so despised and hated by them? I don't wonder about that any more—not because I ever found the answer. I didn't. I stopped wondering because some things just are.

Occasionally you have to accept the fact that certain things are just reality and there's nothing you can do about them. In a more naive period of my life I used to think of cops as being just average working-class guys who would have no reason for being hostile to other working class guys who might happen to be just a little more down on their luck. I've altered my views on that. In fact, I've quit trying to figure out why cops think the way they do about anything—such as, for instance, why they're always so rabidly right wing. Some things just are.

Maybe the same is true of racism, sexism, homophobia and all the other -isms. They just are. Maybe we'll never solve it and get rid of all this hate. But getting back to my original question: Why do cops hate homeless people? The best answer I've ever been able to come up with is: they're just plain old plug mean and they'll do anything for a paycheck. And believe me, cops are drawing some pretty grand paychecks these days.

So there I was staring into the face of a killer, and not just any killer, but a killer who hated my guts, mostly on general principles. To make matters worse it was pitch dark, 3 in the morning, and nobody around for a half mile or more. How had I gotten myself into this? Suddenly my heart began to pound hard as an appalling thought floated into my tired head: this guy could kill me and claim it was in self defense—that I had attacked him, etc.—and he could probably get away with it. No, change that: he could *definitely* get away with it. He could pull out his pistol, pump five or six shots in me, and more than likely no one would even question his version of events except maybe for a few homeless people I knew in Santa Rosa.

Resolving to give him no reason to bash my head in or shoot me, I stood quietly in the dark while he ran, I guess, every conceivable kind of check on my I.D. and license plate, looking for anything he could possibly find to take me to jail on. But there wasn't anything.

"Get out of here," he told me at last, handing back my license. His anger seemed to have subsided just a slight tad. It was definitely capable of rekindling, I decided. "Don't come around here again." Clearly he meant it. He babbled some other stuff in a flat, killer's tone of voice, but my mind was racing too fast to pick it up. "Just get out of here," was pretty much all I thought. At last he told me I could go.

My hand shook on the gear shift stick as I drove away. I drove for a long time, until I was sure I was well out of his jurisdiction. He had not, perhaps, put the fear of God into me, but he had definitely put the fear of fascism.

***

It was sometime during the summer of 1990 that I came to San Francisco. By chance I went to a poetry reading in North Beach, where I met one of the most remarkable men I've ever met. Jack Hirschman was the featured reader that day. It was a Sunday afternoon. I watched and listened, amazed, as this man Hirschman read a series of poems, first in English and then in Italian. I've also heard him speak Spanish and Russian. I have no idea how many different languages he actually speaks.

I thought I had heard it all—that I had more or less plumbed the depths of his knowledge, at least to the extent that I was in for no more surprises—when one day he came over to the SFLR studio with a poet from Haiti, and to my astonishment he and this Haitian poet, named Boadiba, began reading poems together in French Creole! The way some people pull an ink pen out of their pocket and offer it to you, Hirschman casually hands you a whole language you didn't know he had.

He's one of the smartest men I think I've ever met. He used to teach at Dartmouth, I would later learn. But that day in 1990, after finishing his bilingual performance in North Beach, he announced there was going to be a protest that evening. It had something or other to do with homeless people being harassed by the police. My ears perked up. I had been jerked around by so many different cops on so many different occasions by then that I was ready to join anything. In reality, however, this was the first time I had ever encountered homeless people who were organizing to fight back. In my own provincial experience, homeless people invariably did nothing but stammer and cower and cringe when in the presence of abusive cops. I resolved to go to this demonstration which Hirschman had announced.

It was at Civic Center Plaza. When I got there only a few people were present. One of these was Hirschman, who was standing at the front of the fountain talking with someone. I went up and said hello. Hirschman smiled, recognizing me from earlier this afternoon. Along with his powerful intellect he has a wonderful, warm smile coupled with an irrepressible enthusiasm. I judged him to be in his early to mid-fifties. He was old enough to be my father.

He stood slightly over six feet, with broad shoulders and twinkling eyes. While his personal manner was warm and affectionate, his poetry, on the other hand, smoldered with rage, I was beginning to learn. Under his arm he carried a stack of radical newspapers—*The Peoples Tribune,* put out by the League of Revolutionaries for a New America, or what came later to be known by that name. Hirschman, in short, was a poet, an intellectual, a radical, and an organizer—a passel of traits which, taken and mixed up all together in one human being, made him precisely the sort of person who gets killed by U.S.-trained death squads in Third World countries.

In Guatemala or El Salvador, or some other U.S.-supported "democracy," Hirschman would be a dead man. How long before these policies, conducted and carried out by our government in other countries, come home and get put into place against us—this is a question Americans need to seriously ask themselves. Chicago Black Panther leader Fred Hampton, for one, might, if he could speak today, answer that the chickens have already come home. But, again, if they have, you won't read about it in the *New York Times.*

***

The issue that night was something called "647-i." It was some obscure law the cops were using to arrest homeless people who lay on or underneath blankets or sleeping bags. Such an act—laying under a blanket—was considered to be evidence of an "intent to lodge," and was therefore unlawful. Evidently it was legal to be homeless in San Francisco as long as you remained in a sitting-up position and didn't attempt to cover yourself to keep warm.

Mark Twain once remarked that the coldest winter he had ever lived through was the summer he'd spent in San Francisco. Twain made that statement for a very good reason: it gets downright cold here in the summer. It has something to do with the bay drawing the fog in from the ocean at that time of year. I don't exactly understand the meteorological phenomenon at work here. I just know it gets cold. I was wearing a long sleeve sweatshirt and a jacket that night. Now note the absurdity: here you have a law—647-

i—that makes it illegal for people to try and protect themselves from the cold.

Now think about it! Think about the fact that we live in a society that would rather have a stupid, illogical, jack-ass law like that on the books—rather than a society which would prefer to cease creating the conditions which bring about homelessness in the first place. Think about the implications of that! It's a sad, crazy commentary on the insanity of America, and it all gets back to seeing that pile of feces on the ground and getting it straight in your mind who is really to blame for it.

More and more people were arriving now. Somebody called for a circle to be formed. There were about 40 or 50 people present. It made for a very large circle, the circular pattern materializing on the sidewalk in front of the fountain. (The fountain didn't have any water in it in those days; it was just a big, long rectangular hole lined with tile and concrete, like an empty swimming pool.

People sat on the sidewalk breathing in the cold, foggy air and exhaling clouds of the same, some with back packs or other bundles resting beside them. Traveling puffs and wisps of low-hanging fog streamed across the grey ceiling overhead, giving the impression that the world was moving. It was in a way. I could feel power flowing through that circle. Yet not in my wildest dreams did I imagine I was on my way to putting a radio station on the air.

There were men and women of all ages, although for the most part it was a young crowd, with a fair prevalence of Doc Martins shoes, a few pierced noses and lips, some brightly dyed heads of hair here and there. What was going to happen is a small number of people were going to commit civil disobedience, challenging the 647-i law by laying out sleeping bags and climbing into them. It was fully expected that these would be arrested.

A few more people arrived, the circle growing as it stretched to accommodate them. A large man a little ways to my right in the circle began to speak. "So I guess I'll facilitate since I have the loudest voice out here," he joked. Certainly his voice carried, I noticed. He was bearded, blonde-haired, burly-chested and square jawed. Around his middle he carried a pouch of fat, yet the wideness of his chest precluded, for the most part, any thought of him as "fat." A truer description would be "big." He looked, moreover, like an NFL lineman who had decided to give up football, grow his hair and beard out, and live the bohemian life for a while. His blonde hair, a shade or two lighter than his beard, hung almost to his shoulders, but not straight and limp like fine hair. Rather it had a steel-wool-like quality, traveling downward but at the same time frizzing outward, giving the impression of broadening his already-wide shoulders even more. Beneath the beard was the hint of a ruddy-cheeked complexion, as if he spent a lot of time outdoors—time, perhaps, standing or moving about in ultra-violet sunlight, on city concrete baked by global warming.

For all his size, by far the most striking thing about him, however, was the way he spoke. His enunciation of each word was careful, precise—almost loving. He possessed an articulateness that belied his bulky physiognomy. But there was something else about him as well, some intangible trait that I at first couldn't define because it's something you so rarely see. But then I had it. It sort of hit me—not exactly like a bolt of lightning, but more like a feeling or a certainty that sort of descended down and settled comfortably over me. At any rate, suddenly I felt: I was in the presence of a being with a genuinely good soul. A sort of ethereal goodness emanated from his inner being.

Now this is a trait that, when encountered, as it often is in priests and ministers, is never unexpected. Here, however, was someone with no pretense of being a "man of God," and who certainly wasn't wearing any clerical collar—here, moreover, was just a guy on the street—but who seemed to radiate that quality of inner spirituality—that or at least its close cousin. It was unusual. Not unprecedented in my singular experience, but definitely unusual.

I looked around the rest of the circle. What I saw and sensed in the others present, were souls, pretty much like my own, beset by feelings of jealousy, greed, lust, self-aggrandizement and all the other usual human foibles. Despite the prevalence of leather jackets and body piercings it was an otherwise unremarkable cross-section of humanity.

Yet here was someone who seemed, at least for the moment, to have risen above such concerns. Here was someone focused—at least for the moment—entirely upon the purpose at hand. And that purpose was to liberate, not only himself but every single person present in the circle, from police repression. And it was clear that everyone there had experienced repression first hand. It was the common bond that united us all together. This desire that I saw in him, to liberate and deliver from evil, extended, I felt subconsciously, even to me. Even though I was a stranger, and potentially an undercover police informant, I was nevertheless a part of the circle. These are some of the things I felt as I watched him speak, struck by his eloquence.

It was Keith McHenry.

Calmly he began to speak about the upcoming civil disobedience action and of how he felt the police would respond. "My sense is that the police will do this..." he would say, or, "It seems likely that they will do that..." He seemed to have anticipated every move the police would make, perhaps even before they did. Well well, I thought, here's somebody who knows what's what—and although a tense, confrontational situation was developing, I actually found myself relaxing a bit, carried along by the momentum. His presence within that circle was able to do that—to sort of make people feel safe.

There was something else about that circle as well: I didn't know it then, but I had stumbled into my first Food Not Bombs meeting. In those days it was not uncommon for the group to meet in outdoor locations, such as the front steps of City Hall, or, like this evening, in front of the Civic Center fountain. One thing about homeless people, of course, is they have no homes. Thus group meetings, at least in those days, often would be held on some randomly chosen patch of city concrete. That's not to say that everyone present was a homeless person.

You can tell when somebody's carrying their whole life on their back, and the ratio that evening seemed to be about half homeless and half housed persons present. Not that the housed persons seemed to be anything remotely approaching well-to-do—just that it was obvious they had someplace to go after the meeting besides the nearest doorway. As a "vehicle dweller," my whole life was in my camper truck, which I had parked several blocks away. Thus I could have passed for a housed person quite easily—but there was no reason to attempt to do so or pretend to be anything other than what I was. It was clear that within this circle the homeless were treated with just as much respect as the housed. I had seen that instantly. I could share with these people the fact that I was living in my vehicle and no one would think the less of me.

In short, here was a community—a community which took care of its own, much like communities used to do way back in the old days in the event of floods, tornadoes or other natural disasters. And poverty, injustice and police brutality are pretty much the millennial equivalents of natural disasters. Moreover, it had been growing increasingly clear to me for a long time that life as a lone individual would not hold a very high probability of survival in the last decade of the 20th century.

That's why I can never fathom why Americans remain so puzzled over the "phenomenon" of urban street gangs. The word "gang" is simply another word for community. These kids know that in a climate as hostile and divided as that which presently exists in America, their lives would be worth little without the help, support and protection of their community. Listen to the lyrics of rap music. This is stated very clearly. You can learn a lot more about what's really and truly happening in America by listening to rap music than by watching the news with Dan Rather or Ted Koppel or any of those other corporate-owned screen celebrities.

In a world where logic and sense prevailed—instead of money—CBS would fire Dan Rather and hire Ice-T to anchor the evening news. He knows heads and tails more about what's happening in this country and he'd be more bluntly honest with the American people than Rather ever thought about being. No, it's no mystery, as the media would have you believe, why kids join gangs.

And what are the police? The police are maybe a lot of things, but in outward appearance they resemble nothing more than the biggest gang on the street. In terms of their group dynamics they function as a gang. There's a gang mentality operative that you can detect, especially in the more loyal, gung-ho types, a sense that they will support each other and back each other up whether for right or wrong, or good or evil. The reason they are the biggest, baddest, meanest gang on the streets is very simple: They get government funding. Can you imagine if the Crips or Bloods got funding at the level of the police? It would be a whole different story.

This makes the government's whims and desires, backed up as they are by a powerful gang, come closer and closer to resembling nothing more so than the whims and desires of an organized crime ring. And certainly it's possible to get along in a system controlled by organized crime—as long as you play by the rules the crime bosses set.

This being de facto the biggest gang around is why the police get very nervous when other gangs start holding truces. If the smaller gangs ever united and became one big gang they might usurp that position of power. That's pretty much the law of the jungle. This is also why, whenever a cop gets shot, or even just punched, the whole police department goes berserk and practically kills the suspect. They are sending a message to all the other gangs: if anyone out there dares to so much as raise a hand against us we will make sure they pay a heavy price—maybe, even, the ultimate price.

Living under such a system of gang rule might not be so bad if it were a gang-ruled system predicated upon justice. Unfortunately, justice for the individual is not what concerns the crime bosses in power. They have grown rather indolent, lazy and self-satisfied and have cast aside even the flimsiest of concerns over whether or not it's possible, under the rules they have set up, for those at the bottom to eke out even the basest, barest survival.

Since none of us bottom-dwellers wanted to get torn limb from limb that night, and thus have that law-of-the-jungle message transmitted over our broken, bleeding bodies, not a single one of us planned on raising a hand against the police in the upcoming protest. The police, not us, were the most powerful gang on the street.

This is something I think virtually all protest groups recognize without the slightest hesitation or delusion, and that's why when cops go blaming violence on protestors it should always be taken with a grain of salt—which is another reason why Ice-T would be a better anchorman than Dan Rather: unlike Rather, Ice-T would question the cops' version of events. The overwhelming majority of violence at demonstrations is committed by cops against demonstrators. That's a blue chip stock you can invest in, a truth you can take to the bank.

The meeting broke up. The protest got underway. Night had fallen. The sleeping bags were unrolled and people got into them, while others shouted and chanted things like "Food Not Bombs!" and "Stop the war on the poor!"

The police arrived, materializing suddenly out of the surrounding darkness as if they'd been beamed down a la *Star Trek*. The San Francisco police have a way of doing that—just materializing out of thin air when you think they're not around. A moment ago I hadn't seen a cop anywhere, not a one in sight. Then there were about 10 of them.

Like oysters from a shell, the people engaging in civil disobedience were pried loose from their sleeping bags—arrested for the crime of trying to keep warm on a cold night. I stood glued to the spot I was standing on, my eyes riveted to the incredible scene. The defiant protestors were placed in the back of police vans, and the doors shut. After a moment I heard a loud thump thump thump coming from within one of the vans. The people locked inside were kicking the walls of the van—it sounded like some serious kicking going on too. Then the van began to rock from side to side on its axles.

After it was all over I walked away in the cold dark night, furiously mulling over everything I had witnessed, my ears ringing silently after leaving the noisy demonstration.

***

After that I started volunteering regularly with Food Not Bombs. One of the first meal servings I attended was in UN Plaza. UN Plaza and Civic Center Plaza are very close to each other. You can walk from one to the other in roughly 3-4 minutes. After finishing with the food serving in UN Plaza that evening, some of the FNB people—Keith McHenry was not with us at the time—drifted on foot over to Civic Center. Nobody told me not to, so I tagged along.

Now, in those days there was a cop named Blackwell who used to harass FNB a lot. His first name was Thomas, but everybody just called him Blackboot Blackwell. He was built kind of like Arnold Schwarzenegger, and looked a little bit like him too. He was also a sergeant, which made him kind of a big banana with the other cops.

Well, we were all standing there in the fog talking when all of a sudden, cruising slowly up Polk Street in his black and white cop car, came Blackwell. I was standing next to Peter Donahue at the time. Peter would later torch a police motorcycle during the Rodney King uprising. He was a young guy in his mid-twenties with long, blonde dreadlocks, which were held in check to some degree by a bandana tied broadly around his forehead. He also wore thin, wire-rimmed glasses which gave him a sort of studious air, and in fact, underneath the dreadlocks there burned a pretty sharp mind, I had begun to discover.

Whenever he opened his mouth in FNB meetings it was usually to offer some comment or other that made a tremendous amount of sense, and people had a lot of respect for him. I think he and Blackwell may have had some run-in in the past, however, because as the black and white car inched closer to us, he murmured under his breath, "Here comes Sergeant Blackwell. This guy is really bad news." Something about the way he said it gave me to understand that he wasn't kidding in the slightest. Outwardly Peter remained calm, but in his voice I detected an unmistakable note of fear.

Blackwell stopped his cop car about three feet away from us and glared balefully through the open window. Had any of us been serving food that evening? he asked. I'm sure he already knew the answer. "Oh no," someone denied, just for the record, "no not at all." As much as I had felt that ethereal goodness in the presence of McHenry, I now detected wave upon wave of spiritual blackness emanating from Blackwell.

"If I catch any of you serving food around here you're going to jail," he said malignantly, and drove off.

Now the interesting thing about Blackwell is he later committed suicide. He put a pistol to his head and offed himself. Just as statistics should be kept on homeless people's deaths, I contend that statistics should also be kept on how many cops commit suicide every year. I have an idea that the number is fairly high in relation to other occupations. Now you can speculate all you want on why Blackwell committed suicide, theorizing, if you like, that maybe he was depressed over the fact that his job required him to take food out of the mouths of hungry people, but such speculating and psychoanalyzing after the fact strike me as the ruminations of a Monday morning quarterback. The fact is he did it. Who really knows why? I still think it would be useful though for statisticians, if they've not already done so, to start taking note of cop suicides.

***

Those FNB meetings I began going to at that time were my first introduction to anarchy. Contrary to popular opinion, the words "anarchy" and "chaos" are not synonyms. Anarchy, in reality, is a system of government—self government. It is decision-making by a group as a whole, instead of by elected representatives. Anarchy was used as a form of government in certain areas of Spain prior to the civil war. So far to date, Spain in the 1930s had been anarchy's greatest shining moment in history. It probably would have lasted, or so many modern-day anarchists will tell you, if the communists and the fascists hadn't come along and ruined everything. This is of course all speculative.

My own attitude toward anarchy is one of keeping an open mind. It seems moreover to be the only thing we, that is to say the people of the planet Earth, haven't yet tried. We've tried communism and that didn't work. We've tried capitalism. That hasn't worked. Maybe it's time to give anarchy a go. Do I then consider myself an "anarchist?" No, but I jump on bandwagons far less today than I did at a much earlier time in my life. The only thing I know for sure is that what we have in America now is not working—is in fact killing people.

Central to the Food Not Bombs philosophy is consensus decision making. At a Food Not Bombs meeting, once a proposal is put out on the floor, every single member of the group must agree to it or it's no-go. Now, coming to decisions in such a manner sounds like it would make for a very difficult and cantankerous process. This isn't always the case, however, especially when a group has come together for a specific reason—such as opposing war and poverty—and has established itself around certain principles of unity—such as the use of non-violence—as a means of achieving its goals. This is not to say that all is bliss and happiness. I've been to FNB meetings that have turned into marathon wrangles lasting late into the night until I was pretty much sick of the sound of the human voice.

The Achilles heel of such a system is that it leaves a group open to disruption by undercover police informants. In the classic scenario, a cop will infiltrate a group and then block every good proposal that comes along, while promoting or advocating potentially destructive courses of action. This is why many people feel that once the state is finally overthrown, anarchy could potentially come into its own finally as a smooth running system.

The idea is that with global capitalism overturned and multi-national corporations de-chartered and broken up, the police would cease to have political repression as one of their objectives. Their concerns would then become limited to their social service functions in society. This would not only make life easier for the people who live under such a system, it would also be beneficial for the police themselves.

Many cops I think are fundamentally confused about what their role in society is, which probably accounts for their high rate of suicides. In a post-revolutionary era, under a new system predicated upon justice, I think there would be far fewer ideological splits and divisions within society. Some people theorize that whole cities could be organized under a system of consensus decision-making. This would not be inconceivable in a community setting wherein everyone were oriented around the idea of the survival and well-being of the community as a whole.

In Food Not Bombs there is no hierarchy, no chain of command, and no one gives orders to anyone else. In those days in the early nineties, though, there *were* people within the group whose hard work, sacrifice and commitment—and whose wise counsel in group meetings—gave extra weight to their words. When those people spoke others would listen. Keith was such a person. Peter Donahue was too. Never once, however, did I see either of them issue an order to anyone. Both had the ability to speak with eloquence. To the degree that people heeded their counsel, it was because they chose to do so. That's how consensus decision making works.

Not to overly romanticize indigenous peoples or anything, but I think Native American societies, prior to European colonization, must have been organized along somewhat similar lines. I don't believe the Hunkpapa Lakota, for instance, followed Sitting Bull because he ordered them too. I think they simply chose to follow such a man. Similarly, I don't think the Oglalla people followed Crazy Horse under orders. I think they decided simply that he was a man of great wisdom and bravery and, above all else, that he was devoted to his people. People don't have to be ordered to follow such leaders.

America today is run by "leaders" for whom we have little or no respect, and who have no regard for us. Yet we are forced, in lock step, to follow them. Something is wrong with this picture.

So Peter and Keith, while not formal leaders, were listened to for their wise counsel. There were other people in the group who fit that description too. Sheila Cummings was one. She was a woman with red hair who hailed from L.A., and who taught school in the San Francisco school system. She had a peculiar mix of soft-spoken gentility on the one hand, and tough street-smarts on the other. With a flaming spirit that matched her hair, she sometimes acted as a media spokesperson, spinning FNB's position in careful, precise terms, elucidating details of the latest police attacks with vivid clarity. In meetings she could always be counted upon to say something powerful and to the point, and, again, when she spoke people listened.

***

The police, to a large degree, hated FNB with an incomprehensible, unfathomable passion, but they hated Keith most of all, mainly, I think, because he wasn't afraid of them. Sometimes they would arrest him when he was actually "breaking the law" by serving food; other times they would just walk up and claim to have warrants. Sometimes these warrants would be real. Sometimes they'd be phony. Sometimes they would arrest him while he was walking down the sidewalk. Other times they pulled him over in his truck. Once they arrested him right outside a courtroom not more than five minutes after a judge had turned him loose. They pretty much were the law unto themselves.

I had by this time begun to regard Keith as a friend. He and his wife, Andrea, lived in an apartment on Clement Street, and both I and Elsa had been welcomed guests over there on several occasions. The usual procedure when these arbitrary arrests took place was to call Andrea, who had sort of a hotline to all of FNB's lawyers. While the lawyers were often able to get him out of jail, there was little they could do to stop the arrests from happening. These were the days when we realized that something had to change, and that we needed some kind of power on our side to turn the tables. That power later came in the form of radio.

The courtroom arrest alluded to above occurred on March 22, 1991. It was a Friday. I remember because I was arrested that day too and it was Saturday night before I got out of jail. It was my first arrest as a member of FNB.

Keith had gone to court that day on a contempt of court charge. Specifically, he had violated a court order against serving food without a permit. The charge carried a 40-day jail sentence. Keith's friends and supporters went to court with him. I guess there were about forty or fifty of us there, filing quietly into the courtroom and taking seats. Keith had worn a dark grey suit that day. With hair neatly brushed and combed, he looked as if he had put forth a genuinely sincere effort to make a favorable impression on the judge.

Now that day Superior Court Judge Daniel Hanlon ruled that the city's permit process had been flawed in the manner in which it had been applied to FNB. The upshot of this decision was that FNB was ordered to begin the permit application process again. Now, folks had already spent hundreds of hours over the past 3 years negotiating with city officials over permit applications. Essentially what the judge was saying was that members of the group had to now start that process all over again from square one. So that was the dopey aspect of the ruling. Negotiating with the city hadn't led anywhere before—had in fact been a huge drain of time and energy. What reason was there to believe it would turn out any different this time?

The good part of the ruling was that the charges against Keith were dropped. He was free to go. At this point all 50 or so of us rose and began filing out of the courtroom, most of us being generally pretty pleased with the way things had turned out. At least no one was going to jail, or so we thought.

When we left the courtroom we were startled to discover the hallway outside jam-packed with cops. There were cops of every stripe and variety. There were San Francisco cops, California Highway Patrol cops, Sheriff's Department cops...there were uniformed cops, plain clothes cops, grungy-looking undercover cops, and guys in suits and dark glasses who looked like FBI. At first it looked like they were all just standing out there casually lounging around for no particular reason. Then suddenly Keith was grabbed and re-arrested. Supposedly there was an outstanding traffic warrant. At that point all hell broke loose.

Now in my mind, and in the minds of a lot of others, there's always been something real suspicious about the timing of that arrest. Here was Keith leaving court with a crowd of Food Not Bombs supporters. Everyone's in kind of jubilant spirits. Then suddenly this ton of bricks falls on us. It was as if the arrest had been deliberately timed to provoke trouble. If so, it worked.

Suddenly all around me people were screaming. Pandemonium erupted. Now, some people who were there that day say it was the cops who started pushing first. I can't honestly say who started it. Suddenly, however, I was at the top of a stairway in the midst of a crowd of pushing, jostling, screaming people. Like a lump of freshly chewed meat being swallowed slowly down an esophagus, the knot of pushing, scuffling humanity made its way slowly down the stairway. Keith, still in custody of the cops, had lost his footing and somehow gotten flipped over onto his back.

The cops were dragging him head first down the stairs, yet he must have been the only one in all of City Hall who wasn't screaming. His body was straight. He was not struggling. He was completely off the floor, and it looked like he was simply being carried along by the momentum, as if he were riding a wave—a wave leading him head-first down the stairs. His legs were outstretched, his eyes were open, and his mouth was closed. There was a nonplussed expression on his face. Seeing this gentle, loving, kind man dragged down like that, I guess, just triggered something in me, and suddenly I flipped.

All at once I was screaming along with everyone else.

"Nazis! Nazis! You Nazis!" I screamed. It was the worst insult I could think of to call anyone. We had reached the bottom of that flight of stairs now, although we were still on one of the upper levels of City Hall. The cops had formed a cordon, cutting off the hallway to the left. A wall of angry, screaming people confronted that cordon now, yelling stuff in the cops' faces.

By chance, one of the cops in the line was Sergeant Blackwell. In addition there was a guy in a white shirt and a tie there who was kind of directing the cops. I think he was from the D.A.'s office. I had been continuing to yell "Nazis!" all this time when suddenly this guy from the D.A.'s office commanded Blackwell, "Get that one!" pointing directly at me. Well there were about 50 of us there in the narrow corridor, all yelling in kind of a crazed manner, and at first Blackwell just stood there as if he hadn't heard, or was unsure who he'd been ordered to get. If I'd been smart then I would have stepped back and disappeared into the crowd. But I didn't. I just stood there and kept yelling "Nazis!" at a fairly high decibel level until this guy from the D.A.'s office repeated insistently, "Get that one!" and pointed again at me.

This time there was no mistaking. I was tackled by Blackboot Blackwell and brought down with a thud. Before I could recover, I was handcuffed and dragged like a sack of oats into and on through the police line, down a deserted corridor, where I was deposited at last in a tiny room that looked kind of like a miniature law library. There were some law books on some shelves, and a big mahogany table in the center of the room. The room held two other captives besides myself—Keith and another FNB person, Eric Warren. There were about 4 or 5 cops in the room too, all kind of standing around. Keith and Eric were sitting quietly, but the cops were sort of laughing and shooting the breeze with each other, as if it were all just another day's work to them.

Then all the cops left the room except one, who remained standing guard over us. Eric, Keith and I talked quietly for a moment or two, but then the three of us simply began listening to the police radio—the cop in the room with us had one of those walkie-talkie cop radios on his belt. With rapt attention, we all, including the cop, began monitoring the progress of what was going on outside. There were, after all, still 40 or 50 screaming FNB members loose in City Hall.

Suddenly the tone of the chatter on the radio changed subtly, becoming slightly less bored and more tinged with urgency. It transpired that somewhere in City Hall a cop had lost his gun. We all listened intently. There was a lot of back and forth conversation on the radio about the gun. This went on for several minutes, during which time we tried to formulate a clear picture of events unfolding outside, but the traffic you hear over police scanners often bears little relation to what's happening in reality. Try as we might, the only thing we could ascertain for sure was that something had happened and that it involved a cop's gun.

Then the other cops came back to the room and we were told, "Alright let's go." We were on our way to jail, but before we got out of the building a fourth captive was added to our number: Tom Osher, who had worn white face paint and a red clown nose to our little protest on the front steps this morning. Most of the face paint had worn off, but the clown nose was still there, although looking a tad bereft and somewhat the worse for wear.

Still handcuffed, we were placed in the back of a police van. Two cops got in front and began to drive. On the way to jail, it seemed, they made a lot of hard, whipping turns and sudden halts, as if to deliberately toss us around a lot. With our hands cuffed we had no way of bracing ourselves, and mostly we just bobbed, bounced and crashed around back there like 4 bowling pins—or at least like 3 bowling pins, for Keith, maybe because his bulk and size served him as anchor, seemed hardly affected at all. Nonetheless the two cops seemed pretty amused by our predicament, looking back and laughing from time to time as Eric and I and Tom fought to maintain our equilibrium.

After we were booked into the jail we were placed into dormitory cells containing about 20 prisoners each. Keith, Eric, and Tom were put in one cell, while I got broken off from the group and placed in another. The overwhelming majority of the prisoners in my cell were black and brown. Most all of them had heard of FNB, although maybe it was hard for them not to have heard, since there was FNB graffiti scratched everywhere all over the jail. But most everyone there knew at least some little something about FNB and its fight to serve food to the needy, and once word got around that I had been arrested with the group I was befriended and treated exceptionally well. It was touching that people wanted to share their food with me. I was feeling pretty hungry by then, and so some of the extra portions that came my way were especially welcomed.

***

San Francisco Chronicle March 23, 1991

City Hall Melee
After Arrest of
Food Distributor

By George Markell
Chronicle Staff Writer

City Hall looked like a riot zone briefly yesterday morning after a plainclothes police officer had his gun snatched during a melee after the arrest of Keith McHenry, leader of Food Not Bombs, a group of anarchist food distributors.

McHenry was leaving a fourth floor courtroom after contempt charges against him were dismissed, when officers arrested him on a traffic warrant. As he was being led away in handcuffs, McHenry began shouting incitements to his followers, according to police.

McHenry's lawyer, Sarge Holtzman, said the trouble began when a police officer pushed McHenry on the way down a stairwell.

At that point about three dozen of the Food Not Bombs group engaged in a shoving match in which a patrol officer was roughed up and a plainclothes officer had his service pistol snatched by someone in the crowd.

City Hall was immediately swarming with cops, including police in riot gear. When the pushing and shoving broke up, about 40 Food Not Bombs supporters and hangers-on surrounded a police car parked outside. Someone smashed a window with the missing gun and dropped it inside, said Captain Tim Hettrich, commander of Northern Station. [27]

The above *San Francisco Chronicle* article makes us seem like some pretty rough and tumble pistol-grabbing, cop-fighting pugilists. As flattering as that image may be, very little of what the newspaper had to say about that day was true. Four people were arrested—yes—but from there the story pretty much drifts off into cop-inspired fiction.

While there are any number of reasons why someone might want to steal a cop's gun, for that person then to not only have a change of heart and decide to return the gun, but to go to all the risk and trouble of breaking out the window of a cop car in order to do so, seems peculiar indeed. While Hettrich's story would account for how the gun at last came to be found inside the cop car, a much more likely explanation perhaps might be that the cop in question was drunk, dropped the gun on the floorboard of his car, and only realized it was missing once he got inside City Hall and the scuffle started—whereupon he leaped to the conclusion that someone in the crowd had snatched it. That at least is the theory.

The cop whose gun went missing that day was a detective named Broadnick. Several people reported seeing Broadnick drunk that morning, even witnessing other cops remonstrating with him over his public condition. Admittedly the people who say this are members of FNB and you might be tempted to make the claim, "Well, they're biased observers." But since the *Chronicle* printed the police department's version so unhesitatingly, I thought it only fair to give the FNB side of the story here. As for myself, having been knocked to the floor, dragged along like a corpse, and locked up in a little room in an upper floor of City Hall, I'm not really in a position to say exactly what happened outside the building.

But the premise that FNB was responsible for stealing a cop's gun that day was challenged in a letter-to-the-editor written by Andrea McHenry and sent to the *Chronicle*. I don't know if the *Chronicle* ever printed the letter—I don't think it did, although maybe it did and it just got by me. At any rate the letter has been preserved. Here is what Andrea wrote:

Editor
San Francisco Chronicle
901 Mission St.
San Francisco, CA 94103

Dear Editor:

George Markell's article on Saturday, March 23, 1991 about the police riot after the FNB contempt hearing in the City Hall contains statements which are not true.

Mr. Markell states that "a plainclothes officer had his service pistol snatched by someone in the crowd." This statement is not attributed to either the police or the Food Not Bombs members. George Markell was not even present. No gun was ever taken by anyone at City Hall on March 22.

The traffic warrant resulting in Mr. McHenry's arrest also was false. Judge Donaldson ruled that Assistant

District Attorney Petroni had issued two complaints for the same incident. McHenry had made all court appearances on the complaint.

Food Not Bombs has asked the *Chronicle* for a true and accurate account of the police riot, but so far none has been published.

Sincerely,
Andrea McHenry

As far as I know, the *Chronicle* stuck with its story, never printing a retraction.

The jails are so damn full in San Francisco that it's pretty easy to get "OR'd out," or released on your "own recognizance," if you've only been arrested on a minor charge. We were all charged with assaulting police officers, but apparently the jails were so overcrowded that that was considered minor enough. Certainly the charges were bogus—I hadn't assaulted anyone—and judging from the comments from some of the jail staff doing booking and intake, they seemed to be in the know that the charges were bogus too. The sheriff of San Francisco had, as well, become a frequent complainer about the ongoing FNB arrests making the space in his jail, already scarce enough as it was, even scarcer.

Another factor in my getting sprung—I didn't know this at the time but learned it later—was that Andrea McHenry had phoned the OR office and sworn that I had a valid San Francisco address. This was a lie, but so lax were the policies and so full the jail that the OR people were willing to take such affirmations on faith.

Nevertheless, by Saturday night we had been locked up in excess of 24 hours. I was worried about Elsa. I had left her locked up in the truck, which I had left parked at the Marina. The wind blows a lot there, and I knew that with the sunroof and the vents open she'd stay pretty cool. But I was anxious—both for her and our little home on wheels. Thus when the deputy unlocked the cell door and called out my name, it was a welcomed relief.

He led me down a long corridor, past one overcrowded cell after another, and finally out front near the elevators where people were booked in and out of the jail. Here I encountered Keith, who had just been brought up from his own cell. It was the first time I had laid eyes on him since the day before when we'd been brought in. He was still wearing his suit, although by now it was looking pretty rumpled, and he'd taken off the tie. We had barely had time to greet each other when they grabbed us and hustled us up to a counter where we were supposed to go through some sort of check-out paper work process.

There were several male deputies working behind the counter but the one assigned to us took Keith first. He handed Keith a form to sign but Keith refused to sign it. The deputy began to grow angry. Keith informed him politely that a signature was impossible because we had been falsely arrested. By way of response, the deputy simply stared back at Keith as if he had spoken gibberish.

"This is not an admission of guilt or innocence," the deputy explained, as if perhaps Keith couldn't read or had not understood the gist of what was being called for at the moment. "I just need your signature so we can release you."

They argued back and forth for a couple of minutes until finally Keith took the form and wrote the words "In protest of these lies"—and filled in his signature

When the deputy glanced down and saw what was written, his little boiler needle rose dangerously into the red.

"I already told you this is not an admission of guilt or innocence!!"

Keith replied evenly that that's what he had in fact said.

"Then why," the deputy demanded shrilly, "would you write what you did?"

When things reach an impasse in such a manner, the train of officialdom invariably assumes the prerogative of having the right of way. Keith was grabbed and hustled back in the direction from which we had both been brought. They were putting him back in the cell.

My turn.

I stepped up to the counter. The deputy who'd gotten in such a tempest was just then being told something in sort of hushed tones by another deputy behind the counter. "Oh, is that who that sonofabitch is!" he exclaimed now.

A sucker for punishment, I intruded, "You may as well put me back in the cell too, 'cause I'm not leaving until Keith is released."

"Oh yes you are!" the deputy came striding out from behind the counter. Suddenly there were two other deputies with him—three in all. "Come with us."

They didn't lay a hand on me until we got out by the elevator where there was no one around. In front of the elevator were some bars that basically formed a little cage. To get into the elevator you had to go into the cage, which was open on one end. It was deserted and quiet out there. They hustled me into the cage, grabbed handfuls of my hair, and yanked my head around, ramming my face into the bars. At last they pinned me to the floor.

"Why don't you try *really* assaulting a police officer some time and see what happens!"

I was dumbstruck—not only by the attack on me—I guess I had more or less expected, albeit naively, to be simply taken, as Keith had been, back to a cell and locked up—but also by their words: they knew damn well I was no pugnacious, street-fighting cop-puncher, as the charge against me might indicate, and they were telling me they knew. In doing so they were also asserting the supremacy of their gang over mine. Then they left me.

Afterwards I staggered slowly to my feet. There was only one place to go: into the elevator. I had just been thrown out of the San Francisco County Jail.

It was about 10 p.m. I walked from the jail into the Tenderloin, where I grabbed a Geary Street bus and rode it out to the Richmond District, knocking at last at Keith and Andrea's door, where I resolved to tell what I knew about Keith's fate and to inquire of any news. Andrea opened the door. Robert Norse Kahn, of FNB, had moved my truck and parked it safely a street away from the apartment. And there, safe and sound inside the apartment, was Elsa! I was as glad to see her as she was to see me.

Keith arrived at the apartment about an hour after I did. Tom got out of jail the next day, and Eric was released on Monday morning. On Monday night FNB held an emergency meeting to discuss the latest police attack against the group. It was one of the largest FNB meetings I've ever attended. I was still kind of a novice in the ways of repression at that time, and when it came my turn to speak I said, as if I'd hit upon some great discovery or anomaly, "You know, it's ironic—they charged me with assaulting them, when in reality they assaulted *me*!"

About three-fourths of the room replied at once, "THAT'S WHAT THEY ALWAYS DO!."

Chapter 3
Re-Inventing the Wheel

I used to lie awake a lot at night and listen to the radio. A lot of vehicle dwellers I know do that, the reason being that once the sun goes down there's not a whole lot else to do. Yes, it would be nice to read, but the light from a reading lamp would be detectable outside the vehicle, and would alert the police to your presence. The key to survival as a vehicle dweller in America is to blend in. That means making your vehicle no more noticeable or distinctive than any other car or truck in whatever area you happen to be. So no lights, because once the cops figure out you're living in your vehicle, and that you're in fact in there at that very moment, possibly sleeping, they'll be all over you like a cheap suit, and they'll have you move without giving two hoots in hell about the fact that you have nowhere else to go.

Actually, maybe I shouldn't say that since it's not uniformly true. Once I was parked in the lot of an Albertson's supermarket in Oceanside, California, when a plain clothes cop banged on my back door, which I had left only loosely latched. When I opened the door his hand was resting nervously on his gun.

"Are you sleeping in here?" he demanded.

"What?"

He was all excited, out of breath and huffy and puffy.

"Just answer the question and tell me the truth! Are you sleeping in here?"

Unable to speak, I simply nodded in the affirmative.

Without elaborating, he told me that he was hot on the trail of some fugitive or other. I gathered intuitively that someone had been assaulted or robbed in the shopping center. I can only speculate on why I wasn't a suspect, but it was clear he had taken one glance at me and decided I wasn't the man for whom he was looking. Maybe I was the wrong height or skin color, or maybe it was the fact that Elsa was champing at the bit to get at him—I had to keep a firm grip on her collar, or she would have gone right for him—but for some reason the picture simply didn't add up to me being the guy he was chasing. In a flash he was gone, but he left me with what I'm sure he felt was a judicious piece of advice: In the future I should keep my door firmly locked.

Now, leaving the door unlocked that night had been a slight oversight, but in reality I've never worried much about burglars or bandits. Having Elsa around, at least in those days when she was young and in her prime, was kind of the equivalent of having a loaded gun.

Elsa, I should mention, was a German Shepherd. She has since died of old age, and I miss her greatly. Back in those days, in the prime of her life, she was something fierce to behold. When she bared her teeth people froze in their tracks. She was the law—and since neither she nor I looked very prosperous anyway, getting robbed was never very high on my list of concerns.

I've pretty much always felt there was more to fear from the police than from society's so-called "criminal element," and I think people who feel differently have either had life experiences which have been radically different from mine, which is possible, or else have watched too many cop shows on TV, which is the more likely. But at any rate, here was this cop telling me to keep my doors locked—then he dashed away into the night.

Now, having a cop express concern for my safety was new to me, and after my heart stopped pounding and I had a chance to reflect, it also occurred to me that he had not told me to move on. Most cops would have said, "Get out of here! I don't care where you go, just get out of here!" He had not.

At first I thought this was merely because he was too busy chasing somebody else to worry about me, but then a second possibility occurred to me: Maybe he was a cop who had recognized the fact that millions of Americans are now sleeping on the streets and who was merely dealing with that reality. He had not ordered me to disappear off the face of the earth in an arrogant, stupid and idiotic manner because rationally he had recognized and dealt with the reality that it would be impossible for me to do so. Running into a cop like that, as I say, is rare, and it gave me a hunch: notwithstanding the fact that a would-be dangerous criminal was on the loose, I was struck suddenly by the thought that I could probably spend the entire night here, on this very spot, unmolested.

This I did. Not a single cop (or criminal, for that matter) showed up the rest of the night to bother me. I even slept peacefully. It's kind of a comforting feeling going to sleep at night knowing that the cop who's patrolling your beat isn't some sort of wigged-out right wing psychopath who hates your guts.

As I say, I used to lie awake a lot of nights and listen to the radio, and often, at such times, I would think, "Wouldn't it be nice if there was a radio station on the air that offered a whole different perspective, that came at you from a whole different point of view based upon a completely different set of assumptions about reality?"

***

Now you may not think it, but living in shopping center parking lots and listening to the radio at night offers one a wholly unique vantage point from which to observe America, and one of many things I had begun to notice about this country had to do with its radio stations. That is, that they were all pretty much alike. Oh sure, some radio stations have either this format or that format, but in terms of how they perceive the capitalist system, and their assumptions about its basic correctness, they are all alike.

There are plenty of people in America, who believe that corporate power has gotten way out of hand, and that free-for-all, anything-goes capitalism has failed—that it has failed just as badly, if not worse, than Soviet communism, and worse, that it's wrecking the Earth to boot. There are plenty of people who believe this, and you don't have to look too far to find them. Yet these people do not have a voice in the media. If they phone into an AM talk show they are often ridiculed and generally pretty quickly booted off the air.

One of the things you might wish to do with this new and different kind of radio station is to set aside such labels as *right wing* and *left wing*. These should be set aside because they do not accurately describe the political polar opposites which currently exist in America. Two words which do a much better job representing the opposing ends of the spectrum are *criminals* and *victims*. When I use the word criminal here, as well as its root word, *crime*, I'm referring to something much larger than the robbery which took place in that shopping center parking lot that night in Oceanside.

In America we have two kinds of crime: we have street crime, and then we have the sort of crimes committed by corporations and the government. Street crime occurs randomly and in short bursts; corporate/government crime, however, is organized and sustained, a continuous, never-ending din. Yet overall it's the short bursts to which we pay attention, the continuous and far more annoying din having been shrunk for us, diminished and filtered down to a hardly noticeable background noise. It's a Dolby noise reduction of cognition. The more sharp, clear and resonant the primary sound, the less we notice the background noise. Such is the power of the corporate-controlled media—to expand and contract, to amplify or quiet down—to Dolby-ize.

So why *criminals* and *victims*, as opposed to *right wing* or *left wing*? Because the biggest crime stories of all are the ones that never make the news. The "Republicrats" in the government, along with their bosses in big business, have taken national theft and legitimized it by creating an ideology which supports and justifies such theft. That "ideology" is that it's "good for the economy" ("good for the economy" presumably means good for all of us) for savings and loans companies to rip off billions and never have to pay it back; that it's good for giant industries to release toxic waste, negatively impacting the health of surrounding communities, and then to receive billions in taxpayer subsidies or corporate welfare; that it's good for social programs to be eliminated for the poor, the elderly and the disabled—and so on.

These things, of course, are *not* good, but the officials who have enacted them have constructed an "ideology" which holds them to be good, acceptable, and beneficial. The corporate media have willingly adopted this ideology as its own—an ideology which says, in essence, "crime (or at least crime involving theft of public resources by corporations) is good." On the other hand, the folks who suffer under these crimes view them, in many cases, as just that—crimes. Certainly the perpetration of them produces victims. And who are these victims? Us.

We don't own our own national forests any more. They've been turned over to logging and agribusiness. National parks are being "privatized." Seashores and rivers are being lost to floating garbage and contaminants. The airwaves (as surely a natural resource as water, timber, the Rocky Mountains or Yosemite Park)? Long gone. Given over many years ago to the likes of Disney, GE and Westinghouse.

***

Another thing you might want to do with this new and different sort of radio station, with its wholly different set of assumptions about criminals and victims, is to question why it has become so acceptable in our culture for the government to confiscate—to literally *steal*—the property of private citizens. Our much-ballyhooed, and supposedly sacred and culturally ingrained reverence for property rights has been coming quite unglued of late.

In the name of fighting the war on drugs, police now have extraordinary powers to confiscate property and sell it at public auction. Proceeds from such sales can often be legally retained by local police agencies. Confiscated monies and properties have, in no small number of cases, even ended up in the pockets of individual cops and D.A.s.

There is an excellent book on this subject called *Forfeiting Our Property Rights*, by Rep. Henry Hyde (of Clinton impeachment fame). In the book Hyde documents case after case of innocent Americans who have become victims of property seizures by police—grown to be, what is described in one case as "rabid" in their quest to grab more and more property. [1] The super wealthy, of course, are too insulated and powerful, for the most part, to fear this, while the homeless basically have little or nothing of value—*their* pitifully few belongings, as we have already seen, all to frequently simply end up burned or trash-compacted.

Thus it has been particularly those in between the homeless and the wealthy who have fallen most prey to "asset forfeiture," a term which could be described as legalized theft. Cars, boats, homes and farms have been taken, while the "crime-as-ideology" set, who seem to hold permanent tenure on public office in this country, continue to propagate more laws leaving the weak increasingly vulnerable to the powerful, with fewer and fewer constitutional rights and protections against them. Hyde documents cases wherein police and prosecutors have used seized assets to purchase tennis club memberships, Pontiac Firebirds, guns, computers and new police equipment. On Long Island, in Suffolk County, New York, for instance, District Attorney James Catterson used seized assets to buy a $300 watch for his secretary, while converting to his own use a seized BMW 735i, which he drove instead of a county car. [2]

So broad have police powers become, that in many states cops can seize your assets without even having to charge you with a crime. It should come as no surprise to even the most impaired of individuals that once you give power of such magnitude to someone, even to the most saintly among us, which the police certainly are not, there exists a certain likelihood of abuse. When you're talking about a multi-million dollar a year racket, which the forfeiture industry has become, the temptation is too great. Yet the "crime-as-ideology" set claim not to be able to see a problem here.

One of the sources cited by Hyde in his book is a *San Jose Mercury News* series of articles, entitled "The Forfeiture Racket," which ran in 1993. [3] The series was written by reporter Gary Webb, the same *Mercury News* reporter who later went on, in 1996, to break the newspaper's "Dark Alliance" series disclosing possible CIA connections to the crack cocaine trade in Los Angeles. [4]

In "The Forfeiture Racket," Webb cites example after example of innocent Californians who never were convicted of a crime but who nonetheless got taken to the cleaners by their local cops. A favorite tactic by officers, Webb reports, is to arrest a fairly well-off suspect and allow him to keep some of his assets in exchange for "voluntarily" turning over the rest.

Sergeant Dearl Skinner of the Sutter County, California Sheriff's Department, once worked out a deal with a suspect wherein, "I seized close to $17,000 in a vehicle and negotiated with him, and the guy signed a disclaimer for $10,000, and he kept the car and $7,000." [5] Skinner explained his philosophy of drug enforcement this way: "We may go to the house and seize just the cash, maybe with pay/owe records...I tell them, if you're in agreement here, sign a disclaimer for this cash, which I believe is proceeds (of narcotics trafficking) and I won't take your cars, I won't take your boat, I won't take your motorcycles, that sort of deal. They seem to work out okay." [6]

Again, keep in mind, in many states the cops don't even have to find drugs in your house to be able to do all this. If the government can confiscate the assets of millions of Americans caught with small quantities of drugs, why can't it confiscate the assets of savings and loans and other corporate criminals? The fact that the American people never seem to have even pondered or reflected on this rather glaring inconsistency, at least not to any wide degree, is a real testament to the sciences of propaganda, public opinion manipulation and mind control. The government takes the cars of poor and middle income "drug offenders"— not those of wealthy S&L crooks. That's simply the way it is. Period. No one ever questions it—and no one ever will until we have, again, these new and different radio stations, with their whole different set of assumptions about reality.

There could come a time in this country when the police decide they don't need the wealthy ruling class any more. Who knows? Perhaps one day the wealthy will wake up and realize, albeit belatedly, that in their ceaseless calls for more and more police with greater and greater powers, that they have created a monster they can no longer control. That monster's name, of course, is *fascism*.

In her exquisite novel, *The House of the Spirits*, Isabel Allende paints the portrait of Esteban Trueba, a wealthy landowner who becomes a powerful right wing politician and, of course, a stalwart supporter of the police and the military—until, that is, after the Chilean coup, when Trueba is received at the ministry of defense by an unshaven officer wearing an unbuttoned jacket, who arrogantly props his feet upon a desk and demands Trueba's car keys. Could such a stingingly ironic moment await our own members of Congress in this country? Perhaps fascism in America will never undergo that final metamorphosis into a total, outright military dictatorship. Perhaps, from the standpoint of the multinational corporations who control all the money, it never will need to.

It may come as a surprise to some that a book such as *Forfeiting Our Property Rights* would be written by a Republican congressman like Hyde.

The latter may perhaps hold more traditionally Republican-oriented views on other issues, but at least he has sounded an alarm over the danger of growing police powers in this country. Where have the Democrats been on this issue? Mostly issuing demagogic calls for more and more police with greater and greater powers. Hyde is a prime example of why I say the barriers between *right* and *left* are breaking down and becoming no longer applicable and that a new political spectrum with *criminals* and *victims* as the polar opposites is emerging.

***

The buildup to the Gulf War was an especially fascinating time to observe the dynamics of media censorship in America. The debate was never between those who were for the war and those against. The debate, both in Congress and in the corporate media, was a ballyhoo between those who were for war, and those who favored sanctions—or, in other words, those who merely wanted to starve out the Iraqi people, and those who felt blowing them to smithereens a more appropriate approach. Yet it was a scripted ballyhoo, and you had the feeling all along, or at least I did, that it was written into the script for the let's-blow'em-to-smithereens side to win. In any event, where were the people who were opposed to either one of these "solutions?"

During the buildup to the war, Food Not Bombs moved into Civic Center Plaza with a round-the-clock vigil opposing the war. A group of Vietnam veterans erected a similar vigil right next to ours, and the two vigils coexisted side by side, with Food Not Bombs providing food support for both—much as it had during the tent city protest in 1989. The San Francisco Police, of course, began night attacks on the vigils. Those were the days in which I learned the term "5-0." 5-0 means the police are coming. It can also simply mean—the police.

Most of my own time staffing the vigil was spent during daylight hours, however, I remember the night I volunteered for the "graveyard" shift. It was a rather cold, chilly, ghoulish, nightmarish ordeal. The police in those days were still arresting people on 647-i, the intent-to-lodge ordinance discussed in the previous chapter. So all night long that night every time the police drove by, someone would yell out, "5-0!" and people would suddenly shrug off their blankets, sit up and pretend to be fully awake.

It was hard to tell how many people were out there because it was so dark, but there were maybe as many as two dozen or so folks who weren't "officially" a part of either of the two vigils. Some I couldn't actually see, I could only hear their voices in the dark. One or two that I *could* see, however, looked as young as 14 or 15. A lot of these excess people were homeless folks who had decided, I guess, that a safe place to sleep might be here, sort of nestled in between Food Not Bombs and the Vietnam vets. That was understandable, and it made me feel good knowing I was helping provide them with a safe haven in the night.

That night was alive with an erratic procession of weird, colorful insomniacs who materialized out of the shadows, spent a quarter hour or so at the vigil, and then moved on their restless way. Far from being noisy, this nocturnal life of Civic Center was actually much quieter than that of the day. People were respectful of each other for the most part. These "neighbors" came, chatted for a while, then, like whippoorwills, meandered on into the night. This nocturnal activity lasted virtually until dawn.

Sometime around midnight our own little cluster of humanity, sleeping at the two vigils, began feeling less and less like a bunch of random individuals thrown haphazardly together, and more like a community. I was looking forward to the hot oatmeal Food Not Bombs would be bringing by in the morning. I'm sure I wasn't the only one. As the hours ticked by, however, I grew colder and colder. A few times I nodded off, dozing fitfully until the cry "5-0!" penetrated my dreams, at which time my head would snap up as I shook off the sleep. It was a weird, strange night.

Wednesdays had become my regular day for volunteering with Food Not Bombs. In those days Food Not Bombs had an old bread truck which it used for making food pick ups and deliveries all over the city. Talk about a vehicle with character. It was a two-tone brown and beige truck with a cracked windshield and a big front end grill that looked kind of like a smiling face. It was a really old model, a nineteen-fifty-something-or-other, but like a lot of modern day bread delivery trucks it only had one seat in the whole truck—the driver's seat. Those of us who rode as passengers had to ride either standing up or else sitting impromptu on buckets or fruit crates or the like. If you rode standing up there were these little ridges in the ceiling you could grip onto to keep your balance while the truck was in motion.

I once wrote a poem about that truck. This was back in the days when we were serving at UN Plaza. Back then the Wednesday afternoon cooking was done in a building on O'Farrell St. At six o'clock when the food was prepared, we'd load it into the back of the truck and drive down O'Farrell, hang a right at Jones, and proceed down Jones past St. Anthony's Dining Room, which in those days was serving about 2000 meals a day and *still* turning people away. Then we'd make another right onto McAllister St., and hook into UN Plaza through the little entrance drive off McAllister. Technically, I guess, we weren't supposed to be driving a truck out onto the plaza, but there was really no other way to get the food there.

There were never any parking spaces on McAllister. We could have unloaded from the Market Street side of the plaza, but the same thing applied: no parking spaces. Plus, the Market Street side had the disadvantage of being highly visible and exposed, thereby placing us at greater danger from the police. On the McAllister side at least we were hidden away in a sort of nook.

If the city had cared even so much as an acorn on a tree stump about the homeless, the *least* it could have done would have been to reserve a parking space for Food Not Bombs. God knows there were spaces reserved for cop cars all over creation and back. Setting aside just one space for the Food Not Bombs truck between the hours of noon and one, and six and seven each day wouldn't have been too much of a sacrifice considering the public service the group was providing. But we were an outlawed group, at least as far as the mayor of San Francisco was concerned, and such a notion would have been unthinkable.

So I wrote this poem about the truck and about the whole difficulty getting the food from the cooking site to the people—but mostly about the truck. It's no Shakespearean sonnet, but here it is:

The Bread Truck

It's brown and may have at one time belonged
To an actual bread company in days long since gone.
Now all the homeless on Market Street know it by sight,
For its cracked-glass appearance means dinner tonight.

Its tin-sheet interior always loaded quite hectically
With ripe, aging fruits gathered eclectically,
Buckets, boxes, utensils and such
Left little room otherwise, so we rode standing up,

Gripping the ceiling and riding the waves
Of its rocky motion down Jones where St. Anthony lays,
Rounding the corner to the brick plaza so cold,
In this night so empty, and a flock with no fold.

I wrote another poem in those days too, about a woman from Ireland on whom I had developed kind of a crush. She and some friends of hers who were all from Ireland spent a few months in San Francisco, and while they were here they did some volunteering with Food Not Bombs—cooking, serving a few meals and the like. Around the time of the war they all departed San Francisco and returned to Ireland, and I've never seen her since. But I reproduce the poem here because, like the last one, it gives you a sense of what it was like in those days.

Fionnuala

We were talking about how you were returning to Ireland
That day as we made soup for the poor
Of San Francisco, and the world
Hovered on the brink of war,
And how beautiful you were, I thought,
And how much I would like to kiss you,
Yet how tragically ephemeral and small
Such gifts against these explosions of history,
And all
The homeless lined up when we took the soup
Down to the UN Plaza...
The UN Plaza...where civilization
Seemed to have come full circle at last:
With mankind once again huddled together
In prehistoric-like tribes
For mutual benefit and protection—
And as we served the soup and fruit cups
The evening grew cold, and in the lee
Of the plaza the fog rolled in
From somewhere terribly far out over the sea...

***

Then came the day the bombs started falling and the war was actually on, and the protests on the streets of San Francisco swelled to almost unbelievable proportions. In those days, our mythical radio stations—with their whole different sets of assumptions about reality—might have made a lot of difference. For one thing, the sheer size of the protests which took place on American streets, would have been made known to the American people at large.

I remember one day I was standing in a sea of humanity at Powell and Market Streets holding a sign that said: WHEN THEY MUTINY THEY'LL BE *OUR* TROOPS. About 15 or 20 feet away from me, mounted on a platform some six feet above the heads of the crowd, was a TV news cameraman. He was an old geezer who looked like he was about ready for retirement. And, moreover, he didn't appear to be having a good time. I watched his face as he scanned the crowd, his eyes coming at last to rest on my sign.

Now all around me people were yelling stuff like, "Victory to Iraq!" and "George Bush! You liar! We'll set your ass on fire!" There were a lot of protestors there that day, believe me. What you saw when you looked out over the heads of the crowd was, as I say, a sea of humanity. There were so many people, in fact, that the police, unable to contain the demonstration any longer, had given up their positions, falling back, ceding all of Market Street to the crowd—the whole street in both directions. This is something the police *never* do, or hardly ever, but they did it that day, and they did it because of the numbers: they simply had been unable to contain the protest on the sidewalk any longer.

Now a couple of things should be said here about the people who were yelling "Victory to Iraq." First of all, they were a small minority. Secondly, they weren't really, deep in their hearts, anti-American. No, I *mean* that. Scoff if you want, but I believe it's true. What they were calling for was not so much the defeat of America, but the demise and downfall of the crime-as-ideology set running the country. It's not "un-American" to long for the collapse and ruin of the criminals who have taken over your country. In fact, it's the opposite.

This is an important distinction to make, yet it's one which was lost on the old TV camera guy sitting on his platform a few feet above the crowd. A sour, somewhat sick look had settled on his face as he scanned over the crowd—until at last his eyes—and I could see them clear as day—came to rest on my sign: WHEN THEY MUTINY THEY'LL BE *OUR* TROOPS. Suddenly a momentous intensification transformed his face from mere sourness to what might be described as appalled horror—it was kind of funny, although I suppose maybe you had to be there, like they say.

When the police retreated from their positions, people surged into Market Street with a joyousness that was unparalleled to anything I've ever seen. What was making people so joyful was not any special illusion about being able to end the war, although at that particular moment maybe even *that too* seemed possible. But what was *really* making people happy just then was the pride and elation they felt at having finally taken over their own streets.

The protest had reached that "critical mass" point at which the police could no longer control it. Not that there was any violence—there assuredly wasn't. Who needed it? Traffic was stopped. Market Street looked like a huge football field buried under an ocean of humanity. We were standing on ground which we, ourselves, had liberated. It was a heady feeling. People were respectful of each other. There was an enormous sense of cooperation. If you've never been in a protest of that size and magnitude all I can tell you is that it's really heady. No high from cocaine or marijuana or any other drug on earth can come close to matching it. It's the exhilaration and the high of freedom.

We controlled that street, and nothing much beyond that really mattered. The crime-as-ideology might take all the bribes from all the multi-national corporations it wanted. But we controlled that street. The supreme court might be as horrifyingly oblivious to justice as it wished. But we controlled that street. We were standing in liberated territory. Small as it may be, we had our own country. Suffice to say, nobody here in our country would go to bed hungry, or be arrested for serving food or for sleeping under blankets. No one would have their assets confiscated. Those things didn't happen in a free country, and this 5 or 6 block stretch of Market Street was now free.

That's what it felt like standing in that crowd that day. And that, too, is why the old TV news cameraman had become so sourly appalled: for however brief a moment, his class—the criminal class—had lost control of that street.

***

Pronouncements about the alleged demise of the "Vietnam syndrome" aside, it seems clear that the size of anti-war protests in 1991 caught the government by surprise, or at least proved its worst fears to be true. During the war I heard reports of L.A. and New York protests reaching up to 20,000. This would have been small by Bay Area standards, but of course the reliability of those figures might be questioned. Almost surely, attendance estimates in those cities were distorted by police and the corporate-owned media. It may well be that San Francisco had the largest anti-war demonstrations in the country, yet even the corporate-owned media carried little blurb stories about protests in Atlanta, Georgia, Missoula, Montana, and elsewhere.

It's interesting to note that it wasn't until after the Gulf War, and the L.A. Rebellion which followed it, that the Justice Department, under Janet Reno, embarked upon a program of tapping into military technology—particularly that which fell under the category of "non-lethal weapons"—and of making such technology available to local police departments. I first read about this in 1993 in *Mondo 2000*, a publication dealing with futuristic trends in society. By 1996 the program, under the National Institute of Justice, a little-known division within the Justice Department, had advanced significantly. An April 9, 1997 article in the *San Francisco Bay Guardian* reports infrared tracking technology, similar to that used in the Gulf War, in place in police departments in New York and Pasadena, California, while San Francisco Police were seeking a similar system in their 1997-98 budget request. [7] The *Guardian* also gave a brief rundown on other technologies either currently in use or presently offered to police departments, including:

- **Anti-riot foam** This super-concentrated sticky foam, marketed by Sandia Laboratories, is shot from a nozzle and can fill a room with "extremely tacky, nontoxic" sudsy goo, thus blinding and immobilizing those inside. The foam can also be used for sealing off rooms during drug raids and prison riots. Though the foam has already been used in Somalia on rioting crowds, the NIJ notes, "How to effect rapid and safe emergency-removal procedures for face and eye contact remain significant issues."

- **Disabling Net and Launcher** Straight from the pages of Spiderman, this product from Foster Miller Inc., allows law enforcement officials to fire a disabling and sticky (and optionally electrified) net, thus "neutralizing an uncooperative and fleeing felon." The disabling net is also being marketed to the military for its post-cold war peacekeeping operations.

- **Liquid Stun Gun** This device, brainchild of the San Diego-based JAYCOR, can, according to promotional material, "bring down multiple hostilities without interruptive reloading." Through an electrified stream of liquid, police can shock whole crowds into submission. It's the water cannon as Taser.

- **Car-stopping projectiles and pulses** The high-speed chase may soon be a thing of the past Numerous weapons manufacturers have developed such mechanisms as magnetic projectiles that can be shot at a speeding car. Once attached to the vehicle, the projectile sends an electronic pulse through the automobile, short-circuiting its electrical system. The Finnish police have already bought a few of these high-voltage harpoons.

- **Fleeing-Vehicle Tagging System** This product, also a projectile, does not shut down a car but tags it with a radio transmitter that can be monitored by police. Idaho National Engineering Laboratory, makers of the FVTS, like to point out that the tagging system means police no longer have to chase down every suspect, but can track and follow them from afar. Even the uninitiated can see the surveillance potential.

- **Remote frisking** The Millivision Camera crafted by Millitech Corporation reads the electromagnetic fields of one's body and thus "sees through" heavy clothing and detects concealed "metallic and nonmetallic weapons, plastic explosives, drugs, and other contraband." The Millivision Camera can be hand-held by roving police officers or mounted atop a building entrance, perhaps by a private-security firm, to secretly search all those entering. [8]

One thing that hosts of mythical radio stations might want to make clear to their listeners is that the millions of dollars being spent on weapons such as these are not for their own "protection."

***

On April 30, 1992, the city of San Francisco, again, erupted into protest, following the acquittal of four Los Angeles cops in the beating of Rodney King. About 5,000 people gathered in front of the State building at McAllister and Van Ness for a scheduled rally at 5 p.m. that evening. It was a large protest by most standards, yet tiny and miniscule compared to those during the Gulf War the year previous. The reason for the difference was that people were afraid. This was personal in a way the Gulf War had not been. What was going to happen at McAllister and Van Ness that evening was not simply about four cops in L.A., or some lunatic U.S.-instigated war on the other side of the world. What was coming to a head at 5 o'clock that evening was a long history of personal animosity between the people of San Francisco and the police of San Francisco.

Before the night would end, windows would be broken, stores looted, hundreds of arrests would be made and a member of Food Not Bombs would set fire to a police motorcycle.

While many of those who had surged so joyously into Market Street the year before were absent that evening, the ones who did show up were responding to years of police violence, mistreatment, and abuse; to years of spying, infiltration and disruption of legitimate, lawful political groups; and to years of cops getting away, quite literally, with murder.

While the protest was smaller than those of the Gulf War, it equaled or even surpassed the war in another, different respect, however, by attracting a "rainbow" of different people. Blacks, browns, whites and Asians were all pretty equally represented that day—indicating what? That the police had spared no one in their efforts to suppress dissent and maintain power and control over the city, I guess. At any rate, racial unity was high. Despite the purely racist nature of the Rodney King beating, per se, those 5,000 people there that day had come to the realization that the enemy was not, after all, the other race. This probably had the effect of making police nerves even more taut than they otherwise would have been that day.

I arrived at McAllister and Van Ness not with a protest sign, but with a tape recorder. Covering the April 30 demonstration was my first act as a reporter for the nascent Food Not Bombs Radio Network. I started recording some of the speeches, then ran into Andrea McHenry. Keith was somewhere in the crowd too, she said, but I didn't see him. I talked with Andrea, who seemed ill at ease. There were a large number of cops on the sidewalks at the four corners of the intersection, while the protest had settled farther away from the street, on the broad, flat steps leading up to the State building, with its giant seal of the State of California. At the very top of the steps, however, were more cops. In a long line, these riot police, standing shoulder to shoulder, sealed off the building plaza and entrance.

The speeches went on for the better part of an hour, then a march moved off from the State Building and started east on McAllister Street, stopping traffic and filling up all of the street. I walked with Andrea, who was growing increasingly nervous and was beginning to talk about leaving. We found ourselves more or less in the center of the march—not too close to the front and not too far back toward the rear, pretty much just keeping up with the people around us. The pace was leisurely. I still had the tape recorder on, getting just random sounds of the crowd. We were still on McAllister at this point, but suddenly we heard the sound of windows breaking a block away, on Market.

Pop...pop...pop...there was an interval of 15 or 20 seconds between each pop—as if it were one person making his or her way from store window to store window, singly, rather than many people all throwing rocks at once. Nonetheless the breaking glass put Andrea even more on edge; my own instincts were to get over to Market Street and see what was happening. This I didn't do, however, out of reluctance to leave Andrea by herself.

We were still on McAllister when we ran into Peter Donahue. Peter was pushing a bicycle—the street being too crowded presently for riding. He had on a bicycle helmet, a back pack and was wearing a reflector vest. We chatted for a few moments about the rather incredible event that was taking place all around us. Then we parted, Peter headed more or less toward Market Street. By this time reality had pretty universally settled in on McAllister: it was pretty clear, I think to all, that this was no longer a peaceful, orderly, nonviolent protest, but a civilian uprising, and those who couldn't deal with that were now leaving. At the same time others were joining.

Andrea, however, had determined, with no further deliberation, to leave.

There was nothing further I could do or say to talk her out of it: she was going home. For a moment I stood rooted to the spot, torn between whether to follow Peter down to Market, which was where I really wanted to be with my tape recorder, or whether to accompany Andrea. Maybe it's the rather old-fashioned upbringing my parents gave me, but I've always had a chivalrous streak in my soul. I decided, rather nobly, that I had a duty to perform, and that there was no way I was going to let a friend's wife try to make her way out of there alone. After all, we were in the middle of a riot zone. I went with Andrea.

It's with a sense of reluctance that I sometimes recall now how I missed the greater part of the events which happened that night, and which I've already in part described. On the other hand, had I not departed with Andrea, almost surely would I have been arrested or worse. At any rate, my knowledge of what happened the remainder of that night comes second hand. Here, though, is what I've been able to piece together...

***

After leaving us, Peter, still pushing his bicycle, made his way over to Market Street, where a surreal sight greeted his eyes. As in the Gulf War, traffic was stopped, but this time, rather than dancing in the streets people were breaking up chunks of it and hurling the chunks—along with an assortment of other missiles—at the police. A contingent of the latter had grouped up at 7th Street and were shielding themselves as best as they could from the rain of flying objects, refusing to come out from behind their barricades. Thousands of people filled Market. The pavement was littered with broken glass and store-looted merchandise which had been either dropped in the confusion or discarded as not worth keeping.

Earlier in the day students from City College had attempted to hold a peaceful protest and a march out onto the freeway, but had been arrested. This was followed by a second march, which had formed at 24th and Mission and which had proceeded from there into and through the Western Addition, picking up approximately 2000 people. Along the way, police attempted to shut down this group as well, as they had done earlier with the students at City College, but were repelled by bottles, rocks and fists. This second group made it at last to McAllister and Van Ness, joining up with the larger, main rally in front of the State building.

"I talked to some police that I knew," Donahue recalls. "I had been arrested by Northern Precinct people before, so I knew them and they knew me. They seemed pretty frightened by the crowd. I tried to talk to them about how they felt. They were pretty incoherent at that time, so I felt that something was definitely gonna happen.

"They were swearing a lot," he continued. "They were very agitated, smoking cigarettes and chewing gum. When they talked to me they used a lot of profanity, referring to people in a derogatory way—just beginning the process of dehumanizing the protestors."

Sometime after the glass began to break on Market Street a large formation of police moved in and succeeded in dividing the crowd. One of the main two splinter groups marched up to Nob Hill. Within this column was a contingent of Food Not Bombs people, which included Keith McHenry and a few others. Meanwhile, the other large splinter group remained on Market battling with police. A third, much smaller faction, which included Donahue, attempted to do a sit-down in front of Glide Memorial Church, but were pushed up the street by police.

The marchers which had ascended Nob Hill eventually made their way back to Market Street, as did the contingent which had traipsed to Glide Memorial Church. This reuniting of the three factions at first gave renewed life to the rebellion. Soon, however, Market was completely overrun by police, who apparently concentrated all of their forces now into this area.

The arrival of a squadron of motorcycle cops resulted in a substantial division of the crowd once more. Meanwhile, a tactical unit had moved in on the other side of the intersection and begun to contain people. The police on motorcycles parked their bikes and waded into the crowd with clubs swinging. One of them ran up to Keith and yelled, "Hey McHenry!" Hearing his name called, Keith turned and was hit hard right between the eyes with the butt-end of a wooden night stick, smashing the bridge of his nose. A second blow—across his upraised arm—miraculously only bruised his arm but splintered the night stick.

All of this was being observed from about 20 yards away by Peter Donahue, still on his bicycle, which he had been either alternately pushing or riding all night. He remembers seeing not only Keith but a second Food Not Bombs member, Angelina Ramsay, being pummelled especially hard with night sticks. He also remembers seeing people attempt to escape from the police by climbing onto a scaffolding. These people, however, were pursued by officers and thrown off the scaffold and back into the street, a distance of some 15 feet.

A youth took this opportunity to kick over one of the unattended police motorcycles, but then had to tear off into the night, hotly pursued by angry cops. Lying on its side, however, the huge motorcycle began to leak fluid from its gas tank, the flammable liquid trickling out onto the pavement. The toppled machine lay no further than a few feet from Peter. A conversation subsequently developed   amongst standers-around as to whether anyone had a match.

Peter Donahue extracted a lighter from his back pack and, from the seat of his bicycle, leaned over and clicked it once, twice, and then a third time...

***

Now elsewhere along that block of Market, police were still involved in confrontations with protestors. However, by this time a sizeable number, including Keith and Angelina, had been corralled, subdued, and brought together into the center of the intersection, where they were ordered by booted, beefy officers to sit in a circle on the pavement. With blood streaming down his face, Keith McHenry sat down in the street. Suddenly, hearing an explosion, he and others looked up and saw flames leap into the sky.

A raging fire quickly engulfed the motorcycle, melting and rendering it into a bursting, burgeoning inferno. Peter began to move away. A moment later, however, the street slammed up into his face as he was tackled from behind.

"Who's motorcycle is that? Is that one of ours?"

So spectacular was the blaze it was hard to tell it was even a police motorcycle any more.

Cops swarmed all over Peter's prone body like a cloud of flies feasting on live meat. Located at last, the cop "owner" of the motorcycle lost no time joining in the mob violence, his face contorted as he commenced to kick Peter, breaking one of Peter's ribs. About this time a TV news crew from KPIX channel 5 rushed up to the police and announced that they had caught the torching of the motorcycle on videotape.

Meanwhile out on the street more and more protestors were added to the circle. The rebellion was over.

***

Much later what would occur to Peter would be the enormous irony—of his being sent to jail on the basis of videotaped evidence (the news film from channel 5), while the cops who had been videotaped beating Rodney King, had gotten off. With no funds for a lawyer and little hope of obtaining justice in the courts, Peter accepted a plea bargain for a reduced sentence on arson. In December when he got out of jail I interviewed him for the Food Not Bombs Radio Network. We talked a lot about the role Channel

5 had played in his conviction. The TV news crews filming the rebellion had been afraid, he felt, and had "sought the police out at every opportunity for protection."

> I think that the camera people were basically all white, and that they were filming events that were taking place, and they were afraid of what was going on. And they were attacked by looters, who also perceived them as part of the problem...putting the image of greed being the motivation for the riots, and not being sympathetic to or understanding their cause—and, yeah, it disturbed me the entire time the amount of cooperation between the media and the police.

Needless to say, the corporate-owned *San Francisco Examiner* saw things differently. When its reporters and editors had looked out their window upon the crowds filling Market Street, they had seen greed-driven looters—not idealistic young protestors with a legitimate complaint about police brutality and the lack of justice. Especially notable were the *Examiner's* comments regarding Donahue himself. Though not charged with looting, Donahue, the newspaper apparently believed, had participated in a "feeding frenzy." In a story under the headline "Many S.F. looters got caught in feeding frenzy," the newspaper reported:

> One of the more serious charges was leveled against Peter Donahue, who Beckwith said had some affiliation with Food Not Bombs, the organization that consistently runs afoul of the law for trying to feed the homeless at Golden Gate Park or at the Civic Center.
> Donahue is charged with arson—the torching of a policeman's motorcycle as it lay on Market Street after a colleague allegedly knocked it over. Prosecutors allege that Donahue, who was riding a bicycle, rolled up to the downed motorbike and ignited gasoline leaking from the tank. He was arrested on the spot. [9]

It was about this same time that I taped an interview with another Food Not Bombs member, Sheila Cummings. Sheila had been present at one of the more outlandish police attacks against Food Not Bombs—the May 6, 1991 incident in which the cops had dumped the soup into the Civic Center fountain. She said:

This was one of the times that right in front of these homeless people's—*faces*—the police dumped the food into the fountain, the fountain which was right near where we were standing...It was—it was—incredibly upsetting for everyone involved, the homeless people. Some people started yelling. Most people just stood there kind of in shock—or I don't know if they were in shock, but (laughs) it seemed like they were. And meanwhile I was...told by a police officer to leave the scene... I told him, again, "I have a right to be here." And he said, "You're a piece of shit—you're a piece of crap." And so it's like—*these* are the police—these are the *protectors* of our city—stealing food away from us, throwing it onto the ground in front of hundreds of hungry people, and then calling the people who are providing the free food foul names. It just seems like there was no justice at all.

With the two interviews, first Peter's and then Sheila's, we had two very strong, very dynamite pieces of audio tape which, if only they could be heard on our theoretical radio stations with the unique perspective on reality, could conceivably have a powerful impact on the public.

***

It was around the time of the soup-in-the-fountain incident that Food Not Bombs *did* get a peculiar, odd-ball sort of boost from a local mainstream media outlet. KCBS is a news station which also airs a food and wine program hosted by well known connoisseur and food critic Narcai David. KCBS reporter Mike Sugarman paid a surprise visit to a Food Not Bombs meal serving, collected food, took it back to the station and offered some to David, who sampled it and gave his verdict.

The two-and-a-half minute report Sugarman produced contained a sound bite from Agnos in which the mayor could be heard savagely disparaging the quality of Food Not Bombs food, which he referred to as "cold gruel." This was followed by a sound bite of the station's premiere food critic.

Narcai David (munching): That's wonderful. This sauce on top (laughing) is really delicious. It's got, ah, yellow squash that's not overcooked, I mean, it's really al dente. There are nice chunks of yellow squash. The *seasoning* is kind of mild, but there's a wonderful sweet flavor from these vegetables (more chewing) mmm, I'll tell you it's delicious!

***

As it turned out, the soup-in-the-fountain incident was one of the last Food Not Bombs arrests to occur under the administration of Art Agnos. By May of 1991, Agnos was in a hot race for re-election. His main rival was former police chief Frank Jordan. Around May or June of that year the arrests of Food Not Bombs trickled to a halt. If this was Agnos' way of trying to shore up his sagging popularity, it was too little too late. For his nearly four years in office the mayor had largely turned his back on his natural liberal constituency. At the same time, what support, if any, he had ever enjoyed from the progressive/radical community had long since disintegrated. Having burned his bridges to his own base of support, Agnos was dumped by the voters of San Francisco, leaving the mayor's office substantially wide open for the conservative ex-police chief.

For the first year and a half of his term Jordan, remarkably, laid off Food Not Bombs, leaving the group free to serve food without arrest. But in August of 1993 Jordan announced what he called his "Matrix Quality of Life Program," which entailed a harsh crackdown on homeless people. This included sweeps, property destruction, and the issuing of thousands of citations. When the homeless people were unable to pay the fines, the citations matured into arrest warrants.

The Matrix Program went far beyond 647-i, the old law used against homeless folks during the Agnos years. Under Jordan, people, by the thousands, were cited for sitting on the sidewalk or carrying backpacks. According to the ACLU, even possession of a dinner spoon could be construed as illegal under Matrix. Food Not Bombs held protests against the mayor's new policies and one month later—in September of 1993—Matrix was, in essence, expanded to include arrests of Food Not Bombs as well.

But the two-year abatement of arrests had given Food Not Bombs a breather. It had left members of the group free for things other than sitting in jail, making endless court appearances, or trying to get confiscated property returned. It was in this somnambulant, Agnos-to-Jordan transition period that the micro radio movement in the Bay Area was born.

One of the things to which my own attention turned during this time was romance. When I met Jo Swanson it was pretty much love at first sight. She had it all, I guess. Beauty, brains, and a great personality. I fell immediately in love with her. The amazing thing was she fell in love with me too. She was full of energy and had an enormous reservoir of talent and creativity, having somehow balanced acting, puppet-making and puppeteering with a career teaching pre-school, and also with a long history in radical politics. She came to San Francisco in 1991—from Boston, where she had been one of the original 8 founders of Food Not Bombs.

Jo became an instant, enthusiastic supporter of pirate radio long before it became a concrete reality. Her support and encouragement had a lot to do with making me think that starting our own radio station was actually possible. Even later—after we got going, and the frustration and anger brought on by repeated equipment failure threatened to swamp us—it was largely her counsel of patience that kept me from scrapping the whole endeavor. I don't know much about religion, but I sometimes think supernatural forces were at work. How else can you explain her coming along at precisely the time she did?

One summer day in 1991 she had simply packed everything into her Toyota station wagon and set out for San Francisco. On her way west—she swears it's true—she had stopped at Yosemite Park, climbed to the top of a boulder, and, upon reaching the summit, had found a number of small stones shaped into a heart. She took the stones as a sign that she was destined to find love where she was going. When she got to San Francisco I was the first person she met.

***

I don't want to give the impression that San Francisco was the only place in the Bay Area where political repression was taking place in those days. In 1991, civil disturbances erupted in the city of Berkeley when the University of California, over widespread opposition from the activist community, initiated construction of volleyball courts in a small, one-square-block piece of land known as "People's Park." Homeless people viewed the courts, with some justification, as a prelude to a full-scale class cleansing of the area. Park political activists shared similar concerns, additionally regarding the construction as not respectful of the park's historic past (the park had grown out of the Berkeley free speech movement of the sixties).

During the uprising, windows were broken along Telegraph Avenue, and hundreds of police were deployed to quell the disturbances. Cops were stationed at the volleyball courts around the-clock to guard the courts from vandalism, all of this police protection coming, of course, at a cost to the taxpayers of millions of dollars.

The following year a 19-year-old homeless woman—a child, really—who called herself Rosebud Denovo, broke into the campus mansion of UC Chancellor Chang-Lin Tien. Ostensibly—at least according to the police—she was armed with a machete. Rosebud was widely known and liked by homeless people and park activists alike. Though only 19, she was well versed in the park's rich history and loved the little plot of ground with a fervency so peculiar to many Berkeley-ites. Some speculate she was driven by desperation and nightly police attacks on the homeless into taking the course of action upon which she set out. At any rate, after entering the chancellor's residence, she was shot dead by Oakland Police. Chancellor Tien emerged unscathed.

In a lot of respects, the micro radio movement in the East Bay grew out of the People's Park struggle. When asked, Stephen Dunifer today usually points to the Gulf War as being the one incident, above many, which led him to put his own radio station on the air, but I think People's Park had a lot to do with it too. Certainly there was dissatisfaction with the coverage the issue got in the media.

"It was never about volleyball," says park activist Carol Denney. The real issue, she says, was the increasing number of homeless people who had nowhere else to go. "They (the university) wanted to run them out and absorb all of the acreage under the heading of 'sports facility.'"

In the wake of the unrest, Denney and three other activists were accused of fostering the disturbances in a lawsuit brought by UC. The legal action was of a form known as a Strategic Lawsuit Against Public Participation, or SLAPP. After a five-year legal battle the suit was summarily adjudicated in favor of UC.

Central to the People's Park struggle was how it would be covered on KPFA, Berkeley's Pacifica-owned community radio station. No one really expected the corporate-owned media to do a fair job presenting both sides of the story. KPFA was another matter, though. Would the radio station, despite its sympathies toward the city's liberal power structure, report on the nightly police harassment of homeless people? Denney says that while the SLAPP suit "was covered beautifully by KPFA," the station on the other hand substantially failed to focus on the homeless issues involved, and in fact took little notice of events in People's Park until the outbreak of the '91 disturbances and the subsequent filing of the SLAPP suit by UC attorneys.

After the founding of Free Radio Berkeley in April 1993, Denney gravitated toward that station, where she and Dunifer began to co-host a weekly show together.

"They (the university) had the media sewn up, and so we created our own," she said.

"Creating our own" was a lot easier said than done. For those of us involved in the Food Not Bombs struggle in San Francisco, the development and use of micro radio was roughly our own equivalent to the Manhattan Project. And Dunifer was our Oppenheimer—maybe even our Einstein. Few of us had any illusions that the arrests of Food Not Bombs were over for good—not with Frank Jordan in the mayor's office. After all, Jordan, from 1988-90, had presided over something like 300 Food Not Bombs arrests as police chief. In those days, from late '92 through early '93, we were merely in the eye of the storm. Nothing was over. In fact, the worst was yet to come.

***

Thus we began—those of us in San Francisco as well as the folks in Berkeley—the work of making those mythical radio stations a reality.

When I became involved in the micro radio movement in late 1992 it was a challenge just learning the names of everything in Dunifer's lab. There were capacitors—ceramic and variable—resistors, coils, inductors, transistors, ferrite beads, solid wire, stranded wire, heat sinks, dummy loads, power supply units and on and on. There were also potentiometers, which, when I picked one up and examined it, I vaguely associated with the little thing you find underneath the volume control knob on your car radio when the latter comes loose and falls off. All the parts, or components, had values. Capacitors were rated in "pf's" while resistors were rated by the number of "k's" each had. A small ceramic capacitor might have a value, say, of 56pf, while a somewhat larger one might read 100pf.

To confuse matters further, the parts were additionally assigned numbers in terms of the order in which they appeared on a schematic, or diagram. Again, to use capacitors as an example, there would be C1, C2, C3 and so on. Frequently in the early going I found myself getting the value numbers mixed up with the order numbers. It was all pretty technical stuff, from my point of view.

And this all, mind you, was just in terms of learning what everything was and what each part was called. Then consider, that each transmitter, once fully constructed, would have perhaps 50-100 such parts all total. Now try to fathom, if you will, understanding what each part does and how they all interact with each other—this will give you some idea of where Dunifer was in his level of understanding of it all. He was there—and more. He had surpassed the stage of merely following schematics designed and engineered by other people; he was creating his own designs. In doing so, he was constantly coming up with what could only be termed as "new and improved" transmitters.

In the main there were five of us who became Stephen's helpers in those early days. In addition to myself, there were Doug Forbes, Paul

Griffin, Joe Williams, and Carol Denney. By early 1993 we had reached the point where we were doing small tests at night on transmitters Stephen had built. This would involve supplying power to a transmitter in the lab, while one of us would go out on the street with a radio to see how far the signal carried. Stephen, of course, had a power/SWR meter in the lab that theoretically told us if the transmitter and antenna were doing their jobs or not. Switch the meter to gage power and it measured watt output from the transmitter. Switch it back to SWR, or "standing wave ratio," and it told you how much energy was being reflected from the antenna back into the transmitter—hopefully not much.

The idea, of course, was to get the energy waves to radiate out into the atmosphere, not back into the transmitter. If the power reading were high (that is, somewhere in the vicinity of the presumed actual watt capacity of the transmitter) and the SWR were low, it was fair to assume that both transmitter and antenna were functioning harmoniously in relation to each other. But taking readings off a meter and making theoretical assumptions about them are not the same as actually hearing the results for yourself. Often there would be hums or crackles in the signal. The crackles would register on the meter as small, quick darts of the needle, pulsing in rhythm with the crackle. Hums, on the other hand, were a different matter. The only way to detect them was to simply turn the radio on, tune in the right frequency and listen for them. Stephen was able to eradicate a lot of these hums by placing ferrite beads at strategic locations within the circuitry of the transmitter. What the beads did or why they often eliminated the hums, I had no idea.

We were re-inventing the wheel, in a lot of respects, in those days in that lab in Berkeley. Re-inventing the wheel—or, at least, the radio. It was 1895 when a young Guglielmo Marconi invented "wireless telegraphy," causing his invention to transmit a tapped signal for more than a mile. Unfortunately, Marconi handed over his wonderful device to corporations and governments, and there it has pretty much remained ever since. Perhaps the first bust of a radio pirate took place in England in 1914 when a nineteen-year-old youth was caught transmitting illegally from his grandfather's garden. According to Marconi's biographers, B.L. Jacot and D.M.B. Collier, British authorities were able to discover the whereabouts of the young man by means of a device, obligingly invented by Marconi himself, for tracking down illegal stations. The culprit was given a 14 day jail sentence. According to Jacot and Collier,

> With war fever running high and the fact that the young
> fellow lived with his German grandfather, it is surprising

he did not receive a more severe sentence. His installation
was dismantled. [10]

It's interesting to note that by 1935 Marconi had become not only a
supporter of Mussolini, but a friend of the Italian dictator as well, receiving
Il Duce on his yacht on several occasions. Irregardless of any fascist
sympathies he may have had—perhaps, to be charitable, it was only Italian
patriotism that led to his association with Mussolini—Marconi has
nonetheless been credited with one of the world's most amazing inventions.
Yet for nearly two decades after its discovery radio communications
consisted of nothing more than messages tapped in Morse code. It wasn't
until 1912 that "wireless telephony" made it possible to hear voices; not until
1919 that speech was transmitted across the Atlantic; and only in the early
1920's did the world see the rise of the "broadcast entertainment industry."
Fortunately, thanks to the trail having been blazed for us by Marconi and
other scientists, we were making better time than that in our Berkeley lab.

In April of 1993 Free Radio Berkeley went on the air at the 88.1
frequency. Stephen, Carol, Paul and Joe began driving up into the Berkeley
hills on Sunday nights, setting up the transmitter in a clandestine location,
and going on the air from nine till midnight. One of the first broadcasts was
monitored by Keith, Andrea, and myself from Coit Tower on top of Russian
Hill in San Francisco. I'm not sure exactly what the distance was from where
the Berkeley folks set up that night, to our own location at Coit Tower, but it
would have been something like 7-12 miles, much of it over water with no
obstructions. The signal came through on the radio in Keith and Andrea's
Nissan truck clear as a bell.

Earlier in the week I had given Stephen a tape of the latest Food Not
Bombs Radio Network program. It was in the days not long after the
assassination of Dr. David Gunn in Florida. A group known as the Bay Area
Coalition for Our Reproductive Rights, or simply BACORR, had blockaded
a Baptist Church in Freemont, California, where Operation Rescue had
planned to hold an organizational meeting. I had gone down there to cover
the event for the Food Not Bombs Radio Network. "Kill a Doctor for Jesus!"
read some of the signs as people stood out in front of the church and yelled
"Murderers!!" So intense was it, that Operation Rescue, despite a generous
supply of local police support, had been forced to cancel the meeting.

"This is one of the more successful protests that have been held
recently," Stephen intoned, introducing the program that night, while we
listened at Coit Tower. Then it was on, our own program coming at us from
far across the black water and the twinkling lights of the distant East Bay
shores, transported on invisible waves through the air. Wireless telephony.

Suddenly we were laughing. It was an emotional moment, and what we were laughing about had nothing to do with abortion rights or the murder in Florida. We were laughing at the sound of ourselves coming out of the radio.

Sports metaphors are a tremendously overused speech mechanism in American culture, put to work in an especially tiresome manner every time America gets involved in another war, but there's one which comes to mind here that fits perfectly. So at the risk of sounding like a bloated Pentagon general briefing the press on the latest bombing run over Baghdad, I'll use it: we had just done an end run around corporate America and moved the ball 10 yards up field. There was another implication to all of this that became immediately clear: if the San Francisco Police unleashed a new wave of attacks against Food Not Bombs, we now had a potent new weapon with which to fight back. Our laughter spilled out of us uncontrollably.

***

By late May both Free Radio Berkeley and San Francisco Liberation Radio were operational one night a week. With FRB hitting the airwaves on Sunday nights, we had chosen Saturday nights as our broadcast time in San Francisco. After the highway crash in Bakersfield I had bought a new camper, or at any rate a new used one. This now became our mobile broadcast unit.

We conceived the notion that we would have a better chance of eluding the police, or the FCC, or whoever might come after us—we didn't know, at that point, who might take an interest in our activities—by rotating broadcast sites. This is what the Berkeley crew were doing, keeping mainly to the Oakland/Berkeley hills, yet always setting up at a different site each night. In San Francisco we picked five locations. The most advantageous, we felt, in terms of enabling us to reach the largest number of people, was Twin Peaks. This, coincidentally, was also by far the easiest to get to. All you had to do was drive the truck up to the top, park, raise the antenna through the roof, and go on the air. Other sites we used, such as Mount Davidson or Marin Headlands, were inaccessible by vehicle, necessitating hikes of some distance, laden with a hundred pounds or more of equipment. Carrying the equipment from the truck to the top of Mount Davidson was especially strenuous, requiring that we mount a narrow, rocky trail that wound its way up to the summit.

Getting everything set up took time. We began to realize that in order to start a broadcast at 8 o'clock we needed to be at the broadcast site by 7:15. Our transmitter was designed to run on 12-volt DC. Thus, doing a mobile, outdoor broadcast of this type necessitated carrying along a car battery and—yes—hiking it up to the various mountain peaks we regularly visited. At first we tried backpacking the battery, but this turned out to be a disaster because battery acid leaked out and got all over everything else in the backpacks.

We next tried making a sling, hooking the strap over our shoulders and letting the battery dangle at or near waist level during transport, but this turned out to be problematic as well, as the battery acid continued to leak, this time burning holes in our clothes. Then we tried holding the battery by the sling a foot or so out and away from our bodies as we walked. It was awkward and a strain carrying it that way, and the end result was that it still leaked acid and burned our clothes—only not as much. Regardless, this, finally, became the preferred method of battery transport. But our clothes took a beating, and after a while we began to look like a couple of Raggedy-Anns.

Below is a partial list of things we had to buy. No single item, as you can see, amounted to anything all that particularly staggering. Yet everything taken together was far more than we could afford. The conventional wisdom that had been going around back in 1992 was, "Oh, you can start a pirate radio station for around $50." This figure was, to some degree, accurate—but *only* if you were talking about the parts that went in to making up the transmitter alone. The transmitter, however, was only the beginning. If we had known how much it was all really going to cost, perhaps we would never have embarked upon the undertaking. Powering the transmitter with a 12-volt car battery, of course, meant not only the purchase of a battery, but also a battery charger for re-charging in between broadcasts. But there was more. Here are some of the things with which we had to outfit ourselves just to get started:

- parts for the transmitter
- parts for the amplifier
- re-chargeable size D batteries (to power two boom boxes and a flashlight)
- flashlight battery re-charger.
- car batter re-charger
- hardware for the antenna, including approximately 18 feet of copper tubing
- PVC for antenna mast
- coaxial cable—50 feet
- nylon cord
- miscellaneous electrical cords, cables, connectors and couplers—all from Radio Shack at approximately $3-7 each

We had also sprung for a soldering iron, and midway through that summer we came to the conclusion that we would be unable to continue without our own power/SWR meter as well: another $40 to Radio Shack. We were literally being nickeled and dimed to death

Even with all the toil, trouble and financial resources that went into giving birth to the station, I have happy memories of those nights. These broadcast outings of ours became a cheap date for Jo and I every Saturday night. Cheap dates were about all we could afford by then. Often we would take a picnic supper, into which we would dive after we got all the equipment set up and the program tape running.

As I mentioned, Stephen was constantly improving the transmitter designs. One of the improvements he made later on was the inclusion of a PLL, or phase loop lock, system, giving us frequency stability. The transmitters in use back in 1993, however, had no such stability. Approximately every fifteen minutes during operation our frequency would drift and have to be re-set back at 93.7. This frequency accuracy was checked by means of a device known as a frequency counter, which, depending upon the model you had, could look something like a walkie talkie radio, replete with a telescoping antenna you pull out of the top. To check the frequency of your transmitter you extended the antenna and held the tip a few inches above the transmitter, right in close where it could absorb the energy. The numbers on the counter flicker rapidly, but after a few seconds it usually settles down and gives you a fairly stable, accurate reading.

From Stephen, I had learned to reset the frequency by turning a little screw on top of one of the variable capacitors. Jo and I were fortunate in that Doug Forbes was able to loan us his frequency counter for our own use in San Francisco, and later, after Doug moved, Paul Griffin kindly furnished us with his. It was only the generosity of these two, however, that saved us from shelling out another hundred and twenty-five bucks to Radio Shack.

We discovered that if we stuck to a schedule of one frequency check every quarter of an hour, the drift that would have occurred would be minimal. The drift that took place usually was downward. We found that a 15-minute interval might result in a drift downward to, say, 93.6950 from the desired level of 93.7000. A drift of such diminished magnitude would be undetectable to the listener. Yet it's this reputed threat of frequency drift from "pirate radio operators" that the FCC had traditionally waved as a red flag to keep independent voices off the air.

The problem with this argument is that it completely ignores the reality that it's in the "pirate's" own best interest to stay off of the frequencies of commercially licensed stations whose signals, more often than not, are going to be many, many more times powerful than his or her own. Any attempt by two FM stations to broadcast over the same frequency will result in the weaker signal's being obliterated and stomped upon by the more powerful—not the other way around. While a drift from 93.7000 down to 93.6000 would be a fairly substantial drift, relatively speaking, it would still be only barely detectable by the listener. Moreover, it bears keeping in mind that our nearest neighbors on the dial at that time were KYA, an oldies station, at 93.3000, and KPFA at 94.1000. As long as we stayed sandwiched in between, somewhere at or near 93.7000, we weren't interfering with anyone.

And, of course, all this frequency drift stuff became a moot point a year later when the lab in Berkeley started turning out PLL-equipped transmitters that were one hundred percent frequency stable.

***

Outdoor broadcasts were preferable, we felt, to setting up the radio station in our apartment. This was for a couple of reasons. First of all, the outdoor peaks and promontories we chose afforded us far more elevation for our antenna than we could have gotten at our apartment. However, this was not our foremost reason for "going mobile." Our main, overriding concern was the fear of having police or government agents come into our home and confiscate literally everything we owned.

Not only was our mixer and all the rest of our audio equipment necessary for producing the Food Not Bombs programs at risk, but even our TV and our toaster could have been up for grabs as well. We had seen the San Francisco Police clean out Food Not Bombs over and over again, confiscating everything from vehicles to propane stoves to folding tables, and the like. There were also the state's assets forfeiture laws, giving police the right to confiscate your property without even having to charge you with a crime.

At least if we got caught doing an illegal broadcast outdoors, the only thing we risked losing, presumably, was the equipment in our possession at the time. As much money as we had sunk into our mobile broadcasting, we had much, much more at stake—our whole lives—at home. We were willing to risk fines for the radio station—even jail—but we were not willing to risk losing everything we owned. This fear of property confiscation is one of the most powerful tools the government uses to control the American people.

Just as Free Radio Berkeley's signal was audible in San Francisco under optimum conditions, so, too, could our own signal be heard in

Berkeley. On nights when we broadcast from Twin Peaks we could be received on University Avenue loud and clear. Originating from Marin Headlands, we could still be heard in Berkeley, though not as well. Marin Headlands was great, however, for reaching the west side of San Francisco, where we actually lived. It was on a Marin Headlands broadcast one night that our signal was received by Keith in the Cala Foods parking lot at 4th and Geary.

"It was the most amazing thing!" he exclaimed the next day. "I wanted to grab other people in the parking lot and say, 'Here! Listen to this!'" Bubbling with enthusiasm—that was Keith, our greatest supporter. Another really wonderful supporter—and loyal listener—we picked up in those days was Matt Dodt of Food Not Bombs. When we heard that Matt had begun setting up a table with a portable radio on Market Street on Saturday nights and playing our broadcast for anyone who would stop and listen, we were a little overwhelmed—it made us feel so good.

Invariably, when doing these outdoor broadcasts, we encountered other people—joggers, tourists, hikers, or, more commonly, just folks hanging out. Encumbered as we were with equipment, some of it, such as our antenna, of a rather peculiar-looking nature, it was inevitable perhaps that our activity ignited curiosity and prompted comments from passersby. At first we tried affecting nonchalance. When it became obvious that this wasn't going to work, we opted for the truth, there being little else we could think of to explain away our rather mysterious preoccupations. "Oh, we're just operating a pirate radio station."

Now, reactions to this announcement ranged from the mildly bemused to a highly vociferous enthusiasm. Never, however, did the information fail to transform the expression of the onlooker into one of lively animation, and always were we wished good luck.

While having such bystanders "in-the-know" as to our illegal activity made us nervous, their presence, on the other hand, was comforting to us. At least if the government sent a death squad to snuff us out, there would be witnesses, we figured. Now, talk of government death squads being put on the trail of unlicensed broadcasters may sound paranoid at present, but back in those days we really had no idea at all what we were up against or what level of repression to which the government might resort to stop us.

We had heard stories about a pirate radio station on board a ship in New York harbor, and the ship being boarded by government agents—but no one had died in that incident as far as we knew. We were aware, too, of Mbanna Kantako, the blind broadcaster in Springfield, Illinois, who was the voice of Black Liberation Radio. Kantako was still around, so maybe we were safe, we thought. We *thought*—but were not one hundred percent sure.

As far as death squads went—certainly the U.S. Government was involved with death squads in Central America, and if that was the case, why not San Francisco? The San Francisco Police had more than amply demonstrated their complete, unutterable hatred for Food Not Bombs. And then there had been the car bombing in Oakland a few years earlier of Earth First! activists Judi Bari and Daryl Cherney. *That* had certainly had the flavor of a political hit. Bari and Cherney had only thwarted their would-be killers by miraculously surviving. There was no doubt in our minds that we were living in a police state. What we were doing was irrefutably against the law—but was it really dangerous to our safety?

***

We squelched our fears, which we decided were probably mostly in our imaginations anyway, and did a seven hour broadcast on the fourth of July. We originated the broadcast from Potrero Hill, which has a pretty good line-of-sight into Dolores Park. We were particularly concerned with reaching Dolores Park because the San Francisco Mime Troupe was doing a free performance there that day and there would be thousands of people present. We had found an abandoned lot on Potrero Hill that was perfect for our needs. It was reedy and weed-filled and possessed a lone tree which provided a modicum of shade. Though across the street from a school, it was, to a remarkable degree, secluded from the road. And the view was spectacular, capturing all of the Mission District.

A friend of ours had come up with the idea of standing on the side of a busy street with a hand-lettered sign advertising the station. Ideally the sign might say something like "93.7 FM—TUNE IN NOW!!"—the theory being that people would do so, if only out of curiosity. We decided to try it.

On the morning of the fourth we packed a picnic lunch, loaded the broadcast equipment into the truck, and piled in ourselves, along with Elsa. By 1 p.m. we were set up on Potrero Hill. Taking the sign we had made, Jo hot-footed it down to the park while I stayed with the equipment, monitoring the broadcast and keeping tabs on the frequency drift. The Mime Troupe was scheduled to begin its performance at two. From one till two Jo stood on Dolores Street in front of the park as traffic crawled by. People must have been intent on making it to the Mime Troupe on time, however, for when Jo returned to Potrero Hill she reported that few had taken much notice of her or her sign. Oh well. With our program tapes rolling, we sat down to lunch, Elsa watching us greedily and being rewarded now and then with a handout.

We had planned to be out there for seven or eight hours, if the battery lasted that long. In preparation for the day we had each recorded two hours worth of programming. Jo had taken to calling herself "Annie Voice" over the air. We started out with "Annie's" program, followed by my own two hours, at the end of which we simply began a rebroadcast of the two. Around four o'clock Jo took the sign back to the park and caught the rush of people leaving at the conclusion of the Mime Troupe's show. This time the results were far different. She came back up the hill brimming with excitement.

"One woman stopped and said, 'Well, what is it, honey?' and I said, 'It's a—a—a—' I didn't know what to say, so I finally said, 'It's a pirate radio station.' And I could see a whole line of people, one right after another, reaching for their radio dials as they drove by me!"

Chapter 4
The Matrix Program

Both San Francisco Liberation Radio and Free Radio Berkeley were barely up and running, broadcasting only one to two nights a week, when the mayor of San Francisco unveiled his new "Matrix Program." Under Matrix, thousands of homeless people would be cited for "nuisance" crimes, such as sleeping or urinating in public. The program was officially launched in August of 1993. By the end of November the police had issued more than 1,000 citations. When homeless people were unable to pay the fines—usually in the amount of $76—warrants were issued for their arrest.

Matrix also involved extensive property confiscation, with blankets, clothing, sleeping bags and more all seized—and often thrown into garbage trucks.

The program was the brainchild of police-chief-turned-mayor Frank Jordan, who had swept into office after Art Agnos had abandoned his liberal base of support. (In 1995 Jordan's successor, Willie Brown, campaigned on a promise of ending Matrix. Once elected, however, Brown, the city's first African-American mayor, continued the program in all but name only, thus perpetuating the legacy of generations of San Francisco mayors who have campaigned as compassionate liberals only to swing to the right upon taking office.)

The so-called "nuisance" crimes Matrix targeted included sleeping or camping in city parks or upon city land, urinating in public, and "aggressive panhandling." According to Jordan, laws against these crimes had been only loosely enforced in the past (this was news to the city's homeless), but henceforth, under Matrix, police would be "cracking down."

The program lost no time developing a whole host of detractors, who saw through its transparent attempt to make political hay with the law and order set, and who labeled it as everything from "inhumane" to a waste of "police resources." Prominent among the critics were city religious leaders, as well as Jordan's political rival Angela Alioto. [1]

Responding to these antagonists, Jordan re-tuned his rhetoric somewhat and began to speak of Matrix in terms of its being an "outreach" program designed to "help" homeless people. Indeed, Matrix was gussied up in a certain amount of finery, including roving patrols of social workers. It remained, however, fundamentally a police operation—and the social workers were able to do little more than refer people to already-overcrowded shelters.

Jordan and his staff assured the public that police officers would merely be enforcing existing laws against nuisance crimes and issuing violators citations. This is what the public was told time and again. Anyone familiar with past patterns of police interaction with homeless persons, however, knew there was likely to be a sizeable gap between what the city admitted to publicly, and the reality of actual encounters between police and homeless people on the streets.

Then there was the rhetoric of Jordan and the media. If the mayor was going to launch a crackdown against the poor, it was necessary, of course, to make the poor appear less than human. Jordan's comments to the media seemed not only to have that as an objective, but, looked at on a slightly different level, they could have been interpreted as a coded signal—to Jordan's law and order constituency—that police would indeed be operating under far fewer restrictions than those expressly implied. Said Jordan, "It's not a crime to be out there looking like an unmade bed, but if criminal behavior begins—trespassing, urinating in public, aggressive panhandling—then we will step in and enforce the law." [2]

As bad as it was, Jordan's anti-homeless discourse was actually mild compared to that employed by *San Francisco Chronicle* columnist Debra J. Saunders, whose musings on the city's destitute frequently included such appellations as "bums," "shirkers," and "the work allergic." [3] For Saunders, skyrocketing rents and cutbacks in social services apparently had nothing to do with the explosion of homelessness in the 1980s. Contributing factors to this national problem have not and do not include governmental policies favoring the rich, in Saunders' view—and homeless people have nothing to blame but their own decadence, stupidity, and indolence.

"Compassion fatigue sets in when drug addicts and alcoholics receive money with no strings attached," she stresses. [4]

When the Matrix program commenced in late summer 1993, Saunders' columns took a literary leap for joy, bestowing generous praise upon Jordan, who she believed had elected upon a "path of righteousness." She wrote,

> Voters elected Jordan because he said he would do
> something about anti-social spongers who flout the law,
> break the rules and degrade the quality of city life. It took a

while, but with the dawn of Matrix, the mayor has begun
to deliver. [5]

San Francisco television stations, too, presented less-than-flattering
views of homeless people, one of the more noteworthy being a series
reported by Greg Lyon of KRON-TV. Lyon and his producer, Jonathan
Dann, summed up their views of the homeless—i.e. that they aren't "like
you and me"— in a guest column in the *Chronicle* on June 24, 1993. The
headline over the piece purported it to contain "The Truth About the City's
Homeless." Wrote Lyon and Dann,

> Much of what we think we know about America's
> homeless population is wrong. That may go a long way
> toward explaining why after more than a decade and
> billions of dollars spent, we see more, not fewer, people on
> our streets.
> But it just doesn't work.
> The "big lie" on America's streets is that the homeless
> are just like you and me. But for a bad break, lost health
> insurance, or a death in the family, you and I easily could
> be out there too...
> But the poster child stereotype does not begin to
> describe the majority of those we see. They are much more
> than an unemployed workforce looking for a job. Mental
> illness, alcoholism and drug addiction are rampant among
> them. You do not have to be an investigative reporter to
> figure this out. We all see, hear and smell the evidence
> every day. [6]

While the pervasive smells on San Francisco's streets might, as Dann
and Lyon infer, be somehow connected to the various "rampant" inferiorities
of the homeless, a less nebulous explanation might be simply an acute
shortage of restroom facilities available for them to use. This much was at
least conceded by *San Francisco Examiner* columnist Stephanie Salter:

> Do you want to understand why people urinate and
> defecate in the streets and doorways of 1993 San
> Francisco? You don't have to try to empathize with a
> psychotic or an alcoholic. All you have to do is eat and
> drink as you usually do, then operate for the rest of the day
> under these conditions:

No using your own toilet, your office toilet or 99 percent of the "public" toilets in restaurants, hotels, office buildings, department stores or bars. (If you are homeless, you usually look it and smell it. Nobody from Wendy's to the St. Francis Hotel wants to provide relief for that kind of person.)

If you're lucky you might find an unlocked toilet in a government building or public park. If so, go for it. But don't bring along all your worldly goods in a Safeway shopping cart or stay too long in the stall.

One sweep of the mayor's Matrix broom and you could be cited for possession of stolen property or intent to lodge. [7]

Salter's solution to the problem—the installation of pay toilets on city streets—leaves something to be desired as a comprehensive answer to the homeless crisis. Yet Salter, perhaps more so than anyone else in the city's mainstream media, at least came somewhat close to identifying the real problem:

What kind of people use the public streets, sidewalks, doorways and alleys for a toilet?

That's an easy one. Desperate people with no more privacy or dignity to lose.

The really challenging question is this: what kind of people make it nearly impossible for other human beings to move their bowels and empty their bladders anywhere but in public?

And is it ignorance or just plain meanness that then inspires these people to despise the desperation? [8]

Another aspect of Dann and Lyon's analysis of the homeless (see "The Truth About the City's Homeless," footnote 6) is their assertion that drug addicts, alcoholics and the mentally ill make up "the majority of those we see." I'm not trying to suggest that all homeless people are angels. Far from it. There are, no doubt about it, some hostile, demented homeless people out there—people whom you absolutely would not want to invite home for dinner. But there are perhaps just as many who are good, wholesome and honest folks.

The most you can say of homeless people is the same as you can say of any other population group: that there are both good and bad within. This, however, is, I guess, what Dann and Lyon would refer to as "the big lie." Yet in assuming the "majority" of homeless people are slothful degenerates, they are making a classic mistake: they are basing their assumption on that segment of the homeless population who are the most visible. Many homeless people, despite their hardships and obstacles, make the effort—and somehow succeed—in keeping themselves clean and groomed. I offer myself as a case in point.

When I was living in my vehicle I could, though without a regular place to shower, walk into any Macy's department store in any suburban shopping mall in California—and I could do so without drawing the slightest attention to myself. No one knew I was a homeless vehicle dweller. To be sure, keeping oneself clean under such circumstances is difficult, requiring a certain amount of creativity and sometimes monumental effort—and so many homeless people succumb to the temptation of letting themselves go. Many—but not all.

Dann and Lyon presume to have gauged "the majority" of the homeless population. Yet how many people such as myself have they walked by on the street without ever suspecting they were passing shoulder to shoulder with a homeless person? The real "poster child" stereotype of homeless people is the one being presented by Dann, Lyons and Saunders in their TV reports and newspaper columns.

***

In the "main news" pages of the newspaper, where information supposedly is balanced, the image presented is often no better. "How Homeless Avoid Long Arm of the Law" was the headline over one story in the *Chronicle* which quoted a homeless man who sleeps with a "grimy, battered spy novel" over his face so as to "try to look like an office guy on a break." According to this report,

> If San Francisco police have targeted a long list of "quality of life offenses" to enforce against those who spend their days and nights on the city's sidewalks, homeless people have quickly learned almost as many ways to get around them.
>
> Keep your bedroll out of sight, so you can't get cited for violating camping laws. Keep the shopping cart that holds most of your possessions tidy. Don't sleep where many people can see you, and don't use a blanket if you can help it.

> "People definitely have to watch it," said Sally Vegas,
> a homeless woman sitting half hidden behind a box hedge
> in Union Square. "You can't just not pay attention to
> things or you'll get in trouble." [9]

While the above story is not wholly without sympathetic notes, its upshot seems to be that homeless people are mostly devious-minded individuals intent upon evading society's laws—and often they're not that bright about how to go about it, either. Slothful, dumb, ignorant, and lazy are again the images presented, and perhaps only in the world of mainstream media coverage of homelessness could going without a blanket at night be equated with avoiding "the long arm of the law." Clearly, to some mainstream media, homeless people are second class citizens, who don't even deserve to have a blanket with which to cover up at night. Having a blanket, after all, is a human right. But are homeless people even human? The implication in the *Chronicle* is that they are not.

Would the *Chronicle* have run a story purporting to show how African Americans or Jews "avoid the long arm of the law?" Perhaps in earlier decades of this century, but not in the 1990s. The truly telling irony, of course, is that, with regard to Jews, there almost certainly, no doubt, appeared such stories in German newspapers in the 1930's.

Media coverage of the homeless during Matrix worked not unlike a symphony orchestra. Jordan was the conductor. His Matrix program was the baton. And dutifully the media picked up on the theme and sounded the proper notes. The reporters who wrote the above-cited story are probably not to blame. Censorship at newspapers occurs higher up. Editors change what reporters write. But even beyond that—let's say you're a reporter working under a deadline. You're assigned to write a story on the Matrix program.

If you're going to quote a homeless person or two in your story (after first, of course, giving plenty of space to police and government officials to state fully their own views), you're in all likelihood going to rush out on the street and approach the first person, or persons, who look the most "visibly" homeless, i.e. the most dirty and disheveled. That person will then be interviewed, and his or her thoughts will represent those of the "typical" homeless person. Homeless advocacy groups such as FNB, or the San Francisco Coalition on Homelessness, attempting to overcome such negative imagery in the media, found themselves labeled by Saunders as "the see-no-evil homeless lobby." [10]

The commanding officer in charge of Matrix was Commander Dennis Martel. Not unlike any war in Central America, Matrix produced refugees. Martel's comments to the media were often less than circumspect, occasionally hinting, in practically genocidal overtones, that the program's real goal was class cleansing and banishment of homeless people from San Francisco. In a story about how "as many as 100" of San Francisco's homeless people had turned up in Berkeley since the onset of Matrix, Martel was quoted as saying,

> "I'd find that encouraging. We don't want to make our nuisance criminals a problem for other cities. But if people are now finding they can't do whatever they want here, and that makes them uncomfortable, then that is good news." [11]

But what was life truly like for homeless people under Matrix? Occasionally the media let slip a glimpse of the true reality.

> According to the latest report on people being turned away, the city's shelters had to say no to people more than 14,000 times in June alone. With the city telling people to get off the streets or get a ticket or a jail cell, competition for what little space there is has become intense. [12]

The above evoked in me images—once again—of Jews in Germany in the 1930s.

***

Police seizures of homeless people's shopping carts became an issue on Saturday, November 13, when the *Chronicle* reported officers had been "quietly confiscating" the carts for "more than a month." City officials professed shock at the news.

> Chagrined city leaders vowed the cart round-ups would stop, although no immediate disciplinary action will be brought against the police officers involved. Both Mayor Frank Jordan and Police chief Anthony Ribera said they had no prior knowledge of the cart seizures.
>
> "These actions were taken independently of any direction from the administration of this department and will cease immediately," Ribera said. [13]

This notion suffers from an even further erosion of credibility in light of the fact that Operation Shopping Cart was a fairly large undertaking, involving not just one city department, but two. In addition to the police department, the city's Department of Public Works also played a role in the confiscations. This much was even admitted by Public Works supervisor Jere Driscoll, who was quoted as saying the cart seizures were "an ongoing thing." Said Driscoll,

> "Yesterday the police asked us to pick up some carts along Mission Street and we did. We gave some people (duffel) bags for their things. We are trying to be as gentle as possible...but the public wants the streets cleaned up, and we are getting hammered by the public for debris on the streets." [14]

Driscoll's comments about the duffel bags are most interesting. Nearly two months before this, Jordan's office had floated a proposal to seize shopping carts and reimburse homeless people with duffel bags. The plan was hastily withdrawn after meeting with much derision. Yet, if Driscoll's comments are to be believed, it appears as if the city "quietly" went ahead and acquired the duffel bags, anyway.

Columnist Saunders weighed in on the shopping cart issue, too—surprisingly, perhaps, against the seizures. Oddly, Saunders seemed to feel that the homeless who pushed shopping carts were the *good* homeless, or, as she described, they were but mere "gentle rogues" who could often be found going "laughing into the night."

"Why pick on these guys?" Saunders wrote, lamenting that she "doesn't want to see the good Matrix has done undermined by one unpopular action." [15]

Chronicle reporters April Lynch and Clarence Johnson, to their immense credit, reported on the sorry consequences the confiscations had had on one homeless man.

> Kendall Griffitts, a 25-year old homeless man, lost photographs, blankets, a new sleeping bag, all his freshly laundered clothes and a radio when his cart was seized at about 8 a.m. near the Civic Center. Griffitts had left the cart with a friend for safekeeping while he waited in the breakfast line at Glide Memorial Church.

"I didn't believe it at first," Griffitts said. "My friend was told he couldn't move my cart, that I had abandoned it and it was now something like garbage, even though we can't take the carts into Glide with us...Now everything is gone. I don't think I can replace everything..."

"The weather is just getting cold now," Griffitts said, sitting on a bench in Civic Center Plaza and fingering a new blanket someone had donated. "I've lost things before but nothing like this." [16]

No word on whether Griffitts ever received his complimentary duffel bag.

***

For the mayor and police chief to have been unaware of the shopping cart confiscations prior to the *Chronicle's* report of November 13 would have almost required the wearing of blinders and ear plugs. Certainly the "see-no-evil homeless lobby" had complained loudly, as far back as August, practically pleading with government officials to stop the seizures—and with reporters to report on them. And even the *Chronicle* itself had reported the story—though only in a minor way—as early as September. For instance, in paragraph 10 of a story which ran on September 1 there appeared the following: "In some cases, police have called in garbage trucks and thrown away mattresses or other items they say have been abandoned—even though critics say such destruction of property is illegal." [17]

Under international law, homeless people in San Francisco would have been justified in picking up arms to resist the theft of their property and to fight for their right to at least occupy space somewhere on the Earth.

Article 25 of the Universal Declaration of Human Rights, to which the United States is a signatory, states:

Everyone has a right to a standard of living adequate for the health and well being of himself and his family, including food, clothing, housing and medical care and necessary social services, and the right to security in the event of unemployment, sickness, disability, widowhood, old age or other lack of livelihood in circumstance beyond his control.

Food, clothing, housing and medical care clearly are human rights which the U.S. government is failing to ensure for its citizens. But in the matter of the confiscation of homeless people's property—in San Francisco and other U.S. cities—the U.S. is moving beyond the category of mere "human rights violations" and stepping toward the shadowy realm of genocide. The deprivations of homeless people's belongings—let's take "clothing," for example, since that's one of the items specifically cited in Article 25—creates adverse conditions that become precarious to life. Was the confiscation of homeless people's property by San Francisco officials done deliberately with the intention of creating conditions precarious to life?

The UN Convention on the Prevention and Punishment of the Crime of Genocide, to which the U.S. is also a signatory, defines genocide in precise terms:

> In the present Convention, genocide means any of the following acts committed with intent to destroy, in whole or in part, a national, ethnical, racial or religious group, as such:
>
> (a) Killing members of the group;
> (b) Causing serious bodily or mental harm to members of the group;
> (c) Deliberately inflicting on the group conditions of life calculated to bring about its physical destruction in whole or in part;
> (d) Imposing measures to prevent births within the group;
> (e) Forcibly transferring children of the group to another group.

There are doubtless those who would argue that the term genocide cannot possibly apply to homeless people because they do not constitute a recognized "ethnic group." This is mere sophistry. Discrimination based upon condition or status is as real as that based upon race, gender, religion or sexual preference. The pivotal question, then, becomes one of intent: What was the intent of the San Francisco officials who implemented the Matrix program?

* * *

FNB responded to Matrix by organizing protests in front of City Hall. These would invariably be observed by high-ranking officials of the police department, who stood out on Jordan's office balcony, from which they were able to gain a bird's eye view of all that was going on in the plaza below. This went on throughout August. Then on September 2 the state of affairs shifted substantially. Twelve members of FNB were arrested and charged with illegal food serving, followed by 11 more arrests the next day. Jordan had just upped the ante.

For more than a year, the new mayoral administration had left FNB alone. The September 2 arrests, however, marked the beginning for FNB, of what became an even uglier period of repression than had occurred under Agnos.

September was also a fateful point in the history of San Francisco Liberation Radio as well; it was the month in which we were finally tracked down and caught by the FCC.

***

Public opposition to the FNB arrests was expressed by Angela Alioto, president of the city's Board of Supervisors. In Alioto's view, "The mayor is doing something outrageously wrong in calling for a crackdown against the homeless and the people who are helping them. It's like arresting Mother Teresa and her nuns for feeding the hungry on the streets of Calcutta." [18] Alioto's words would prove truer than even she realized at the time. This would occur later on, when priests and nuns joined with FNB and were arrested.

If homeless people were given an overall unsympathetic slamming by the San Francisco media, how, praytell, did the defenders of homeless people fare with the same press corps? Over the years both the *Chronicle* and the *Examiner*, needless to say, had published quite a few news articles, as well as opinion pieces, about FNB. It's important to stress that not all of these were wholly negative, and that a few even portrayed the group in a favorable light. Even so, FNB took regular beatings in the media.

As early as 1988 *Examiner* columnist Rob Morse claimed there was "something fishy about this group tendentiously named Food Not Bombs." Morse believed Food Not Bombs was "more interested in feeding its political agenda than feeding the homeless," and he felt that group members were engaging in "exploitation of the homeless" for purposes of calling "attention to themselves." [19]

By 1993, having racked up hundreds of arrests, FNB had established for itself, more or less by default, a fairly notorious reputation. The city's conservative pundits were quick to capitalize on this. The most vitriolic of all, perhaps predictably, was *Chronicle* columnist Saunders.

On September 10, Saunders took the opportunity to lambast both FNB and Angela Alioto in one column, citing an incident in which the liberal supervisor had been witness to an FNB arrest. Alioto had earlier made use of a campaign slogan, in which she had promoted herself on bumper stickers and billboards as: "Angela: the ♥ of San Francisco." In her column, Saunders, showing her readers her jousting skills, referred to Alioto not by name, at one point, but as "♥." Saunders began her attack by touting the virtues of the Matrix program and referring to homeless people as "anti-social spongers." Then:

> But there is an obstacle in the mayor's path of righteousness. It is the school of thought that says unless you can *solve* homelessness, you are not free to deal with lawlessness. Dean of that school is Angela ("The ♥ of San Francisco") Alioto. Alioto has introduced a measure that would give legal amnesty to derelicts cited under Matrix.
>
> Last week, police arrested two men attending an Alioto press conference because they were violating a 1991 court order forbidding them from serving food without a permit; one also was in violation of a court order to keep away from City Hall. Alioto was indignant. "To arrest people that are that poor and that underrepresented—I hope they sue the mayor tomorrow." [20]

Saunders added,

> Of course they can't sue the mayor without suing the city, but then again ♥ isn't know for her compassion toward the taxpayers. [21]

At this point the text broke for a bold face subhead, which read, "Bomb Throwers, Not Food." Saunders then shared,

> A few words about the gents who were arrested. They belong to a group called Food Not Bombs, which has few reservations about suing the city. In 1992, Keith McHenry, head of FNB, and two other members filed a $24 million lawsuit against the city and officials. McHenry and FNB have filed some six suits against the city; three have been dismissed. [22]

The columnist claimed television news reports about FNB arrests had served "the group's propaganda goals." She then quoted a city health department functionary's warning that FNB's buckets of all-vegetarian soup could be dangerous reservoirs of "salmonella, hepatitis (and) diarrhea." Finally Saunders rendered her coup de grace, branding FNB as "ruthless, lawless and anti-social." Wrote Saunders,

> McHenry has boasted that FNB's have been arrested hundreds of times, the group has treated the court restraining order the way a dog treats a bush, yet those cited rarely spend time behind bars...
>
> Alioto says these guys are "underrepresented." In her dreams. In *my* dreams. The people of this city who truly are underrepresented are the folks who play by the rules and pay their taxes. A person who wants to start a business faces more roadblocks than an advocacy group that spits on the law.
>
> As it turns out, you *can* beat City Hall. But only if you're ruthless, lawless and anti-social. [23]

Of course, it wasn't FNB, but the police who were "ruthlessly" and "lawlessly"confiscating homeless people's belongings in violation of the constitution. And no one seems less "underrepresented" in San Francisco than right wing pundits who are given prominent space in the *Chronicle* every day to express their views.

On October 20, John Crew of the American Civil Liberties Union spoke before the San Francisco Police Commission, questioning the legality of the Matrix program. Crew's comments were reported in a short blurb in the October 21 edition of the *Chronicle*. "Winter is fast approaching. The rains have already started falling and unless we allow people to cover themselves, people will be dying in the streets," Crew said. [24] Instead of presenting Crew's remarks as reasonable, however, the *Chronicle* characterized the civil rights attorney as being "angry." [25]

Did the Matrix program and its accompanying negative stereotyping of homeless people in the media create a backlash of public sentiment against homeless people? It's hard to see how it could not have. Yet what soon happened to one homeless man, described by a housed neighbor as "a street bum who never bothered anybody," would shock even Jordan and the police. [26]

On November 16—just 27 days after Crew's address to the police commission—47-year-old Dennis McCormick was asleep in a doorway on Geary Street when he was doused with alcohol, set on fire, and burned over 30 percent of his body. According to the *Chronicle*, "Veteran officers, including Police Chief Anthony Ribera, were shocked by the savagery of the attack." [27] Even so, McCormick's assailants were described variously in the media as "irrational street thugs." [28]

Any possible cause-and-effect relationship between the climate engendered by Matrix, and McCormick's infernal tragedy was overall carefully avoided by the media."The Burning of a Man," read the headline over a Rob Morse column in the *Examiner*—however Morse seemed less concerned with McCormick's life, as it then hung in the balance, than with the crime-ridden conditions in the neighborhood.

After a foray into the area, Morse was able to deliver the following scoop to his readers: the "thugs" who set fire to McCormick were part of a gang, perhaps "40 or 50" strong, whose members "prowl like sharks on Geary, selling drugs to the young and following the elderly on the 1st and 15th of every month to steal their social security checks." [29] In articulating the above, Morse, who had once accused FNB of "exploiting the homeless," had essentially used the attack on McCormick as an opportunity to call for more police. One neighborhood resident who spoke to Morse wanted to see a "RICO" investigation of the alleged gang.

The columnist did admit, in the closing paragraphs of his expose, to having encountered a woman—only one—who suspected McCormick's torching may have had something to do with the anti-homeless climate created by Matrix, however, according to Morse, "I scoffed" at that. [30]

***

City officials, indeed, were shocked by what happened to McCormick. (Jordan even put up a $10,000 reward.) Yet what had they expected? Did they really expect that their characterizations and depictions of homeless people as subhuman would have no effect on an impressionable public? Had colonial-era characterizations of Native Americans as "merciless savages" been without their effect on the citizenry of that time? Had Hitler's denigration of the Jews been without impact or effect on the German public? Does anything on this Earth really exist wholly within a vacuum? Or do we all, to one degree or another, affect somebody or something else around us?

A rally to protest the attack on McCormick was held in Civic Center Plaza, ending with a march to St. Francis Memorial Hospital, where

McCormick lay in critical condition on the hospital burn unit. The procession was joined by Vietnam veteran Ron Kovic, author of the book, *Born on the Fourth of July.*

Jo covered the march for San Francisco Liberation Radio. Of that night, she remembers Kovic's quiet dignity and his eloquent words on behalf of San Francisco's homeless, any one of whom, said Kovic, "could be a veteran." She remembers, too, that even the San Francisco police seemed affected by Kovic's presence, recalling that the cops that night—while treating FNB members with their usual rudeness and contempt—responded to the wheel-chair-bound Vietnam vet with deference and respect.

A little in awe of Kovic's celebrity status herself, Jo nonetheless, with tape recorder in hand, approached the author for an interview. Finding him pleasant and willing to speak, she inquired of him what he would do to change the system, if he had the power. We still have the tape on which can be heard his reply,

> I would begin to be more positive, begin to teach people that these are our fellow citizens—the people sleeping in the parks, the people sleeping in the streets. These are our brothers and our sisters. These people are a part of our family, and we must see them as valuable resources, as important men and women, as people who can help us help our society become a better place...we (need to) begin to change our attitude toward the homeless, toward, the poor, and realize that they are just as important, just as valuable as anyone else in this society.

The prayers offered up to heaven that night on McCormick's behalf were answered, it seems. It's a good thing the homeless man's attackers had only used alcohol. Had the flammable liquid poured over him been gasoline the result might have been different. As it was, McCormick continued receiving treatment at the St. Francis burn unit up until his release in January 1995.

***

Had Frank Jordan and his supporters, both in and out of the media, contributed, with their anti-homeless rhetoric, to the vicious attack on Dennis McCormick? Although not in depth, or to any great degree of seriousness—this very question was actually addressed on a radio talk show. In January of 1994, after the shock of McCormick's death had substantially worn off—Jordan made an appearance on the Peter B. Collins show on KSFO.

Many an aggressive talk show host might have considered the prospect of having Jordan on a hot seat in front of a live mike to be a golden, god-sent opportunity. It became clear, however, that nothing really challenging was going to be put forth when Collins began the interview with a bouquet of flattery for the mayor, which included a compliment on Jordan's being a "good listener."

Finally, Collins lobbed a question about the Matrix program. Positioning himself as a moderate, the talk show host remarked that he had "criticisms" of Matrix—yet so irrevocably "moderate" was he that it was difficult to ascertain exactly what those criticisms were, at least, insofar as to whether Collins felt the mayor's homeless program was too draconian or too lenient. Any empathy Collins may have felt toward those who were suffering police persecution under Matrix took on the form of a mirage, disappearing and reappearing at various times throughout the interview.

At one point on the program, Collins referred to homeless people as "bums"; then, having expressed mild concern about members of the public "disposing" of homeless people, he brought up the sound effect of a gasoline-powered leaf blower. Purportedly, this latter showed how the Matrix program merely dispersed the homeless to various parts of the city without actually addressing the real problem.

This sort of fatuous line of questioning was adhered to by Collins pretty much throughout the interview. Thus it should come as no surprise that it was not Collins who initially raised the subject of the attack on Dennis McCormick. This—amazingly—was done by Jordan himself:

> Jordan: You've seen one in a door where they lit an individual on fire. I've seen them where we have people using shopping carts in Civic Center Plaza acting as a homeless person selling drugs out of the shopping cart. That to me is a situation where the police have to do something to deal with it because there are people taking advantage of all of us under the guise of being homeless. There is a connotation, and rightly so, that anyone who is, quote, homeless, we should be sensitive and caring and compassionate to them. But we also have to separate homeless from street people—

Thus it was Jordan himself who opened up the Pandora's box of the attack on McCormick—an opportunity that was seized upon later by a phone caller into the program.

Jordan next introduced the theme of "fraud" and the possibility that some homeless people were receiving "duplication and triplication" of social services. One manner of welfare fraud which worried Jordan was the one clearly recognized and defined by law as illegal: that of welfare recipients signing up and receiving benefits in more than one county. Considering the extensive identification demands and the onerous General Assistance (GA) application process, the incidents of this were probably quite low. Yet Jordan felt it necessary to institute, at considerable cost, a program of electronic fingerprinting of all welfare applicants.

The mayor believed there was a danger of homeless people receiving "duplication" in other ways as well. Specifically, he said, there was a widespread problem of GA recipients sleeping in homeless shelters. This constituted duplication because the people receiving GA benefits—set at $345 a month—were supposed to be using that money to pay rent on hotel rooms or apartments (an absurd expectation in a city where the average one-bedroom apartment went for $600 a month.) If they were sleeping in shelters and using the money for other purposes they were, to Jordan's way of thinking, guilty of duplication.

"What are they doing in the shelters?" he asked Collins rhetorically. "We've already given them money for housing."

Obviously in a city with a cost of living as high as San Francisco, GA recipients living on $345 a month were not likely to find much, if anything at all, in the way of shelter. But Jordan had an answer for this too: mandatory rent payments. Under this system the city would automatically deduct $280 from each GA recipient's $345 allotment. With this money the city would then contract with slum hotel owners, securing reduced rent by obtaining transient rooms on a steady package basis.

This left the GA recipient with no choice, of course, in how or where to spend his or her money, raising civil liberties questions. But there were other concerns as well. The hotels selected for the program were invariably some of the most rancid, decrepit, stench-permeated abodes in hell's creation. Many homeless people considered them little more than disease-ridden fire traps.

Indicative of this, perhaps, is the experience of FNB member Stuart "Hambone" McKillip. A resident of one of the hotels in the spring of 1995, McKillip stepped on a used syringe while taking a shower in the communal bathroom shared with the hotel's other tenants. McKillip, who was not an IV drug user, told friends about the incident, expressing concern over possibly having contracted AIDS. McKillip, as it turned out, had plenty of reason to fear—though not from AIDS. Two weeks after stepping on the syringe, McKillip came down with a particularly virulent strain of hepatitis. A Vietnam vet, he was taken to the Veterans Hospital in San Francisco's Richmond District.

In those days San Francisco Liberation Radio was broadcasting just a scant few blocks away from the hospital. I didn't really know "Hambone" all that well due to the fact that by this time I had substantially ceased as an active member of FNB, at least insofar as cooking and serving food were concerned, spending all my free time now with the radio station. Keep in mind this was 1995. Many new faces had come into FNB since those painful, turbulent days of the early nineties. Some of these, such as Hambone, I scarcely knew at all. Nonetheless I went to see him when he ended up at the VA hospital. He was, after all, only a few blocks away.

Standing at his bedside, I regretted having never taken the time to get to know him better. In those days I was heavily immersed in the day-to-day operation of the station, as well as supporting, in various ways, our legal challenge to the FCC. Both SFLR and Free Radio Berkeley had begun to receive a lot of publicity in the media. Hosting reporters on a tour of the station (i.e. the tiny apartment Jo and I shared) and giving extensive interviews had become a time-draining activity. Perhaps Hambone had some inkling of this, for he said, "It's so cool that you came, man!" He flashed a smile, though speech was obviously difficult for him.

He was on the intensive care unit, meaning there was a nurse hovering about constantly. His bones stood out starkly in his face, and the pallor of his skin was alarmingly yellow. Again there washed over me a feeling of regret—and guilt—that I had never gotten to know him better, coupled also with a sensation of awkwardness in standing, so intimately, at the bedside of a near stranger. Knowing the SFLR signal would surely be received loud and clear at the hospital, I had brought along a battery-powered radio for him to listen to while he recuperated—but the nurse refused to allow me to leave it with him.

Though it was around 11 a.m., for some reason the breakfast trays had not been collected. His breakfast remained by his bed, and from the looks of things it had gone untouched. With my assistance, however, he began to take in food. I watched as he consumed about half the scrambled eggs and a few bites of the cold oatmeal. We chatted for a while, though he was in a groggy state, and speech remained a difficult task for him. Encouraged, nonetheless, by his display of appetite, I left, assuming he was more or less on the road to recovery. It thus came as a shock to me a few days later when I heard he had died, still in the hospital.

He had spent his last days, prior to becoming ill, working with FNB. I guess you could say he had been "killed" by that residential slum hotel in which he had been living—or if that sounds a bit too overstated, maybe it suffices simply to say he was a "casualty of poverty—" having survived the Vietnam war only to become such a casualty in the very country for which he had fought.

***

San Francisco's slum hotels had taken other tolls in human life, too. A fire at the Folsom Street Hotel on September 8, 1993—just over one month into the Matrix program—killed 51-year-old John Franklin Jordan (no relation to the mayor) and injured 13 others, two critically. According to the *Chronicle,* "city officials were red-faced to learn they had placed homeless welfare clients in the facility although it had been cited for serious building code violations." [31]   Arson was suspected as the cause of the 5 a.m. fire. "It appears that an accelerant was used," commented Police Homicide Inspector Alex Fagen on the morning of the blaze. [32]

Records listed Chhotubhai B. (Charlie) Patel and C. Savitaben as the owners of the hotel, according to the *Examiner*. Interestingly, Patel, viewed as a "key player" in the city's mandatory rent program, owned a total of 10 hotels that "primarily" served the poor.

The string of Patel rental properties in San Francisco was valued at $14 million. Yet Patel had a lengthy history of code violation citations and had been the target of fourteen lawsuits, five of which had been brought by the San Francisco city attorney's office, dating back to the early 1980s. The most recent of the city-initiated suits had been dropped in the fall of 1992-shortly after Jordan took office- after city officials deemed that the violations had been "cleared." Whether this was the case or not, the history of Patel's troubles, just with regard to the Folsom Street Hotel alone, the one which burned, makes for riveting reading. The building had been constructed in 1906—the year of the San Francisco earthquake. Patel had acquired it in 1986 for $729,412. According to the *Examiner,*

> Records show that the hotel had been cited 12 times since 1986 for building code violations, including the lack of smoke detectors in halls and rooms, inadequate fire hydrants and obstructions to fire escapes.
>
> The most recent inspection came March 26, 1991,during which it was noted that windows to fire escapes were nailed shut. The inspector ordered them

made openable. He also ordered the owners to recharge fire extinguishers.

On May 14, 1991 the hotel management issued a "self certification" declaring that a battery-powered smoke detection system had been installed throughout the building.

The building inspection department apparently accepted the certification with no further inspections. [33]

The September 8 fire at the Folsom Street establishment was not the first fire at a Patel-owned hotel. In 1990 a blaze at the Patel-owned Hotel Abbey gutted 20 units, leaving one man injured and 50 people homeless. As if that weren't enough, there were others, according to the *Chronicle:*

Last year, two suspicious fires damaged another of Patel's properties, the Lyric Hotel at 132 Jones Street in the Tenderloin. Investigators suspect arson in the fires, which occurred at different times. [34]

Despite these occurrences, Patel appears never to have been a suspect in any of the arson investigations surrounding his hotels. The Abbey fire was judged to have been an accident.

As in the matter of the shopping carts, city officials were once again professing shock to the public—this time over the news that GA recipients had been placed in hotels with serious code violations.

It should be noted that at the time of the Folsom Street fire on September 8, 1993—one month into the Matrix program—the mandatory rent program had not yet become law, still being only a proposal at that point, albeit one which was rapidly gaining support. Jordan administration officials assured reporters on the day of the fire that all the hotels currently under consideration for use in the program had been "rigorously" inspected and found to be "clear of violations." Yet even before the fire and the program's commencement, homeless people had been placed in the hotels, including the Folsom Street, by the Tenderloin Housing Clinic, a private, non-profit organization, using city money.

Even as officials rushed to minimize the PR damage brought about by the fire, the truth was starting to come out about sub-standard housing for the homeless in San Francisco. On September 16, a week after the fire, it was reported by the *Chronicle*, in a page one story, that of the 22 hotels used by the city to house the homeless, only one had not been cited by city inspectors for code violations during their most recent inspections. "The other 21 were cited for multiple violations—including such potentially life-threatening deficiencies as failing to provide smoke detectors." [35]

Many, particularly in the "see-no-evil homeless lobby," suspected cross-purposes to be at work with regard to the city and its proposed mandatory rent program. Specifically it was felt that city officials had more interest in rounding up homeless people and removing them from the streets, than with forcing slum lords to bring their buildings up to code standards. It should be kept in mind that under Jordan's plan, hotels would accept city-referred tenants at the rate of $280 per month. This was substantially less than "market value," even given the dilapidated conditions of the hotels. What were the hotel owners to get in return? Could it be lenient code inspections—or even no inspections at all?

Indeed a symbiotic relationship seemed to have developed between the owners and the city. Despite the below-market rentals, the arrangement was nonetheless a lucrative one for hotel owners, as the *Examiner* reported in its September 9 story on the fire: "The (mandatory rent) program is expected to generate about $140,000 a month for the hotel owners, depending on the number of tenants involved." [36] Patel, as the owner of 10 hotels (worth $14 million in assets) and a "key player" in the program, stood to become a significant beneficiary of this money. Frank Jordan—the mayor of San Francisco—had thus made common cause with Charlie Patel, the city's most preeminent slum lord.

Yet all these issues seemed to get swiftly pushed aside. Jordan, unable to get his GA fingerprinting and mandatory rent programs passed through the board of supervisors, placed the issues on the ballot—in November as proposition V, and the following year as Proposition N. For all the revelations that had emerged in September in the wake of the fire, by election day the issue had been largely forgotten.

***

Although in another city, in a different state, I, myself, had once lived in a slum hotel similar to those which abound in certain parts of San Francisco. The experience had been a negative one, to put it mildly. While the sheets and pillowcases had been clean, the pillow itself on my bed had smelled partly of whiskey and partly of vomit, the two odors competing with each other for ascendance. Nightly I did battle with cockroaches, who retreated during the day, but seemed literally to hemorrhage out of the walls at night.

During this time I became soundly convinced that it was far healthier to live outdoors where the grass was green, the air fresh and the only things moving overhead were the moon and stars. This had been in the mid 1980s. I had paid $75 a week for that room. The cockroaches got to live there for free. That experience is what set me irrevocably upon the course of becoming a vehicle dweller. As long as I owned my own vehicle, I reasoned, never again would I have to lay my head down in such a place.

Ironically, the city government which allowed such hotels to remain open, was the same city government which so had it in for FNB. By January, when Jordan did his interview with KSFO, the Folsom Street fire had receded into history; proposition V had passed; and the issue of housing for the homeless was once again on the back burner—only kept alive at all by the efforts of groups like FNB.

In fact, FNB at one point became a focal point for discussion in the KSFO interview. Completely ignoring the issue of substandard conditions in the slum hotels, Jordan commented to Collins: "Food Not Bombs is the *only* entity that I know in San Francisco that refuses to comply with the health regulations."

***

Given the conditions in the hotels, is it any wonder that many homeless people preferred to live outdoors? Such freedom of choice, however, was precisely what Jordan was not prepared to tolerate from the homeless. A further remark to Collins is revealing:

> Jordan: ...If we can find a better place than a doorway on the streets of San Francisco in a business entranceway, let's try to do it. But at the same time, if we also find out through this Matrix program that the individual is already receiving help and is not using the funds properly, then we call that person out and get them into the system some way. That's what we're trying to do.

"Into the system" obviously meant into the slum hotels.

The KSFO dialogue between Jordan and Collins droned offensively on. With revolting patronization of the poor, Jordan professed to offer quotes from homeless people, ostensibly made to Matrix officials. In summing up their existence on the streets, these homeless people are said to have told Jordan's Matrix team, "We can't help ourselves."

The latter comment was a nice touch on Jordan's part, even further reducing homeless people to the status of children, thereby, conveniently, further justifying government control over the spending of their funds.

The pace of the interview picked up when Collins started allowing phone-in callers. The first caller, as it happened—identified as "Ethan from San Francisco—" turned out to be Ethan Davidson of FNB.

I knew Ethan, having cooked and served food with him. Had he been allowed to remain on the air, he likely would have made a formidable sparring partner for Jordan, however, he was quickly cut off—though not before re-introducing an important component into the discussion.

> "Ethan from San Francisco: He (the mayor) mentioned the guy who was set on fire—I think that was mostly because of Matrix creating this climate that it's—um—open season on the homeless and that they should cease to exist, and that they're fair game—
>
> Collins (interrupting): Alright, Ethan, let's let the mayor respond to these comments.

Ethan was hung up on. Jordan responded:

> Jordan: Well first I would say, Ethan, that's an outrageous statement to make, that—uh—by trying to protect even the homeless themselves that somehow it's Matrix's fault...

To this Collins followed up, "Mayor Jordan, I echo the caller's sentiments that you personally are not responsible for the torching of Dennis McCormick..." Ethan had never, in fact, granted the mayor such absolution. Collins resumed:

> But I think that I'm not alone in feeling that a climate has been created here by your aggressive approach to the homeless problem using law enforcement in particular—uh—and that that climate has given some people who are not good citizens a sense that they have permission to dispose of homeless people. And that they're some kind of animal life that exists beneath the rest of us. And I wanna give you an opportunity to respond to that because I think it's significant and I know you don't agree.
>
> Jordan: Well, Peter, yes, I don't agree, but I can understand the perception of what you're stating here, but, uh, put yourself in the position of a police officer, number

one. You have people every day in San Francisco who are just hounding them, saying, "Will you please do something about the problems we see in the streets of San Francisco?" You have business owners who say, "Will you please not allow this person to sleep in front of that doorway or urinate in front of that doorway?" They're making tremendous demands on the police officers all over town.

A later caller, identified as "Jason in the city," was also an FNB activist—Jason Corder, who, spoke of being arrested while doing nothing more than holding a "Food not Bombs" sign, and who urged Jordan to "give your police force a lesson in democracy."

By way of response, Jordan took the opportunity to assert, "Food Not Bombs is the *only* entity that I know in San Francisco that refuses to comply with the health regulations." The mayor expanded:

If you take a look at how it's being served—they take food and maybe go out to different supermarkets, throw the products in the back of a pick up truck, or like an old bakery wagon truck, all thrown together, and then they serve it in plastic buckets. If you take a look at it I don't think you'd—uh—want to eat it. But the danger here is that they refuse to comply with healthcare regulations—

What Jordan failed to say here is that one reason FNB served food out of plastic buckets was to protect its giant, stainless steel cooking pots from police confiscation. The food was always cooked in the big cook pots, then poured into the hard-plastic buckets for transport to the serving site. The cook pot remained behind in safe storage, out of reach of the police. Jordan continued, focusing his remarks now specifically on Keith McHenry:

Jordan: I've talked to Keith McHenry myself, the head of Food Not Bombs, and I've said, 'We will help you set up a food kitchen. We'll help you cooperate and serve food, but you have to comply with health and public safety standards.' He just refuses to do so. Why are the other thirteen (soup kitchens) complying? Is he the only one who should have an exception to the rule? He's not going to have an exception to the rule as long as I'm the mayor of San Francisco.

Collins: Jason, you have a follow up?

Jason: We've tried to—uh—get a health permit for three years. We had one and we complied with it fully, and it was taken away from us, and we tried over and over again to get it, so that line is just absolutely untrue. Keith McHenry is in jail right now as we speak, and he's been in jail for over two days. He was arrested for three counts of felony, grand robbery and two counts of battery. He himself was actually attacked—by a person who is associated with the mayor—inside City Hall, and when that person called 911, the cops came and arrested Keith. The bail has been set at $10,000. He is hurt and he has not been able to see a doctor, and this is just outrageous civil rights abuse—I don't even know what country you think you're in, Mayor Jordan—

At this point Jason was cut off by Jordan, who, despite his alleged prowess as a "good listener," began now to refer to Jason as "Roger."

Jordan: Well, I'll tell you, Roger, the-the problem—what you're doing is spreading misinformation here too because I've seen the reports and I know exactly what happened! Let me tell the public what happened here! Keith McHenry was outside of City Hall. He was haranguing a parking controller and pounding on his—uh—chest—parking controller's chest—because he was parked in an illegal—Keith McHenry was parked in an illegal parking space, and he was wanting to stay there. And an aid of—uh—the—my office came over and told him, 'Do you need help?' to the parking controller. And the next thing you know, Keith McHenry assaulted him! He chased him inside of City Hall, grabbed his beeper off his belt—we don't know where the beeper is now—and he struck him in the back of the head and spit right in his face. Now that's Keith McHenry!   That's the person that you're representing here as a wonderful, outstanding citizen! I think the man needs to grow up! I think he needs to start being professional in his conduct, and then maybe people will start paying attention to him!

Collins: Thank you very much for your call, Jason. More of your calls coming up for Mayor Frank Jordan in a moment...

***

In August of 1993, at the very outset of Matrix, I interviewed Keith for San Francisco Liberation Radio. The subject was the Matrix program—or as the word "Matrix" had not, as of yet, become a household word in San Francisco politics, rather the new program known by that name.

In a rational, normal world, someone with thirteen years experience working with homeless people on a daily basis would be considered eminently qualified—an ideal candidate for an interview discussing the Matrix program's impact on the homeless. Yet outside of a few appearances on KPFA, Keith was shut out of the Matrix media debate virtually everywhere except on San Francisco Liberation Radio.

One really interesting thing about this interview is the timing of it in relation to the sequence of events. Keith knew about the shopping cart confiscations at the time the interview was conducted—mid-August—and spoke of such confiscations having taken place as early as June—two months before the "official" onset of Matrix and fully five months before the *Chronicle's* grand revelation about the carts on Nov. 13. What had come to light even prior to this interview—and had even been reported on earlier SFLR broadcasts—were incidents of homeless people's blankets and other belongings, irrespective of shopping carts, being loaded into garbage trucks.

The interview also provides some historical insights into the roots of the Matrix program. While the name "Matrix Program," eventually became synonymous to a large degree with persecution of the homeless, the program didn't initially start out as an anti-homeless measure, having rather taken on that characteristic as it evolved.

In it's initial concept, the "Matrix Unit" appears to have been a roving police task force set up to deal with violent crimes—specifically including car-jacking, of which there had been a rash earlier in the year. Perhaps Matrix, in keeping with the dictionary definition of the word, was envisioned as a mold, out of which future similar police units would be cast. It was probably sometime during the spring or summer of 1993 that Jordan got the idea of applying Matrix enforcement to the homeless population—in his stated quest of stamping out "nuisance crimes." If so, this would have coincided with protests against the removal of homeless people from Transbay Terminal, as well as a protracted series of takeovers by Homes Not

Jails (HNJ)—a Food Not Bombs offshoot group—of an empty building on Polk Street.

Perhaps noteworthy about the latter is that it had involved not only squatters occupying the inside of the building, but also a number of homeless youths camping out at night on the sidewalk in front. One day while doing radio interviews there, I encountered an HNJ squatter who related an incident wherein Jordan and his driver had pulled to the curb on the opposite side of Polk Street, across from the squatted building. Jordan had seemed to stare, transfixed, at the activity in and around the building.

Even then, prior to the onset of Matrix, the mayor had in no way been loved or admired by the homeless community. According to the squatter, the young people, both inside the building and out, upon becoming aware of being observed by so dignified a presence as the mayor of San Francisco, had begun to shout insults and wave middle finger gestures as Jordan had gazed out from his car window.

This continued for a long, embarrassing moment—until the mayoral car pulled away without the city leader's ever having emerged from within. How significant or pivotal this incident was in Jordan's decision to turn the Matrix program against homeless people can only be speculated upon.

During our interview, Keith said:

> The other portion of this is they've contracted, somehow loosely—I'm not—I think what has happened is they've encouraged a person who does the shopping cart pick ups for the regular supermarkets—instead of concentrating on picking up the shopping carts surrounding the supermarkets, they're just concentrating on picking up the shopping carts from Civic Center Plaza, which means these private individuals have to wrestle homeless people—um—you know, wrestle the carts from them...
>
> This has been going on for August, um, it did—there was in June a sporadic—the same man was coming around Civic Center. In June the police were going around saying, 'There's no shopping carts allowed in front of City Hall,' and we were able to stop that in June, but then it's now started up again.

We ended the interview with Keith pointing out one of the more glaring ironies of life in Frank Jordan's San Francisco. Said McHenry, "They (police) are out there just *agitating*; calling homeless people names;

giving them a hard time; kicking them; citing them; telling them to move along; pushing them around physically; stealing their belongings from them...and *they* (police and government authorities) want everyone to be *mellow*!"

The Matrix program was an all-out war upon the poor and homeless population of San Francisco. And the time had come for micro radio to join that war and mount a fight back.

Chapter 5
The Jolly Roger Comedy Troupe and the Rise of Clandestine Radio in the Bay Area

It was on a Sunday night that the FCC came to Stephen's door. Discarding their usual routine of driving up into the Berkeley hills on Sunday nights, the Berkeley crew, opting perhaps for convenience, chose to broadcast that evening from Stephen's living room. While this had saved much time and effort, it also led the feds right to Stephen's lair.

There was something else about the visit too: it was the beginning of a noticeable pattern of reluctance on the part of FCC agents to pursue micro broadcasters up into rugged, hilly terrain. How long had they known about the Sunday night broadcasts? Fliers had been circulating for months. There had even been an ad in a local underground newspaper, *The Slingshot*. I had heard it said—and in my opinion it's a fairly credible notion—that the FCC is able to pinpoint an illegal signal within five minutes of it's going on the air. So where had the feds been all this time? Not trekking up into the Berkeley Hills, that's for sure.

A visitor at Stephen's house that night got up to answer the door. She found two men, dressed, truly appropriately, in black, standing on the doorstep. They identified themselves as agents of the Federal Communications Commission, flashing IDs in the fashion of scores of celluloid G-men out of movie screen history. So true to form was their demeanor that she almost laughed.

"We're looking for an unlicensed radio signal that seems to be coming from around here somewhere," they told her. "Is anyone inside operating a transmitter?"

"Oh no!" she replied, feigning innocence. "There's *nothing* like that going on *here*."

They thanked her and went away—not fooled in the least. She returned to the living room with her heart pounding. Thus began the case of *The United States of America vs. Stephen Dunifer*. Six weeks later Stephen got a "Notice of Apparent Liability" in the mail from the FCC, informing him he was being fined $20,000. (The fine was later reduced to a mere $10,000.) He was instructed to respond within 30 days.

While I didn't say anything, privately I thought the Berkeley crew had gotten careless, and I resolved not to let the same thing happen to us in San Francisco. Fear of violence from the San Francisco police provided us with additional incentive for caution in that regard. At that time we were still doing our broadcasts on Saturday nights, but then came the Matrix program and we felt we had to be more bold. We expanded our broadcast schedule, first to Wednesday nights, and then to other nights of the week as well.

The Matrix program as well as the resumption of the arrests of Food Not Bombs may not seem like things which could be laughed at—but as it turned out, they were. Humans are singular in the animal world, I suppose, in their ability to laugh, but even within that ability lies an even more singular ability: the capacity to laugh under the most trying of circumstances. Here we were, afloat in a stream of human rights violations—with our friends in FNB under constant police attack; with ourselves being chased by the FCC; and thousands of the city's homeless suffering under what amounted to a government removal program—yet not only were we able to laugh, but we ultimately adopted humor, in the absence of guns, as our weapon.

***

The Jolly Roger Comedy Troupe was born in the grand tradition, more or less, of the National Lampoon, with a little Jonathan Swift and some Franz Kafka thrown in for good measure. It started out with just Jo and I resolving to do a satirization, for one of our Saturday night broadcasts. This was to be of Frank Jordan stealing a homeless woman's shopping cart. We set up the microphones in our living room, then got oven racks out of our oven and clanged them together so as to approximate the sound of a shopping cart. Summoning up my best weasely tone of voice, I played Jordan, while Jo played the homeless woman. The latter screamed for help as the former bellowed, "Go to Berkeley! Go to Berkeley!"—while attempting to rip the "cart" from her grasp.

Finally the homeless woman pulls out a cane and bats "Jordan" over the head with it, sending him to the hospital, where neurosurgeons open him up and discover that he has no brain. The skit ends with a newsboy, played by Jo, hawking papers on the street with the shout, "Extra! Extra! Doctors discover medical miracle in San Francisco! Mayor runs city for two years without brain! Extra!"

Another skit, in a parody of Dickens' *A Christmas Carol*, also attacked Jordan. It consisted of three characters. The first, played by myself and dubbed "the ghost of homeless past," appears to "Frank" late at night, confounding him with terror as he recalls how the mayor had made a secret pact with NASA to "send all the homeless people to Mars." The second character to appear was "Frank's" mother—played by Jo in an aged, pitiable voice. In this segment "Mom" recalls for Frank how she and Frank's father had always given Frank everything he wanted, including—for his 16th birthday—a police car "with a real siren on it to drive to school."

Lately, however, the elderly couple had fallen on hard times, currently living on the streets after having had to sell their house to pay the bills. Arrested during a Matrix sweep of Civic Center Plaza, "Mom" wails accusingly, "We went to your office in City Hall to ask for help!" But "Frank" was far too busy to lend a hand to his homeless parents. Instead, "Mom" recalls bitterly that they had been referred to "Eleanor Jacobs, your homeless coordinator who makes $80,000 a year!"

In the final segment Jo played "Frank's" therapist. It was done very "California." Using a lot of highfalutin psychiatric terms, Jo diagnoses "Frank's" mental breakdown, ending with the dire warning: "My advice Frank? Get into therapy—quick!"

The Jolly Roger material was, if nothing else, different from anything else then airing on San Francisco radio. There was nothing even remotely like it. But was anybody listening? We had no way of knowing, but were eager to find out, or at least to get some kind of gage or indication. To this end we set up a voicemail account.

On our next broadcast we began giving out the number over the air and asking people to call in and leave us messages. We got a tiny little smattering of calls, one of them from a man who criticized and berated us in blisteringly sarcastic tones, and who became a regular caller. He never told us his name, but he always prefaced his message with the greeting, rendered jeeringly and caustically, "Hey Pirate!" (Mainly this was aimed at me.) Following this contemptuous salutation, he then would deliver his verbal tracheotomy of the day—usually something about how badly our frequency was drifting. It became apparent after a while that he had some knowledge of radio frequency engineering. Usually we could expect a call from him about once a week.

Other callers, fortunately, were not as bad. One guy called in to say that his message to the world was that people should stop voting. The so-called "democracy" we have in this country is a sham, he felt, and by voting people only further legitimized it. We recorded his message off the phone and played it over the air on our next broadcast. A few other folks called in as well—mainly just to say they were listening and to give us signal clarity reports. All of this, even our vituperative critic, gave us a degree of confirmation: people were listening—certainly not in large numbers—but they were listening.

After these initial comedy skits produced by Jo and I, Carol Denney and others began to collaborate with us, and we officially came to be known as "The Jolly Roger Comedy Troupe." Of all of us, only Jo had formal acting experience. However, we were soon joined by a prodigiously talented actor named Richard Cicerone. Jo and Richard had been in the same theater group for a while—until the run of the play they were in had ended. Richard went on to other acting jobs, but was able to come over to our house on Sunday afternoons and lend his talent to the skits.

One skit we did with Richard's help was called "The Sally Sullivan Show," which was a takeoff on daytime TV talk shows. Jo played Sally, an effusive and rather bubble-brained talk show host, while Richard was her guest—Jay Carlisle Rockemorgan, who was "one of the wealthiest men in the world." We had acquired some sound effects CDs with, among other things, canned audience applause and laughter. These we brought up at the appropriate moments as Sally walked on stage to greet her wildly enthusiastic audience.

> Sally: Boy, do we have a fascinating show lined up for you today! Wealth! Privilege! Power! That's what it's all about here in America! But most of us never get a chance to experience up close just what it's like to be rich! Well, we're gonna change all that for you today. (Laughs) No! No! No! We're not handing out bags of cash—
>
> (audience laughter)
>
> Sally (more seriously): But we *are* going to give you a rare glimpse into the mind of one of the wealthiest men in the world, who's going to demystify for us just a little bit today the aura surrounding the ruling class of America! Our guest today is Mr. Jay Carlisle Rockemorgan!—
>
> (Murmur of excitement)
>
> Sally: —who, indeed, is one of the wealthiest men in the world, and who has graciously consented today to a rare, on-camera interview. I first met Mr. Rockemorgan two years ago, and for all his wealth and power found him to be amazingly warm, open and frank. And he's agreed to be

here today to talk candidly about what rich people *really* think—and what they're *really* like! You've read about his financial empire in the *Wall Street Journal!* You saw his patriot missiles grinding Iraqi cities to rubble! You saw his grandfather's ships carrying armaments to the Germans in World War II! Please welcome if you will—Mr. *Jay Carlisle Rockemorgan*!!!!

(sustained audience applause)

Jo was superb as the daffy talk show host, Sally, while Richard breathed a dynamism into the skit that made it unforgettable. Richard played Rockemorgan in a manner positively oozing with upper crust suavity and cultivation. The result was an urbane unctuousness that bordered hilariously on pomposity. In reply to Sally's query regarding what rich people "talk about when they get together for dinner," Richard/Rockemorgan itemizes a "wide variety of topics." These include: a) who's got "the best Rolls Royce mechanic," b) "the inferiority of the lower classes," and c) the "purchasing of political favors." Here Sally picks up on the issue of political favors, inquiring, "Do rich people really buy off politicians?" Rockemorgan's astonished reply: "Oh, oh yes! Certainly! It's a time honored tradition!" He then elaborates that it was his great-grandfather who...

...first fashioned the idea of giving equal amounts of cash to both presidential candidates. Heh heh heh. And look around you today—who does that? Virtually *everyone!* Great Granddad always was a trendsetter. 'We can't lose!' he said. And naturally he was right!

This prompts a discussion on the whole issue of manipulation of elections in America, with Sally commenting, "It must be a great source of amusement to you and other members of the ruling class to watch millions of Americans streaming to the polls on election day, as if their vote actually *means* something, when in reality the outcome has already been predetermined, and the candidates bought and paid for, long before election day rolls around." Rockemorgan, bemused, responds,

We *do* get quite a few chuckles out of that, I must confess—Sally—*millions* of people wearing buttons, pasting bumper stickers, palms sweating as they stand in line to vote for candidates they sincerely believe in...all in all it's worth *some* laughs, really, I suppose, and that's not *bad*, is it? Ha ha. I mean, after all, *humor* is a necessary ingredient for maintaining one's overall good health and physical well-being—even for us in the *ruling* class.

The issue of how much it cost to buy the average presidential election was raised, with Sally questioning why Rockemorgan and his fellow members of the ruling class didn't just save their time and money by simply doing away with the elections? The aristocrat acknowledges that holding elections every four years is a "nuisance," but adds that "it is a necessary one," insofar as it "gives you in the lower classes a reason to *live*—justifies your *faith*—sustains your continued belief in the system."

Sally: Explain what you mean by 'the system?'

Rockemorgan (patiently elaborating): The *system* which we set up, wherein *we* rule and *you* serve *us*. You see, a long time ago my great-grandfather—I hate to keep bringing him up but he really was a remarkable man—got the idea that a system of high prices for consumer goods and low wages for the workers who produced those goods could sustain itself if you could instill among the workers the ridiculous illusion that somehow such a system worked for them. You see, the 'democratic process'—that *name*, of course was our invention—is a necessary tool...nothing more than pure slight of hand—but a necessary tool nonetheless.

In a case of art mimicking life, the subject of "free trade" was broached, with Sally inquiring as to Rockemorgan's hand in setting up the General Agreement on Tariffs and Trade, and the North American Free Trade Agreement. Observed Sally, "A lot of people are saying that with GATT and NAFTA you guys in the ruling class have gone just a little too far this time, and that 'free trade' is nothing more than a power play—a greedy, bald-faced attempt to set yourselves up as the ultimate power on the planet, as Kiplingesque 'kings' over the entire Earth. How would you react to that?"

Here Rockemorgan is, for once, truly and fundamentally at a loss for words, finally stammering, "Uh—would you repeat the question please?"

Sally (patiently probing): *Is* NAFTA a power play? And what are you going to do about the millions who will be homeless and unemployed once their jobs have left the country?

Rockemorgan: Ahh! Unemployed workers—I'm glad you brought that up. You see, we here in America must exercise a predisposition toward adjustment to flux and prevailing market and economic trends, gradually realigning the work force in the direction of optimum free trade demands.

Sally: And translated into *English* that means?

Rockemorgan (offhandedly): We'll give them all jobs as prison guards, I suppose.

Sally compliments Rockemorgan on his candidness, and asks "one final question." She then inquires: "Candidly—do *poor people* have just as much right to *live* as rich people?"
Rockemorgan's succinct reply: "Of course not, Sally."
The talk show host then turns to her audience and gushes, "Well, there you have it! I wanna thank you for being with us today—ladies and gentlemen—Mr. Jay Carlisle Rockemorgan!!!"
The skit closes with applause and Sally Sullivan's theme music.

*****

One by one The Jolly Roger Comedy Troupe took America's sacred cows to the slaughter house and turned them into hamburger. In two skits, written by Carol Denney and lampooning the Federal Communications Commission, FCC agents were depicted alternately as either cockroaches, or as bumbling fools losing their footing and rolling down hillsides in a vain attempt to track down pirate radio broadcasters. In the latter, two FCC agents—Harvey and Larry—blunder exhaustedly through a densely wooded area in search of an unlicensed radio signal.
Richard played Harvey, while the part of Larry was filled by a guy who had simply dropped by our house that day and been hastily recruited. We dipped once more into our bag of sound effects and came up with one called "crickets" that provided a night time ambience for the dialog between the two government agents. We also created a few of our own sound effects by breaking small twigs. The overall impression was of two guys—exhausted but determined—crashing through the woods at night.

Harvey (huffing and puffing): Geez Larry, slow down, will ya?

Larry: I know we're getting closer, Harve, I can feel it. (Pause) Harvey! I see something! There's something in that tree over there!

Harvey (still struggling): Ughh! We gotta *get* those radio pirates now! We gotta get'em! We'll show them you can't play games with the Federal Communications Commission! No sir!

Again Jo's acting friend, Richard, playing Harvey, gave a really top-notch performance. When the two agents, peering through binoculars, discover that what's actually tied to the tree-top is a flag with the words, "Screw the FCC," Richard/Harvey explodes, "Arrest 'em Larry!"

After the latter replies that this cannot be done, Richard then thunders, "Well then fine 'em! Give 'em a big fine!"

"We can't do that either," Larry informs his friend, to which Harvey replies: "Well then sue them in civil court!"

Larry: We can't do that *either*, Harve.

Harvey: *WHY NOT???*

Larry: Because it's a piece of *cloth*, Harve!

Suddenly the two spy a cabin resting in a clearing in the woods. "Let's investigate!" Their knock upon the door is answered by an elderly woman, played by Carol.

Larry: We're the Federal Communications Commission, ma'am. We think there's an unlicensed broadcast coming from somewhere in the vicinity.

Old Woman: Oh my! That's terrible!

Larry: Yes! It's an insult to the authority of the federal government and a brazen challenge to the corporate control of the airwaves.

Old Woman: It certainly is indeed! Oh my! My!

When Larry asks for permission to inspect her house, however, the old woman's demeanor suddenly turns hostile. "Well," she drawls, "do you young men have a search warrant?"

Harvey: Not exactly, ma'am.

Old Woman: Then you can kiss my *butt!*

This is followed by the sound of a slamming door, to which an aghast Larry exclaims, "Well, that was certainly a deplorable display of disrespect for a federal official!" His voice cracking, he adds: "I think I'm gonna cry!"

Harvey: Aww, forget about it Larry. She's no radio pirate.
(pause) Oh! Let's look over here next to this rocky cliff!

At this point both actors stepped back several feet from the microphone to give the impression of their voices receding into the distance.

Harvey: Watch your step!

Larry: Look out!

Both together: Aaagggghhhhhh!!!!!!

Once again our sound effects CD handed us a gem: "rockslide." The two FCC men are last heard from rolling perilously down the mountain. Suddenly, however, the scene shifts to the inside of the cabin, where the old woman chuckles to her husband, "Take a gander outside the window, Grandpa. We bagged us another couple of feds!"

Grandpa: Hell, they sure roll a long way!

Grandma: Well, Grandpa, they get lots of practice!

Both guffaw at this observation, but then, the episode over, it's back down to business for the old couple:

> Grandma: Crank it up, Grandpa!

Suddenly rock music swells into the background.

> Grandpa: You got it, Grandma! (speaking now into the microphone and addressing his listeners): This is Pirate Radio, saying, 'Reclaim the airwaves—and *screw* the FCC!!!

The skit ends with the old couple chuckling delightedly as they spin their favorite rock songs on the turntable.

***

The FCC took another beating, in a second skit written by Carol, which featured a character, a la Sam Spade, private detective. With a sort of smoky-nightclub jazz ambience in the background, "Spade," in a movie-voice-over style of narration, gives the listeners the dope on what's happening:

"They knocked on my door about 4 p.m...."

Again Richard Cicerone came through with another sterling performance, this time as the hard-nosed, tough talking private detective. The skit, however, contained just a touch of Franz Kafka. Gradually, as "Spade" weaves his narrative, the listener becomes aware—even though the private detective never says so directly—that the "clients" who have engaged his services are cockroaches.

> Spade: They had 'feds' written all over them I could tell by the wriggling antenna, the six legs, and the brittle metathorax that they were the FCC. They told me they were tracking pirate radio broadcasters. Smart ones. Broadcasting from cars—broadcasting from inaccessible mountaintops—broadcasting fresh perspectives and unusual music. It was their job to put a stop to it. And they needed my help.
>
> The money was good, so I took the job—although the FCC guys gave me the creeps. They kept running behind the refrigerator whenever I turned the lights on.
>
> We tracked a signal to a private residence near Brisbane. We could hear them laughing inside of the house...

Here we employed a few sound effects, deciding that our "audience laughter" effect could pass for a party coming from inside a house if the volume were kept low and slightly muffled. The "party" effect was enhanced by adding "loud" rock music into the mix—though again with a low-volume, muffled damper on it. Our private detective hero continued his narration:

Spade: It sounded like a real *party*! We were there to spoil that party. The way the FCC explained it, the airwaves belonged to them.

'Why's that?' I asked them, as they got ready to slip in through the cracks in the floorboards.

'Because they didn't buy a license,' they answered, their trochanters rubbing in anticipation.

'How much *is* a license?' I asked.

'Between fifty and a hundred grand,' they answered.

Suddenly I realized I was at the *wrong* party. The micro broadcasters weren't hurting anybody. As a matter of fact, their music was fresh—their perspectives unusual, and the flavor was decidedly *not* corporate.

'HOLD IT RIGHT THERE, RADIO PEOPLE! WE'RE THE FCC!' they said, antenna waving. And they banged on the door.

But these radio people were smart! Very smart! They knew the FCC had no warrant, and—they knew the FCC. They turned some bright porch lights on and the FCC scuttled away into the foggy night. I stood there on the porch for a moment wondering whether to tell the radio pirates how much I'd liked the program. As I walked away I heard them talking:

Pirate #1: Hey man! How often does *that* happen.

Pirate #2: Awww, don't worry about it! You sprinkle a little boric acid near the baseboards and they *never* come back!

Pirate #1: I heard diatomaceous earth works too!

At this point "Spade's" narrative continues, though unfolding now toward its conclusion—another case solved:

Spade: I knew boric acid was non-toxic—but I knew it *could* kill. It crossed my mind to warn the FCC in case they ever came back. After all they *were* my clients. And then I thought: nah!

The skit ends with the jazz music fading and "Spade" walking slowly away.

***

If we were to be in the business of slaughtering sacred cows, under no circumstances, we decided, could we leave out the corporate-owned news media or their blow-dried anchors. In a wonderful skit written by Jo, we contrasted what the evening news *ought* to sound like, with its bleak reality. The skit pairs off a "good anchor" with a not-so-good one, the scene alternately shifting back and forth until the end of the skit when the two realities collide, this happening as an angry mob of media consumers, tired of "happy news," storm the ABC building in New York.

Being bigger'n the broad side of a barn, the media made a nice fat target, as did politicians, corporations and the like. But I'd have to say that overall the majority of our satirical ammunition was aimed at San Francisco's Matrix program. In one skit, entitled "A Hunting We Will Go!"—we had Jordan and one of his aids enjoying an afternoon of male bonding. The two are standing on City Hall balcony dressed in camouflage hunting fatigues, sport shooting at the homeless in Civic Center Plaza below. This skit was followed by "The Matrix Diet Plan," under which homeless people grow ever more slim and trim while dashing to avoid the police under a new, medically approved weight loss regimen.

One routine we did I would hesitate to even call a "skit," as it left the comedic realm behind to a considerable degree, venturing into what I would almost describe as "serious opera." Changing the words so as to depict the plight of the poor, we performed the piece, "O Sole Mio." This would have been reduced to the level of a poorly rendered, not-so-funny farce had we not had the singing talent necessary to do a reasonably convincing job of sounding like opera singers. Fortunately, however, two in our group had trained singing voices: Carol Denney and Mug Muggles.

The newly penned lyrics lent themselves quite well to two voices: a tenor and a soprano. Like two characters on an opera stage, Mugg and Carol wailed their miseries across the room to each other. Not having a symphony orchestra handy at our disposal, an acoustic guitar was the best we could do for accompanying instrumentation, but nonetheless the whole thing came together. It really sounded good! And while it depended much less on comedy as a vehicle than anything we had previously done, it still got its shots in. There were dagger sticks here and there at the Matrix program, as well as at Berkeley's version of Matrix, a series of "anti-poor laws" aimed at, among other things, curtailing panhandling. Under the strict letter of the law, the singing of the song, "Buddy Can You Spare a Dime?" would be illegal on public streets in Berkeley.

The opening passage belonged to the soprano, with the tenor following in the next verse, the two alternating back and forth until the piece's dramatic conclusion, when the tenor vows to pick up a gun and fight back against the crushing injustices.

Soprano
O Sole Mio, O star of night
O Sole Mio, I'm in a plight
The corporate freight train is on its way
And on the tracks our bodies lay.

Tenor
O Sole Mio, I've been misused
The Matrix cops, they stole my shoes.
Now hunger and cold are all I know
And Rush Limbaugh on the radio.

Soprano
O Sole Mio, life on the wing
No more in Berkeley, 'tis legal to sing
I sang 'Brother Can You Spare a Dime?'
They locked me up, now I do hard time.

Tenor
O Sole Mio, I'm feeling sick.
My candle's burned down right to the wick.
It's been so long since I've seen the sun,
In my final hour, I pick up a gun.

Soprano
O Sole Mio, the journey starts.
The desperate beating of our two hearts
Means all may not be lost.

O Sole Mio, who'll pay the cost?

Together
O Sole Mio, we know not hate
But act we must before it's too late.
Our children are cold and in despair
O New World Order, ye'd best beware!

***

Potrero Hill is a lovely little area of San Francisco. From the top its views are spectacular, not, perhaps, so much so as at Twin Peaks, but impressive nonetheless. Moreover, Potrero Hill has a charm and uniqueness of its own. On the night of September 22, 1993—the night the FCC entered my life—I was on Potrero Hill doing a broadcast by myself.

In those days Jo was working as a teacher at a pre-school. Her job required that she get up some mornings as early as 5 a.m. Thus, I had begun occasionally taking the radio station out by myself. We continued to do our Saturday night broadcasts together. However, for SFLR broadcasts on weeknights I often went solo. So that's how I came to be on Potrero Hill alone on a Wednesday night when FCC Agent David Doon drove up behind me with his bright lights on.

That night, rather than go backpacking with all the equipment as Jo and I had often done at Mount Davidson, Marin Headlands, and other locations, I decided simply to park on the side of the street and do the broadcast from within the truck—a risky thing, but I decided to chance it.

There were a fair number of vacant parking spaces but I deliberately chose one underneath some trees, reasoning that the overhanging branches might provide a degree of camouflage for the antenna. After hoisting the antenna up, I stood back a ways to admire my handiwork. I had been right about the camouflage. The cover was pretty good. The camper, of course, was plainly visible resting under the trees, but you would have had to look closely to discern the antenna rising up and through the branches above it. Satisfied, I hooked up the transmitter and began the broadcast.

One of the things I had on the program that night was a tape of Jack Hirschman, discussing the homeless situation and reading from his wonderful poetry. About an hour and fifteen minutes into the broadcast—it was around 9:15—a car pulled up behind me. Its headlights were extremely bright. I assumed it was someone who lived in one of the surrounding houses, parking his or her beloved auto for the night. But the brightness of the headlamps bothered me. Though my windows were adorned with curtains, the blazing yellow beams penetrated piercingly through the fabric and lit up the gloom inside the camper. The car behind me didn't appear to be a cop car—though beyond that, blinded as I was, there was not much else I could tell about it.

Minutes went by and I began to grow annoyed. Of all the parking places on the street this guy had chosen to drive up directly behind *me*. More time ticked by. Now I began to grow doubtful. Maybe this *wasn't* just somebody who lived in the neighborhood. Suddenly my old fear of being knocked off by a government death squad loomed up into my imagination. Was I going to die here on Potrero Hill? What was this guy *doing* back here? (Naturally I assumed it was a man, and my imagination, by now in overdrive, obligingly supplied me with a theatric image of a hand, encased in a black leather glove, gripping a revolver with a silencer.)

I decided the time had come to go off the air. This was not an especially logical move on my part, since if I was about to be murdered the best thing I could do (from my point of view) would be to broadcast it. However, the only thing I could think of, fighting back rising panic as I was, was to disconnect the transmitter. This I did, my fingers scrabbling nervously for the alligator clips on the battery.

Dead silence.

The station was off the air now. But now what? The lights, so close to my rear bumper, continued to blaze through my back window. If the person behind me were deliberately trying to scare me, he, or she, was succeeding. I took a deep breath as I realized the only thing to do at this point was to go out and confront face to face whoever it was. Face to face was exactly where we both were a moment later.

Resolutely, I got up, stalked to the back of the camper, and opened the door, preparing to step out into the night to get a better look at my antagonist. But I didn't need to do even that. He was standing right there at my back door.

"I'm with the FCC," he said. "Do you have a license to broadcast at 93.7?"

As he spoke he flashed his government I.D.—not that I could possibly have read it there in the dark, even with his headlights blazing so gaudily. For a moment I stared dumfounded. So! It's finally happened, I thought. I've been tracked down by the FCC! And with that came flooding the realization that anyone intending to murder me would likely have done so and been long gone by now. "Whew!" I thought. "It's only the FCC!"

***

At that point, with my fear dissipating, my manner became one of somewhat apologetic, yet firm, non-cooperation. He asked for permission to come in and inspect the equipment. I refused. He inquired if I was the only person inside the camper. I declined to say. "If you're not going to cooperate I'm going to have to call the police," he said. He was calm. There was nothing hostile or threatening in his manner. He was almost, to a degree even, polite. Suddenly I saw us for what we were: two men standing in the dark with nothing personal against each other, yet cast in opposing roles by the government.

"I guess you got your job to do and I've got mine," I replied, and suddenly that was indeed how I looked at it. I had been performing a role, doing my "job." My job, as I saw it, was to broadcast the truth. His was to stop me. Nothing personal. Now that it had come down to this, my job, further, I felt, was to refuse to grant permission to a federal agent to enter my camper. Again nothing personal.

"Okay," he said, leaving my back door and returning to his car.

Okay. Fine, I thought. Probably his federal car was equipped with a radio with a police channel. Through the course of our exchange it had become clear to me that this guy had no enforcement powers, no powers to arrest me. So the police were coming. Fine. But they weren't here yet, and I didn't feel obligated to wait for them to arrive. Partly to get out of the area, but partly, also, out of curiosity to see what he would do, I decided, without further adieu, to scram.

Quickly, I climbed up to the roof of the camper and took down the antenna. I was obviously in a hurry, but I wasn't going to go breaking the antenna off on low hanging tree limbs. The tearing-down process took two to three minutes. Through it all I was curiously aware of his eyes on me, watching from his car, yet I proceeded slowly and methodically, knowing that if I got in a panic it would only cost me more time in the long run. With the antenna dismantled and stowed safely away in the back, I climbed into the cab of the truck and started up the engine. Pulling away, I looked in the side-view mirror and saw that he had begun to follow me.

What then ensued did not, in any way, even *remotely* resemble a high speed chase. In tandem we came down off Potrero Hill, but slowly, as if we were both driving to church. I got onto the 101 freeway and his headlights got lost more or less in the jumble of all the other traffic behind—but I knew he was back there. I suppose somewhere in the back of my mind lay the hope that if I could lose him, the FCC—even though he by now surely had my license plate number—could never prove in court that it was me who had actually been in the truck and doing the broadcast that night. This was a rather dim hope, of course, but there was little else to hope for at this point.

A realistic appraisal told me how hopeless the odds were against my ever shaking him off my tail. I mean, here I was in this great, big, awkward, lumbering camper, and there *he* was following along behind, pretty as you please, in a standard passenger car. Yet shake him I in fact did.

I chose the 9th Street-Civic Center exit off the freeway and watched, through the side view mirror, as a lone set of headlights disengaged itself from all the others and followed me down the exit ramp. Was it him? I squinted a little harder in the mirror to be sure. Yep!

Still puttering along at 30-40 miles an hour, we cruised up 9th Street until we stalled completely in a yellow snarl of traffic around Civic Center. It must have been an opera or a symphony night. The traffic was bumper to bumper. Pedestrians on the sidewalks were dressed in formal eveningwear. As we inched west along Grove Street, I looked off into the darkened expanse of the plaza, where I had served innumerable meals to the homeless. Civic Center Plaza was dark and it was impossible to see if there was anyone out there, but I knew they were there: America's invisible army of poor people. I longed to be out there—in that friendly darkness, perhaps with a few companionable shopping cart pushers, the lot of us on our way, "laughing into the night." I longed to be anywhere. Instead, though, here I was, being chased—even if only in slow motion—by the government.

Suddenly a silent police car—silent except for wildly flashing lights on top—whipped erratically around the corner of Polk and Grove and sped toward me from the oncoming direction. Arrowing east at high speed, it shot on past, moving off urgently—kind of as if looking for someone, I thought. "That has nothing to do with you," I told myself reassuringly. In sharp contrast to the rest of the traffic, the motion of the cop car had been fast and violent. "He went right by you. See? That *proves* it has nothing to do with you."

I continued to inch forward, with the rest of this jammed mass of traffic, west along Grove, across Van Ness, to Franklin, and then right. Headed, more or less, in the direction of home (another stupid idea, no doubt), my plan was to turn left onto Fulton. But Franklin was a one way street and at that moment it was completely clogged with northbound traffic. Jockeying into position for the left turn onto Fulton necessitated crossing three solid lanes of bumper to bumper traffic, and it necessitated doing it fast. I looked in the mirror. The guy from the FCC was still in pursuit, though now several car lengths behind.

Suddenly I saw the opening for which I had prayed; quickly I shot into it. Then, almost miraculously, came another in the lane abreast. Finally I was precisely where I had wanted to be: turning west onto Fulton. Again my eyes shot toward the rear view mirror: the guy from the FCC, still locked into one of the center lanes, was forced, like a drifting cork, to continue north on Franklin. I had done it! I had actually lost him!

Exultant, I *did*, finally, step on the gas a little at this point. Hoping to make the separation final, I executed a series of zig-zags, from Fulton, to Laguna, to Hayes, and finally out onto a wide, four lane boulevard with a median in the middle which I think must have been Webster. In the mirror, however, I caught a glimpse of flashing colors behind me. A cop car. Then I noticed another cop car behind that, and another after that. Cop cars were also approaching from the oncoming direction. The entire northbound lane of Webster seemed as if it had been closed to traffic and suddenly my camper was entirely surrounded by cops. I braked to a halt.

"Get your hands up in the air and keep 'em up!"

***

I was amazed at how fast they had swooped down on me. It had all happened in less time than it takes a dog to sit down and start scratching its behind. More orders were shouted at me. The cops were clearly adrenaline-pumped to the gills. "Get out of the vehicle now!!" I don't know what the FCC had told them about me, but from the looks of things these cops may have thought they had just captured the Unabomber. "Get out of the vehicle slowly and keep your hands up in the air!"

I did as I was told, resolved not to give them any excuse to shoot me. My arms were wrenched roughly behind my body and plastic handcuffs were placed on my wrists. At this point, now that I had been safely subdued, a curious confusion seemed to descend down upon the ranks as they looked at each other: "Who is this guy and why do we have him here?" someone asked. One cop seemed to have a vague idea, but no one really seemed to know the answer to that question for sure.

The cop who seemed more or less in charge was a great, big, beefy, mustachioed Italian-looking guy, who seemed to have decided that the best way to keep me respectful and mindful of my place was to heap upon me a great deal of verbal abuse and contempt. Upon trying to speak I was promptly told to shut up. There followed from him a string of words, which contained a thinly veiled threat of violence.

Of the remaining cops, most of these seemed to be Asians. The most striking thing about them was the way they stood in silence, eyes averted, as the Italian bellowed, bullied and raged. The confusion as to my crime and identity was quickly cleared up as the FCC guy arrived. I recognized the car right away as it drove up abreast of our little street party. Where had *he* been? Better late than never, I thought.

The agent, whose name, I would subsequently learn, was David Doon, got out of his car and began talking with some of the cops. I saw now that there was what appeared to be a slightly Asian cast to his looks, something I had only partially noted earlier in the dark. Around his face was a trace of refinement. Oddly, my first sensation upon seeing him show up now, was one of relief, a sense of kinship. After all, we were both radio guys, right? These cops were just paid thugs. As I stood there bathed in the red and blue flashing light, I became aware of involuntary spasms in my legs, causing my knees to knock together uncontrollably. I was scared to death.

A cop came over and said they needed my I.D. With my hands still cuffed behind me, I replied that my I.D. was in my back pocket. I acquiesced as he turned me around and dug the I.D. out. I figured my truck keys would be next. I looked over to where the camper sat parked, envisioning how it would, no doubt, be rummaged through and torn apart. I assumed they would confiscate my truck and everything in it, most especially the transmitter. I was wrong.

David Doon had my I.D. now. Using the hood of a cop car as a writing desk, he was busily taking down the vital information on my license. Then he came over and stood next to me, his face expressionless. He was dressed in casual attire—not sloppy, like jeans or sneakers or anything, more like he had simply taken off a coat and tie and put on a zip up windbreaker for the occasion. He inquired if the address was my current one. I replied that it was, then started to add something as an afterthought, but was again told to shut up by the Italian cop.

"Am I under arrest?" I asked.

"I'M NOT GONNA TELL YOU AGAIN!" the Italian roared.

"No, you're just being detained," answered another cop.

I stood there in silence. Finally a cop came over and said, "Okay, we're releasing you," and removed the handcuffs. I was given back my I.D., while David Doon handed me his business card with his name on it.

I stared dumfounded at this turn of events. Not only was I being released, but I was being let go with my truck still intact. No tearing up the panels as the cops ransacked the interior for drugs, "contraband," or whatever. I thought in amazement. The most astonishing thing of all was that they had not even gone inside to take the transmitter, as I had fully expected they would.

Always, I had thought, did the FCC confiscate equipment when they raided pirate radio stations. This was just what you always heard. It was why Jo and I had deliberately begun the practice of traveling as light as possible on these mobile broadcasts. We had made a conscious decision to expose as little of our equipment as possible to government seizure, to the extent of even pre-taping our programs at home. Never in my wildest dreams, as I had stood there on the street with my hands cuffed, had I imagined I would be allowed to leave and simply drive away with our transmitter. I had not only envisioned spending several hours and several hundred dollars the next day getting my truck out of police tow, but I had also fully entertained the possibility of spending a night in jail.

"Is that it?" I asked with a quaver, not daring to hope. David Doon, I noticed, seemed to be hastily departing. The cops, on the other hand, were obviously, to a large degree, planning to linger on the spot and have one of those group cop chats on the street.

"Yeah, you're free to go."

I couldn't believe my luck. I reached for my keys and started walking.

"Hey!" called one of the cops, one of the younger ones, who inquired now with a grin, "what frequency do you broadcast on?"

"93.7"

"What times?"

I told him, and, with a small wave, drove away.

                              ***

I've often wondered why I was treated with such kid gloves that night. Possibly my race was a factor. In encounters with the police, it is almost invariably true that white people fare better than do people of color.

Has this same pattern of discrimination held true with regard to enforcement against the micro radio movement? The question has been raised, more than once, as to whether micro stations run primarily by people of color have not suffered more door breaking and equipment confiscation than have stations in which white involvement outnumbers that of black. Certainly the example of Napoleon Williams, of Black Liberation Radio in Decatur, Illinois, would tend to support this notion (although Williams' troubles seem to have far less to do with the FCC than with problems with local authorities). Since their radio station went on the air in 1990, the Williams family have endured multiple raids on their home—not, as it so happens, by the FCC, but by state and local authorities—as well as equipment confiscations and even the taking of their children.

So, while it was a white broadcaster—Stephen Dunifer—whom the FCC ultimately chose to go after and make a test case out of—it *does* seem as if black or Latino stations have been dealt with more severely—or at least it *did* up until November 19, 1997. On that day the FCC raided three white-owned stations in the Tampa, Florida area, confiscating thousands of dollars worth of broadcast equipment and taking two people to jail. At six o'clock that morning the FCC, accompanied by an armed multi-jurisdictional task force, broke down the front door of Doug Brewer, whose 102.1 FM station, the "Party Pirate," operated out of his garage. Helmeted police, armed with weapons equipped with infrared scopes terrorized Brewer and his wife at gunpoint. The couple was placed in handcuffs and forced to sit for 12 hours as agents ransacked their home. The homes of two other Tampa broadcasters, Lonnie Kobres and Kelley Benjamin, were raided as well.

Compared to the raid on Brewer in 1997, my own FCC bust in 1993 had been a cakewalk. Why? It was after I read Allan Weiner's story that I began to be aware that possibly there was a pendulum swing at work. Weiner was the owner/operator of a pirate radio ship in the late 1980s. The ship, the M/V Sarah, broadcast from off the coast of New York, though far enough out to sea so as to be in international waters. In addition to that safeguard, Weiner had also taken the precaution of obtaining for the ship a Honduran registration. The U.S. government had no legal right to interfere with that ship's operation in any manner whatsoever. Yet this didn't stop the U.S. Coast Guard, accompanied by the FCC, from boarding the vessel at gunpoint. This took place in international waters, making it essentially an act of piracy (in the more traditional sense of the word) on the high seas. Once on board, FCC agents proceeded to virtually destroy Weiner's ship. The story is told in Weiner's book, *Access to the Airwaves*:

> The FCC had a party. They were running around taking videotapes, snapshots, and Polaroids. They cut all the cable harnesses and transmission lines with hacksaws, ripped everything out, and threw it in the middle of the deck. And of course they damaged quite a bit of the equipment. They basically destroyed everything that it took me a year and a half to put together. The FCC knew that we were outside of their jurisdiction and were not violating the law. But they wanted to make damn well sure that we didn't go back on the air after they left.
>
> I asked the Coast Guard, "Why are you letting these people do this? We have violated no laws, and you've come on board, seized our ship—as far as I'm concerned illegally—and are letting the FCC tear up our station. Why are you letting this happen?"
>
> One of the men admitted that he didn't understand why the FCC was destroying equipment and breaking stuff up. He didn't feel that was right, but he was under orders. [1]

The FCC's lawless thuggery initially began to backfire when it turned out that one of the passengers on Weiner's ship was a reporter for the *Village Voice*. The story was picked up by other New York newspapers, radio and TV stations, plus CNN and the major television networks. From a PR standpoint, the FCC got substantially creamed. As Weiner reports:

> Of course the press was there. They asked me what happened, and I yelled out to them, "Free form rock and roll radio had been snuffed out by the United States government!" [2]

The boarding and ransacking of Weiner's ship occurred on July 28, 1987. On July 30 Weiner recorded in his ship's log:

> On Tuesday July 28, we were boarded. Ivan, myself and R.J. Smith were arrested and the ship was seized. The FCC came on board and tore apart the radio station. It hurts to talk about it. I've tried very hard. I wanted to bring Free Radio to New York. Please, no failure this time. We need a solution. So many people have hoped and dreamed. To let them down is a pain. I guess it's part of the learning process. Love, peace and understanding. [3]

Could the bad press sustained by the FCC in the wake of its attack on Weiner in 1987 have been the reason the federal agency adopted a significantly different strategy with unlicensed broadcasters in the Bay Area in 1993? Could it also be why the agency distanced itself from the ruthless assaults on Napoleon Williams beginning in 1990? By the same token, could it be that, by the time of the FCC's raid against Brewer in 1997, the pendulum had swung back the other way?

These are possibilities; there are a couple of others: a) perhaps it was simply that David Doon, the FCC agent assigned to cover the Bay Area, had less of a tendency to be a cowboy than agents operating in other areas of the country; or, b) perhaps—strange as it may seem—the SFPD had nixed any requests from Doon that my vehicle be impounded. When I recall the attitude of those police that night—upon ascertaining that I was neither a murderer, terrorist or drug dealer (nor, worst of all from the SFPD's point of view, a criminal purveyor of vegetarian soup)—and recollecting most of all the one cop who had asked for our broadcast times, this seems not beyond the realm of possibility. Perhaps it was any one of these factors—or perhaps it was a combination of them all.

When I arrived home that night, later than usual, Jo was, naturally, worried. The later it had gotten, the more fearful she had grown. She had imagined, she confessed later, all sorts of frightful scenarios befalling me, though had never once considered, as it turned out, the possibility of what had truly taken place. This is typical of the way activists often underestimate the effectiveness of what we do. The *government* afraid of *us?* Actually alarmed at the thought of something *we* could do to *them?* Yes, actually, it *does* happen, and more often than we think—and not altogether without reason. We, collectively as a people, are stronger than we give ourselves credit.

"Where have you been?" she asked.

I was dead tired and perhaps it was for this reason that my voice didn't convey the emotion that might normally be present when imparting such news: "I was tracked down by the FCC and then I was pulled over by all these cops."

She gave a sarcastic laugh, obviously of the opinion that I was putting her on.

"Sure!" she replied.

She didn't believe me!

"No, it's true, that's really what happened!"

And suddenly I couldn't help myself. I began to laugh at the absurdity of it all.

Chapter 6
Justice Delayed, Justice Denied

K eep in mind that the political persecution of Food Not Bombs (FNB) was a big reason why we started our own radio station.

It's difficult for me to write about the FNB case objectively, having been taken to jail myself for the "crime" of serving food to homeless people. Therefore I can make no plausible claim to objectivity. All I can do is tell you the story the way I saw it and perceived it. Perhaps one day someone with the city government will write his or her own book on the matter, and the reader will have the two points of view from which to choose.

Forming a judgement of it all, of course, requires evaluating an eight-year history. From 1988 to 1996 there were more than a thousand arrests of FNB members for serving food to poor people. In virtually every case the charges were dropped by the district attorney's office. An impartial observer might be tempted to view this as one thousand-plus cases of false arrest and imprisonment. Suffice to say, that is *not* how the courts viewed it. Over the years, FNB's efforts to gain justice through the judicial system, going all the way up to the U.S. Ninth Circuit Court of Appeals, amounted substantially to nil.

The legal struggle between FNB and the City of San Francisco was like an octopus with many tentacles, including one designated "omnibus" case, with each lawsuit forming a different tentacle of the octopus. While all the cases listed multiple causes of action, the main thrust of each were allegations of selective, punitive measures against FNB members based on their membership in an unpopular (from the point of view of the authorities) group. The result of such selective measures was that, without any statute so saying, the "punishment" for serving food as an FNB activist was arrest, a night or so in jail, and property seizure, including vehicle impoundment. It was a punishment carried out entirely at the discretion of the police, in total absence of a jury trial.

While the City of San Francisco justified its actions on the basis of alleged health code violations by FNB, the latter argued repeatedly over the years that the manner in which it served food—to homeless people in outdoor locations—was a form of free speech, protected under the first amendment. Just as the Supreme Court had declared flag burning to be protected speech, so too, argued FNB attorneys, must distribution of food to the poor, underneath a banner reading "Food Not Bombs" be so regarded.

With regard to allegations of health code violations, the city was on shaky ground due to its own Health Department having issued permits to the group—in September 1989, and again in March of 1990. To be sure, the permits were extremely restrictive in nature, limiting food serving to only two designated locations—Golden Gate Park and Civic Center Plaza—and allowing the serving of only one meal per week at each location. The permits were issued only after FNB had complied, at some considerable cost, with Health Department demands regarding the way food was stored, prepared, covered and served. One of the demands was that meals be served from within a large tent: FNB acquired such a structure only to have it later confiscated by the police.

While the two Health Department permits were never officially rescinded, they were later rendered obsolete when the city Recreation and Parks Department adopted a rule change making it illegal to serve food to groups of more than twenty-five people in city parks.

All of this bureaucratic nitpicking could have been avoided had the city adopted a more humane approach to dealing with its homeless population, as FNB, through all of its protests, was attempting to force it to do. Yet the city named after St. Francis seemed forever intent upon a path of repression, rather than one of compassion and enlightenment. Perhaps, in fairness to the city, it had no other choice. After all, there was, and still remains, no leadership at the national level concerning the problem of homelessness in America.

How can one city implement progressive solutions to homelessness while the rest of the cities across the U.S.A. continue to offer little or nothing? Such a city, so the argument has been made, would run the risk of becoming a Mecca for every homeless person in the country. Perhaps there is some merit to this argument. Clearly leadership from Washington is desperately needed on this issue.

Yet there are distinct measures which *could* be taken by local governments to significantly ease the plight of their homeless populations—like *not* confiscating their property or moving them about from place to place by force of police sweeps. This would require nothing more strenuous than simply obeying the Constitution.

How could the city argue health problems with FNB's food if its own Health Department had issued permits to the group, regardless of how restrictive? After all, if the food were deemed sufficiently sanitary to be served two days a week, why not all seven? San Francisco City Attorney

Louise Renne, however, was determined, if possible, to reduce the number of meal servings per week down to zero.

It's fair to say that FNB did not, in all probability, abide by the place and time restrictions on the permits. To do so, went the argument, would have been to ignore the reality that people need food all seven days of the week, and not just one or two—and the city, thank you, had already done quite enough ignoring of hard realities when it came to homelessness. For the city, on the other hand, such a failure to abide by restrictions probably only reinforced its perception of FNB members as bad-faith negotiators. But if such a view was held by city officials toward FNB, a similar one was held by FNB with regard to the city, which seemed, much of the time, to be employing a strategy of laying down as many obstacles in FNB's path as possible.

If such obstacle laying was being employed it was not new, but rather a continuum of a practice begun the year before, in 1988, during the city's earliest dealings with FNB. A sort of daily diary of the period, encompassed within an FNB civil suit in Superior Court, is revealing. The incidents alleged are presented in chronological order, with each separate incident numbered by paragraph. The time period covered in the suit begins at December 1987.

Skipping ahead, the following passage from the sixty-six page document lays out a sequence of events beginning with September of 1988:

> 47. On September 14, 1988 plaintiff Keith McHenry met with Jack Breslin of the Health Department to review the California Public Health Code to negotiate Food Not Bombs' compliance with these rules.
>
> 48. On September 19, 1988 defendant Al Chin of the San Francisco Health Department inspected Food Not Bombs and issued a new list of requirements to meet. Food Not Bombs acquired the designated items.
>
> 49. On September 26, 1988 Defendant Al Chin inspected Food Not Bombs again and issued a different list of requirements for Food Not Bombs. Food Not Bombs again acquired the designated items.
>
> 50. On October 3, 1988 defendant Al Chin inspected Food Not Bombs again and issued still a different list of requirements for Food Not Bombs. Food Not Bombs once again raised money for the new items and requested a final list of required items from Chin.

51. On October 10, 1988 the defendant City and County of
San Francisco's Recreation and Parks Department issued
Food Not Bombs a new permit for Haight and Stanyan
streets. On that day defendant Al Chin inspected Food Not
Bombs again. [1]

At this point the officious Al Chin dropped from sight for a few days.
Intervening events included a protest at the Presidio Army Base, at which
Keith, without warning, was attacked from behind by a group of police and
beaten to the ground. By the 17th, however, Chin was once more dogging
Food Not Bombs' trail.

54. On October 17, 1988, defendant Al Chin inspected
Food Not Bombs again and provided a list of still more
demands to change their food distribution. [2]

It must be kept in mind that Chin was employed by the city and thus
getting paid for his time. The FNB members who were jumping through
Chin's hoops were volunteers, putting their time in for free. With the
ushering in of the new year, Chin was once more back on the job:

59. On January 15, 1989, defendant Al Chin adduced still
new reasons to deny Food Not Bombs a health permit.
Plaintiff Keith McHenry and Food Not Bombs requested
and were granted another meeting with Health Department
officials to establish definitive standards for the operation
of Food Not Bombs.
60. In February 1989 a final meeting between plaintiff
Keith McHenry and Food Not Bombs and the Health
Department occurred at which Food Not Bombs was told
that no further meetings would be needed. Food Not
Bombs implemented the agreed-to changes. However,
defendant Al Chin subsequently inspected and stated that
there were further problems with Food Not Bombs' food
distribution. [3]

On July 14, the city petitioned the Superior Court for an injunction
forbidding FNB from further food serving. The court granted the request.
Meanwhile the arrests continued to pile up. While many of these were
documented in the suit, it is highly unlikely, in the confusion of events, that
all were so recorded.

One which *was*, however, was an incident taking place five days before Christmas 1989. Distinguishing this arrest from the many others was the presence of high ranking city officials, and the suggestion of an inter-departmental collaboration in the repression—in this case between the police department and the city attorney's office.

> 70. On December 20, 1989, plaintiff Keith McHenry was arrested while talking to journalists in United Nations Plaza by defendant San Francisco Police Department Captain Dennis Martel and other defendant (John) Doe uniformed officers in the presence of, and on information and belief, under the supervision of defendant Commander Michael Lennon and Executive Deputy City Attorney George Riley. Doe defendant police officers also arrested other Food Not Bombs volunteers at this time and location. The defendant Doe officers took into custody the food and other equipment which had been in the possession of the Food Not Bombs volunteers. Plaintiff Keith McHenry and the arrested volunteers were held in jail over night. [4]

Throughout this time (and for years into the future) city officials repeatedly painted a false picture for the media regarding the whole permit controversy. Time and again officials spoke of how the city had attempted to *assist* FNB in obtaining the necessary permits. The problem, they would say, lay simply in FNB's intransigence—its refusal to get permits or to obey even minimal food safety standards.

"They refuse to comply with health care regulations," asserted Jordan in the interview (cited extensively in chapter four) on KSFO in January 1994. Health officials, Jordan added, had offered to "help" FNB achieve this longed-for compliance, to no avail. Such patently false statements were even made before judges.

On July 21, 1989, Deputy City Attorney Riley declared before Superior Court Judge Ralph Flageollet, "The city stands ready today, as it has since September, to waive fees, to assist Food Not Bombs in meeting these minimal requirements so that a permit can issue." Riley added, "All we ask is that minimal compliance with law." [5]

Another deputy city attorney, Paula Jesson, stated in a December 18, 1989 letter to Federal Judge William Schwarzer, "...the city has engaged in numerous attempts to assist plaintiffs to obtain the health and park permits that they need..."

Upon first venturing into federal court in 1989, Food Not Bombs encountered a judge, The Honorable William Schwarzer, who evinced a striking degree of understanding of the issues at hand. Unfortunately, Schwarzer was about to leave San Francisco.

According to FNB attorney Dennis Cunningham, Schwarzer "was—and is—a district court judge with an extremely sharp mind and a devotion to the first amendment, I would say." But Schwarzer, shortly after taking the FNB case, took a leave of absence from the bench. From then on, federal court became a far different place as FNB consistently ended up before the more conservative Judge Vaughn Walker.

"Walker came on the bench and he got it (the FNB case)," said Cunningham. "He might have taken Judge Schwarzer's whole case load, or it might have been that his case load was broken up and reassigned. I can't remember what happened with that, but he succeeded to it and he had the opposite view (from that which had been held by Schwarzer)." In successive cases brought thereafter, FNB struck out under Walker.

Were the arrests of FNB members for serving food to the poor a violation of the first amendment? The more liberal Schwarzer had shown indications of believing that they were.

"Judge Schwarzer reacted to it by saying, 'If this is what's happening, the city's got a problem,'" said Cunningham. "His impulse, I think, was not to bring this to litigation, to tell the city it ought to back off and accommodate this."

Handling FNB's challenge to the legal establishment were Cunningham and two other attorneys, Randy Baker and Sarge Holtzman. Of the three, Cunningham, with a career in public interest law that spanned more than two decades, was the more experienced—though much of the work on the main "omnibus" case that went before Walker was spearheaded by Baker.

Leading the charge for San Francisco officialdom was City Attorney Louise Renne. The city attorney's job was an elected position, though it came with a staff of more than 60, including 18 attorneys. Renne thus had the luxury of delegating much of her responsibilities to her own staff, and did so much of the time. In addition, the office occasionally contracts with private, downtown lawfirms to "assist with its workload." [6]

Cunningham, Holtzman and Baker, on the other hand, having no such reserves upon which to draw, were on the front line every day. Representing FNB consistently drained them of time, energy and resources.

The three put in literally thousands of hours of legal work, over the course of more than five years, hoping for a jury verdict resulting in a civil judgment that would make it in the end all worth while. That hope proved, ultimately, futile. In virtually every instance, the cases were thrown out of court by judges who had no desire to see justice done. Thus, other than the small amount FNB was able to raise for their attorneys through the holding of fundraisers, Cunningham, Holtzman, and Baker were never compensated for the massive amount of work they performed.

Bringing a civil case requires considerable out-of-pocket expenses necessary simply to move the case forward from square A to square B. Such requirements essentially make justice in the courts for sale, available only to those who can afford it. Under such a system, poor people are, again, at an extreme disadvantage.

One of the costliest expenses in a lawsuit is the deposing of witnesses. This takes place in what is known as the "discovery" phase of the legal proceeding.

"In a civil case," says Cunningham, "each side has the right—and, more or less, the obligation—in preparing their case, to learn all the evidence on the other side, what the testimony of all the witnesses will be. So you do that by taking a deposition, which is sworn testimony in a non-court setting.

"It's very expensive because it involves the services of a court reporter, who sits there and takes everything down in one of these hand-held machines and then types it up in a prepared transcript so that it can be used, it can be read by the court, it can be excerpted in a brief. And those (transcripts) cost typically about four dollars a page.

"So if you take a person's deposition for two hours, that's likely to cost three or four hundred dollars," he added."

Given that some cases may involve deposing ten or more witnesses, and that the deposition times may vary, in some instances drastically, the cost of deposing witnesses may quickly grow into a bankrupting enterprise.

"We had a couple of witnesses in the Judi Bari case (a client of Cunningham's who sued the FBI) that testified for three or four days," said Cunningham. "So that cost a few thousand dollars just for one witness."

For an indigent client, such amounts of money are colossal. Little wonder, then, that San Francisco police officers, in the course of carrying out FNB arrests, often would remark, "We don't care if you sue us. Go ahead." [7]

In defending the city against the FNB lawsuits, Louise Renne employed a strategy of chipping away at them, one small piece at a time, until almost nothing remained. One of FNB's suits listed a total of 81 causes of action against the city. In a demurrer to the complaint, Renne stated,

> ...several causes of action fail on their face. Six...are barred
> by plaintiffs' failure to comply with the claims filing
> requirements of the Government Tort Claims Act...six

more causes of action are deficient because Civil Code 52
does not support a cause of action for coercive denial of
constitutional rights. [8]

In such a manner did Renne and her staff, probing for minor statuary
or procedural flaws, chip away tirelessly at the very substantive claims in
each suit, whittling away first here, then there.

A view of Cunningham and Renne provides a study in contrasts.

***

Cunningham got his start in law in the city of Chicago in 1967.
Among his clients at that time were members of the Chicago chapter of the
Black Panther Party, including party leader Fred Hampton, who was
murdered by a police death squad on December 4, 1969.

Cunningham's life has been strangely interwoven with other historic
episodes of state violence as well. The Chicago convention of 1968 was one.
There were many, many other arrests at that convention besides those of the
eight people who eventually went to trial in the famous conspiracy case.
Like many other local attorneys, Cunningham defended his share of young
people swept up in that rampage of police brutality.

But it was the inmate takeover at Attica State Prison in New York, on
September 9, 1971, which initiated the toughest legal fight of Cunningham's
career. Retaliations by guards against prisoners after the prison was retaken
were swift and brutal. The charges included stripping inmates naked, burning
them with cigarettes and hot shell casings, and forcing inmates into games of
Russian Roulette." To say that justice for the Attica prisoners has been slow
in coming would be an understatement.

After the rebellion, Cunningham joined a team of lawyers that
struggled with the Attica case for the next two and a half decades. In
1997—twenty six years after the fact—a jury awarded Frank Smith,
Cunningham's client, $4 million. Smith was the first Attica inmate to push
his case to a successful conclusion. Other cases are still waiting in the wings.

Dennis Cunningham has, then, essentially spent a lifetime defending
the wretched of the Earth, or at least the wretched of America.

In the 1980s Cunningham moved to the San Francisco Bay Area,
where another strange collision with fate occurred.

After her car was bombed in 1990, Earth First! activist Judi Bari
became Cunningham's client. The bomb that destroyed Bari's car had been
planted under the driver's seat. When it exploded, it blew straight up into the
young activist's body. Bari miraculously survived that attempt on her life,

yet succumbed to cancer in 1997. Despite her passing, Cunningham continued to forge on ahead with her lawsuit against the FBI.

***

The professional life of Louise Renne, on the other hand, has taken a far different path from Cunningham's.

Renne was elected to the office of San Francisco City Attorney in 1986. Over the years she has been accused of being close—too close—to big business. Such closeness reportedly has extended to certain large corporations with whom the city does business, particularly Pacific Gas & Electric (PG&E).

According to a *Bay Guardian* editorial,

> The reign of secrecy continues unchecked at the San Francisco City Attorney's Office. In the past two weeks alone, Louise Renne and her staff have:
>
> - signed off on a deal to keep under court seal the records of the city's legal case charging PG&E with bid rigging in the 1994 Presidio electricity supply contract;
> - lied to a Board of Supervisors committee about the status of the case, and only under blistering interrogation admitted that the city had lost the suit;
> - refused to draft legislation, as requested by the Sunshine Task Force, that would open up to public scrutiny information on single source contracts.
> - insisted that the City Attorney's Office documents are not subject to the Sunshine Ordinance. [9]

Advocates of public power have long had a gripe with Renne as well. A congressional act, signed into law in 1913, authorized the City of San Francisco to dam the Tuolomne River in Yosemite National Park. Under the *Raker Act* the city was given water rights to the resulting Hetch Hetchy Reservoir, but along with this gift came an obligation: that the electricity generated at the dam would be used to provide the citizens of San Francisco with cheap, publicly owned power. The loser in the creation of such a public power utility would stand to be the privately owned PG&E. The fact that this congressional mandate has never been fulfilled is testimony to the influence wielded by PG&E over successive generations of San Francisco politicians. Again, from the *Guardian:*

> For more than 80 years, San Francisco city attorneys and public utilities commissioners have operated as if they're in a state of denial: they've refused to acknowledge that the federal law that gave San Francisco the right to dam the Tuolomne River in Yosemite National Park for the city's water system also came with an obligation—to provide the citizens with cheap, public electricity generated at the dam. [10]

As if to dispel any doubt, the *Guardian* also supplied a quote from Supreme Court Justice Hugo Black. In a 1940 case, Black, writing for the majority, stated,

> Congress clearly intended to require—as a condition of its grant—sale and distribution of Hetch Hetchy power exclusively by San Francisco and municipal agencies directly to consumers in the belief that consumers would thus be afforded power at cheap rates in competition with private power companies, particularly Pacific Gas and Electric. [11]

In 1996 Renne "blocked" [12] the creation of a citizens advisory committee to focus on public power and to possibly award a contract for a feasibility study. The citizen's panel had been advocated by liberal supervisor Angela Alioto, whose efforts were described by the *Guardian* as a "courageous solo crusade." In these days Alioto, forbidden by term limitations from seeking re-election, was in the waning months of her term on the city's Board of Supervisors. Ironically, no such term limitations hindered Renne's re-election aspirations the following year.

Renne concluded that the creation of a citizen's committee such as that proposed by Alioto would be a violation of the city charter. Was the city attorney deliberately laying down obstacles to thwart the creation of a public power utility in San Francisco?

The *Guardian* observed, "The city attorney's determination is the most recent in a long history of actions that have obstructed implementation of a public power system in San Francisco."

Later on in 1996, after Renne's office was accused of "taking a dive" in a multi-million dollar suit against PG&E, the *Guardian* wrote,

> Renne's staff never raised the question of the Raker Act, never challenged the federal judge's connections to PG&E—and then tried to keep the whole outcome secret. [13]

The judge with "connections" to PG&E was none other than FNB's eternal nemesis, Vaughn Walker—who had, according to the Guardian, worked for "a PG&E-connected law firm as recently as 1990." [14]

The 1996 case centered around the question of who would provide power to the Presidio—the city or PG&E—following the conversion of the area from a military base to a national park.

> The issue goes back to 1993 when PG&E submitted the only bid to provide power to the new Presidio National Park. In its proposal the private utility first suggested that it would ask the taxpayers to fork over $22 million to replace the aging system of poles, wires and meters at the Army base.
>
> But there were two serious problems with that picture. For starters PG&E did something federal law prohibits: It provided the design and specifications for the new park electrical system and then turned around and submitted the bid that met those specifications.
>
> At the same time the Presidio is within the city limits of San Francisco, which, under federal law is required to operate a public power system. [15]

Potentially, with such a power system in place, the city would have stood to make millions supplying electrical power to the new national park. It was not to be. Renne lost the case.

Having earlier "blocked" the creation of a citizens advisory committee to study public power, the City Attorney now found it difficult to present the pertinent evidence in court. "I always thought the lawsuit was totally phony," said Neil Eisenberg, who had run against Renne in 1993. "She was pulled into court kicking and screaming, then kept the decision sub rosa and wouldn't tell anybody they lost. They blew it—that's why they lost." [16] According to the *Guardian,*

> The situation has gotten completely out of control. Renne is demonstrating more and more every day her utter

incompetence and her inability to run one of the most important offices in San Francisco.

The PG&E case is a disturbing, if not terribly surprising, example of how the City Attorney's Office has helped the utility maintain its illegal private-power monopoly in San Francisco for more than 80 years...Renne's office, which from the start resisted filing the PG&E Presidio case, wound up bungling it so badly that it's hard to believe the city's legal advocates actually intended to win. [17]

Perhaps the City Attorney's Office had indeed "taken a dive" in its square-off against corporate giant PG&E. But when it came to representing San Francisco's interest against the likes of Food Not Bombs, Renne was a *tiger.*

* * *

Charging FNB with being a "public nuisance" and with creating a "health emergency," the city attorney filed a motion for an injunction in Superior Court on July 14, 1989. The motion sought to have FNB enjoined from food serving "without first obtaining the appropriate permits" from Rec and Park and the Health Department.

In moving for the injunction, Renne and her staff expressed concern for the health and well-being of homeless people. "The continuing threat to the health, safety and welfare of the patrons of Defendants and of other citizens constitutes irreparable injury to the public," stated the motion. [18] The steadfast efforts of that devoted public servant, Al Chin, were also duly noted.

> Inspector Chin has testified that defendant has regularly failed to provide an enclosure for its food handling operations, has failed to keep the food in proper containers, has failed to prevent unnecessary handling of food by allowing the general public to serve itself from bins and boxes, has failed to provide soap and towels (and often water) for hand washing by employees and operators, and has failed to provide waste disposal facilities. [19]

Specifically, Renne's office charged, FNB had violated regulations requiring that: a) food be distributed from an enclosed booth, b) food beverages and utensils be covered, c) food be kept at least six inches off the ground and be dispensed by operators, d) food handlers wash their hands with soap and water before food preparation, and that hand washing facilities be available at all times, (a difficult requirement for food distribution occurring in outdoor settings) and e) that there be adequate garbage containers and that plastic bags be used in the food booth.

Renne's office, naturally, was able to summon up expert testimony—from the city's own public health department—to warn of the consequences of such failures.

State Health Code section 27551, as well as section 452 of the San Francisco Health and Safety Code regulating restaurants, or, more specifically, "food preparation and service establishments," were both cited by Renne's office. By way of rebuttal, attorney Sarge Holtzman, for Food Not Bombs, zeroed in on the latter citation and found fault with it.

> Section 452 of the Health Code applies on its terms to food preparation and service establishments. Food and service establishments are defined in section 451 to "mean and include any restaurant or itinerant restaurant."

> Defendants and his associates are alleged to have distributed free food to indigent individuals in the Civic Center Plaza of San Francisco. Plaintiffs offer no explanation as to the manner in which these activities should be deemed the operation of a restaurant.

> Section 451 (b) does not encompass the noncommercial preparation and distribution of food by an individual. To establish that a violation has occurred, plaintiffs must demonstrate by competent evidence that Food Not Bombs constitutes a food preparation and service establishment. The only allegations made concerning the status of Food Not Bombs are made on information and belief. Statements offered on information and belief cannot support an injunction and must be disregarded. *Low v. Low* 143 Cal.app.2d 650, 654 1956...The grounds for relief must be established by dentiary facts and not conclusory allegations. [20]

Having pretty much established what FNB was *not*—namely a restaurant—Holtzman then tackled the problem of identifying precisely what it *was*.

The fact as established by the declaration of Keith McHenry is that Food Not Bombs is not an organization in any traditional sense. It has no membership nor any qualification for membership. It is merely a designation for a shared philosophical and political precept that the resources of the country should be dedicated to the distribution of food rather than the proliferation of weapons. [21]

Not an organization, but a "shared precept?" It was perhaps a bit too esoteric and avant-garde for the average person, much less a conservative judge, to fathom. If all those people serving food out there on the street were not "organization members," then what were they? Identifying them merely as "holders of shared precepts" seemed a bit hazy. Was FNB, then, an organization after all? Perhaps, but even if so, city code was *still* inadequate, as written, to halt the group's challenge, as Holtzman pointed out:

If Food Not Bombs were to be deemed an organization then it would be on the basis that its defining characteristic was a shared conceptual ground. Anyone who shared the conceptual commitment would be a member. Section 452 specifically excludes social and political organizations which provide free food to their members. [22]

The above argument would appear to pose a serious problem for Renne and her staff. Clearly what was transpiring with the rise of Food Not Bombs in the city of San Francisco was the establishment of a new social order, a completely new paradigm. That paradigm had arisen in response to a changing, shifting America, an America which bore little or no resemblance to the one in which the elders of our society had grown up. The city was ill-equipped to deal with the demands of the changing times—the explosion in the numbers of homeless people, and the deteriorating quality of life under a system that simply wasn't working any more. Furthermore, the rise of this new social system made the keepers of the old, corrupt system as skittish as a frightened horse. Again from Holtzman:

A comprehensive evaluation of the Health Code renders it abundantly clear that it was never designed to apply to a situation such as that of the instant case any more than it would to casual picnics in the park. The only

> difference is that in the instant case it is a matter of survival as opposed to recreation.
>
> The guidelines that the Health Department is attempting to impose are those for street fairs and carnivals. The absence of standards for free distribution of food by individuals is indicative of the fact that this is not an activity that the city in its more rational periods ever envisioned as being subject to regulation. [23]

In those days Holtzman was a young lawyer practicing in a district of San Francisco where he came inordinately face to face, on a daily basis, with the social consequences, the *enfants perdu*, of a decade of unbridled corporate greed: The Haight Ashbury District. If ever there was a legal brief which could be said to read like poetry, Holtzman's answer to Renne's injunction motion seems to soar to that height in places.

> The constitutions of the United States and the State of California establish a right of privacy. This doctrine prevents unwarranted interference with certain forms of human interaction. Providing food to someone who is starving is an act of charity and compassion. It cannot be regulated under provisions designed to regulate commercial transactions.
>
> An aspect of the defendants' activities is the dramatization of the fact that the needs of the citizens are not being met by the government. The food program is clearly expressive in character and subject to constitutional protection. Although symbolic speech is subject to reasonable regulation regarding time, place or manner, such regulation must be narrowly directed toward the realization of legitimate state interests. [24]

The Supreme Court had ruled (in an earlier case) that restrictions on First Amendment activity must serve a "siginificant governmental interest." It had also said that consideration should be given as to whether there existed "alternative channels for communication of the information." Did the city's response to FNB adhere to these standards?

Holtzman argued:

Plaintiffs make no effort to isolate legitimate health concerns but rather seek a sweeping injunction to prevent any aspect of defendants' expressive activities.

Plaintiffs' evidence fails to establish any legitimate health hazard. Plaintiffs have alleged that defendants have engaged in the conduct subject to complaint since September of 1988. They fail to indicate any instance in which an individual suffered any affliction as a consequence of the food distribution of defendants. Defendants have been engaged in food distribution for over nine years and (have) been involved with the preparation of over one million meals. There remains not one known instance in which anyone has become ill as a result of these activities. Therefore, plaintiffs motion must fail for the failure to demonstrate irreparable injury. [25]

If there was no health hazard, what, then, was the city's motive for bringing the current proceeding against FNB? According to Holtzman:

Relief must be denied in situations where the plaintiff is proceeding in bad faith. The recognized maxim is He who comes into equity must come with clean hands...It is inconceivable that anyone familiar with the facts of the instant cases could conclude that the motivation of the plaintiffs in this action is concern for the health and welfare of the homeless who consume the food distributed by the defendants. Plaintiffs' action is a thinly veiled effort to eliminate a factor which has focused attention on the failure of the administration to adequately address the problems of the homeless. Plaintiffs' allegations of Health and Park Code violations are clearly pretextual. If plaintiffs could not interfere with defendants' activities on the basis of their actual political interests, then they should not be entitled to invoke equity to accomplish this end through subterfuge. [26]

Thus were the positions of the opposing sides delineated. The case was set for oral arguments on Friday, July 21, 1989 in the courtroom of Judge Ralph Flageollet, Department 9, Superior Court of the State of California, City and County of San Francisco. Appearing on behalf of the city were Deputy City Attorneys George Riley and Randy Riddle. A transcript of the proceeding is nineteen pages long and shows Riley referring to the FNB giveaways as "a criminal act." [27] According to Riley, it was "clear" that FNB was a food preparation and service establishment under section 451, and that also:

> This case is not about providing food for the poor. It is about whether there will be a double standard, a standard that differs between the activities of an establishment that regularly gives food to the public. Other organizations have met these minimal requirements and given away food to the poor with some measure of safety and dignity. [28]

As much as Riley tried to depoliticize the argument, Holtzman, whose oral arguments were, if anything, even more eloquent that had been his written brief, placed the issue squarely within its political context and left little doubt as to the possible "ideological" motivations on the part of the city. He said:

> The court must also consider the good faith of the people in bringing this action. Are we really to believe that the motivation for this action is concern for the health and well-being of the individuals in the Civic Center? If that were the case, would the plaintiff at this very day be depriving them of their tents and their other means of subsistence within the Civic Center? It is not a health question that is involved. It is an ideological question. [29]

Holtzman presented to the court papers containing "over 50 statements" from homeless people who had been served meals by FNB. According to the attorney, this evidence showed "an overwhelming need" for the service being provided by FNB. Holtzman argued that the court must "balance" the "very remote possibility" of a health hazard against "the very real privation" that would result if FNB were to cease operations. A major fault with the city's motion, he said, is that "rather than isolating the conduct which the plaintiff contends constitutes a nuisance," it instead sought a "sweeping" injunction shutting down FNB's entire food serving operation.

"If there are nuisance conditions, if this action is really about the question of whether food should be stored six inches above the ground or not, then an injunction should be framed that way." [30]

The discussion next shifted to Health Department regulations, one of which, it must be remembered, was a requirement that FNB obtain a tent, or an enclosed canopy from which to serve its food. Riley brought up the subject of the canopy, but then, omitting to mention that it had been the SFPD which had confiscated the structure, claimed FNB had "abandoned" its use. In the course of the whole exchange, Riley, once again, asserted that the city had "worked with" FNB to help bring the group into compliance with codes.

> The Health Department worked with them. They erected overhead cover and provided some safety for their food. They've now abandoned it and are asserting a blanket exemption to the law itself, and this is the activity which must be enjoined, [31]

Riley said, to which Holtzman responded:

> When they brought that canopy to the Civic Center the police took it from them. So now they're being told by the city that because they don't have that canopy, they are exposing the people the city is so concerned about to an unreasonable health risk from health hazards. [32]

Why would FNB go to all the trouble and expense of acquiring a tent that would meet Health Department specifications, only to later "abandon" it? In granting the city's injunction request, Judge Flageollet seems not to have given that question much, if any, consideration. In fact, Flageollet's comments, at the close of oral arguments, were exceedingly brief: the issue, said the judge, was "strictly" one of health and "not any ideological problems that might exist." [33]

Flageollet also apparently disregarded whether sections 451 and 452, regulating a "food preparation and service establishment," were even applicable to Food Not Bombs any more than they were applicable to a company picnic in Golden Gate Park.

From the day of Flageollet's order, FNB members arrested for serving food would henceforth be charged with "violating a court order."

That year FNB filed a $50 million suit against the city of San Francisco in federal court, naming as defendants Mayor Art Agnos, (then) Police Chief Frank Jordan, the SFPD, and the San Francisco Superior Court. The suit, which was thrown out by Walker, also sought an order enjoining police from further arrests of FNB.

***

"We do not dispute that the health department code applies to Food Not Bombs," said FNB attorney Randy Baker. "The point of issue in this case is that the health code *changes* when it's applied to Food Not Bombs from time to time."

A hearing in the FNB federal case took place in Walker's courtroom on August 7, 1990. In contrast to Flageollet, Walker appeared to be fully engaged. A transcript of the proceeding, in fact, reveals a judge with an extraordinarily keen mind and a high degree of mental agility. It also suggests, on the part of Walker, a mischievous delight in verbal jousting, and with playing devil's advocate with opposing counsels.

Riley, once again appearing for the city, fixated on a Washington DC case entitled *Clark v. The Community for Non-violence*, in which the court had ruled *against* the forces of protest. The case involved an encampment of homeless people in a park across the street from the White House, known as Lafayette Park. Unbeknownst to the courtroom antagonists that day, Lafayette Park was to be the scene of a police murder. Just four years after Riley cited the *Clark* case as a just ruling in the matter of homeless protestors, U.S. Park Police would gun down homeless father Marcelino Corniel in front of the White House (covered in chapter two).

Said Riley that day in 1990,

> And I think what is most instructive on this basis is the Clark case, Clark versus the Community for Non-violence in Washington D.C.
>
> There a group of homeless advocates staged an encampment in Lafayette Park right across from the White House. They alleged that their activity of calling attention to the plight of the homeless was protected by the First Amendment and, therefore, the National Park Service was obligated to open the parks for that activity.
>
> And the Supreme Court held that that conduct, that camping in the park, was not protected by the first amendment. [34]

In the *Clark* case, Riley added, the government had an "overwhelming public interest in managing public property" to the benefit of everyone.

Cunningham, however, disputed the applicability of the *Clark* case to the FNB matter:

> I think when they (the court) got down to it, what they barred them from doing was sleeping. They couldn't say

they couldn't be there holding a banner. But if they fell asleep, they were camping, and that was beyond the free speech protection.

So they said you can't do that. But they didn't say that they couldn't carry out mixed conduct. [35]

Addressing the court now, Baker added,

Your honor, I'm somewhat familiar with the case. I think a critical difference in *Clark* versus this one is there was a categorical ban on sleeping in the park in that case.

Here people eat in the park all the time. So we have the paradoxical case of people who aren't engaged in First Amendment activity being allowed to go in the park and serve food, have class picnics, but people who are trying to make a point to the public being categorically banned. [36]

There followed an exchange between Walker and Baker, with the former evidencing a relishing of the debate. The transcript reads:

The court: I'm not sure that helps your side, though, does it?

Mr. Baker: As I understand the First Amendment, people exercising their First Amendment rights are entitled to at least the same leeway as people who aren't exercising First Amendment rights.

The court: Well, if there is a First Amendment right to this conduct, you may have an equal protection argument that has been implicated. But the fact that the city allowed some people to go into the park and eat, picnics, and so forth, that doesn't help you in this case, does it?

Mr. Baker: My understanding is Food Not Bombs is engaging in expressive conduct.

The court: I understand that is your argument. The fact that the city permits people to picnic in the park doesn't mean picnicking is a First Amendment activity. [37]

Walker ruled against FNB, tossing the case out of court. The judge commented:

First I don't believe that there is a communicative aspect...That alone should be sufficient to support summary judgement on the first amendment. But even if there were a communicative element to that activity, the city and county's interest in regulating public health and the use of the parks is an exercise of the city's traditional and substantial government interest...

In effect the plaintiff is claiming that he has a protective right to communicate through the distribution of food in a manner that the city has found to be unsafe or unsanitary. And it seems to me that the distribution in this manner is not safe or sanitary. [38]

Was the judge saying that he was a greater expert than the San Francisco Health Department in determining what was "safe and sanitary?" The Health Department, after all, had *granted* FNB a permit. (The health permit, it must be remembered, was rendered null and void after the city's Rec and Park Department adopted a measure disallowing food serving to groups of 25 or more in city parks.) At any rate, thus did Walker shoot down FNB's First Amendment argument.

The hearing in federal court was over. FNB, if it wanted justice in the courts, had no recourse now but to go back to the State Court. It did just that.

***

In subsequent cases back in California Superior Court FNB accused the city of an "unlawful conspiracy." One suit listed 32 causes of action, including an incident in which Keith had been stripped of his clothes and beaten while in custody of police and sheriff's deputies.

In responding, Renne and her staff accused McHenry of "artful pleading," [39] and declared, "It is untenable to suggest that anytime an individual in the custody of police charges that he has been battered, the government also must anticipate a claim of false arrest." [40] The charges of false arrest, stated Renne's office, couldn't hold water because, "since July 21, 1989 an order of this court has enjoined Keith McHenry and Food Not Bombs from distributing food without appropriate permits."

Renne also scoffed sneeringly at FNB's claim of a city-wide conspiracy, calling it "defective." [41]

The case further took into account the toll on plaintiffs' personal lives brought about by Keith's constantly being arrested. The "battery of unconstitutional arrests, imprisonments, and physical attacks" created, as may well be imagined, immeasurable stress upon Keith and Andrea's marriage.

The suffering and stress engendered by the city's campaign against FNB was felt by no one perhaps more acutely than Andrea McHenry. One can easily imagine the fears of a wife whose husband has been subjected to police beatings and death threats, and who faces the prospect of being arrested literally every time he sets foot out upon the street. Yet for Andrea, no sympathy was accorded by the City Attorney's Office. The McHenrys' claim of interference with their marriage was "absurd" and "untenable," responded Renne and company. [42]

Alas a jury was never given the opportunity to decide. The case was thrown out of court. Still seeking justice, FNB went back into the federal court—and into the waiting arms of Judge Walker.

The year was 1992. The "omnibus" federal case was assigned the number 92-1154 VRW. A second plaintiff in the case, after Keith, was Eric Warren, who had been arrested (along with Keith, Tom Osher and myself) during the police riot at City Hall on March 22 the year before (described in chapter two). Named as defendants in 92-1154 VRW were Renne; numerous police officers, including Thomas (Blackboot) Blackwell; Jordan; Agnos; and other city officials, including employees of the Office of Citizens' Complaints, which had, to date, never sustained a single complaint brought by any FNB member against a police officer; plus the Superior Court.

In shooting down the case, Walker wrote,

> Plaintiffs request the court to order the city to refrain from interfering with plaintiffs' activities and to reform its police disciplinary procedures. This court cannot order the city not to enforce the law; to the extent that plaintiff seeks an order regarding any city enforcement activities, defendants' motion to dismiss is granted. [43]

***

FNB fared no better in the U.S. Court of Appeals than it had in either Walker's courtroom or the state courts. In a written decision released July 21, 1993, the three-judge panel declined to issue an opinion on whether FNB food giveaways constituted First Amendment activity, finding instead that the city's permit requirements amounted to "reasonable" time, place and manner restrictions. Therefore, opined the court, no decision on the free speech issue was required in this case.

Moreover, said the venerated body, the city's ordinances "do not foreclose McHenry from alternative forms of communication: feeding the homeless in public parks is not the only way to call attention to their plight." [44] It was the only way which had ever been effective, though.

Completely ignoring the trials and tribulations undergone by FNB members in an effort to comply with permit requirements, the court included the following incredible passage in its decision:

> In fact, these ordinances do not foreclose McHenry from feeding the homeless or otherwise demonstrating in public parks at all. As stated above, they merely require that he obtain the necessary permits before doing so. [45]

The city had once again emerged victorious. Should FNB now take its case to the U.S. Supreme Court? To do so would have been a crap shoot, played for high stakes, with no realistic hope that the outcome would be any different. Could FNB afford to fly attorneys back and forth from San Francisco to Washington D.C.? The answer, of course, was no. Justice once again was available only to the wealthy, and completely out of reach of the poor.

Having succeeded Art Agnos as mayor, Frank Jordan, running into vocal opposition to his Matrix program in September 1993, initiated a new wave of FNB arrests, the first of his administration. The arrests later combined with a pattern of sexual harassment of women FNB members by arresting officers, resulting in what some FNB members began to believe was a "psychological operation" being waged by the city against the group.

***

A look over the list of persons arrested in the first days of this new wave leaves one struck by the incredible youthfulness, for the most part, of the offenders. Though not necessarily all members of FNB—some simply were bystanders at the time, while others might more accurately be described as FNB "supporters"—the arrested included: Brian Wickenheiser, 36, Kim Argula, 27, James Tracy, 23, Michael Linde, 32, Simon Penland, 21, Julie Schweit, 24, David Grace, 37, Matt Bouvier, 27, Brett Parker, 29, Matt Dodt, 36, Richard Chandler, 50, Paul Lesneski, 24, Emily Murdock, 24, Vincent Giacomini, 29, Mario Martinez, 29, Nicholas Alesandro, 25, Michael Reinsborough, 24, Robert Kahn, 44, David Modersbach, 27, Christa Reiff, 21, William Rubley, 27, Anil Nair, 28, Teal Dixon, 25, Greg Price, 23,

Judith Kalloch, 26, Victor Vasquez, 28, Tristan Anderson, 22, Louisa Krupp, 23.

The above is only a partial list. The arrests in the post-September '93-era went on until after Jordan left office in January 1996, with a sizeable cluster, around 200 or so, occurring in June 1995 during the FNB International Gathering. Whatever satisfaction the city may have derived from throwing all these people in jail, ultimately it was Keith McHenry that the Jordan administration considered public enemy number one. Arrests occurring in early 1994 left Keith facing multiple felony charges which jeopardized him under the California "three strikes" law. Throughout this time, too, there continued police confiscation of vehicles, food, food containers, and cooking equipment.

Despite such an incredible record of civil rights abuse, the city seemed to have no trouble blocking and frustrating FNB's efforts to get justice in the courts. In the court of public opinion, however, we were on the fast lane of the freeway. In September four members of the clergy were inspired to take up soup ladles and serve food with FNB. Arrested right alongside FNB members, were Father Louis Vitale, 61, Father Stephen Kelly, 44, Sister Bernie Galvin, 59, and Father Cornelius Leehan, 72.

Father Vitale, pastor at St. Bonifice's Catholic Church, in the heart of San Francisco's economically ravaged Tenderloin District, and Sister Galvin, especially, became the nucleus of what would later be called Religious Witness with Homeless People. The latter grew into a large coalition of clergy from all over the city, representing many different faiths, which came together in opposition to the Matrix program.

By early 1994, Religious Witness was holding demonstrations of its own, attracting large turnouts and a fair amount of media coverage. While using civil disobedience tactics similar to those employed by FNB, Religious Witness adopted a less militant tone at its protests. Nonetheless, the group's very existence was a powerful testament to the injustice and inhumanity of the Matrix program. For FNB, the entrance of Religious Witness with Homeless People into the public arena was enormously welcomed. Notwithstanding, there was a difference in treatment meted out to the two groups by police. A food giveaway organized by Religious Witness in the spring of 1994 was allowed to proceed without incident. This inequality, however, would actually work to the favor of FNB criminal defendants later on.

By May of that year, the cases of those who had been caught up in the previous September's arrests were about to go to trial, and in this new "get tough" climate, initiated by the Jordan administration, it looked as if the D.A. might be planning to press ahead with prosecutions. Suddenly, however, these efforts collapsed. A legal maneuver executed by an FNB attorney stopped the D.A.'s office dead in its tracks.

Frances Pinnock, attorney for FNB member Brian Wickenheiser, filed a "Murgia" motion on behalf of her client. The motion, charging discriminatory enforcement of the law, was eventually signed onto by attorneys for all FNB defendants save for one: Robert Kahn, who had unwisely separated his case from the others and elected to proceed to early trial in February. (In so doing, Kahn was convicted and sentenced to 60 days in jail—for handing a bagel to a homeless woman. He remains, to this day, the only San Francisco FNB member to ever be so convicted.)

"Murgia" motion is a petition charging selective law enforcement and prosecution based on one's membership in an unpopular or disfavored group. The original Murgia defendants (in a 1975 case) had been members of the United Farm Workers in Kern County, California. In that case, the defendants alleged they had been arrested and prosecuted for criminal offenses solely because of their union membership and organizing activities. In pressing for a Murgia ruling in the case of FNB, Pinnock filed a supplemental declaration with the court that makes for riveting reading.

The document cites numerous instances of outdoor food giveaways—carried out by organizations and individuals other than FNB—which had been allowed to proceed without interference from the police, despite the absence of permits. These included the Religious Witness giveaway, as well as distributions by the Buddhist Church, the Church of Jesus Christ, and one Father Town Flower. Also cited in the motion were the activities of a group calling itself the Richmond Anti Graffiti Squad whose fliers promised free "juice and doughnuts" to members of the public participating in graffiti cleanup.

Most stingingly ironic of all, however, was the evidence, including photographic, of food giveaways by Jordan himself. In 1991, when running for mayor, Jordan had thrown a series of campaign events dubbed "Franks with Frank." The gatherings had been held in city parks and had involved the giving away of hot dogs to the public.

Sated Pinnock:

> I am informed and believe that the mayor of the City of San Francisco, Frank Jordan, and his associates, participated in the distribution of free food on public land. Attached as Exhibit A is a copy of a flier distributed by the mayor and his associates in connection with his food distribution at Delores Park on Nov. 30, 1991.

The intent of Mayor Jordan and his associates was strictly political. Mayor Jordan and his associates did not have a permit for this activity. In fact, Mayor Jordan was quoted in the *SF Weekly* newspaper as saying: "So far no one has said anything (about permits). If they do, we'll go down and get the proper permits." Attached as Exhibit B is a copy of the *SF Weekly* article. Mayor Jordan and his associates were not subjected to a warning, citation or arrest by law enforcement representatives, including himself, at any time. [46]

Resting under the headline, "Hotdog-gate: Does 'Franks with Frank' violate the law?" the *SF Weekly* article, stated in part:

During the weekend "franks with Frank" outdoor soirees, the mayoral candidate has been giving away free hotdogs and Cokes to large, hungry crowds. But when Food Not Bombs tried to do the very same thing—give food away without a permit—Jordan, as police chief, personally had the activists arrested. [47]

The story noted the numerous FNB arrests, and observed that Jordan, in giving away his "sodium nitrate-riddled hotdogs," was "now guilty" of violating park and health codes by failure to obtain permits.

Did "Franks with Frank" not constitute clear evidence of selective enforcement of the law? I put the question to attorney Sarge Holtzman in an interview in April of 1998.

"There were two differences in terms of Food Not Bombs—one, Food Not Bombs was giving it (food) to people who were poor, who were actually hungry," said Holtzman. "The other is that their (FNB's) food wasn't carcinogenic."

Pinnock said that in filing her Murgia motion, "We were trying to politicize the case and win some leverage with the District Attorney's Office." It worked. Faced with a choice between dropping the charges or opening up a whole Pandora's box of constitutional questions, the D.A.'s Office dropped all charges against the FNB defendants. But that old revolving door to the jail kept on revolving for the next two years.

While the Murgia motion perhaps did save a lot of people from extended jail stays, its drawback was that, as an aspect of a criminal proceeding, it had no bearing on any of the civil cases. For the civil courts, the charges of conspiracy and selective enforcement still remained but a theory, or mere "narrative ramblings," as Walker had once termed them. And while the D.A. was dropping charges like hot potatoes in the courts, in the streets—scene of the age-old, eternal struggle between FNB and the police—something far different was happening.

The arrests were continuing, true, but now, with the assignment of two African-American officers to the "Special Operations Division" (Special Operations was currently in charge of arresting FNB), enforcement measures suddenly began to take on a new, more menacing aspect.

***

The arrival on the scene of Officers LeRoy Lindo and Cornelius "Con" Johnson brought about a definite change in the weather. Some in FNB assumed, naively, that because the officers were black they must share some sense of kinship as fellow victims of oppression. "We know you're only doing your job," these FNB folks would proclaim understandingly to the pair.

In those days when I attended FNB protests I would inevitably arrive only to find at least one or two members of the group engaged in seemingly endless philosophical discussions—about racism, poverty, injustice, or whatever—with smirking, grinning cops, attempting to "reason" with such miserable specimens of humanity as if they were normal human beings capable of being reasoned with. Sometimes the level of naivete could rise pretty high. In the case of Lindo and Johnson, though, I think it may have risen, in the initial going at any rate, pretty close to the top of the scale.

A video which shows the two black officers arresting David Grace on December 29 is illustrative. As Grace is worked over by Lindo (Johnson played only an assisting role in the arrest), someone off-camera can be heard screaming repeatedly—over and over—"What if this were Alabama and Woolworth's?" In the film footage Grace is thrown by Lindo onto the hood of a police car, his body flung so hard that he rolls off the other side, where he is dropped to the ground like a sack of oats—with Lindo after him all the way.

Not only were Lindo and Johnson decidedly *not* kindred spirits with the white radicals of FNB, but there are indications that their intentions, or at least the intentions of those who had assigned them to Special Operations, may have been subtly nefarious. Johnson and Lindo, to be sure, were only "doing their jobs." It's what their "jobs" consisted of that became the subject of speculation. Some in FNB, Keith McHenry included, felt at the time—and do today—that the task meted out to Johnson and Lindo was, in a sort of

Food Not Bombs members serve food to homeless people in Civic Center Plaza.

Homeless people sit in the empty Civic Center fountain during the Agnos years. When Frank Jordan was elected mayor the fountain was refilled.

San Francisco police welcome Food Not Bombs to City Hall.

Richard Edmondson (left) with Keith McHenry and Elsa, Pluto, and Bear near the Golden Gate Bridge.

The Food Not Bombs bread truck. San Francisco Police routinely confiscated vehicles while making arrests of Food Not Bombs members.

Jennifer Baker is handcuffed by Officer LeRoy Lindo.

"Franks with Frank:" The Jordan for mayor campaign serves free food in the park without a permit.

Holding bagles aloft, Food Not Bombs members Vincent Giacomini (right) and Tristan Anderson serve food from the Civic Center fountain.

Father Father Cornelius Leehan (left) and Father Stephen Kelley serve food with Food Not Bombs while Sister Bernie Galvin stands (center) in the background.

Officer Lindo wades into the fountain to make arrests.

Officer Lindo whistles a happy tune while confiscating food from the homeless.

Keith McHenry address a crowd with authors Ron Kovic
(center seated) and Howard Zinn in attendance.

Jo and Elsa.

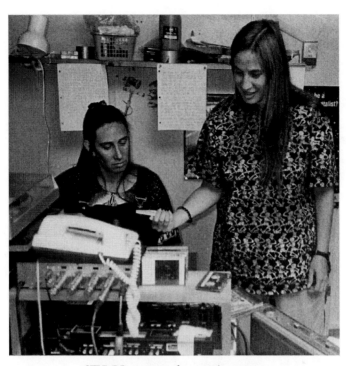

SFLR DJs prepare the evening news.

The offending transmitter.

Keith McHenry is arrested by San Francisco Police. There were more than 1,000 arrests of Food Not Bombs members. McHenry was arrested more than 100 times.

Kiilu Nyasha and Richard Edmondson

"FBI-COINTELPRO-like" fashion, to sow divisions between FNB and the African-American community.

Certainly such an endeavor might have been worthy of the late J. Edgar Hoover, who, in his lifetime, proved himself quite equal to the challenge of sowing strife and divisions within and between groups. For years FNB had attempted to build bridges of solidarity to the African-American community. These efforts had included food giveaways at local housing projects. Yet for all that, FNB remained, in 1993, primarily a white activist group. Be that as it may, there is no greater fear among those in power than unity among the masses, and they must always be on their guard to stamp it out whenever and wherever it threatens to occur.

If the goal were indeed racial discord, what better way of achieving that end than to—if such were possible anyway—ignite the ancient flash point between the white and black races in this country: the fear among white men, resonating and head-rearing down the spiral of time from antebellum history, of black men making sexual advances toward white women. This view of the whole Lindo/Johnson affair is held, at any rate, by FNB member Mike Linde, who described the pair's entrance onto center stage as a case of the city's having "played the race card."

"It was intended to be inflammatory," Linde said. "I always felt it was not by accident that it was two black police officers, and that this was directed primarily against white women."

The same view, more or less, is shared by FNB member Vincent Giacomini, while a third, Andrew Rose, who kept a journal of the period, described the Lindo-Johnson affair as "a psychological operation." The brunt of the sexual harassment was borne by two FNB members in particular, Catherine Marsh and Anastasia Jones.

While Lindo was accused often times of physical violence upon FNB members, the charges of sexual harassment fell squarely upon Johnson, who was not assigned to Special Operations until approximately December—well after Lindo. The latter, on the other hand, seems to have been already on the Special Operations team with the first FNB arrest (to occur under the Jordan administration) on September 2.

These September arrests were amazing, videotaped spectacles in which emotions grew as springy as a stretched out piece of bubble gum. The incidents unfolded noisily during the noon lunch hour, in Civic Center Plaza, across the street from the mayor's balcony. Film footage shows FNB members linking arms, in an effort to protect the food, as hundreds of bystanders scream angrily at arresting officers.

Much of the film was shot by FNB member Hugh Mejia. Significant about the footage is the degree of racial unity documented. Among the crowd, in the highly charged atmosphere, can be seen both whites and blacks—vociferously denouncing the actions of the police, and voicing support for FNB. The crescendo reaches fever pitch as police, stepping upon spilled food, begin dragging FNB members across the pavement to the waiting paddy wagons.

In most cases FNB members simply go limp after being pried loose from the circle, however, in one scene Linde mounts a fierce resistance to the police manhandling. Linde's struggles are entirely of a non-violent nature, consisting of nothing more than a wrestler's arm-lock around the knees and ankles of the officers who are attempting to drag him away. Yet the act is sufficiently discombobulating to the cops, who find themselves incapable of forward motion with their legs hopelessly entwined in the folds of Linde's elbow, the grip of the FNB member seemingly vice-like.

Perhaps without the presence of TV cameras and hundreds of witnesses, Linde would have been clubbed for this act of unruliness. In this case, however, his resistance is finally overcome as up to five officers pile on top of him with knees in neck, chest and groin. At last he is dragged away and put in the paddy wagon along with the others.

In a September 11 entry in his journal, Andrew Rose wrote, "Thanks to all who have come before who have made such a 'San Francisco standoff' possible, and prayers to those who face oppression of a more brutal kind."

The September arrests did, indeed, garner quite a bit of media coverage, a surprising amount of it not entirely unsympathetic to FNB. In one TV report Commander Dennis Martel can be seen telling a reporter, "They obviously don't want to feed the hungry, they just want to make an anarchist-type statement, and we're not gonna allow it. It's that simple." [48] These comments were seized upon by FNB members—and their attorneys—as further evidence of an illegal campaign of repression against the group. It was another case of foot-in-mouth disease for Martel, who seemed to have forgotten that "statements" are allowed under the U.S. Constitution.

Clearly, as had been the case earlier under Agnos, the City of San Francisco had once again encountered, in its arrests of FNB, a public relations problem of no mean proportions. But the media, if nothing else, are fickle. The TV reporters quickly lost interest in the arrests, and soon the only camera left remaining to witness the confrontations in Civic Center Plaza became Mejia's.

By December, when Johnson arrived on the scene, the press coverage had trickled to a halt. In his journal Rose wrote, "We have lost the attention of the media because our methods are non-violent and therefore unattractive to the corporate-owned war makers."

Johnson's arrival on the scene came curiously on the heels of an article in the *San Francisco Chronicle* in which the officer was reported to have been the subject of an internal affairs investigation. The charges stemmed from an October 16 incident in which Johnson was alleged to have struck his girlfriend, a woman by the name of Rathany Nahul, "who worked at a doughnut shop on 24th Street, where the incident occurred," according to the *Chronicle*. [49]

The case was said to be "making waves" in police circles "because of Johnson's high-profile political role in the department." Johnson was described in the article as being "president of the black officers' organization in the department," a group calling itself "Officers for Justice." [50] One interesting aspect of the *Chronicle* article is its implications of racial antagonisms between black and white officers.

The case had apparently not gone unnoticed by the command staff of the police department. Deputy Chief Fred Lau, who later became chief, told the *Chronicle*, "We are gathering the facts," and that "we are treating this like any other case—in a fair, professional manner." [51]

If the *Chronicle* report is to be believed, there is an indication, then, that Johnson had a problem with women. Further, judging from the *Chronicle*, the police command staff knew about that problem prior to assigning him to Special Operations and placing him on the detail to arrest FNB.

The *Chronicle* did not give the story about Johnson much play, relegating it to a position on the lower front page of the metro section. The story would have been easy to miss. Now I would not describe FNB members, in a general manner of speaking, as being avid daily readers of the *Chronicle*. Yet somehow the allegations that Johnson had "beaten up his girl friend" became common knowledge among FNB folk within days after his transfer to Special Operations. At any rate by December Lindo and Johnson were operating as a team and cruising the Civic Center area in the same car.

***

Mejia says that one particularly favored modus operandi of Lindo and Johnson was to pull out food belonging to themselves, and then, in a very public manner, begin eating it—this after confiscating the food of FNB. Indeed, one of Mejia's videos—the one depicting the arrest of David Grace—shows Lindo at the end of the sequence, eating a candy bar. In the scene Lindo, having just confiscated from FNB all of its bread and buckets of soup, is sitting in the front seat passenger side of the patrol car. Looking out the window, Lindo comments for the camera, "Snickers—a fistful of peanuts in every chewy bite."

Of more concern than such would-be comical theatrics, however, was sexual harassment. The latter would obviously be more difficult to document, however, since the overtures were never made in the presence of a video camera. Nonetheless, in February of 1994 Jo and I had over to our apartment (which had long since doubled as a radio production studio) two women upon whom the brunt of the alleged sexual harassment had fallen, Catherine Marsh and Anastasia Jones.

Our intention was to tape an interview and air it on our next broadcast. Discussing it beforehand, Jo and I had decided that *she* would conduct the interview while I would clear out of the apartment entirely for the duration of the pair's visit. This was on the assumption that the two women would feel more comfortable talking with another woman. We probably needn't have bothered with this measure. Marsh and Jones showed up with a third FNB member, Greg Price. The latter, as it turned out, also had a story to tell.

Price told of an incident in which he had jokingly made some sort of off-the-cuff remark to Lindo about coming over to his (Lindo's) grandmother's house for Thanksgiving dinner. Lindo, according to Price, had responded, "You leave my grandmother alone or I'll kill you," which Price interpreted, somewhat dubiously, as a "death threat."

If it was a death threat, it was not a very compelling or convincing one—although we had no doubt that Greg probably was genuinely afraid of Lindo. Much more disturbing, however, were statements given by Marsh and Jones regarding alleged sexual harassment—from Johnson—plus an additional story related by Catherine in which, having been denied access to a toilet, she had been obliged, finally, to urinate in the presence of four male officers. The incident had occurred at Northern Police Station, where Marsh had been locked up in a holding area with no waste disposal facility. Marsh, who was 22 years old at the time, was arrested a total of 25 times—mainly by Lindo and Johnson—for serving food.

Both Marsh and Jones told similar stories about sexual come-ons from Johnson, often made while they were under arrest and in the officer's custody. On one such occasion, Jones said, she found herself being told her life story, as interpreted by Johnson.

"I was the only one serving that day, so I was the only one arrested," Anastasia explained to Jo.

During the ride to Northern Station Lindo drove, Johnson sat in the front passenger seat, while Jones—the prisoner—sat in the back. In route Officer Johnson "turned himself around," said Anastasia, "and he proceeded basically to comment on my appearance, on my physical stature." At this point Jo wanted to know specifically what words the officer had used.

> Anastasia: Well, he first of all started saying, "Oh you've got such a cute smile. What's a hot babe like you doing—" I can't specifically say that he used the word "hot babe," but he more or less commented to that regard, and said, what are you doing being an anarchist and being so stupid, you should just be at school being a good little white girl, etcetera.
>
> Jo: Did he say "white girl?"
>
> Anastasia: He *did* say "a good little white girl," and then he said, "Let me tell you about yourself"—and basically decided he was gonna tell me my life story from the time I was born.
>
> Jo: And what did he say? What *was* your life story, according to him?
>
> Anastasia: This is my life story, he said, "Your daddy's a banker and your mom is an alcoholic. They sent you away to college, but you're just a little bit bored, so you're gonna get this out of your system. You don't know what you're doing. You're gonna be lucky if you finish college, then you're gonna proceed to marry a dickless fucker who won't be able to satisfy you like I could.

Marsh spoke of an occasion when, as Johnson's prisoner, she was made to take an elevator ride at 850 Bryant Street. The two were alone in the elevator at the time, Marsh recalled.

"We got into the elevator and I'm, like, totally worried," said Catherine. "And the whole time he's, like, standing right in my face, and he's like, again saying, 'Why don't you smile for me, you have such pretty eyes.' That's what was so weird about it. He kept saying the whole thing over and over."

Marsh also was allegedly told by Johnson, "If you were my woman you'd have nothing to worry about," while at other times he reportedly showed her how he could make the squad car door close all by itself—by pressing suddenly on the accelerator.

The incident in which Marsh was denied access to a bathroom—which did *not* involve either Lindo or Johnson—took place at Northern Station, where there existed a "stall" designated for women, said Marsh. She added, however, that "it has no toilet in it because they don't want women peeing in front of all the men, and there's tons of men around all the time. So what they do is then they call a female officer and they take you over to the bathroom."

On the day in question, however, there were "no women around," said Catherine, "and I yelled out, and I knocked on the window, and I'm, like, 'Can I go to the bathroom?'

"He (a male officer) goes, 'We don't have one!'—and started laughing, and there was another guy next to him, and he started laughing too," she said.

After repeatedly being denied access to a bathroom in such a manner, Marsh proceeded to urinate into a drain in the floor, at which time, "all the officers turned around and watched me for a little bit, and then they, like, snickered, and then went back to doing whatever they were doing."

***

The interview, if not Catherine's experience in jail, had gone well. Jo had asked good questions and had handled the whole interview very smoothly. We now had Catherine's and Anastasia's comments on tape. Our intention was to get them on the air on our next broadcast, which was a Wednesday. However, when that night came we were thwarted once more—not by the FCC this time, but by nature.

Because it was a weeknight I had, again, to do the broadcast without Jo, who had to get up at five the next morning to go teach pre-school. I chose Twin Peaks as a broadcast location since it had the easiest access—a paved drive right up to the top. But what I found when I arrived were the most savage, despotically howling winds I have ever encountered. Standing outside the truck, I took an assessment of the situation and realized I would never get the antenna up in this wind.

It was that night, in February of 1994, that I decided we simply *had* to come in out of the cold. What we needed was a *real* radio station—enclosed in a building—as well as a *real* antenna, mounted on a steel mast anchored by guy wires. The only place that afforded us the means and the space for such a set up, of course, was our apartment—but it would be a while yet before I would convince Jo that installing an FM radio station in our living room was the thing we ought to do.

We aired Catherine and Anastasia on Saturday, our next night out. The elements were tamer. The broadcast went off without a hitch.

***

Anytime an FNB member was arrested and taken to jail there was a definite fear and intimidation factor involved. Brian Wickenheiser tells of a time in which he was arrested by Lindo and Johnson, who, while driving him around in a squad car, talked of taking him out to China Basin and dumping his body. Wickenheiser, described by his attorney, Frances Pinnock, as a "devout, spiritual man," said Lindo and Johnson "were driving around the fountain (in Civic Center Plaza) and deciding what they should do with me."

According to Wickenheiser, the suggestion was made by Johnson that "we could go out to China Basin" and that "people disappear out there all the time." Wickenheiser says he rode along in silence as Johnson began to address him directly, commenting "how I was a white middle class male with all these altruistic ideas, and how in reality that people could see the white devil behind my blue eyes."

It is perhaps easy to imagine the incident as nothing more than two officers deriving amusement out of scaring the bejeesus out of a frightened prisoner. Yet from Wickenheiser's point of view, the ride was frightening—especially given that, in those days, he was only just becoming aware of U.S. support for death squads abroad.

"I realize now that they (the officers' remarks) were only psychological tactics," said Wickenheiser. "But I'm also aware of how psychological tactics have escalated in places like Argentina, Guatemala and El Salvador, and at the time it was pretty terrifying."

Perhaps helping to fuel Wickenheiser's fears were revelations, then coming out, about the extent of the Gerard spy scandal, a domestic surveillance operation which gathered data on hundreds of Bay Area activists groups and their members. One of the central figures in the controversy was Tom Gerard, a San Francisco police officer with a shadowy CIA past. After disclosures about the operation appeared in the *Examiner*, Gerard was denounced by the SFPD command staff as a "rogue officer" acting on his own, a notion which the corporate-owned media accepted without question.

One of the more delightfully titillating aspects of the case were disclosures concerning the contents of Gerard's locker, opened by investigators after the "rogue officer" had departed the city and surfaced in the Philippines. Reportedly among the contents were a black hood with draw strings, as well as photographs of blindfolded men under interrogation, presumably made during Gerard's alleged CIA work in Central America.

While Wickenheiser and others were fearful for their safety, it was ultimately Greg Price and Catherine Marsh who sought help from the courts, however. Now, expecting the courts to offer protection from the police was probably a naive hope to begin with. Add to that the element of amateurish subterfuge surrounding the plot from the start, and it was clear the initiative had little hope of succeeding. Yet what Marsh and Price hadn't reckoned upon was how truly close criminal charges came to being filed—not against Lindo and Johnson, but against themselves.

On February 2, 1994 Marsh and Price filed for separate stay-away orders, naming their alleged tormentors—Lindo in Price's case, and Johnson in that of Marsh's—yet significantly, in both cases, omitting to mention the two men were police officers. "Defendant (Lindo) has repeatedly threatened the life of plaintiff, causing plaintiff to alter daily activities to avoid contact with defendant," Price alleged in his handwritten complaint. Cited was an incident in which Lindo had allegedly attempted to run down Price with a car. Here again, however, Price's claims, as in the matter regarding Lindo's grandmother, were, perhaps, a bit dubious and open to subjective interpretation.

Other FNB members remembered the incident concerning the car—actually a police car—as being a case of Price's having attempted to block Lindo's way. "There was an incident where Greg was blocking something—or he was standing there—and LeRoy just muscled on through in his car and knocked into him," recalls Vincent Giacomini. Obviously the brush-by with the auto had not been an attempt by Lindo to murder Price—and indeed the complaint fell short of making that charge. Yet the court, ignorant of Lindo's employment as a police officer, granted the injunction.

Marsh, too, filed a complaint without mentioning that the defendant in her case—Johnson—was a police officer. Marsh, too, like Price, was granted her stay-away request.

For Catherine, the way was fraught with trepidation and uncertainty, perhaps even more so than had been the case with Price. In Catherine's case, the current court action not only risked an angry backlash from Johnson, but also condemnation from within her own peer group.

According to Giacomini, there were those within FNB who urged Marsh not to file for the court order, fearing such an action would be viewed as racist. "So many people called up Catherine and told her at the time, 'Don't file this complaint against this guy. Don't think of suing this guy or getting a restraining order against him. You're being divisive.'" recalled Giacomini.

"They felt simply because this guy was a black officer and she was this white woman, that she was being racist or causing divisiveness between these two groups (African Americans and FNB) by bringing this complaint forward—even if it was real," he added.

In the end, Marsh went forward with the complaint, yet, recognizing the political reality of the unlikelihood of the court sustaining any kind of action against a police officer, she, like Price, omitted that small detail.

The complaint alleged,

> He (Johnson) was staring at me and making faces. He asked me several times to smile at him regardless of my requests for him to stop. He proceeded to say, "Catherine, if you were my woman you'd have nothing to worry about." He asked if I'd ever go out with him... He stared at me for at least 10-15 minutes, even after I asked him to stop. This is an ongoing thing and I'm extremely upset. I wish he would just stop it and leave me alone. [52]

As would perhaps be expected, the efforts by Price and Marsh to gain the safety and protection of the courts blew up in their faces. Under California law, victims of harassment are allowed to seek a restraining order if: a) the defendant's conduct is *intentional,* b) the defendant has committed a *series of acts* alarming, annoying or harassing plaintiff, c) the plaintiff has suffered emotional distress, and, d) the defendant's conduct has "no legitimate reason and is not protected by the constitution."

Despite these provisions, the law never worked to the favor of the two young FNB members. Louise Renne's office filed a declaration by Lindo stating he and Johnson had had no contact, other than through their duties as police officers, with Price and Marsh. At this point Superior Court Judge Raymond J. Arata acted swiftly to protect not Marsh and Price, but the city. Not only did Arata dissolve the restraining orders, but the judge also threatened Marsh and Price with prosecution for "obtaining an injunction under false pretenses and abusing the lawful processes of the San Francisco Superior Court." [53]

In leaving the two young petitioners exposed to the not-so-tender mercies of the police, was Arata merely ignorant of the illegal tactics used by law enforcement agencies to suppress dissident groups in this country in the past? Or did he simply not care? Not only were Catherine and Greg cut loose to fend for themselves, but ultimately they were left facing the prospect of jail. So serious was the judge's threat of prosecution that Cunningham was forced to come into court and plead on Marsh's and Price's behalf.

***

Ultimately, however, it was McHenry—not Marsh and Price—who the city wanted behind bars and out of commission.

On January 4, 1994—just two days before Jordan's interview on the Peter B. Collins show on KSFO (covered in Chapter 4)—Keith was arrested and charged with assaulting and robbing Nick Roomel, film commissioner for the City of San Francisco and a close Jordan ally. Bail was set at $10,000. Roomel claimed McHenry had struck him in the back of the neck in a deserted corridor in City Hall, spat in his face, and stolen his phone pager. For Keith it was the first of two City Hall arrests on serious felony charges that would leave him jeopardized under California's new "three strikes" law.

According to Keith, an assault did indeed take place in City Hall on the day in question, but in the latter's version it was Roomel who had assaulted *him* (McHenry)—not the other way around. Further, stated Keith, he had spotted Roomel on the mayor's balcony, in the company of a San Francisco police officer—the very officer who would later make the arrest—only minutes before the incident. "It was a set up, pure and simple," Keith was quoted in an *SF Weekly* article which appeared a week after the incident.

Embarrassingly for the prosecution, the *Weekly* story was accompanied by a photo of Roomel dressed in drag. The caption under the photo read: "FRANK'S EMPRESS: Film Commissioner Nick Roomel may look like a pussycat in this glamorous photo op, but Food Not Bombs activist Keith McHenry accuses the mayoral appointee/sometime drag queen of roughing him up." [54] In the photo Roomel can be seen wearing a blonde wig, hoop earrings and a dress.

Further damaging to the prosecution were the story's allegations that Roomel had "stalked" McHenry for months prior to the incident. "A Frank Jordan loyalist's crusade against Food Not Bombs leader Keith McHenry erupted into a one punch attack at City Hall last week. The question: Did Film commissioner Nick Roomel slug one of the mayor's chief antagonists, or did McHenry punch the man who was stalking him?" the story asked. [55] And later on:

> Roomel admitted he has spent months gathering information on McHenry out of disgust at his do-good reputation. "When Keith McHenry presented himself as a saviour of the homeless, I just wanted to expose that issue," he said. "He's nothing more than a politician who serves food to demonstrate against the system." [56]

Roomel, who described Jordan as "a wonderful, wonderful man," claimed to have been compiling a "fact sheet" on McHenry for the mayor's administration, however, Jordan spokesman Noah Griffin "tried to distance himself" from the film commissioner, saying, "No one in the Jordan administration asked Roomel to do anything." [57]

How strong, then, was the prosecution's case against Keith, given that Roomel was not likely to make the most sympathetic of victims? Would the D.A.'s office need more artillery than the alleged City Hall assault/robbery to put Keith in prison?

In seeking a solution to this problem, the police blundered, coming up with some charges so laughable they would ultimately prove more embarrassing to the city than any kind of threat to Keith. On May 10 Keith was arrested on charges of receiving and concealing stolen property. The property in question: approximately four plastic milk crates which some FNB members had used for the purpose of carrying around food and literature. The charges were ludicrous, and as news of the arrest got out, an embarrassed D.A.'s office quickly stepped in.

"The district attorneys found out about it, realized they were stupid charges, and released him," said attorney Mary Stearns, who was now working with Dennis Cunningham in representing Keith.

Happily, the milk crate charge didn't keep Keith behind bars more than 24 hours. While he was in, however, he *did* manage to make a phone call out—to Jo and I—at which time we put him on the air live to tell the story of the great milk crate caper.

***

The biggest change at San Francisco Liberation Radio at this time was that we had just recently gone from mobile, to fixed-location, broadcasting. It was different and more risky from anything we had done in the past. The radio station was now in our apartment—rooted there permanently like a thousand year old redwood.

It had taken Jo and I a long time to reach an agreement to make this step. The wind storms through which I had struggled back in February had been the deciding factor for me. The FCC already knows who I am, I had thought. They know where I live. What am I doing out here fighting the elements? But Jo had resisted a move to the apartment. What if the government should raid our home and take everything we owned? That was always a possibility, I had replied. Community support was in our favor. Yet we had talked about it and argued for two months. In the end, I had prevailed.

In coming down off Twin Peaks we were sacrificing a lot. The reduction in antenna height meant a drastically reduced signal coverage area. What we were getting in return, however, was the ability to be on the air a steady seven nights a week: regular hours our listeners could count on. We hoped, despite the reduction in signal area, that the expanded hours coupled with schedule regularity would mean, ultimately, more listeners for us, not less.

So that was the state of affairs when Keith called us from jail on May 10 and informed us he had been arrested for felony possession of stolen milk crates. He also informed us that while handcuffed to a bench at Northern Station he had been threatened with death by a San Francisco police captain. All of this went out live over the air.

Prisoners doing interviews live from jail—as far as I know it was another first for San Francisco radio. Yet how many people could hear us? Without the height advantage of Twin Peaks, our signal could no longer reach the vast majority of the east side of San Francisco, much less the East Bay. Twin Peaks in fact had now become our enemy rather than our friend, bottling up our signal and confining it to a relatively small pocket of territory out on the west side—while the majority of San Francisco's population lay to the east. In terms of land mass, we estimated we were now reaching perhaps only a third to a half of the total geographical area of the city.

Despite these concerns, we gritted our teeth and simply did what we had to do. Actually, from our standpoint, the task was easy. All we had to do was put Keith on the air. He did the rest. The ability he has to speak to people was precisely, to our way of thinking, what the city feared most about him. That was why they were so intent on stopping him. That evening—live—our new audience in western San Francisco got an earful as Keith's account of the day's events poured forth eloquently.

The police captain who had threatened him that that day, had also threatened him on a previous occasion.

"He threatened to kill me again today," said Keith that night. "He tried to whisper, or speak quietly, and he came over to me and said, 'This is now more than just fun and games. This is serious. I'm going to follow you around and when you least expect it, I'm going to off you.'"

For Keith, such threats of violence were not new. For the listeners who heard us that night, however, it was assuredly *not* the usual fare for talk radio—either for the west side of San Francisco, the east, or anywhere else.

***

Keith was cut loose from the slammer later that night. Had his swift release been solely the result of the efforts made by attorneys Cunningham and Stearns? Or had our broadcast had something to do with it as well? Given that city officials seemed to be sticking to an unstated policy of never publicly commenting on pirate radio broadcasts—and given, too, that the major media also seemed to have a policy of ignoring us—it was impossible to say what impact, if any, we had had on the whole affair.

Yet the FNB meal servings were continuing in Civic Center, and these clearly *were* having an impact.

One tactic which had been developed by FNB servers by now as a means of evading arrest was the practice of "fountain hopping." The Civic Center Plaza fountain, which had remained bone dry throughout the Agnos years, had been suddenly filled with water under the beautifying hand of the new mayor. Now, consequently, when the police showed up to make arrests, the servers simply jumped into the fountain and waded out to the center—out of reach of the officers, who, in lieu of getting their uniforms wet, were reduced to threatening and cajoling from the sidelines. Eventually the cops would tire of the effort and simply leave—at which time the server would hop out of the fountain and head, lickety-split, for the hills, eluding the police and avoiding a night in jail.

One of the more congenial aspects of fountain hopping was that it never placed too severe a disruption on the serving of food. How appetizing it may have been for homeless people to be served a lukewarm cup of soup from a bucket held by a server standing waist deep in cold water, was another matter. Yet the serving nonetheless did go on. Despite the conditions, people were still willing to take the food. Police attempts at interference were usually thwarted by simple strategic re-locations: when the police approached too close, the serving line simply shifted to another point along the periphery of the fountain. The homeless people who wanted the food seemed to readily adapt.

In what must surely have been a humiliating experience for Lindo, the African American officer, enduring shouts of "lackey" from the crowd, waded into the fountain to make an arrest. "His boss ordered him to get in," said Vincent Giacomini, who was one of the two people in the fountain that day. "Tristan (Anderson) and I—we went underneath where the water was coming down from the fountain, in the middle of the pool. LeRoy...had to come out in the middle and get soaking wet...

"He was going to put his waders on, and he kind of realized that that was going to weigh him down. I was alright getting out. He (Lindo) was a little bit rough with Tristan. He really managed to choke Tristan quite a bit and hold him under the water for an extra long period of time," Giacomini said.

The police had apparently been particularly intent on making an arrest that day, and the wade-in to the fountain by Lindo had evidently come only as a last resort. According to Giacomini, the officers had earlier summoned a Fire Department hook and ladder truck to the scene. However, city firefighters "took one look at the situation" and then left, leaving the Special Operations squad to cope with the fountain extraction on its own.

***

On May 13, a second City Hall incident took place resulting in Keith's arrest on felony charges. Stemming from the breaking of a window in the office of conservative City Supervisor Barbara Kaufman, the charges were serious enough that they had many in FNB, including the group's lawyers, contemplating the prospect of Keith being packed off to San Quentin Prison for a long period of time.

It had been the delivery of an $800 bill which had brought Keith to the offices of Kaufman and other members of the Board of Supervisors that day. Presentation of the bill had been nothing more than political theater. No one, least of all Keith, expected the Board of Supervisors to appropriate money to reimburse FNB for anything.

The bill was to cover repairs to Keith's truck, which had been vandalized—while in police custody—after the milk crate arrest a few days earlier. After charging Keith in the milk crate caper, the police had towed his truck. Upon his release from jail late that night—following the interview on SFLR—McHenry had gone over to the City Tow garage on Mission Street to retrieve his vehicle. Upon securing release of his truck, he discovered that someone had damaged the steering column, inserting an object, possibly a screw driver, into the small gap left by moving the turn signal lever either up or down. As a result of the jamming, the wiring inside the column was all haywire, leaving the truck's electrical system disabled. The cost of repairs, combined with towing charges, had come to $800.

Accompanying Keith into City Hall that day had been Jess Mejia (father of Hugh). Jess Mejia was a 71-year-old veteran of World War II and a long-standing friend of Keith's. The pair delivered the repair bills to each member of the Board of Supervisors' offices without incident. However, upon arriving at conservative member Kaufman's office, the day's calm was shattered.

As in the Roomel case, what happened depends on whose version you believe. Kaufman was not present at the time. However, her legislative aide

Nancy Kitz, reported Keith had verbally abused her (Kitz) and punched his fist through a glass panel in the door. Keith's version, substantiated by Mejia, had Kitz screaming "Get out!" and attempting to slam the door on Mejia. The window had broken when Keith had stuck out his hand to protect the older man. In both versions, the broken glass resulted in profuse bleeding from Keith's hand.

Unlike in the Roomel case, the prosecution had an eyewitness other than the principle parties involved. The eyewitness was Randy Riddle, an employee of the City Attorney's Office (the same Randy Riddle who had, along with George Riley, represented the city in court actions against FNB). Riddle claimed to have seen Keith drive his fist through the window and then walk away with blood dripping from his hand.

The arresting officer was John Nevin, an SFPD officer who also served as Frank Jordan's bodyguard. Nevin coincidentally had also been the arresting officer in the Roomel case, and was — again coincidentally — spotted on the mayor's balcony — in the company of Roomel — just minutes prior to the January 4 altercation between Roomel and McHenry, according to Keith.

Nevin's arrest report on the Kitz incident gave Riddle to say Keith had smacked his fist through the window "in a manner consistent of a boxer throwing a punch." Nevin's report also had Keith, during the course of the incident, "violently swearing" at Kitz, "Your (sic) the lowest Mother-Fucker (sic) piece of shit, what are you doing here." Keith, in Nevins' narrative, was also alleged to have demanded "I want to be reimbursed $800." Nevin further stated, "The impact of the punch shattered 3/4 of the glass door right onto Kitz's shirt and narrowly missed her facial area." [58]

Nevin charged Keith with threatening a public employee, aggravated assault, and trespassing. The mayoral bodyguard also tacked on a charge of resisting arrest, even though his own written narrative of events described Keith as having been taken into custody "without incident" after officers followed a "trail of blood" from City Hall to Opera Plaza.

Jess Mejia, described in Nevin's report as "an unidentified WM (white male) Hispanic type," was not arrested.

Once again events at City Hall had people wondering openly if Keith were being framed—while others considered the possibility that the "leader" of FNB had finally begun to "crack" after all the years of getting arrested. Who was telling the truth? Keith or Kaufman's aid, Kitz? Keith or Roomel? How badly did city officials hate Keith McHenry and want to be rid of him? To what lengths would they go? And to what extent would they have the cooperation of the judiciary?

An answer to the last question can perhaps be gleaned from a decision by Judge Jerome Benson to quash a defense subpoena for Jordan to testify in the Roomel case. Jordan had not been a witness to the confrontation between Roomel and McHenry, and, indeed, at a hearing on February 1, Deputy City Attorney Loretta Giorgi professed her office to be "perplexed" as to why the mayor had been called. However, defense attorney Mary Stearns cited Jordan's interview on KSFO in which the mayor had claimed to know "exactly" what had transpired between McHenry and Roomel.

> In essence, your Honor, I believe the evidence will show that the mayor intensely dislikes my client, that he has a political vendetta against my client, that this has been a long standing political vendetta, and that this dislike had been conveyed to the victim in this case, who works for Mayor Jordan, and that this dislike has been conveyed to the arresting officer, who was his driver, and, I'm not sure, bodyguard, but an officer which works closely with Mayor Jordan.
>
> I believe that the evidence will show that the victim in this case handed out a letter, handed out by Mayor Jordan at a Board of Supervisors' meeting, that discredited my client. And I think the political vendetta that Mayor Jordan has against my client is completely connected to the allegations in this case made by Mr. Roomel. [59]

Mary Stearns, only a young attorney at the time, had made a great presentation. Deputy City Attorney Giorgi, by way of response, however, didn't find the reasons outlined by Stearns to be "compelling enough to have the mayor leave his very busy schedule" to come to court and testify. Judge Benson agreed and quashed the subpoena. Jordan, who, either as police chief or mayor, had presided over more than 800 FNB arrests (the figure would eventually rise to over a thousand), never had to appear in court—either in that or any other FNB case.

***

Out on the streets, the racial animosities that seemingly were being deliberately sowed, came at last to a head in the form of a guttural racial epithet hurled at Lindo after the latter had confiscated a bucket of soup during an arrest incident in March. Events leading up to the incident had included a violent arrest of FNB member Jennifer Baker by Lindo on March 1 in Civic Center Plaza. This incident, too, was videotaped.

On the tape Lindo implores Baker to cooperate in her arrest, however, the young woman's body goes limp to the ground each time Lindo initiates the arrest procedure, frustrating the officer. In the early phases of the tango which ensues, Baker is sent sprawling into a homeless person's shopping cart. Subsequently she ends up rolling on the ground as Lindo, first alone and then aided by another officer, wrestles her furiously, finding the limpness of her body coupled with her prone position and her passive resistance, difficult to overcome.

At last the two officers get the cuffs on and "secure" their prisoner, however, by the time it's over Lindo's manhandling of Baker has rivaled in roughness his arrest of Grace a few months earlier. The difference is that in the Baker arrest, which, as the videotape reveals, is replete with a lot of physical groping, the black man/white woman template has again been in evidence.

How big a part, if any, this played in the racial tension which followed, is difficult really to say. But at any rate, when, on a subsequent day, Lindo returned to Civic Center Plaza and resumed arresting and harassing people, the word "nigger" flew out of the mouth of one of the food servers, and once the racial epithet had taken flight, it was too late to recapture it. The damage was done.

"If it was a plan to make FNB look racist, I was a dupe, and it worked," commented the server who had uttered the slur and who asked to remain unidentified.

The invective was overheard by dozens, if not hundreds of witnesses. Stating that he had "snapped," the server admitted, "This was calamitous. It was on a day when East Bay FNB (the East Bay chapter of Food Not Bombs) was over and they had signs and street theater and were being nice demonstrators. I don't think they were aware how tense and burnt San Francisco Food Not Bombs was, or the recent events. Lindo did this (confiscated a bucket of soup) and I called him that, and all of a sudden all the East Bay folks, especially two big guys, were pushing me and yelling 'racist!' 'get out of here!' and Lindo was laughing. It was awful."

While the incident was never reported in the media, news of it did, nonetheless, travel through the black community.

"I heard in the next few days that _____ (a prominent African American activist) was saying 'Food Not Bombs is racist' and I got kind of freaked. I totally realized what I had done reflected on the group. So I called _____ and talked to him and told him that it was totally my action...and that, of course, Food Not Bombs wasn't racist. He hardly said a word and I am still pained about it," the server said.

Apologies were even made to Lindo.

"I did apologize over and over again to Lindo, who simply smiled at me and said things like, 'You have a lot of work to do' and 'See how you are?'...Lindo was not about to let me off the hook," said the server, adding, "I left Food Not Bombs a depressed wreck in April of '94."

***

The broken-window arrest, occurring as it did on May 13, came while Keith was still free on bail in the Roomel case. If he was in hot water before, the temperature was approaching the boiling point now. On May 20 the District Attorney's Office requested that Keith's bail be increased to $250,000, from its then-present level of $10,000.

"The witnesses and victim in the defendant's new case fear for their safety (and) believe that the defendant is a dangerous individual," asserted Assistant D.A. James Chou. "The defendant has demonstrated through his subsequent actions that he is a threat to public safety."

Chou cited Keith's "escalating violence" in calling for the increased bail.

Judge Alfred Chiantelli did not give the D.A.'s office everything it asked for, but *did*, nonetheless, place a substantial price on Keith's head: $75,000.

Defense attorney Stearns commented for San Francisco Liberation Radio afterward, "Seventy five thousand dollars in bail for this kind of offense is very unusual—breaking a window in a situation like that never gets a $75,000 bail."

Dennis Cunningham also commented, "The city political machine has succeeded in silencing this man. They've been able to create a situation of pressure and confrontation that has gone so far as to persuade a man who is basically a reasonable judge and an honest judge that there's a problem here which I don't think really exists."

Madeline Muir, longtime friend of Keith and Andrea, was less charitable to Chiantelli in her remarks than Cunningham, saying, "To hear the judge say he (Keith) was a threat—for giving food to the homeless—he (Chiantelli) just didn't want to hear the facts. He was just a closed man."

With bail set at $75,000 it was beginning to look like Keith was going to be stuck in jail for a long time. This proved not to be the case, however, for suddenly Berkeley night club owner David Nadel came forward and put his club, The Ashkenaz Music and Dance Cafe, up as collateral on Keith's bond. [60]

With Keith now free to help organize in his own defense, what emerged was a massive public letter writing campaign targeting the D.A.'s office with demands to drop the charges.

At San Francisco Liberation Radio we put together a 30 minute program entitled "Special Report on the Jailing of Keith McHenry." Included on the program, in addition to the comments by Muir and Keith's two attorneys, were sound bites from Father Louis Vitale, Sister Bernie Galvin and the Rev. Phil Lawson—prominent members of Religious Witness with Homeless People—all denouncing the Matrix program.

We also included a segment from author and syndicated columnist Norman Solomon. Addressing a rally in San Francisco organized in Keith's support, Solomon, a co-founder of the media watchdog group FAIR, said, "Recently I spoke with Keith McHenry and he told me about one of the times he was in jail in this city. He'd been arrested for serving food to hungry people, and a person in the next cell had been arrested for stealing food from a supermarket. And that says a lot about the situation that we're in today."

The request for a bombardment of letters to the D.A. was made not only at the public rallies held in Keith's support, but also over our airwaves. People were requested to send copies of their letters to FNB. More than 100 letters were received. Petitions were circulated gathering even more names. Many of the letter writers spoke of Keith's dedication to non-violence. Some compared him to Gandhi. Others drew religious parallels, speaking of Christ's compassion for the poor. One letter writer prefaced his missive with a quote from Psalms:

> The wicked in his pride doth persecute the poor: let them be taken in the devices that they have imagined.
> For the wicked boasteth of his heart's desire, and blesseth the covetous, whom the Lord abhorreth. [61]

So who—or what—was Keith? Was he a "threat to public safety," as the assistant D.A. had branded him in court? Or was he a man whose life had in some ways emulated that of Christ's?

Perhaps biblical imagery was not far from the mind of author Alexander Cockburn, either. In his column "Beat the Devil," Cockburn took up Keith's cause in *The Nation*, writing in the magazine's July 4 issue,

So here in a supposedly enlightened city we have the
late-twentieth-century spectacle of a man facing life
behind bars for giving food to the down and out...It's
difficult to imagine McHenry may end up with hard time
for trying to feed people. But then it's difficult to accept
that the way many cities and states are confronting social
misery is to criminalize poverty. Close down public
assistance, close down welfare, close your eyes and hope
the homeless, the single mothers, the down and out will
disappear. Jail them and maybe sterilize them. America is
a society hot for final solutions. [62]

The column appeared under the headline, "Beat the Devil. Cut out his
heart in San Francisco."

Many of the letters defending Keith were read aloud over San
Francisco Liberation Radio, though again, how much of an impact we had on
the situation would be difficult to gage, for the police, the mayor and other
city officials continued to pointedly ignore our presence on the airwaves.
Ignoring us, at least, was preferable to coming to our house and raiding us.

There *were* those, however, who were *not* ignoring events in San
Francisco. That late summer/early fall both Amnesty International and the
UN Human Rights Commission took an interest in the FNB case.

"Amnesty International is concerned that the Food Not Bombs
activists may have been targeted on account of their beliefs and effectively
prohibited from exercising their right to freedom of expression, assembly,
and the right to impart information," Amnesty announced on Oct 28. "If this
were found to be the case, the city of San Francisco would be in breach of
international law and Amnesty International would adopt those imprisoned
as 'Prisoners of Conscience' and would work for their unconditional
release."

The announcement was made from Amnesty's London office. But in
addition to ignoring San Francisco Liberation Radio, local officials also took
no heed of Amnesty International. The organization never received a single
reply to any of its letters to District Attorney Arlo Smith, Mayor Frank
Jordan, or California Governor Pete Wilson.

At around the same time, Karen Parker, a San Francisco attorney
specializing in international human rights and armed conflict law, took the
case of Food Not Bombs before the UN Human Rights Commission in
Geneva, Switzerland. In her specialty of the law, Parker had argued cases
before the Organization of American States and the International Court of
Justice. Her credentials were about as impressive as you can get. Yet the

major media virtually ignored the story of her trip to Geneva on behalf of FNB.

In an interview which aired over SFLR, Parker told me, "This is an issue that strikes at the core of international human rights law—people have a right to food. They have a right to shelter. It's not discretionary. It's not 'when we get around to it.' It's not 'you have a right to see if you can get charity to be interested in you.' It's 'you have a binding international law right, that is applicable in the United States, to shelter and food.'"

Parker, who won one of the first human rights judgements against the U.S. in any international forum—in a case involving the U.S. bombing of a mental hospital in Grenada—read for our microphones the verbatim text of her speech in Geneva. Here is an excerpt.

> Food Not Bombs has established programs in many U.S. cities to feed the homeless and the poor and to distribute literature on food, housing, peace and social justice issues. The group in San Francisco alone has suffered hundreds of arrests. Now the local mayor, Frank Jordan, has unleashed a personal vendetta against both the homeless and Food Not Bombs. Jesuit brothers, the pastor of St. Boniface Church, and 72-year old Rev. Patrick Leehan, join the hundreds arrested.

Parker's speech also cited the jailing of Keith McHenry, who "clearly is subject to personal persecution with a mayoral zeal rarely seen," and closed with a quote from Cockburn's July 4 column in *The Nation*—the quote ending with the words, "America is a society hot for final solutions."

During our interview I commented to Parker, "I sometimes wonder how officials in other countries such as India or Ethiopia—places where there's famine and hunger on a large scale—would view, if they knew about it, what's happening in San Francisco. Of course, the routine procedure for San Francisco police when arresting Food Not Bombs is to arrest the food server and then *dump out the food*. How do you think a mayor, say, or a government official in India, or Somalia, or Ethiopia would view an act like that?" Parker responded:

> Well one of the reasons I made the public statement is so I could legitimately talk to members of the subcommission and governments without disclosing any information that I might have been privy to, and one of the people I talked to is the Ethiopian member of the

> subcommission, who of course is totally appalled—not only by the audacity of destroying food and lives...but also the audacity of thinking one can completely ignore human rights law.
>
> The Ethiopian member of the subcommission has been there just about as long as I have, and is there because he, like myself, I believe, is committed to international law and human rights. Regardless of the different regimes (in Ethiopia) that have nominated him, he comes there and he has a concern, a legitimate concern, for human rights, is able to discuss it in a scholarly way. On occasion we differ on interpretation, but this is a human rights person who comes with a background and knowledge of international and human rights law and talks about it as law—not like, say, the American member, who only talks Reaganomics. I can tell you personally that that delegate is simply shocked.

It's significant to note that before appealing to the international community, FNB had made entreaties to the U.S. Justice Department, asking for intervention in San Francisco. These entreaties had begun as early as 1992. In April of 1995, Deval L. Patrick, Assistant Attorney General of the Civil Rights Division of the Clinton Justice Department, informed Keith in a letter,

> We have previously reviewed a videotape forwarded to this office regarding this matter, and we concluded that no prosecutable violation of federal criminal civil rights statutes was disclosed. In subsequent telephone calls to this section, you were informed by paralegal specialist Moira Dawson that you were welcome to submit any videotape or letter which might provide more information regarding these allegations. We have since received and reviewed several letters concerning this matter. However, the information contained therein did not provide any details which would alter our original decision. This latest correspondence similarly does not contain any new information. Accordingly, we are unable to assist you.

Bill Clinton, apparently, was too busy at the time signing the Crime Bill into law—placing 100,000 more police on the streets of America—than to bother attempting to curb criminal, unconstitutional acts committed by the police themselves.

Concern about international law was also voiced by local academics. In a September 30, 1993 letter to Jordan, James W. Syfers, Director of the Center for Advancement of the Covenant, School of Humanities, San Francisco State University, wrote, "I respectfully call your attention to the fact that the City and County of San Francisco is failing to enforce international law."

Citing Article 25 of the *Universal Declaration of Human Rights,* Syfers commented that the "programmatic use of...police power...to harass and arrest the homeless and those trying to provide them with food is profoundly contrary to the human rights law that had its origins in our city and that is now endorsed by the majority of nations on earth."

At San Francisco Liberation Radio we aired in October a one hour special we had put together entitled, "Food Not Bombs Appeals to the UN" In producing the program, we solicited reactions from both the offices of the mayor and the district attorney regarding the fact that the United Nations was now investigating the City of San Francisco for human rights violations. Mayor Jordan's office never returned our phone calls, while Assistant District Attorney Terry Jackson came on the line just long enough to issue a brief "no comment."

The one-hour UN program was immediately followed by two half hour specials, one focusing on Amnesty International's having gotten involved in the case and featuring a telephone interview with Mandy Bath of Amnesty's London office. The second was entitled "Four Authors Speak Out" and reported on an October 28 press conference at which FNB had gathered together writers Norman Solomon, Howard Zinn, Ron Kovic and Starhawk to denounce the Matrix program and call for an end to the arrests of FNB. Predictably the press conference was given no coverage by the major media. This was despite the fact that a TV news crew happened by during the course of it. The event was held on a weekday morning in Civic Center Plaza.

"You better come over here and do a story on all these famous authors over here!" Keith bellowed out to the TV crew, which had just then emerged from City Hall after covering an event of the mayor's.

Though apparently annoyed at having been so unceremoniously hailed, the TV reporter nonetheless strolled over, stood around and observed for about ten minutes before leaving. Yet no mention of the press conference made the news. Despite the fact that Solomon was a syndicated columnist with over a million readers—despite Zinn's highly acclaimed text, *A People's History of the United States*—despite Kovic's having been the subject of the film, *Born on the Fourth of July*—despite the fact that Starhawk had developed quite a readership with the publication of her novel, *The Fifth Sacred Thing*—none of their comments in support of FNB were deemed newsworthy that day. Three hours after the press conference, Keith was arrested again on a new felony charge—conspiracy. Two other members of FNB were also taken into custody and similarly charged.

We talked about those arrests later. It was almost as if the cops were thumbing their noses at us and saying, "Go ahead and have your press conference. See if we care."

Yet there were indications that the D.A.'s office was finally weakening under the combined weight of international scrutiny and community protest. In November there began to circulate rumors of a deal being discussed between Cunningham and Stearns on the one hand, and the D.A.'s Office on the other. Finally in February a settlement was announced: Keith would accept a 12 month term of probation in return for a "no contest" plea. The whole thing had wound its way to a jagged edge.

The protests, the community organizing, the broadcasts of San Francisco Liberation Radio, the letter writing campaign, and the international attention—all certainly played a role in weakening the D.A.'s resolve to go through with the case.

Also taking the wind out of the prosecutor's sails, no doubt, was a new revelation about Nick Roomel. This came on August 3, once again in the *SF Weekly*.

"Bizarre court record of Keith McHenry's accuser," read the paper's headline.

The report outlined several instances in which Roomel had made questionable claims in court appearances, in other unrelated cases, dating back to the early 1980s.

One of these was a 1989 probate case in which Roomel allegedly produced a phony will, purported to be that of his mother, whose estate was valued at "several hundred thousand dollars," according to the *Weekly*. The case, involving a dispute between Roomel and a 10-year-old cousin, had resulted in Roomel accepting a "token settlement" of $2,500 after he had undergone a "withering" cross examination said to have left his credibility at "zero," the newspaper reported. [63]

Also demoralizing to the authorities had to be the rise of Radio Libre. San Francisco Liberation Radio was at this time no longer the only micro station in town. Now there were two of us. What we at SFLR were doing west of Twin Peaks, Radio Libre, which also had FNB members among its programmers, was doing in the east. There were now very few places you could go in San Francisco without hearing one or the other of the two stations—although what greatly reduced our effectiveness was that neither of us had begun to broadcast a full 24 hours a day. Both stations were mainly on during the night time hours, and Radio Libre was constantly plagued by a hum in its signal. Even so, having two stations on the air was bound to be better than one—and was also, perhaps, useful as a psychological tool of our own.

As part of the terms of his probation, Keith's attorneys had insisted that nothing short of an arrest on a violent crime would be considered grounds for revoking the probation. Specifically spelled out as being insufficient grounds for sending him to prison would be any and all future food serving arrests. Anxious to put an end to the whole affair, the D.A.'s office agreed to these terms. It was over.

Yet the question still remains, how much of what the city had done, over the past six years and more than 800 arrests, had been a real, true-to-life "COINTELPRO" campaign intended to split FNB and destroy the organization? Could the city credibly claim, as it does to this day, that no such attempt was ever afoot? Had the city spent millions of dollars hauling people to jail and defending itself in court solely out of concern that homeless people might get sick eating FNB's food? Or had it devoted all that time, energy and money in an effort to smash an organization that was attempting to bring homeless people together, uniting them to demand their civil rights?

Insight into this can be gleaned through several internal police memos, obtained by FNB through court discovery motions, including a September 27, 1988 memo from Captain Richard Holder to Deputy Chief Frank Reed. In the memo Holder acknowledges conducting an investigation, "as per your request," into FNB, commenting, "During my investigation I was able to obtain the private phone number of 'Food Not Bombs' organizer Keith McHenry, who, unknowingly was a great asset to this investigation." What did Holder mean when he said Keith had been an unknowing asset to his investigation? Had Holder placed a tap on Keith's phone?

Another insight can perhaps be offered by Andrew Rose.

"It was very unnerving for me," said Rose, "to be told by Lindo that 'these (homeless) people don't care if you help them' and 'why don't you get a job, you've got a college degree'? I should have let this pass but it started to affect me. Lindo was very effective at dividing me against FNB and especially at minimizing Keith and implying we were fools for 'following Keith'—which caused me to question a lot of things."

Rose added: "It was very hard ball psych ops at the time."

The multiple felony prosecution of Keith McHenry was over. With the help of protests in the community, micro radio, and international outreach, Keith had been saved from going to prison.

The FNB lawsuits against the city of San Francisco remained active up until 1995. All but one were thrown out of court before ever reaching a jury. The one case which *did* go before a jury was a 1995 case which ended up being stripped down to its barest essentials. The nearly 1000 arrests; evidence of a city-wide conspiracy against FNB; internal police memos documenting police surveillance against the group, including a possible wiretap on Keith's phone—all were suppressed at the trial. Lacking this essential information, necessary for even a fundamental understanding of the case, the jury found in favor of the police.

Yet we had come away with one victory. We now had our own radio station. In 1995 the voters of San Francisco dumped Jordan after we aired a program entitled: "Frank Jordan and the Politics of Persecution." I mention that not to make the claim that SFLR was responsible for Jordan's political demise—by 1995 many people were against Frank Jordan for many different reasons. I only mention it to show that now, added to the voices of many others, we had one of our own as well. Jordan's successor, Willie Brown, ended the arrests of FNB when he took office in early 1996. However, in late 1999, while Brown was in a hot contest for re-election, the arrests started up again for a short time. This resumption of all the unpleasantness of earlier years prompted Sister Bernie Galvin, of Religious Witness with Homeless People, to launch a hunger strike that lasted 19 days.

The resumption of the arrests of FNB, as well as Sister Bernie's hunger strike, were reported loudly over SFLR. The arrests quickly ceased.

As for the 1995 trial—the one and only FNB civil case that ever went before a jury--had San Francisco City Attorney Louise Renne "bungled" *that* case as she has been alleged to have done in matters regarding PG&E, it's quite likely that FNB would have won the $200,000 the suit had sought. And just as likely that money would have been spent feeding the poor or in some way helping to alleviate homelessness in San Francisco—a problem which, after an eight year period of arresting FNB, the city has still not adequately addressed.

A long time ago, back in 1989, FNB had circulated a questionnaire among homeless people. The form had been handed out at a meal serving in Civic Center Plaza during that summer's Tent City occupation of the plaza. On it were three questions. While the filling in of the questionnaire was only voluntary, more than 50 people responded. The reason FNB had gone to the trouble of such an exercise was that the city, as described earlier in this chapter, was seeking an injunction stopping FNB from further food distribution in San Francisco.

The responses of those who had answered the questionnaire were submitted to the court by attorney Sarge Holtzman, in arguments against the city's motion. As we know now, the injunction was ultimately granted, on July 21, by Judge Ralph Flageollet. The judge's decision was unfortunate, as a look back at some of the handwritten answers on these records now reveals.

The three questions on the forms were quite simple:

1. We need to know your name
2. How the Food Not Bombs effort helps you?
3. Why do you eat at Food Not Bombs instead of other free food programs?

"Food Not Bombs is interested in knowing if our food service has been any help to you and your food needs," the form stated. "We are going to need your comments for our defense against the court order this Friday at 10:00 at Department 9 City Hall."

A homeless person identifying himself only as "B.J.," responded to question number three, "It is close to camp so I can watch my stuff." Another man, Keith Truitt, wrote, "I have no friends here in S.F. My only friend, Leonard (last name illegible) died of AIDS last year." Truitt, who commented that he was not sleeping on the streets but rather living in a transient hotel in the Tenderloin, added, "I have no cooking facilities where I currently reside."

During the tent city, FNB had operated a 24-hour-a-day outdoor soup kitchen. The presence of the FNB facility, within the very boundaries of the encampment, was obviously a great source of comfort to many of the questionnaire respondents. In answer to question number three, Joseph Callahan wrote, "Being ill, I'm unable to go to the other food programs," while Cyndie Crenshaw remarked, "They serve good food and are always there." Crenshaw's remarks were echoed by Reginald Carnegie, who wrote, "Other programs are opened for a few hours a day, but Food Not Bombs is there 24 hours a day."

By being there "24-hours-a-day," FNB and the tent city organizers had obviously constructed, for many of these homeless people, a civil society that had previously been absent, essentially bringing "order out of chaos." This was, to some, perhaps, doubly ironic given the adherence to "anarchist principles" in the running of the tent city. This relief at being able to rein in out of the chaos of life on the streets was expressed by Raymond S.

Saunders, who answered question three with, "Because I really enjoy the outdoors food. Please let our people stay in your space," and by John M. Boyce, who wrote simply, "Because this is a hell of a lot better than all of the places I've been."

Kevin Moore wrote simply from the heart, "They care. Look at their efforts. Thank You Food Not Bombs," while another man, after leaving questions one and two blank, responded to question number three, "We need Food Not Bombs. Thank you. C.C. Kavanaugh."

Many of the responses were indicative of at least some degree of mental illness. In response to question number two, one man wrote, "Keeps me from stelling (sic)—selling drugs and dooing (sic) thangs (sic) against my will." Had San Francisco authorities not broken up the tent city, it would have been interesting, from a clinical point of view, to chart the above individual's progress, and to determine whether his mental state had either degenerated or improved after, say, an additional six months in the structured, "anarchistic" environment.

"I eat and don't thieve," wrote another man, while a third, in response to question number three, simply drew a smiling mouth (a mouth only—absent a nose, eyes or facial outline).

Despite the presence of mentally unstable, potentially violent individuals, the tent city was obviously regarded as a haven for the homeless women who responded to the questionnaire. Lisa Ann White wrote, "They bring hot food to me personally. I don't have to wait in a long line with a lot of rude men by myself. All the F.N.B. men are gentlemen." A homeless woman named "Star" commented, "It is much more convenient than walking into the T.L. (Tenderloin) and dealing with the bullshit there."

Perhaps what the authorities feared most about FNB was spelled out in one man's answer to question number two: "supplies food needs, educates me in regards as to what I can do about my homelessness, in a political sense, teaches me to organize with others, and take action by communicating (illegible) to find solutions to problems." Or, to put it another way, it came down to a simple question of loyalties, as one man, identifying himself as "Renegade," remarked: "It (FNB) keeps my belly full. The mayor don't."

With answers such as the above submitted as exhibits to the court, it is perhaps not hard to fathom why Flageollet, as an upholder of the established order, ruled the way he did.

Renegade went on to add, in reply to question number three, "Because at least they don't try to look down on me when they give a plate. They come from the heart."

There were residents of the tent city, such as Ethan Davidson, who became active members of FNB, helping with cooking and serving, and remained active even after the tent city was razed by the police. In response to question number three, Davidson wrote on the questionnaire, "It is more convenient, the food is better, and the surroundings are much more pleasant."

The actual *joining* of FNB, by people who were literally living on the streets, was, perhaps, more so than anything else, the greatest source of concern to the authorities. The court injunction—the 1000-plus arrests—the eight years of property confiscations and attacks against food servers—were, when it came right down to it, perhaps nothing more than an attempt by one social order to keep from being supplanted by another. This is certainly how the police viewed it (what else, after all, could conceivably inspire such unmollifiable hatred?), as well, quite likely, as those who gave the police their orders.

"It effected Mayor Agnos, it effected Mayor Jordan—they couldn't stand it. They were being shown up," Cunningham said. "Somehow—I'll never understand it—but they (FNB) got so deeply under the skin of official San Francisco."

Perhaps most importantly, the questionnaires revealed, for anyone with eyes to see in 1989, the deepening crisis of homelessness in America. Yet today judges go on gaveling down the poor in their courtrooms—as meanwhile more and more people continue to die in the streets—in a country which continues to ignore international human rights standards.

Chapter 7
The People of the United States vs.
The Government of the United States

The struggle over the nation's airwaves began to revolve around Free Radio Berkeley in 1994 when the FCC, citing "irreparable harm" to the public, filed for an injunction. In addition to fining Stephen Dunifer $20,000, the federal agency was now seeking to silence his radio station by court order.

If the FCC succeeded at this, presumably we would be next in San Francisco. However, the agency seemed at this point to put my case on the back burner as it focused more and more of its time and energy into getting Stephen. Perhaps it perceived Stephen to be the "ringleader" of the micro radio movement. If so, it was not an altogether illogical assumption.

By 1994 Stephen had already begun to make transmitter kits—complete with prefabricated circuit boards, parts, schematics, and loading diagrams—available, either through direct purchase or mail order. (The sale of fully assembled transmitters was prohibited under federal law, however, there was no law against selling someone a random package of disconnected parts.) Those kits, coupled with Stephen's expertise in designing and building them, gave the micro radio movement the wherewithal to "be fruitful and multiply."

Nineteen-ninety-four had seen the taking to the air of Radio Libre in San Francisco, but the movement was destined to spread wildly beyond the confines of the Bay Area. Such was the demand for free speech, that by early 1995, when oral arguments were first heard in the Dunifer case, the landscape had become sparsely dotted with additional stations, such as Free Radio Santa Cruz, in Santa Cruz, California. In addition the rock group Pearl Jam had taken a micro transmitter on tour and begun to broadcast their own concerts.

The micro radio movement had even begun to creep outside California, into such disparate locales as Tampa, Florida, and Seattle, Washington—while in the State of Illinois, Black Liberation Radio in Springfield (now called Human Rights Radio) had, with the help of Stephen and station founder Mbanna Kantako, raised its signal strength from one-half of one watt up to a whopping powerhouse of 30 watts.

While BLR's commercial neighbors on the dial were operating at wattages vastly above that figure, the 29 and a half watt increase did, nonetheless, give Kantako the means of being heard, along with his family (the members of which all took turns at the microphone), in areas of Springfield which lay well beyond the narrow confines of the Kantako home in the John Hayes Homes Housing Project.

The FCC may have well thought to put a stop to all this activity by putting a stop to Stephen. And they might have succeeded had not they run into one completely unexpected obstacle—a federal judge who still believed in the constitution (at least somewhat). The FCC chose as its entryway into the judicial system the U.S. District Court for the Northern District of California. This was necessary because it was in Northern California that Stephen was committing his alleged crime, i.e. flouting the authority of the FCC.

Now keep in mind the nature of some of the despicable scoundrels who call themselves judges in this part of the world—and keep in mind that the FCC had never—and this is an historical fact—lost a single court action against an unlicensed broadcaster—either here or in any other court in the land—and you begin to see how truly taken aback the federal agency must have been by Judge Claudia Wilken's upsetting of the apple cart on January 20, 1995.

Keep in mind, further, that the Federal District Court of Northern California was also the seat of the royal throne of Vaughn Walker, Food Not Bombs' nominee for the title of the World's Number One Thwarter of Justice. This will probably get Walker nominated to the supreme court by some future jackass American president in the 21st century, but I can't help it, it needs to be said: had the FCC drawn Walker instead of Wilken, in the Dunifer case, it's quite likely that the former would have promptly unleashed the apparatus of state repression, possibly giving the micro radio movement a premature death in early 1995. The FCC had every reason to expect just that—from Walker, from Wilken, from any judge.

Wilken, to be sure, went on to betray the micro radio movement, not to mention her own ethics, as all good red-blooded American judges do sooner or later. But her betrayal didn't occur until nearly four years later. Having strayed from the judicial fold, Wilken regained her senses, granting the FCC its injunction on June 16, 1998. During the intervening time, however, an enormous change had taken place. America—though most Americans remained oblivious to the fact—witnessed a literal radio revolution, with hundreds of unlicensed stations becoming active, in challenge to the corporate domination of the airwaves.

These included Radio Mutiny in Philadelphia; Steal This Radio in New York City; Radio Free Allston in Boston; micro KIND in San Marcos, Texas; as well as three additional stations operating under the widening umbrella of "Black Liberation Radio"—there were now a total of six "BLR" stations: in Fresno, California; Kansas City; Chattanooga, Tennessee; Richmond, Virginia; and in the towns of Decatur and Springfield, Illinois.

But the list didn't stop there. There were also 87 X FM, Lutz Community Radio, and the Party Pirate, all operating in the Tampa, Florida area; Beat Radio in Minneapolis; Fantom 101 in Oklahoma City; Raindrop Radio in Juneau, Alaska; KAW Radio in Leavenworth, Kansas; Excellent Radio in Grover Beach, California; Radio Clandestina in Los Angeles; and finally, retracing our steps back to Northern California, "KBUDS" in the pot-growing region of Mendocino County. There were many, many others as well.

At the time of the Wilken decision in 1998, the FCC estimated a total of 112 unlicensed stations operating nationally. This figure presumably represented only those stations on-air at the time the figure was compiled, and did not take into account the hundreds more which, lacking staying power, had come and gone in the intervening years. Many of these stations took to the air using Free Radio Berkeley transmitter kits; many had had the courage to make that step due to the pending status of Stephen's case and the holding in limbo by Wilken of the FCC's injunction. This is not to say that the FCC left everybody alone until the injunction's issue in 1998. Far from it. There was widespread harassment.

Beat Radio became an early casualty, in 1996, after a federal judge in Minneapolis ruled in favor of the FCC's right to seize the station's equipment. The same year also saw a raid against Lutz Community Radio in Tampa, Florida. Again equipment was seized. The following year Lutz was raided a second time, along with two other Tampa stations. This time FCC agents from the Tampa field office brought with them a retinue of heavily armed U.S. Marshals, and state and local law enforcement personnel, all brandishing automatic weapons.

At the Party Pirate, the party was over as Doug Brewer and his wife were terrorized at gunpoint for 9 hours while cops ransacked their home and carted away their belongings. The multi-jurisdictional task force even brought in a crane and dismantled the Brewer's antenna from on top of their house, knocking holes in the roof in the process.

Elsewhere in Tampa, Kelly Benjamin, the young twenty-two-year-old who had started up 87 X FM, watched in dismay as agents seized not only his broadcast equipment, but also carted away his rare record collection—while a second federal swoop upon Lutz Community Radio, which had recovered from the previous year's raid and gone back on the air, resulted in the confiscation of the station's *new* equipment. Lutz founder Lonnie Kobres, this being his second offense, was charged with 14 counts of broadcasting without a license. Kobres was convicted by a jury and sentenced to a $7,500 fine, six months of house arrest, and three years probation.

While the FCC's enforcement actions in Tampa would appear to be the most draconian in the nation (the Tampa field office seems to be especially rabid in its pursuit of micro broadcasters), other stations throughout the country have been subject to FCC visitations and harassment to one degree or another. This has resulted in numerous "voluntary" station shutdowns, under threat of duress. In some cases, such as that of Steal This Radio in New York, the shutdowns proved to be only temporary after community groups, pulling together in the face of intimidation, debated the issue, weighed the government's threats, and returned to the airwaves, more determined than ever.

In Decatur, Illinois, Black Liberation Radio, operated by Napoleon Williams and his wife, Mildred, was raided repeatedly—not by the FCC but by local authorities. The FCC was far from idle, however. Elsewhere, the agency launched enforcement measures against Free Radio Gainesville, in Gainesville, Florida; Radio Mutiny in Philadelphia; micro KIND in San Marcos, Texas—and in Tioga, North Dakota, where a farmer had set up a transmitter in his house so as to broadcast to himself while he was working out in his fields. Evidently threatened by this potential competition, a local commercial station—the only other station on the dial in Tioga—complained to the FCC. The Commission, backed by the full power of the United States Government, took the farmer to court and won an injunction shutting down the farmer's low-powered radio station.

In the Bay Area, by contrast, where we were under the protection of Judge Wilken, we led, for the most part, a charmed existence. This lasted from 1993 all the way up until June of 1998 when Wilken pulled the rug out from under us. During this time there were no raids. Nonetheless, FCC agents *did* visit the landlord of the building from which Radio X, a new bilingual micro station in San Francisco, had begun to broadcast. Precisely what words were communicated to the landlord during this meeting has been speculated upon widely. In any event, the landlord climbed to the roof of his property and dismantled the station's antenna. The Radio X broadcasters ended up having to get out of the building.

Broadcasting in both English and Spanish, Radio X, using a Free Radio Berkeley transmitter, had sprung up in the city's largely Spanish-speaking Mission District, putting out information on police brutality, INS sweeps against undocumented workers, and news of the Zapatista rebellion in Mexico. Radio X had replaced the now-defunct Radio Libre, whose demise had come about the year previous—*also* as a result of landlord troubles. The silencing of these two stations was a great loss to the city's Mission District.

Despite these unfortunate episodes, FCC enforcement measures remained largely in abeyance in the Bay Area. Out on San Francisco's west side our own station continued to go great guns during this time, as did Free Radio Berkeley over in the East Bay. In San Francisco, we were watching developments very closely in the Dunifer case. Whatever fate awaited Free Radio Berkeley also, obviously, awaited ourselves. Yet we weren't the only ones. Literally all across America, from the corporate boardrooms of the largest broadcast conglomerates, down to the tiniest of micro stations in the most rural, out-of-the-way places, all eyes were on the Stephen Dunifer case.

***

Why, you might wonder, would Corporate America take such a keen interest in a Berkeley activist's challenge to the Federal Communications Commission? The answer is that such a challenge to the FCC essentially amounts to a challenge to Corporate America's right to own, control and use as they see fit the airwaves of this country.

It would be *impossible* to overstate how threatened corporate-owned radio stations feel by micro radio. An inkling of this was hinted at in a speech by Lee Ballinger of *Rock n' Rap Confidential*, a publication reporting on the music industry. Ballinger, who spoke before the 1996 micro radio convention in Oakland, had become an early convert to the cause of micro radio due to the medium's potential for giving exposure to artists who would otherwise never be heard on commercial radio.

Commercial radio is "corrupt" and "undemocratic," gladly "taking money from record companies through third parties," Ballinger said, mentioning the operations of one, perhaps typical, music industry consultant.

Jeff McCloskey sits on his ass in an office in Chicago and tells the radio stations of America what records to play. If you want to get Jeff's attention, send him a check. McCloskey's consulting company has all the major record companies as clients. He maintains what he calls "close relationships" with over 60 of America's biggest radio stations.

Using the $6 million he takes in from record companies, McCloskey pays each station from $15,000 to $100,000 a year in return for exclusive access to the station program directors. These program directors know what to do when McCloskey tells them what records to play. Now, as any regular Jeopardy watcher will tell you, the correct question is: How much airplay does a record get if it's put out by an independent company that can't afford to hire Jeff McCloskey or one of the other parasites of the record promotion industry?

Aside from the question of music censorship, however, was the overall issue of the literal ownership of America's airwaves—a point brought more acutely into focus with the passage earlier that year of the 1996 Telecommunications Act. The Act greatly loosened restrictions on how many broadcast outlets a corporate entity might own. Said Ballinger,

> As a result of the mergers and acquisitions generated by the Telecom Bill, there are already 127 fewer radio station owners now than there were at the same time last year. Several billion dollars worth of broadcasting properties have changed hands. For example, just last month SFX Broadcasting bought Secret Communications for $300 million. SFX now owns 75 stations and is a significant player in 20 major radio markets. In 1995 the top 50 radio chain owners controlled 876 stations. Today the top 50 owners control 1,187 stations—an increase of 40 percent in just twelve months.

In essence, literally billions of dollars are at stake, Ballinger said, as he offered a sober warning to the more than 100 "pirate" broadcasters present that day in 1996: "The huge broadcast chains, having paid hundreds of millions of dollars to expand, will not sit by quietly and allow their investments to be threatened from the likes of you."

Ballinger, quite correctly, perceived the fight for the nation's airwaves as a class struggle between rich and poor.

> Downsizing in manufacturing and service industries continues to sweep across our country. The result has been

extremes of wealth and poverty never before seen in
America. Downsizing has created 80 million people living
below the poverty line. These people have no voice in the
media. Micro power radio must be the voice of America's
poor regardless of age or race. [1]

A voice articulating the concerns of America's poor, however, seems
to be precisely what some in America wish to avoid hearing.

"The harsh truth is that we are up against the people in America who
have all the money and all the power," Ballinger said. "They have already
shown that they will not hesitate to use both."

The latter statement did not require any special insight on Ballinger's
part. If there was ever any doubt of commercial broadcasting's overt hostility
to micro radio it was dispelled in 1995 when the National Association of
Broadcasters (NAB) filed an amicus brief in support of the FCC's efforts to
shut down Free Radio Berkeley. That brief was pretty much Corporate
America's declaration of war against micro radio.

While Dunifer, through his attorneys, had argued that the FCC should
rescind its ban on low-power radio (since 1978 the federal agency had
refused to license stations under 100 watts in power), never had it been said,
either by Dunifer or anyone on his legal team, that the FCC shouldn't exist
or shouldn't perform the function of assigning frequencies and ensuring that
stations don't interfere with each other.

Nevertheless, according to the NAB, "Acceptance of Dunifer's
arguments would jeopardize the entire regulatory program carefully
constructed by Congress in the Communications Act of 1934...and would
deprive the public of the benefits of the diverse, vibrant system of free, over-
the-air broadcasting that FCC policies under the Act have made possible." [2]

It's hard to fathom how returning to a system of regulation similar to
that which had existed in this country prior to 1978, would undermine
everything the FCC had "carefully constructed" since 1934. Further, it
should be kept in mind that the NAB, the supposed upholders of "vibrancy"
on the airwaves, had been lambasted as early as 1961, by no less than the
then-chairman of the FCC, for turning American television into a "vast
wasteland."

The events leading up to the passage of the Communications Act of
1934, and of Corporate America's essential takeover of the airwaves, are
extensively documented in such books as *Telecommunications, Mass Media
and Democracy* by Robert McChesney. There is, therefore, no need to go
into it in great detail here. It might, however, be useful for us to pause here
and scrutinize the NAB—since the widely held view today is that it has been

the NAB over the years which largely has given the FCC its marching orders—rather than the other way around. What follows is an admittedly selective history—of the NAB and its role as the driving force of America's immense broadcast lobby, and of broadcasting in general.

The NAB is essentially the lobbying arm of corporate-owned broadcast conglomerates. It is one of the most powerful lobbies in Washington, with political connections in the highest of places. The organization was formed in 1922, partly as a means for broadcasters to get out of paying artist royalties to ASCAP. [3] It has been pushing its weight around and essentially setting communications laws in this country for three-quarters of a century, since virtually the infancy of radio. The organization was instrumental in the passage of the Telecommunications Act of 1996 and today operates on an annual budget of $35 million.

Historically, however, the NAB's influence, due no doubt to the power accruing to those who control the airwaves, has far superceded the arena of broadcast regulatory policies. Alexander Kendrick, in his *Prime Time: The Life of Edward R. Murrow*, documents NAB opposition, in the years prior to Pearl Harbor, to U.S. support for Great Britain, which at the time was already at war with Nazi Germany.

"America First broadcasts, for example, opposing aid to Britain, would escape the network restrictions on political controversy by being offered, and accepted by the National Association of Broadcasters, as 'nonpartisan,'" writes Kendrick. [4]

Such a "nonpartisan" designation held significance in light of the NAB's adoption, in 1939, of a "revised code of standards for the broadcast industry." That code called for the allotment of airtime "with fairness to all elements in a given controversy." [5]

Much of the 1939 "code of standards" looked good, at least on paper. For instance, the reporting of news was to be done in a fair and even-handed manner without resorting to editorializing. "This means that news shall not be selected for the purpose of furthering or hindering either side of any controversial public issue nor shall it be colored by the opinions or desires of the station or network management...(or) the advertiser."

How closely this standard was adhered to might be wondered about in light of the fact that shortly before its adoption by the NAB—and continuing well after—NBC became the only American network that Hitler allowed to broadcast from Berlin. NBC's favored status with the Nazis is documented by Kendrick, according to whom NBC correspondent Max Jordan enjoyed "excellent relations" with top party officials.

"In Berlin, Goebbels' propaganda ministry had repeatedly denied CBS requests to short wave 'special events' to the United States, and NBC, by virtue of its favored position, had scored a series of broadcasting triumphs." [6]

One might pause and wonder why the world, despite NBC's "broadcasting triumphs" from Nazi Germany, never officially learned of the Nazi concentration camps until the arrival of allied troops at the gates of Buchenwald in the spring of 1945. Whatever the network's "broadcasting triumphs" might have consisted of, they apparently did not include reporting on the extermination of European Jews, says David S. Wyman in his rather definitive work, *The Abandonment of the Jews: America and the Holocaust 1941-1945.*

> All major newspapers carried some Holocaust-related news, but it appeared infrequently and almost always in small items located on inside pages. American mass-circulation magazines all but ignored the Holocaust. Aside from a few paragraphs touching on the subject, silence prevailed in the major news magazines, *Time, Newsweek,* and *Life...*
>
> Radio coverage of Holocaust news was sparse. Those who wrote the newscasts and commentary programs seem hardly to have noticed the slaughter of the Jews. Proponents of rescue managed to put a little information on the air, mainly in Washington and New York. Access to a nationwide audience was very infrequent. The WRB (War Refugee Board) even had difficulty persuading stations to broadcast programs it produced. [7]

Interestingly, Wyman informs us, this silence persisted even in the face of widespread reporting on the slaughter in the Jewish press. Why were American broadcast outlets so silent on the murder of Jews, despite ample evidence that the Nazi concentration camps existed?

***

In 1961 the NAB was verbally lambasted by then-FCC-Chairman Newton Minow. In an address to the association's convention in Washington D.C. on May 9, Minow accused the industry of turning American TV into a "vast wasteland."

At the age of just 35, Minow had been appointed by President John F. Kennedy to head the FCC. In terms of government regulators he was, in essence, one of a kind. Never had there been an FCC chairman who had bucked the broadcast industry to the degree done so by Minow. Never was there one since—until, that is, the ascension into office of FCC Chairman William Kennard in 1997.

Excerpts from Minow's famous "vast wasteland" speech were published in the *New York Times*, May 10, 1961:

> When television is good, nothing...is better. But when television is bad nothing is worse. I invite you to sit down in front of your television set when your station goes on the air and stay there without a book, magazine, newspaper, profit-and-loss sheet or rating book to distract you, and keep your eyes glued to that set until the station signs off. I can assure you that you will observe a vast wasteland.
>
> You will see a procession of game shows, audience participation shows, formula comedies about totally unbelievable families, blood and thunder, mayhem, violence, sadism, murder, western badmen, western goodmen, private eyes, gangsters, more violence, and cartoons. And, endlessly, commercials—many screaming, cajoling and offending. And most of all boredom. True, you will see a few things you will enjoy. But they will be very, very few. And if you think I exaggerate, try it. [8]

Commenting that "never have so few owed so much to so many," Minow informed NAB broadcasters that, "The People own the air. They own it as much in prime evening time as they do 6 o'clock Sunday morning. For every hour that the people give you—you owe them something. I intend to see that your debt is paid with service."

Minow vowed to hold public hearings on whether or not stations had presented sufficient quantities of public affairs programming, and he promised that station license renewals would no longer be automatic, as had been the FCC's tendency to do in the past.

> I intend to find out whether the community which each broadcaster serves believes he has been serving the public interest. When a renewal is set down for hearing I intend—wherever possible—to hold a well advertised public hearing, right in the community you have promised to serve.

> I want the people who own the air and the homes that
> television enters to tell you and the FCC what's been going
> on. I want the people—if they are truly interested in the
> service you give them—to make notes, document cases,
> tell us the facts. [9]

The 1934 Communications Act had mandated broadcasters to serve the "public interest, convenience, or necessity." Clearly Minow felt that standard was not being met, yet the new FCC chairman, perhaps, to be going even a step further, regarding the airwaves as a "natural resource"—a resource which, like any other, was capable of being wasted.

"I did not come to Washington to idly observe this squandering of the public's airwaves," he said. "The squandering of our airwaves is no less important than the lavish waste of any precious natural resource."

Minow also took exception with the broadcast industry's long-stated defense, "We're only giving the public what they want," noting that, "if parents, teachers and ministers conducted their responsibilities by following the ratings, children would have a steady diet of ice cream, school holidays and no Sunday school."

The FCC chairman also provided a valid criticism of the broadcast industry's interpretation of its own ratings process.

> I do not accept the idea that the present over-all
> programming is aimed accurately at the public taste. The
> ratings tell us only that some people have their television
> sets turned on, and of that number, so many are tuned to
> one channel and so many to another. They don't tell us
> what the public might watch if they were offered half a
> dozen more choices. A rating, at best, is an indication of
> how many people saw what you gave them.
>
> Unfortunately it does not reveal the depth of the
> penetration, or the intensity of the reaction, and it never
> reveals what the acceptance would have been if what you
> gave them had been better—if all the forces of art and
> creativity and daring and imagination had been unleashed.
> I believe in the public's good sense and good taste, and I
> am not convinced that the people's taste is as low as some
> of you assume. [10]

Having thus criticized the broadcast industry, Minow also expressed unequivocally his opposition to "government censorship" (corporate censorship not yet widely recognized as a concept in those days).

"There will be no suppression of programming which does not meet with bureaucratic tastes," Minow affirmed, adding that "Censorship strikes at the tap root of our free society."

Yet it was precisely the specter of censorship which the broadcast industry waved in responding to Minow's speech. The young FCC chairman was especially condemned by the head of NBC—the network that had been unable to find Hitler's concentration camps.

"When criticism comes pointedly and suggestively from the voice of governmental authority, speaking softly but carrying a big hint, at what point does criticism become coercion?" queried NBC chairman Robert Sarnoff. "Where does freedom leave off and interference begin?" [11]

Saying NBC had provided the public with "the gift of laughter, the spell of dreams, and the weapons of knowledge," the network head summed up by branding Minow as the purveyor of a "dangerous, mistaken, illiberal doctrine." [12]

Not to be outdone, CBS head Frank Stanton called Minow's comments "sensationalized," and praised the "diversity" of television, while criticizing the FCC chairman for drawing "broad brush conclusions."

"The danger of this kind of sensationalized and oversimplified approach," said Stanton, "is not only that it grotesquely distorts the situation as it is...but also it invites impulsive measures directed at making fundamental changes on the ground that any change is a change for the better." [13]

Stanton let it be known that he, for one, at least, believed in democracy.

"I don't know of any satisfactory or democratic alternative to letting the people set the standards of programming by the simple act of accepting or rejecting what is offered," Stanton said. [14]

Minow's tenure at the FCC, lasting just two short years, was marked by bitter frustration, with the broadcast industry fighting tooth and nail a package of reforms he attempted to implement at the federal agency.

In its war with Minow (as is the case in its present war with Kennard) the broadcast lobby was not in the least shy about enlisting the support of its friends in Congress. These included powerful house speaker Sam Rayburn, whose nephew, Robert Bartley, as it so happened, held a seat on the seven-member Commission. Bartley stridently opposed Minow's reform plan, which would have ceded more authority to the FCC chairman in the granting of station license renewals.

The Minow plan was described by *New York Times* columnist Tom Wicker as "relatively inoffensive and not greatly dissimilar" to three other departmental streamlining measures then being pushed through Congress by the Kennedy administration. While Congress approved the other three measures, the FCC reform suffered a defeat so crushing it was described by Wicker as "the most complete rout the Kennedy administration has suffered in this Congressional session." [15]

> The broadcasters are not much interested in streamlining the FCC. The more it is bogged down in its own procedures, the less effective regulation it provides. For instance under present law, a broadcaster can take separate exception to every line of, say, a sixty page ruling by a hearing examiner and force a full commission hearing on every exception. [16]

The reform package put forth by Minow and the Kennedy administration would have put an end to such a burdensome process. Wicker summed up: "Nobody who watched the fate of (Minow's proposals), however, would discount the broadcasting industry's ability to write its own ticket on Capitol Hill." [17]

On May 14, 1963 Minow quit his post as chief regulator of America's vast wasteland. The former Kennedy Administration official took a job in the private sector—as vice president and general counsel of the Encyclopedia Britannica Company. His tenure at the FCC had not been without certain accomplishments. At his initiative, the Commission had pushed through Congress legislation providing aid to educational television. He had also been chiefly responsible for the opening up of the ultra-high-frequency, or UHF, TV channels. Yet the loftiest of all his goals—a broadcast industry more responsive to the public interest—remained unfulfilled. A *New York Times* editorial marking his departure appeared under the headline, "No Flowering of the Wasteland."

***

Not only did the wasteland fail to bloom, but the programming got even worse as controversial reports such as "Harvest of Shame," produced by veteran CBS reporter Edward R. Murrow, were shunned by network executives, who preferred a more bland diet of sitcoms and crime melodramas. The uproar over "Harvest of Shame" is recorded by Kendrick:

On the Friday after a bountiful Thanksgiving day, and designedly so, *CBS Reports* brought into American living rooms a 1960 *Grapes of Wrath*. It was described by one viewer as "searing and searching," and "a needed indictment of a blight on the American scene." [18]

"Harvest of Shame" was a report on the plight of migrant farm workers in America. "The public reaction to it was one of surprised horror at the conditions portrayed," yet, according to Kendrick, agribusiness interests were "'horrified' for other reasons." Owners charged the program with "deceit" and with containing "highly colored propaganda," while a boycott of the sponsor was threatened.

Following the documentary's airing, *CBS Reports* was relegated to an inferior time slot, while Murrow was rejected as the program's principal reporter, narrator and co-editor. Said Kendrick:

The controversy over "Harvest of Shame" coincided with a kind of phasing-out of CBS public affairs programs—"because they cost too much"—by James Aubrey, the television network president who had succeeded Lou Cowan, and who had dedicated himself to making more money than ever for CBS...The Aubrey regime, which was contemptuous of news and public affairs, was solidly installed with such new, popular entertainment favorites as *The Beverly Hillbillies*. [19]

Besides "Harvest of Shame" another illustration is offered to us by the fate of the *Smothers Brothers Comedy Hour*. Despite being the top-rated TV show in America, the *Smothers Brothers* was cancelled in mid-season 1968-69, says Bert Spector, after a long series of clashes over program content between Tom Smothers and CBS executives. That such issues as racism and the Vietnam War had ever gotten addressed at all on the show was due in large part to the fact that the brothers had been given a significant amount of artistic control in their network contract.

Could the American people handle such bold artistic freedom? Indeed, rather than being repelled or made bored by the airing of controversial issues, the public seemed to embrace wholeheartedly the Smothers brothers' brand of political humor, as evidenced by the show's top ratings. In his essay, "The Smothers Brothers vs. CBS," Spector points out that the *Smothers* show, even more remarkably, was born as a mere mid-season replacement

In the winter of 1966, Sunday night prime-time television was dominated by one show, NBC-TV's venerable family western, *Bonanza*. In an attempt to unseat the Cartwrights from their weekly throne, CBS had called forth some of its high-powered stars. Both Gary Moore and Judy Garland tried and failed to woo viewers from the Ponderosa. *Bonanza* seemed invincible.

Then came the Smothers Brothers. [20]

Despite being on the air just three years, the *Smothers* show "zoomed into the top ten and, remarkably knocked *Bonanza* out of its number-one slot." [21] Yet all was not happiness at CBS. As Tom Smothers recalled, "The whole series was a weekly clash over something," with network executives, including CBS Vice President Perry Lafferty, constantly at odds with the brothers. Political censorship "occurred with regularity," including the excision of a segment from a Joan Baez appearance in which the folksinger expressed support for the antiwar movement by dedicating a song to her husband, who, she told the audience, was then in jail for resisting the draft. Also never making it to the air was a segment featuring Harry Belafonte singing "Lord, Lord, Don't Stop the Carnival" against a backdrop of film clips "from the riot-marred 1968 Democratic Convention in Chicago." [22]

Musicians Tom and Dick Smothers had been invited to do a variety show on CBS in part due to the late '50s/early '60 s boon in popularity of folk music. At the time of the show's debut, TV comedy was dominated by "McHale's Navy," "My Three Sons," and "Gilligan's Island."

Unexpectedly, the Smothers Brothers turned their show into a kind of prime-time showcase for the generally anti-establishment trends of the counterculture. They presented their audience of 30 million viewers with folksingers, little-known rock groups, and social satire of a kind not then seen on television. [23]

Despite the incidents involving Joan Baez and Harry Belafonte, a surprising amount of material *did* escape the censorship net as the show "clearly and openly aligned itself with the anti-war movement." *Smothers* producers opted for such material in order to "let our audience know we know what's going on," said co-producer Saul Ilson. [24]

Yet this provoked endless confrontation. One of the fiercest clashes between the brothers and their network bosses occurred over the appearance of folk-singer Pete Seeger, who had been blacklisted during the McCarthy era. While other blacklistees had gradually been "rehabilitated" back into show business, Seeger had continued to suffer ostracism—perhaps due to his outspoken opposition to the Vietnam War since the war's earliest days. Seeger's 1967 invitation to guest on the *Smothers* show resulted in his first commercial TV appearance in 17 years, and prompted a return appearance after network censors bleeped out his controversial song, "Waist Deep in the Big Muddy."

"We're getting nasty letters now," Lafferty reportedly complained to Tom Smothers. "Now you're going to put this Pete Seeger on? I don't want him!" [25]

After much wrangling with network executives, Tom Smothers won the right to bring Seeger on, not only for one appearance, but also for a return engagement—specifically so as to perform the bleeped-out song, even though, as Lafferty added ominously, "You're going to have to pay the consequences." While "Waist Deep" was given a pass by the network censors on the second go-round, even then the song was edited out by the CBS affiliate in Detroit. [26]

Despite its popularity, the *Smothers* show got the ax in April,1969—just three months after the inauguration of President Richard Nixon. In pulling the plug on the show, Nixon's friend, CBS Chairman of the Board William Paley, who had expressed a desire to be appointed ambassador to Britain (he never received the appointment), "removed from the air the one show that contained any criticism of the president." [27]

The Smothers brothers had certainly been innovators. They had, after all, overcome, at least for a time, the networks' "absolute dread and total rejection of political content." Yet perhaps only within the rather narrow, numerically limited society of presidents, media owners, and network executives had the duo been viewed as "radicals." As Spector observes:

> The significance of the show was that political commentary was there at all. This is not to say that the Smothers Brothers were radicals or that their show represented the coming to prime-time commercial television of political radicalism or the values of the counterculture. They were hardly in the vanguard of public opinion when it came to the war, civil rights, or even drug use. Instead of leading opinion, they seemed to reflect the views already extant in large segments of the public. [28]

Media owners often base their exclusion of "political content" on the grounds that they must avoid favoring one point of view over another. But is that what they're really about in their act of suppression? And is not the complete avoidance of political content in reality a political position in itself? If one considers that there is in existence in the media in this country an "assumed norm" which is not universally accepted in the population, then that would appear to be the case.

"Nobody bothers hawks like Bob Hope," said Tom Smothers.[29]

Effusive expressions of patriotism, for instance, are hardly content-neutral at any time, though this is especially so when a government is embarked upon a policy widely opposed by its population. The *Smothers Brothers* show was not to be used "as a device to push for new standards," instructed CBS-TV President Robert Wood. [30] This policy was apparently to be upheld at CBS, even though the standards being pushed were presumably "already extant in large segments of the public."

The lesson of *Harvest of Shame* and *The Smothers Brothers* show would seem to be, then, that even though a program might be one which, in the words of Minow, "all the forces of art and creativity and daring and imagination had been unleashed"—if it failed to be devoid of "political content," then it must be killed. This holds true even if, as in the case of Pete Seeger, one station owner in Detroit takes exception to the words of a song—in such a case then the whole city of Detroit must be deprived of hearing it.

Imposing an absence of such "political content" upon an entire populace hardly constitutes a politically neutral act. Rather it is an affirmation of the national "assumed norm," a norm which, in the case of the U.S., has been wholly wrought by a small minority of media owners and politicians who have little or nothing in common with the vast majority of Americans. [31]

The cancellation of the Smothers Brothers would appear to give the lie to the broadcast industry's claim, "We're only giving the public what they want." If the ratings were any indication, the public had certainly wanted The Smothers Brothers show.

"Political content," on the other hand, would appear to be acceptable provided it's sufficiently retrospective. In 1977 the networks, specifically ABC, lauded themselves for airing a docudrama depicting the evils of slavery—112 years after slavery had been abolished.

"We've done something in making this that no one has ever done before," ABC executive Fred Silverman reportedly boasted in describing his network's production of the miniseries *Roots*. [32]

Apparently being opposed to slavery was a great leap forward for media owners in 1977 since, as Leslie Fishbein reports, "none of the ABC affiliates north or south rejected *Roots*." [33]

If nothing else, *Roots* was ample testimony to the power of corporate media to reach millions. "The final episode attracted a staggering 80 million viewers, surpassing NBC's screenings of *Gone With the Wind* and the eleven Super Bowls as the highest rated TV show of all time." [34] Moreover, "author Alex Haley was himself deluged with honors, including a National Book Award and a special Pulitzer Prize"—this despite the book's—and the miniseries'—documented genealogical inaccuracies, according to Fishbein.

One wonders if Haley would have been so deluged had his novel depicted the struggle of blacks—not against white antebellum plantation owners but against police brutality in the ghettos of contemporary America.

***

The same year of *Roots*, a little-known but perhaps even more significant event occurred—at a meeting of the National Association of Broadcasters. A measure calling for the creation of thousands of new, low-power FM stations was proposed by the chairman of the House subcommittee having direct oversight over the FCC. Rep. Lionell Van Deerlin, a California Democrat, unveiled his proposal at the NAB's national convention in Washington that year. The story was covered in the *New York Times*:

> Mr. Van Deerlin, chairman of the House Communications Subcommittee, said that engineers on his staff have determined that a new system of low powered FM stations could be established if Channels 67, 68 and 69 on the UHF television band were reallocated for radio.
>
> This system would make possible as many as 450 new radio stations in every metropolitan area, stations that would be distinctly local because their signals would cover a radius of around 10 miles.
>
> These stations could not be received on the FM radio sets that are now on the market, but their frequencies could be added to new sets at a nominal cost. [35]

The addition of many, many new radio stations per market would certainly have greatly enhanced free speech possibilities over the airwaves—yet at the same time its potential to harm the profits of already-existing stations was, perhaps, undeniable. Indeed, NAB broadcasters at the convention were said to be "shaken" by the proposal, fearing that, in the words of the *Times*, "an infusion of thousands of small stations would increase competition for the established broadcasters and dilute their market." [36]

Perhaps even more objectionable, was a Van Deerlin proposal that would have charged commercial broadcasters an annual licensing fee for their use of the public's airwaves. The fees would be based according to ability to pay. An AM station in a small-town market, for instance, would pay less than a TV station in a major market. The money would be used, among other things, to finance public broadcasting.

To make his ideas somewhat more palatable to the NAB media establishment, Van Deerlin coupled them with a proposal to end virtually all government regulations over broadcasters, including the "fairness doctrine." That doctrine, which had been upheld by the Supreme Court, required broadcasters to give equal time to all sides in a controversial issue. Van Deerlin reasoned, not altogether illogically, that with thousands of new low-power stations on the air, the opportunities for all sides to be heard shot up considerably, making the fairness doctrine less necessary.

As things turned out, the broadcast lobby got to have its cake and eat it too. Neither the low-power FM service nor the licensing fee ever became law—while the fairness doctrine ended up being done away with anyway. Van Deerlin, though an incumbent with 18 years in Congress, was defeated in the election of 1980, replaced by someone presumably more acceptable to the NAB.

In the 1980s, Mark Fowler, the Reagan administration's appointee to chair the FCC, pressed for an end to the fairness doctrine, and on August 7, 1985, the Commission, by unanimous vote, labeled the policy constitutionally "suspect," announcing that the doctrine no longer served the "public interest, convenience or necessity." [37]

Far from aiding and abetting free speech, the fairness doctrine "inhibits" and "chills" it, Fowler's FCC decided. The Commission based this rather strained reasoning not only on the burdens of regulation, but also on the fact that there were then (1985) more stations on the air than there had been in 1969 when the Supreme Court had upheld the doctrine (in a landmark case entitled *Red Lion Broadcasting Co. vs. the FCC*). The *New York Times*, frequently a proponent of decreased corporate regulations, supplied the statistics.

> Since the Red Lion decision, commission statistics
> show, the number of radio stations in operation has risen

48 percent, to 9,766 stations in 1985 from 6,595 in 1969.
The number of television stations has increased 44 percent,
to 1,206 in 1985 from 837 in 1969. [38]

What the *Times* and the FCC failed to mention is that virtually all of these stations were full-power stations, requiring for the most part wealthy, corporate ownership. Disingenuously, the *Times* and the FCC also did not acknowledge that while the number of stations had gone up, the overall trend at the time was toward a decrease in the number of station *owners*. While the *Times* may not have been aware of this, the FCC certainly was. The march toward mergers and buyouts was already on, with each broadcast acquisition requiring FCC approval—and even in 1985 the coming of what ultimately became the 1996 Telecommunications Act could have—or at least should have—been anticipated.

The issue of media ownership consolidation has been addressed by Ben Bagdikian in his book, *The Media Monopoly*. In the book's first edition, published in 1983, Bagdikian concluded that U.S. media across the board—from broadcast to print to film—had come to be dominated by just 50 corporations. By the book's fourth edition, published in 1992, that number had dropped to two dozen.

It's testimony to the broadcast lobby's ability to "write its own ticket on Capitol Hill," that of all of Van Deerlin's ideas, only his proposal to eliminate the fairness doctrine survived to become national policy. This stands as an incredibly monumental testimony to one other fact as well: that the airwaves in America are regulated in the corporate—rather than the public—interest, for now that total, unabridged corporate control over the media had become a virtual fait accompli, suddenly America's "leaders" had decided that there was no longer any need for a fairness doctrine.

***

In 1996 the broadcast lobby pulled off one of the greatest coups in history. The feat was described by *New York Times* columnist William Safire as being a "ripoff" occurring "on a scale vaster than dreamed of by yesteryear's robber barons." [39] Safire was referring to provisions in the Telecommunications Act, which basically authorized the giveaway of large chunks of broadcast spectrum for conversion to digital television.

The new digital technology in broadcasting, in addition to bringing sharper, higher definition TV pictures, now makes it possible for up to six separate signals to be broadcast simultaneously over one frequency or channel. In terms of TV, this would make it possible for the same 6-

megahertz-wide portion of the broadcast spectrum—which previously would have accommodated only one analog station—to now be used, not only for the station's digital signal, but also for pagers, cellular phone services, and the like. As if commercial broadcast outlets weren't lucrative enough enterprises before, the new technology makes it possible for them to reap profits exceeding even the obscene. As Safire described, with the advent of the new technology "each broadcasting oil well was transformed into six gushers." [40]

The 1996 Telecommunications Act directed the FCC to issue licenses for digital television to "incumbent" broadcasters. Under the new rules, these incumbents will retain use of their analog frequencies while making the conversion to digital, a process which could take up to ten years depending upon how quickly consumers go out and buy the new digital TV sets. The example provided by WBTV is illustrative.

In October of 1997, WBTV, channel 3 in Charlotte, North Carolina, became the first television station in the continental United States to be issued a commercial permit by the FCC for construction of a digital television facility. Under its FCC license, WBTV will broadcast its digital signal, to be designated "WBTV-DT," over channel 23 in Charlotte, while plain old WBTV will continue to put out its old analog signal on channel 3.

WBTV is an NAB-member station owned by Jefferson-Pilot Communications, a corporation which owns 17 other radio and television stations in the cities of Miami, San Diego, Denver, Atlanta, Richmond, Virginia, and Charleston, South Carolina. Under the Telecommunications Act there are no provisions for Jefferson-Pilot to pay the government a penny for the use of channel 23 during the conversion to digital. It simply gets a free ride off its "six new gushers."

To be sure, there *are* provisions calling upon WBTV to give its old analog frequency back to the government at the end of the conversion period, however, given the broadcast lobby's ability to "write its own ticket on Capitol Hill," there is significant concern that even that requirement may not be met when the time comes. According to a 1997 report by Common Cause entitled "Channeling Influence: The Broadcast Lobby and the $70 Billion Free Ride," broadcasters have already begun to:

> balk at giving back the extra free spectrum being given to them. They have resisted a proposal by the Clinton administration that they give up the use of their analog TV licenses by 2005, arguing that date would be too soon to make the transition, but not suggesting any other date for the swap to be made. Indeed, there is some concern that

broadcasters will never want to give up this extra spectrum. [41]

So how much is all this booty worth to the *real* broadcast pirates who'll be walking off with it? Well, the FCC itself has estimated that were it to auction off these new frequencies—as opposed to simply giving them away—the sale would generate as much as $70 billion.

In 1995 then-Senate-Majority-Leader Bob Dole set out to retrieve this money for the U.S. Treasury, leading a move in Congress to auction the new channels off to the highest bidders. It was basically Van Deerlin's old proposal dusted off and presented in a slightly altered form: broadcasters would pay for the use of the public's airwaves, but by means of a one-time auction rather than an annual fee. With the support of the Senate majority leader, the measure seemed about to gain steam, according to Safire:

> But then the National Association of Broadcasters—the media lobby—went to work. Members of Congress soon felt the hometown heat that the vaunted gun lobby wishes it could generate—not only from the network mega-mergers, but from suffering "mom and pop broadcasters," some worth as little as $100 million, which felt an entitlement to have their primary asset sextupled in the great digital bonanza. [42]

What the broadcast lobby came up with rivaled even its attacks on Minow, three decades earlier, for disingenuousness. In March of 1996 there was launched a series of ads warning the public of a "TV tax." The ad campaign was cited by Common Cause:

> In the prime time viewing hour, an advertisement fills the television screens in millions of American homes. In this ad, a bank of glowing television sets is tuned to one of the highest-rated television programs. One by one the sets go dark. An ominous voice warns that government is about to impose a "TV tax" that would kill free TV. The announcer then urges viewers to call their elected officials and protest the imposition of this "tax" before it's too late. A tag line on similar print ads reads, "Doesn't a free society deserve free TV?"

The listed toll-free number, 1-888-NO-TV-TAX, reportedly logged about 3,500 calls a day while the ads ran. [43]

It should be noted, as it in fact was by one FCC official, that when Disney and Westinghouse had spent billions acquiring, through corporate mergers, their existing analog licenses, there had been no talk of the cost of those mergers resulting in the end of free TV.

Why had broadcasters been able to dupe the public so easily with the "TV tax" ad campaign? Much of the answer certainly lies in the fact that the media had given virtually no news coverage to the issue of the spectrum giveaway. As Common Cause put it, "The decision to threaten the end of free TV was part of a larger campaign strategy by broadcasters to distract attention from the real issue at hand," i.e. the $70 billion giveaway.

**

Digital radio is to differ from digital TV in a number of respects. Perhaps the most important of these, from the standpoint of those who might wish to use the airwaves for community purposes, is the manner in which it is expected to be implemented. Unlike their TV brothers, radio broadcasters plan to acquire no new or additional frequencies. Instead, under a system called IBOC (in-band-on-channel) both digital and analog frequencies will, for the duration of the transition period, be broadcast simultaneously on one frequency. Radio stations will simply remain where they are on the dial as they gradually begin to implement digital.

The significance this holds for micro stations is that the AM and FM bands, already crowded as is, will become even more so, with commercial stations transmitting both a digital and an analog signal in the same amount of spectrum in which there had previously existed only an analog. This poses somewhat dire implications for micro stations, most of which, on the FM band at any rate, broadcast at second and third-adjacent frequencies from large stations.

For instance in San Francisco, in the more than seven years we've been on the air, there have been no significant instances of interference between our own station, broadcasting at 93.7 FM, and our two nearest neighbors on the dial, broadcasting at second-adjacent frequencies above and below us—KYCY at 93.3, and KPFA at 94.1. Should either KYCY or KPFA go digital, however, that may change, causing the chances of interference between our station and theirs to go up. Will second-adjacent spacing between stations then be sufficient?

The question has sparked much-heated debate. IBOC is still in the testing phase. However, if it comes down to a choice between one or the other—large, corporate-owned commercial stations, or small, independent micro stations—you know who will be facing the music. Micro stations with no licenses and no legal standing will be the ones who end up getting squeezed out—if we allow that to happen.

The irony is that IBOC is *not* the system of choice in much of the rest of the world. In Canada, much of Europe, and elsewhere, radio stations will implement a digital system known as Eureka 147. U.S. broadcasters, virtually alone in the world, have opted for IBOC.

Under Eureka, European and Canadian radio stations will be moving completely off the AM and FM bands—in most cases up to a much higher point in the spectrum known as the "L" band. Just as FM offers superior quality sound to AM, so, too, does the L band offer a somewhat similarly enhanced resonance over FM, according to Stephen Provizer, director of the Boston-based Citizens' Media Corps and a founder of the Boston-area micro station, Radio Free Allston.

"The only country in the world that wants to implement digital audio broadcasting on existing AM and FM bands is the U.S.," Provizer told me. "Why? Because generally it means the least possible disruption to business as usual."

Certainly, from the standpoint of spectrum scarcity, it would have been better had the U.S. followed the rest of the world in implementing Eureka. Rather than becoming *more* crowded, as they will under IBOC, the AM and FM bands in the U.S.—had Eureka been the system of choice—would have become far less so—with whole sections of both bands being vacated as large-scale broadcasters made the leap to digital. In Europe, says Provizer, "countries are abandoning their AM and FM bands and several have said they will make frequencies available for small local stations."

The IBOC vs. Eureka issue was examined by the National Lawyers Guild's Committee on Democratic Communications (CDC), which has called for the legalization of micro radio. In comments addressed to the FCC, the CDC stated:

> Nearly the entire industrialized world, including Europe, Australia, and our neighbor, Canada, are moving all of their broadcast radio to the L Band and implementing the Eureka 147 system. The L Band offers far superior engineering advantages over the current radio spectrum. If the United States opts for the IBOC plan, we

will forever be stuck with a system that is not only inferior
in quality, but incompatible with the rest of the world. We
find it particularly ironic that the opposition, who
repeatedly cite their concern over maintaining high
engineering standards in radio, would support the inferior
technical option for implementing digital radio. We
assume this is simply because it is in their short term
financial interest to do so, thereby dooming the U.S. to an
inferior, incompatible service for the foreseeable future. [44]

The manner in which digital radio is implemented, as well as the
overall regulation of the airwaves as a whole, will impact virtually every
single American. Yet these key decisions, in which the NAB exerts
enormous influence, are made wholly outside the arena of public debate.

***

According to Common Cause, the NAB operates on a budget of $35
million a year, making it one of the most well-heeled lobbies in Washington.
But the NAB has something that the other lobbies don't have: the power to
determine what kind of media coverage members of Congress get—or
whether they get any coverage at all. "Washington is a city full of powerful
industry lobbies, but the National Association of Broadcasters seems to
wield more power than most," says Common Cause.

Others have spoken out on the NAB's Washington influence as well.

"The NAB may well be the most powerful lobby in the U.S.," says the
A-Infos Radio Project, another group advocating micro radio legalization.
On a web page entitled "Don't Let Them N.A.B. Our Airwaves," A-Infos
adds of the NAB:

The U.S. Congress dares not cross them. The FCC,
which is supposed to regulate the equitable use of the
public airwaves, serves as their police force. In 1996,
Congress passed the Telecommunications Act which
legalized the theft of the public airwaves by the NAB. The
act lifted restrictions which severely limited the number of
radio and television stations any one entity could own. The
FCC, whose officials often get lucrative employment in the
industry upon leaving government service, was told by the
NAB that if it opposed the 1996 legislation, the NAB
would see to it that the FCC would be disbanded.

Campaign finance reform provisions which would have mandated free air time for political candidates, and thus benefited candidates not backed by big money, were also squashed by pressure from the NAB. [45]

In addition to spectrum giveaways for digital broadcasting, the Telecommunications Act of 1996 also loosened restrictions on radio station ownership, allowing a single corporation to own up to eight stations per market. The Act also made station license renewals much easier, with renewal periods jumping from five to eight years (in the days of Minow they had been three years).

So how much did the NAB spend in its successful efforts to win passage of the Telecommunications Act? The amount, while considerable, was nonetheless miniscule compared to the astounding profits standing to be made off of "gushers" so lucrative they would have aroused the envy of "yesteryear's robber barons." Common Cause followed the money trail:

> The new lobby disclosure act which took effect in 1996 reveals, for the first time, the magnitude of the broadcasters' lobbying effort. Reports filed for the first half of 1996 alone show that NAB spent $2.3 million to lobby Congress, the Administration, and the FCC. That total was enough to land the lobby among the top spenders of 1996. Based on public lobby disclosure reports, NAB spent more on its lobbying efforts for the first six months of 1996 than the Bank of America, Chrysler Corp., or the National Rifle Association.
>
> But industry giants don't just rely on the NAB. ABC, NBC, CBS, Fox, and the Tribune Co. also invested their own millions to influence elected officials and regulators. According to lobbying reports, these largest broadcasters, along with the NAB, spent more than $4 million on lobbying during the first half of 1996. [46]

In addition to spreading around its money, the broadcast lobby also capitalizes on its "24-carat connections to Washington's power elite." These would include a long term relationship between NAB President Edward O. Fritts and Senate Majority Leader Trent Lott—fellow Mississippians and former college roommates, according to Common Cause. That, however, is only the beginning:

Connections to the powerful Lott also enhance the lobbying patina of several firms that work for major broadcasters. Griffith and Rogers, which did $60,000 worth of lobbying for CBS last year is full of Mississippi political hands, including James Johnson, who went to the University of Mississippi with Senator Lott and ran his campaign for student body president. More crucial, Johnson last year ran Lott's leadership PAC.

The firm also was founded by Haley Barbour, who returned to it in 1997 after serving as chairman of the Republican National Committee.

Johnson, Smith, Dover, Kitzmiller & Stewart, which earned $100,000 from CBS, is chock full of Congressional contacts. David Johnson was a former administrative assistant to former Senate Majority Leader Mitchell. W. Michael Kitzmiller was for eight years staff director of the House Commerce Committee.[47]

The House Commerce Committee has oversight over the FCC. Never have truer words been spoken than those uttered by Ballinger at the micro radio convention in Oakland in 1996: "The truth is we are up against the people in America who have all the money and all the power."

And those people appeared to be calling in their chips. After the FCC raids in Tampa, Edward O. Fritts, NAB President and former Trent Lott roommate, issued the following statement: "We are delighted that federal authorities have stepped up enforcement against pirate radio stations. The NAB Radio Board in June asked for the FCC to focus more attention on the growing number of unlicensed stations. We commend the Commission for sending a strong message to broadcast bandits that their illegal activities will not be tolerated."

Fritts' logic, of course, was a tad bit upside down. Who, after all, had only just tapped into "six new gushers" springing from the public airwaves without having to pay a penny? The "broadcast bandits" of the micro radio movement or the NAB?

In 1982 Fritts became president of the NAB at the age of 41. At the time, he and his family controlled a small chain of ten radio stations located in Mississippi, Arkansas, Louisiana, and Kentucky. Today he hobnobs with ex-Presidents, having been a signer, along with Gerald Ford and Jimmy Carter, of the so-called "Williamsburg Charter."

Fritts, who referred to the TV tax commercials as an "educational" campaign, also sits on the board of directors of the Partnership for a Drug

Free America (PDFA). Heavily dependent upon corporate funding, the PDFA has been criticized for harping—to the point of distraction—on the dangers of marijuana use, while ignoring such legal drugs as alcohol and tobacco. *High Times* magazine and others have accused the PDFA of accepting funding from alcohol and tobacco companies, however, the PDFA today denies this is the case.

The PDFA *has*, however, received generous contributions of free airtime, particularly from ABC. While evidently airtime giveaways for anti-marijuana messages are alright, Fritts has staunchly opposed calls for free airtime for political candidates. Do broadcasters, in return for free use of the public's airwaves, at least owe the public that much?

Airtime donations for candidates would, after all, help reduce the corrupting influence of big money on our political system. However, in response to such proposals, made before the Gore Commission, Fritts said, "Broadcasters welcome the opportunity to cooperate with the Gore Commission, but we will be vigilant in our resistance to government mandates that threaten the ability of local stations to determine how best to serve their communities." [48]

***

Opponents of micro radio have most often cited concerns over potential interference with already-existing stations. Assuming such concerns were valid, one remedy would be to allocate new spectrum to the FM band in a manner similar to that proposed by Van Deerlin. This spectrum could be set aside solely for use by micro stations. If, as Van Deerlin suggested more than 20 years ago, each metropolitan area in the country could conceivably, with the right sort of regulatory scheme, accommodate many, many new micro stations, then the free speech potential could be huge while the risk of interference would be nil. The problem, as Van Deerlin stated, would appear, indeed, to be political, rather than technical.

"Whatever technical concerns they may come up with, we can answer them," Stephen Dunifer has said.

In Dunifer's view the desire to repress micro radio stems in part from a desire to impose censorship. Speaking at the Oakland convention, Dunifer said,

> We're seeing a struggle that's going on in this country for self determination, for free speech. We're also seeing it in Chiapas. We're seeing it in El Salvador. We're seeing it in Haiti...Just as this sort of corporate yoke of what I call

> neo-feudalism—they call it neo-liberalism, but let's call it
> what it is—descends around the neck of everyone on this
> planet, they think they have it made, that they can
> somehow pull this off. But I got news for them. People are
> fighting back.

Dunifer's concluding words to the convention that day: "If you can't
communicate, you can't organize. If you can't organize, you can't fight
back."

Since those who seek to suppress micro radio obviously can't and
won't say, "We're opposed to micro radio just because we want to censor
what they have to say," let's examine, then—prior to focusing on the
showdown in Judge Wilken's courtroom—what they *do* say.

> Modern regulation of broadcasting began with the
> Radio Act of 1927, 44 Stat, 1162 (1927). The broadcasting
> provisions of the Communications Act of 1934 were taken
> part and parcel from the Radio Act. The foundation of the
> regulatory structure created by the Radio Act was the
> government's assertion of control over who may broadcast
> and under what terms and conditions.
>
> Without regulation, use of the radio spectrum is futile.
> Because there are more potential broadcasters than
> available frequencies, "if two broadcasters were to attempt
> to transmit over the same frequency in the same locale,
> they would interfere with one another's signals, so that
> neither could be heard at all." ...Prior to 1927 this
> intolerable situation existed. [49]

So said the NAB in its amicus brief in support of the FCC (at the time
the NAB and the FCC were allies in the drive to suppress micro radio) in the
Dunifer case. Though the NAB doesn't say so here, the "intolerable
situation" that existed in those early years was remedied in a very novel
manner—through the elimination from the airwaves of virtually everyone
but large, commercial broadcasters.

Public interest and educational stations were the big losers when
Congress passed new broadcast regulations in 1927 and again in 1934. As
Common Cause noted, the NAB, "founded in 1922, got its first victory in
1927 with the passage of the Radio Act."

The late '20s/early '30s demise of radio stations run by educators and
labor unions is recorded very vividly in Erik Barnouw's *A History of*

Broadcasting in the United States and elsewhere. Non-commercial stations were forced to cut back power levels, while commercial broadcasters were given leave to increase theirs, including NBC "with its powerful line-up of clear-channel stations," says Barnouw. Public interest stations also suffered by being repeatedly forced to switch from one frequency to another, as well as enter into elaborate, often grossly inequitable time-sharing schemes with more powerful commercial stations operating on the same frequency.

The case of WCAJ, operated by Nebraska Wesleyan University, is perhaps illustrative. Reports Barnouw:

> In 1927 the FRC (Federal Radio Commission, predecessor to the FCC) assigned it (WCAJ) to 860 kc.; then moved it to 790, sharing with KMMJ; then in 1928, to 590, sharing with WOW, Omaha, which was given six-sevenths of the time. A hard struggle for the remaining one-seventh followed. WOW applied to the FRC for the full time; when this was denied, appealed to the District of Columbia Court of Appeals; when this action was lost, renewed its petition to the FRC. Each such hearing meant legal and travel costs for the Nebraska Weslyan station...Eventually, worn down by litigation, hearings, and travel costs, the University station sold out—to WOW. [50]

Another historian who has addressed the rise to dominance of commercial broadcasters is Robert McChesney, author of *Telecommunications, Mass Media and Democracy: The Battle for Control of U.S. Broadcasting.* In an affidavit filed in the *Dunifer* case, McChesney states:

> The Radio Act of 1927 and the Communications Act of 1934...were both drafted and passed with minimal public participation. Special interests dominated the legislation. In 1934 corporate broadcasters used their immense political power to see that there was no possibility for Congressional hearings about the legislation before it was passed. Historical research shows that Congress was manipulated against public sentiment in 1934 concerning broadcast legislation. Indeed, in 1927 there was a general consensus that the term public interest as it applied to broadcasting meant that the government should favor nonprofit groups in the allocation of licenses.

> There has never been a subsequent Congressional debate overturning that sentiment. Corporate power has been able to make certain that the FCC has done exactly what corporate power wanted. [51]

Another objection to micro radio centered around the issue of "efficiency" in the use of the broadcast spectrum. The premise here is that large, full power stations make for more efficient use of the available spectrum than do small, low-power stations.

At the heart of this argument lie the buffer zones that separate two stations operating on the same frequency. Low power stations, so the argument goes, require proportionally larger buffer zones than do higher ones. In the following passage from the amicus brief, the NAB, in order to illustrate its point, makes us privy to the FCC's own algebraic conclusions on the matter of spectrum efficiency. From the amicus brief:

> In order to achieve interference-free FM service, stations broadcasting on the same channel must be separated by distances far greater than their respective service areas. For example, FCC rules require that the lowest-powered authorized class of FM service—class A stations—be separated from other class A stations on the same frequency by at least 71 miles...Stations operating on adjacent channels must also be separated to avoid interference. The rules require that a class A FM station be separated by at least 45 miles from a class A station on an adjacent channel. The FCC's licensing rules were established to ensure the most efficient use of the broadcast spectrum with the smallest amount of interference. Thus if a low-powered FM station began operations, it would prevent the authorization of a full-power FM service on either its channel or any adjacent channel for many miles outside the area in which the low-powered station could be heard. The FCC recognized this in affirming the Notice of Proposed Liability against Mr. Dunifer. [52]

We now have the FCC's own precision calculations submitted in Dunifer:

A simple example shows how preclusion and service are related. A 10 watt station with a 100 meter antenna has a service radius of 5.9 kilometers and a service area of 109 square kilometers. To protect this hypothetical low power station from interference by a co-channel Class A FM station operating at 6 kilowatts, we would need to preclude the establishment of that Class A station within a distance of 92.6 kilometers from the transmitter for the low power station. In contrast, one Class A station would preclude another co-channel Class A station within a distance of 115 kilometers. A Class A station, however, operating at 6 kilowatts with a 100 meter has a service radius of 28.3 kilometers and a service area of 2,516 square kilometers. While the preclusive effect of a Class A station is 24 percent greater than the 10 watt station...the service radius of a Class A station is almost 500 percent greater than the smaller station...If we treat preclusion as a cost and service as a benefit, the cost/benefit ratio improves with power; but the ratio is very poor for low powered stations. [53]

By way of response to the above, the first and most obvious answer that comes to mind is that it hardly makes for an "efficient" use of the broadcast spectrum to simply turn the entire spectrum over to corporations. But beyond that, let's look specifically at the engineering arguments, for they have been challenged.

One of those who has posed such a challenge is Harold Hallikainen, a San Luis Obispo, California radio frequency engineer whose engineering firm services several full-power stations in the Central Coast area. Hallikainen, who supports micro radio legalization and has filed comments with the FCC so stating, says the above arguments, while technically accurate, tell only part of the story.

For one, says Hallikainen, "there is substantial area between 'tightly packed' stations where additional low power stations could exist within the existing interference criteria.

In addition, in most cases, stations are not 'tightly packed,' thus making additional space available for low power stations while not providing enough space for a full power station. Failure to use these gaps between stations is inefficient use of the spectrum and deprives the public of a local service." [54]

A graphic, perhaps, helps illustrate Hallikainen's point. The following figure depicts a "tightly packed" cluster of class A stations:

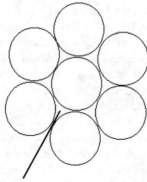

Gaps where micro stations
could fit

In the above figure "the circles represent the 'interference contour' with a radius of one half the required co-channel separation distance. Each of these circles has a radius of 57.5 km. Within this interference circle each station has a protected coverage contour radius of 28.5 km. Thus, the coverage area of the single class A station (in the center of) this tightly packed array of stations is 2552 km2." [55]

Now—if you *really* want to talk about efficiency—and the NAB has implied, after all, that maximum efficiency is their goal—then picture the following: an array of "tightly packed 1 watt stations replacing the class A station in the center of the cluster as follows:

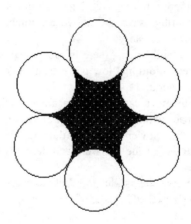

In this illustration we have many tiny circles (representing 1-watt stations) blotting out the center circle (representing the single class A station we are theoretically proposing to replace). In this arrangement, says Hallikainen, "the coverage of each 1-watt station is 7 km2, substantially less than the class A station. However, 1,129 1-watt stations fit, as shown...giving a total coverage area of 7,980 km2, substantially more than the coverage of the single class A station it replaced."

Adds Hallikainen: "No one is suggesting replacing full power stations with low power stations. However, refusing to permit the use of the gaps between existing full power stations is inefficient use of the spectrum and deprives the public of a truly local service." [56]

Another aspect of the whole "efficiency" issue is this: if maximum efficiency is such a strongly desired goal, then why are so-called "FM translators" allowed to exist?

To understand what FM translators are all about, picture this: a full-power FM station serving a large metropolitan area desires to extend its signal into a distant rural or suburban community. Encompassing the people of this community into its listening area would improve the station's Arbitron ratings and boost its advertising revenue.

However, the station's signal is presently cut off from reaching the community by hilly or mountainous terrain. What to do? Set up a small 10-watt transmitter on a hill overlooking the targeted community. That "translator" will then be able to receive the signal from the station's main transmitter and "import" it into the distant community.

The question then becomes, however: are the people of this community well-served by having this imported signal from a distant station filling up their airwaves? Or would they be better off having a community station of their own, originating local programming and focusing on issues of local concern?

By the NAB's own definition of efficiency, FM translators are an inefficient use of the spectrum. They are nothing more than micro stations—with one exception: they are prohibited by law from originating their own programming; they are parrots, giving added reach to the voice of distant, mega-watt stations.

FM translators are yet another example of how the airwaves in this country are regulated in the corporate, rather than the public, interest. In the years since 1993, when the FCC tracked down and initiated enforcement proceedings against micro stations in the Bay Area, it has continued to license new FM translators to large, corporate-owned stations.

***

Another aspect that needs to be considered in all this is the NAB's response to the First Amendment arguments that were raised in *Dunifer*. In the view of the NAB, American citizens have no First Amendment rights when it comes to the use of their own airwaves:

> The sole remaining issue is Dunifer's claim that the First Amendment guarantees him the right to broadcast. Because control over all uses of radio frequencies is, as we have established, the gravamen of the regulatory scheme established in the Communications Act, Dunifer is arguing that the Communications Act unconstitutionally restricts protected speech. The Supreme Court has addressed that issue repeatedly and concluded, without exception, that the Act is constitutional and that "the right of free speech does not include...the right to use the facilities of radio without a license."...The court restated this point two terms ago in *Turner Broadcasting System vs. FCC*...(quoting from the Red Lion case): "'it is idle to posit an unabridgeable First Amendment right to broadcast comparable to the right of every individual to speak, write, or publish.'" [57]

The statement that Dunifer had argued that "the Communications Act unconstitutionally restricts protected speech" is somewhat misleading. Dunifer's attorneys had merely asked the court to take First Amendment issues into consideration in determining whether or not to uphold the FCC's ban against low-power stations. No one had said broadcasters, either large or small, shouldn't have to be licensed.

The free speech issues—as well as the impact of changing technology—were outlined in the Dunifer legal team's very first communication with the FCC, on June 28, 1993.

To enforce its "absolute prohibition" against micro radio, argued Dunifer's lawyers, "the FCC is relying upon regulations which were promulgated long before the advent of the technology that makes possible micro radio; indeed, even before the advent of FM broadcasting." (The changing technology, in fact, was the very reason we had been able to stick micro radio stations in at second adjacent frequencies on the dial without causing interference to already-established stations. Stephen's ability to do this in 1993 would appear to underscore the outdatedness of the FCC's regulations.):

The FCC's application of these regulations violates the First Amendment rights of individuals seeking to exercise those rights via methods and mediums that were technologically impossible when the regulations were created.

The cost of owning and operating a radio station has skyrocketed into the hundreds of thousands and even million dollar range, and participation in the broadcast media has thereby become limited only to large corporations. The individual seeking to communicate and listen to others over the airwaves in his or her local community is completely left out of the licensing scheme if he or she cannot afford the expenses entailed in purchasing, obtaining a license for and operating a commercial broadcast station with at least 100 watts of power. [58]

Dunifer's failure to apply for a license should be considered here, for that failure became an increasingly crucial factor as the case progressed.

Dunifer did not apply for a license prior to putting FRB on the air. Indeed, with FCC regulations prohibiting the licensing of low-power stations it would perhaps have been futile to do so. Nonetheless, it was repeatedly argued by both the NAB and the FCC that Dunifer should have properly submitted an application and then asked the FCC for a waiver of its rules. Failure to do so, it was argued—and the court ultimately agreed—constituted a violation of proper procedure. Such a violation leaves the violator with no standing in a court of law. By law you have no right to go to a court unless you have first availed yourself of all other possible avenues in an effort to remedy your situation.

Should Dunifer have applied for a license? Why did he not do so? The legal team had said that the problem was not that micro broadcasters were refusing to comply with FCC licensing procedures, but that the FCC had failed to provide a means under which they might legally do so. Yet did Dunifer's failure to go to the FCC to seek a waiver render that statement slightly suspect? Perhaps not. Contended Dunifer attorney Luke Hiken in the June 28 communication:

It is the obligation of the FCC to construct and enforce its regulatory framework in such a way as to safeguard the First Amendment right of free speech for all persons, regardless of their economic power. By totally prohibiting low-power radio, the FCC has failed to comply with its congressional mandate to regulate the airwaves in the public interest, has exceeded the limits of the power conferred upon it by Congress, and is violating the constitutional rights of micro radio broadcasters and their listeners. [59]

It should be noted that nothing in the 1934 Communications Act forbids micro radio. The establishment of a 100-watt minimum is entirely "a regulatory creation of the FCC," Hiken said, adding that the agency's "deceptively long" response to *Dunifer* "boils down to 'ask us to change our rules.'"

If the Commission's ban on low-power radio violates the First Amendment, as Dunifer contends, is it incumbent upon Dunifer to ask the Commission to change its rules? Or must the Commission bring its rules into compliance with the First Amendment? Who must act first? Regarding requesting a waiver, Hiken said,

> Given that there are absolutely no standards or limitations governing the Commission's discretion in considering an application for a rule change or a waiver, this "option" is meaningless. It is well established in First Amendment jurisprudence that regulations which vest absolute or near absolute discretion in an agency to approve or deny exceptions to a generally applicable rule are unconstitutional. The forfeiture order seems to suggest that applicant Dunifer has somehow failed to exhaust his administrative remedies because he did not petition for a rule change...If the FCC's rules, as currently formulated and applied, completely prohibit micro radio, then the rules violate the First Amendment. Citizens have no responsibility whatsoever to petition the FCC to change unconstitutional regulations—rather, the FCC is required to structure its regulatory framework so as to comply with the First Amendment. [60]

Another possible explanation for Dunifer's failure to apply comes down to money. Before approving any waiver, the FCC likely would have required that Free Radio Berkeley conduct engineering surveys costing several thousand dollars. Even had such surveys been done there would have been no guarantee that the waiver would ultimately have been granted. Yet in the view of the NAB, Stephen faced a veritable abundance of opportunities.

"Dunifer is free to apply for a license for a full power station, to apply for a license for a low power station and seek a waiver of the FCC's rules, or to buy an existing station." [61]

For the rich in this country, things, perhaps, are that simple. But for the poor they are not.

These, then, are some of the issues that were presented before the court.

The showdown in Wilken's courtroom came on January 20, 1995. That day was a cool winter day in Oakland, California. The wind was brisk but the sun was shining. A crowd of micro radio supporters, including myself, gathered at 9 a.m. in front of the Oakland Federal Building. Some of us carried signs or banners. Some made speeches.

There was a sense that something important was about to happen. The fact that a federal judge had—as Wilken had done just a few months earlier—expressed agreement that there might be some legitimate First Amendment concerns at stake in this case was taken as a good sign. Yet we were in alien territory. We were all about to go into a U.S. federal courtroom—a place where poor people had no right to expect justice.

At 10 o'clock we began filing in, and at 10:30 the hearing began. Present on behalf of Dunifer were attorneys Luke Hiken and Peter Franck. On behalf of the government—David Silberman, an FCC attorney from Washington, and Patricia Duggan, an assistant from the U.S. Attorney's Office in San Francisco. Stephen sat at the defense table with his attorneys. Presiding was Judge Claudia Wilken.

Wilken was young for a judge—a fact which Silberman attempted to underscore during the proceeding, citing at one point a Supreme Court decision rendered in 1943—"right after I was born and before you were born, Your Honor."

Wilken's previously shown tendency to see some validity to the First Amendment issues in the case, had apparently prompted the government to dispatch Silberman from Washington. His role that day seemed to be very much that of troubleshooter, as he took charge of the case, wresting control away from the local U.S. Attorney's Office. His concern was perhaps genuine. No federal judge had ever before so questioned the validity or constitutionality of the FCC's "regulatory scheme."

"Good morning," Wilken said, calling the hearing to order. The oral arguments commenced. Silberman spoke first. There is, he said, an "ongoing violation" of the 1934 Communications Act, and to fail to issue the injunction would allow Dunifer's "lawlessness" to continue. Quoting Silberman from the court transcript:

> In every case where an injunction has been requested by the Government to prevent unlawful, unlicensed broadcasting, the district court has granted the injunction.
>
> There is no case that we are aware of—and the defendant cites none—where a district court has been asked to issue an injunction and the government has proved an unlicensed radio operation where the government has been denied that injunction.
>
> And there's a very good reason for that. Unlicensed broadcasting creates chaos on the airwaves. It's anarchy on the airwaves. And to allow and not to enjoin this kind of operation, the court should consider that in doing so it encourages continuing violations not only by the defendant, but by those who would also see this as a signal that the law is not going to be enforced. [62]

Silberman, predictably, raised the procedural issue. Dunifer, said the Washington attorney, had not exhausted his administrative remedies. Hiken, however, turned Silberman's arguments around, pointing out possible procedural flaws in the FCC's own course of action to date.

After the FCC had issued its $20,000 forfeiture against Stephen, Hiken and the legal team had, on December 2, 1993, appealed to the full board of the FCC in Washington with an "Application for Review." The FCC had allowed that appeal to "languish," said Hiken, and had still, to that day, more than a year later, not ruled on it. Procedurally, then, was not the FCC in error for coming to the court with an injunction request without first ruling on Dunifer's Application for Review?

And then there was the matter of the fine. The FCC had issued a forfeiture order against Stephen in the amount of $20,000. This, said Hiken, automatically gave Stephen "standing" in the federal court. Addressing the FCC's allegations that Stephen's broadcasts caused "irreparable harm" to the public, Hiken cited the case of Mbanna Kantako, the blind broadcaster out of Springfield, Illinois, who was now considered the pioneer of the micro radio movement:

> They gave him a forfeiture order five years ago. If there is an emergency why is it that they haven't done

anything about that? There's no emergency in this case. And we would point out to the Court that the suggestion you were making is exactly what should occur here. We made a request in the forfeiture order that "If there were proceedings or rules or means whereby we can raise this issue for your consideration, please give them to us." We did that a year and a half ago when they filed their first forfeiture order. [63]

Why had the FCC allowed Mbanna Kantako to continue to broadcast for five years without shutting his station down and collecting on his fine? The Kantako case did seem to make a mockery of the FCC's contention that Dunifer was somehow causing "irreparable harm," requiring an emergency injunction to remedy it.

Hiken's arguments were persuasive, yet Silberman cited precedent after precedent in which courts had always granted injunctions against unlicensed broadcasters when requested to do so by the FCC.

Again, Your Honor, in the Medina case and in the McIntire case and in the Weiner case and in cases decided under the Radio Act, every time the Government has asked for an injunction to prevent unlicensed, unlawful, illegal broadcasting, the Government has gotten the injunction for the simple reason that the statute is plain. It requires a license to broadcast. The Defendant admits he doesn't have a license. He admits all the broadcasts that are cited in our complaint. The administrative proceeding is a punitive action for two of the earlier broadcasts.

This proceeding is to enjoin and to prohibit and to prevent further violations of the law. [64]

To this Wilken responded, "Well, it's sort of an odd statutory scheme and regulatory scheme, but what it leaves me with is I have to balance your likelihood of prevailing and the harm to either side..." [65]

Wilken denied the injunction "at this time," staying the proceedings until the Court might obtain the FCC's "guidance with respect to the need for these regulations...against the constitutional interests of people who wish to broadcast." [66]

The ruling did not sit well with Silberman. The FCC attorney complained to the Court:

When we have a rule-making proceeding...there would be a requirement for notice and comment. And it could take months to years to resolve that question. Is Your Honor saying that we would have to have a rule-making proceeding, open up for public comment, have the staff consider the recommendations to the Commission, and then go through the judicial review process if someone were to challenge any new rules or to challenge the decision not to adopt new rules? This could take years. Are we saying—is Your Honor saying that that's what we are going to be going for?...Because that's precisely what's going to happen, Your Honor. Your Honor, this opens up such a can of worms. You don't realize. I mean it. Your Honor, what would happen would be that you've given carte blanche to this group of people who think they can operate a radio station without a license. If Your Honor were to issue the injunction the status quo would be maintained because the Communications Act prohibition against operating a station without a license would be protected, whereas the Defendant and others who want to broadcast could go forward, and then seek to change the rules. [67]

But, of course, as Silberman had noted, a rule-change "could take months to years," during which time, if the judge ruled as Silberman wanted, micro broadcasters would be enjoined from broadcasting.

The upshot of Wilken's ruling that day was that the FCC was directed to "address the constitutional issues" raised in the case and then report back to the court. A brief chronology of ensuing events is helpful here:

Aug. 2, 1995—The FCC denies Dunifer's Application for Review and issues a memorandum opinion and order, affirming its belief in the constitutionality of its ban on low-power radio.

Feb. 1, 1996—Congress passes the Telecommunications Act, consolidating control of the airwaves into fewer and fewer hands.

Feb. 2, 1996—The FCC files for "summary judgement," demanding a permanent injunction against Stephen.

March 15, 1996—Additional brief filed by the FCC argues that Wilken lacks the jurisdiction to decide the constitutional issues raised in the *Dunifer* case. Constitutionality of FCC regulations may only be ruled upon by higher federal courts, states the FCC. In effect, the Commission is saying that while Wilken *does* have authority to issue the injunction, she lacks leeway to rule on the First Amendment concerns. The argument is called "Kafkaesque" by Dunifer's attorneys.

April 12, 1996—Oral arguments are held on the issue of jurisdiction. Appearing in court this time, in addition to Silberman, is Jack Goodman, attorney for the National Association of Broadcasters. When micro radio supporters attempt to witness the proceedings they are locked out of the building by police. On the lingering question of the injunction, Wilken takes the matter under advisement, leaving Dunifer and others again free to broadcast in the meantime.

Nov. 8-10, 1996—Micro radio convention is held in Oakland, California.

April 5-10, 1997—NAB holds its annual convention in Las Vegas, Nevada. Speakers at the convention denounce micro radio, issuing calls for its elimination.

June 20-21, 1997—Second micro radio convention is held, in Los Angeles. Representatives of the A-Infos Radio Project demonstrate their new Website, powered by Cold Fusion software. The Website has both upload and download capabilities, making it possible for micro stations nationwide to send and receive news programming virtually instantaneously over the internet.

Nov. 12, 1997—Wilken denies the FCC injunction "without prejudice," requesting further briefing from the opposing parties. Additional briefs are to address the question of whether the alleged unconstitutionality of the FCC's regulations are a sufficient defense against the injunction. On the issue of jurisdiction, Wilken notes that the FCC's argument in *Dunifer*—that the constitutional questions could only be decided by the higher courts—is exactly the opposite of what it had argued in an earlier case against a micro broadcaster in Arizona.

Nov. 19, 1997—In complete disregard for the Wilken decision of just a week earlier, the FCC carries out armed raids against three Tampa, Florida micro stations. The raids are supervised by Ralph Barlow, head of the FCC's Tampa office. In a reference to Doug Brewer, operator of one of the stations, Barlow had been quoted in the *Wall Street Journal* as saying, "Sooner or later I'll nail him." In the *Tampa Tribune* the general manager of an area commercial station was reported to have praised the operation, saying, "True to their word the FCC did indeed shut down these unlicensed, pseudo-broadcasters."

April 6-10, 1998—NAB holds second convention in Las Vegas. Micro radio broadcasters stage counter convention, picketing NAB festivities at the Las Vegas Convention Center. The NAB convention features a panel discussion entitled, "Pirate Radio Stations: Will They Be Walking the Plank?"

June 16, 1998—Wilken grants "summary judgement" to the FCC, issuing the injunction against Dunifer.

June 17, 1998—San Francisco Liberation Radio and Free Radio Berkeley go off the air in response to the judge's ruling.

June 22, 1998—The FCC raids Radio Mutiny in Philadelphia, seizing the station's equipment. The raid is personally supervised by Richard Lee, head of the FCC's Compliance and Information Bureau from Washington.

June 28, 1998—Clandestine broadcasts begin to emanate from the hills of Berkeley and San Francisco as people begin to defy the injunction.

Dec. 5, 1998—San Francisco Liberation Radio formally applies to the FCC for a license to broadcast, requesting a rule waiver on the ban against stations of under 100 watts in power.

Jan. 28, 1999—The FCC (now under a new chairman) announces a rule-making proposal to study the possibility of legalizing micro radio. Period of public commentary is opened.

Feb. 12, 1999—With still no answer to our license application, San Francisco Liberation Radio calls a press conference and returns to the air.

While Wilken had earlier, back in 1995, directed the FCC to "address the constitutional issues," in the end she, herself, failed to do the same. Her final ruling was based upon procedural grounds only. Dunifer had not sought a waiver of the rules. He therefore lacked standing in the courts, meaning his First Amendment complaints would not even be heard.

"The FCC has dodged the bullet once again and evaded substantive judicial review of its blatantly unconstitutional allocation of the airwaves to the rich, vested interests of the NAB," Hiken commented to reporters in the wake of the decision.

Did the FCC initiate a micro radio legalization procedure out of a sense that such a move would be only the fair thing to do? Or did it realize that its ban would never stand constitutional challenge in a federal court? By filing an application and requesting a waiver of the rules, SFLR had presumably met the conditions set down by the judge in the Dunifer case. Perhaps the FCC had taken a realistic stock of its situation and come to the conclusion that it could not go on indefinitely "dodging the bullet," as Hiken put it—the "bullet" in this case being a constitutional review of the FCC's regulations banning low-power radio. Perhaps, also, the federal agency feared an enforcement nightmare, with more and more stations taking to the airwaves regardless of the FCC or its regulations.

With regard to Wilken's decision of June 16, 1998, the reaction from NAB President Fritts was jubilant.

This decision represents a great victory for legitimate broadcasters who play by the rules...The FCC deserves credit for putting Mr. Dunifer and other broadcast bandits out of business.

***

Interestingly, at virtually the same time that FCC attorney Silberman was in the Oakland court in 1995, defending the public interest from irreparable harm, Reed Hundt, who was on his way out as chairman of the Commission, was traveling about the country giving speeches in which he asserted that the FCC was finding it impossible to even determine what the public interest *was*. In a talk at the University of Pittsburgh School of Law on September 21, 1995, Hundt made the following observations:

> ...The FCC's current implementation of the public interest mandate is intellectually indefensible. Either our rules actually require something—and something unknowable—of broadcasters, in which case they should be rejected as constitutionally intolerable. Or they actually require nothing of broadcasters, in which case they are a meaningless hoax on the American public. In fact the latter statement describes our rules.

How could the FCC defend the public from irreparable harm when it didn't even know what the public interest was? Were the Commission's arguments in the Dunifer case nothing more than a "meaningless hoax on the American public?" And is that perhaps what it realized in 1999 when, under new chairman William Kennard, it began moving toward micro radio legalization?

***

In 1998 the FCC received three formal petitions calling for it to change its rules on low-power radio, and on January 28, 1999 the Commission announced a "Notice of Proposed Rule Making" in which it expressed a view toward legalizing some form of micro radio, possibly on a limited basis. A period of public commentary was opened.

Hundreds of comments poured into the FCC from all over the United States, each one articulating a vision of how micro radio legalization should be implemented. The large, corporate broadcasters, including the NAB, filed their own comments as well—naturally opposing the whole process.

In its pro-legalization comments, the CDC of the National Lawyers Guild, cited what it termed as "Rosa Parks—the Pirate."

In 1955 when Rosa Parks decided to sit on a bus seat reserved for "Whites Only" she was breaking the law. She was "pirating" a seat that did not belong to her. She was right and the law was wrong. And she didn't need to nicely ask permission before violating an immoral and unconstitutional law. That is the essence of civil disobedience. Maybe we should also mention that every signer of the Declaration of Independence was breaking a law—a law punishable by death.

A number of the broadcasters who have opposed micro radio have done so on the grounds that it will reward "pirates." This is equivalent to saying that we should not have compelled integration of public facilities because it would "reward" lawbreakers like Rosa Parks. Or maybe we should not have honored George Washington because it "rewards" traitors to the King?

This broadcasters' response is the arrogance of state-protected monopolists. [68]

To no great surprise, commercial "state-protected monopolists" opposed the micro radio rule-making petitions practically en masse. They have been joined in this opposition, however, by a perhaps unlikely ally—National Public Radio (NPR). The foundation of NPR's opposition to micro radio rests on the "interference" and "inefficiency" arguments. Thus, micro radio should not be allowed, argues NPR.

But what about diversity of voices in the media? Clearly this is an "important" goal, yet the promise of micro radio to bring about an increase in such diversity is "neither self evident nor established," says the public broadcast entity. [69]

NPR evidently assumes that an adequate diversity of media voices is already provided by itself. Not only, of course, is such an assumption "neither self evident nor established," but it borders, in light of public broadcasting's increasing willingness to take money from corporations, upon the paradoxical. While it may sound sanctimonious, NPR's comments have to be examined in light of public broadcasting's ongoing march toward commercialization. They can really be viewed in no other context.

The proposal put forward in excess of 20 years ago by Rep. Lionell Van Deerlin would have involved, as already mentioned, reallocating UHF channels 67, 68, and 69 for FM use. Such a reallocation would have allowed for the addition of many new low-power FM stations per metropolitan area, the congressman stated. This plan would perhaps be less feasible today due to the degree to which the UHF channels have filled up in the more than two decades since Van Deerlin proposed it.

However, an alternate proposal—the conversion of TV channel 6 for FM use—has been put forth by Dunifer, Hallikainen and other engineers. The nationwide conversion to digital TV could allow an opening for such a possibility, says Hallikainen.

"Spectrum could possibly become available in the spectrum shuffle of digital television, possibly leaving television channel 6 vacant nationwide allowing for the expansion of the FM broadcast band down into this spectrum," Hallikainen stated to the FCC during the micro radio public commentary period. [70]

Assignment of all micro stations into this new, expanded portion of the band would virtually eliminate the "interference" argument now used by NPR and all the other "state-protected monopolists." Whether or not the FCC approves such a move, however, will depend ultimately upon its capacity to act independently of "the people in America who have all the money and all the power." As Ballinger correctly pointed out at the micro radio convention in Oakland, the struggle for the airwaves is a class struggle. When you sift aside "interference," "inefficiency" and other more specious arguments, there really is no other issue involved.

One might dare to imagine a collapse of corporate power to be somewhere in America's future. Yet with as many as 8 million homeless and 80 million living below the poverty level in America, Ballinger envisions an important role for micro radio in the coming years—either with or without such a collapse.

> As a result of NAFTA and its ongoing aftermath, the destinies of poor and working people in the U.S., Mexico, and Canada are joined more closely than ever before. In order to control the deteriorating political and economic situation in Mexico, the international bankers are pressing the Mexican military to restore order...Micro power radio must facilitate communication throughout the entire zone of NAFTA occupation, from Chiapas, to the Yukon, to South Carolina. From there micro radio can help us all to extend a hand to the rest of our hemisphere.

> Music is the conscience of the world, and is a prime source of inspiration and information. Yet commercial radio refuses to play much of the music that is on the charts, let alone the wealth of sounds from the underground. Commercial radio is undemocratic, taking its

orders from a handful of professional consultants. Commercial radio is corrupt, gladly taking money from record companies through third parties. Micro power radio must be the voice of our music and our culture.

The Democratic Party has abandoned us. Liberal Democrats were the instigators of the ongoing wave of music censorship. Liberal Democrats were eager partners in passing the Telecom Bill. It passed in the House by a vote of 414-16, and in the Senate by a vote of 91-5. Micro power radio must be the voice of all those striving to break away from the political parties of the corporations. Micro power radio has a role that goes beyond being the voice of a vital, cutting-edge underground. Micro power radio must set its sites on becoming the voice of a new American majority. [71]

Perhaps history has more to teach us here than we think. A couple of quotes on the essence and nature of fascism come to mind, passages that just might have been reflected upon by the broadcasters of Tampa as their homes were ransacked by police—or by Napoleon Williams, or the programmers of Radio Mutiny as they surveyed the ruins of their empty studios.

The first is from Barnouw's *History of Broadcasting*, a passage harkening back to the mid '1930s in the days immediately after passage of the 1934 Communications Act. It has to do with words spoken by Raymond Swing, a radio journalist of the era: "Fascism, said Raymond Swing, was the scuttling of democracy to maintain 'an unequal distribution of economic power.'" [72]

The second quote comes from *For Whom the Bell Tolls*, Ernest Hemingway's classic novel of the Spanish Civil War. During that war many Americans went to Spain to fight for the Republic. The book tells the story of one such American. He is sent to join a band of guerillas working behind fascist lines to blow up a bridge. During a somewhat idyllic interlude, a conversation transpires, with one of the guerillas seeking to know more about life in America:

"But are there not many fascists in your country?" the guerrilla inquires of the novel's protagonist. To this question, the American replies: "There are many who do not know they are fascists but will find it out when the time comes."

The concentration of media ownership into fewer and fewer hands holds undeniable consequences for American democracy. Micro radio may not be a cure-all for America's many problems—of which the "unequal distribution of economic power" is high on the list. Yet with corporate broadcasters pushing strenuously in one direction, and micro broadcasters pushing just as adamantly in the other, clearly the country has come to a strategic crossroad.

Chapter 8
The Death Culture

There is a culture of death in America. It is evident in many facets and avenues of American life and society. We have a death penalty. We have one of the highest murder rates in the world. We have slaughterhouses where animals are butchered for our dinner plates. We have a government which has sponsored death squads in the Third World, our tax dollars financing secret police forces and mercenary armies which have crushed democracy movements and committed human rights atrocities. We have homeless people dying on the streets of our cities. At the same time we have a military in possession of a nuclear arsenal capable of killing off humanity with the press of a button—and since the ending of the Cold War, rather than cut back on that arsenal, we have added to it.

Here in this Death Culture we are out of balance with nature. We have cancer clusters and "downwinders" and Superfund toxic waste sites, and communities, from Love Canal to the San Joaquin Valley of California, where people have sickened and died from exposure to an assortment of chemical poisons. We have environmental racism and classism, and drugs in our communities that were put there by our own police. We have a government, which rails vociferously against biological and chemical weapons in other countries while itself sitting on the largest stockpile of such weapons in the world.

We have changing weather patterns, unprecedented floods and heatwaves, and emerging new diseases, which confound medical science and portend global epidemics and a nightmarish future.

We have a working class growing increasingly poorer, and a homeless population increasingly larger. By no accident, police brutality has risen proportionally. The sodomizing by police of a Haitian immigrant in New York is shrugged off by New York's ruling elite as a minor aberration, and rather than a focused condemnation of such acts, we have television shows which glorify the police. Is it any wonder, then, that the society is schizophrenic?

We have problems with mental illness. We have teen suicides. Suffering and dissatisfaction are widespread, and we attempt to squelch our depression with Prozac so that we may continue to go to our jobs. We have school ground shootings by disturbed, confused teenagers who see no hope for the future. We have joblessness, hunger, and poverty, while we are told that the economy is good. We have a society that is isolated and fearful of itself, and commercials which put a happy face on it all and keep us in a buying mood.

Perhaps most tragically of all, we have a news media that refuses to address these and other problems in a meaningful and substantial manner. In so doing they have avoided, like the plague, what is perhaps the most important issue, the most pertinent and relevant question of all: is it just fortuitous that all these things, these products of a Death Culture, have come about in a society dominated by corporate power (as opposed to popular, democratic rule)? Or is there a possible connection?

It's no coincidence that hundreds of micro radio stations have gone on the air across the land at this particular point in our nation's history. The micro radio movement is a subconscious effort by a society to save itself, to hang onto life, and to break the death grip of the Death Culture. When community groups gather together in protest, as has been done in San Francisco, and sing "Swing Low Sweet Chariot" while calling out the names of community members who have been killed by the police—something is fundamentally wrong. When such a scene is repeated in city after city across an entire country, it is indicative of a society on the breaking point.

America is run by an elected government that is subservient to corporate power. Most Americans view these forces in control of our lives as being basically well intentioned, and guilty only, perhaps, of poor judgement at times, and of misguided policies. While not always pursuing the best course of action, our government is certainly not out to get us, we feel. But is this picture of a basically benign, benevolent, well meaning force an accurate one?

***

Perhaps the most visible and obvious manifestation of the Death Culture, is the death penalty. According to the Department of Justice, there were 3,219 prisoners on Death Row in America as of year-end 1996. The youngest of these was 17; the oldest was 81. In the year 1997, seventy-four executions were carried out. It was the largest number of executions in one year since 1955. One of these was Terry Washington, a mentally retarded man who was put to death in Texas. Another was Pedro Medina, whose head burst into flames on Florida's electric chair after the device malfunctioned. Despite Medina's pyrotechnical exit, the Florida State Supreme Court upheld the state's use of the electric chair, ruling that that particular mode of execution did not constitute cruel and unusual punishment. [1]

Also in 1997, the state of Virginia executed Joseph O'Dell despite pleas on his behalf from the Pope, Mother Teresa, and the Italian Parliament. Evidence which had been introduced at O'Dell's trial was thrown into doubt by subsequent DNA testing.

Nor did serious questions about possible innocence stop the state of Texas from executing David Spence. Two police officials who investigated the murder with which Spence was charged expressed doubt about his guilt, while *New York Times* columnist Bob Herbert concluded, after looking into the case, "Mr. Spence was almost certainly innocent." Spence went to his death based on testimony from prison inmates who were granted generous favors in return for their cooperation. [2]

Washington, the mentally retarded man also executed in Texas, had an IQ of between 58 and 69, and possessed an intellect said to be comparable to an eight-year-old's. The jury that sentenced him was never told about his retardation

Each of these executions took place in the year 1997 alone.

How has such a climate come about in America—in which people are sent to their deaths regardless of their age or mental competence, and despite lingering questions about their guilt? How is it that an American court could, at least by implication, sanction the horrendous immolation suffered by Medina in Florida?

According to the Washington-based Death Penalty Information Center (DPIC), the death penalty process has become "politicized," leading judges to impose more death sentences in an effort to avoid ouster from office, and giving politicians to pander increasingly to right-wing, law-and-order electorates. In a study entitled "Killing for Votes," DPIC found that "the infusion of the death penalty into political races is reaching new extremes and distorting the criminal justice system." [3]

The report cites numerous instances of judges, both elected and appointed, who suffered career setbacks, after issuing death penalty reversals. One of these was Justice Penny White, appointed to the Tennessee Supreme Court in 1994. In the very first capital case to come before her, White upheld the defendant's conviction but overturned the death sentence.

This gave the Tennessee Conservative Union, a far-right anti-tax group, the opening they needed to attack her as an opponent of the death penalty in the judicial election in August, 1996. White's opponents, including the state's Republican leaders, accused her of never voting "to uphold a death penalty conviction" (even though this was her first capital case and she had *upheld the conviction)*, and of wanting to "free more and more criminals and laugh at their victims." Both of the state's Republican senators voted absentee before the official election and then publicly announced that they had voted against Justice White because of her death penalty position in this one case. The Republican governor, Don Sundquist, proclaimed before the election that he would never name someone to a criminal court judgeship unless he was sure the nominee supported the death penalty. [4]

Similar fates to White's were suffered by other judges. All across the country, in fact, "the climate has become increasingly hostile towards any judge who has reservations about the death penalty." [5]

The defeat of conscientious judges invariably opens the door for those who are rabidly pro-death-penalty. In 1992, a pro-death-penalty prosecutor who kept a hangman's noose over her office door defeated Texas District Court Judge Norman Lansford, who had set aside a death sentence due to prosecutorial misconduct. [6] This penchant for morbidity seems to be common now among the Texas judiciary.

One judge set the execution date of a defendant on his clerk's birthday as a "present," while another callously insists on signing his death warrants with "smiley faces." [7] And then there's the Texas D.A. who has on his wall a chart entitled, "The Silver Needle Society," which lists all those from his county who have been executed by lethal injection. This particular D.A., Johnny Holmes, of Harris County, Texas, has literally made a career out of the death penalty. Since 1976 he has sent more people to Death Row than any other state except Texas. [8]

One pandering politician in Arizona so strongly supports the death penalty he announced it was okay with him "if we get a few innocent people," while New Mexico Governor Gary Johnson proposed executing children as young as 13. [9] Former House Speaker Newt Gingrich, who sponsored the "Effective Death Penalty Act" in Congress, had campaigned for mandatory death sentences for drug smugglers while proposing to eliminate most appeals in such cases. Envisioning mass executions of 35 people at a time, Gingrich commented at a fundraiser, "I have made the decision that I love our children enough that we will kill you if you do this."
[10]

The supposed contradiction between Gingrich and Governor Johnson offers a diseased, unwholesome irony: Gingrich, we are expected to believe, wants to protect children, while Johnson wants to execute them.

On the issue of the death penalty, America has grown increasingly isolated from the rest of the world. The UN Commission on Human Rights in 1997 voted overwhelmingly to urge member nations to abolish the death penalty. The vote was 27 for, 11 against, with fourteen abstentions. The resolution was opposed by the U.S. along with such countries as China, Indonesia, and Bangladesh.

According to DPIC, the number of executions dropped off slightly in 1998—down to 68—but rose sharply in 1999, up to 98—the highest for any year since the death penalty was reinstated in 1976. By year-end 1999 the Total number of executions since that reinstatement had risen to 598.

***

Yet it is not only the issue of the death penalty which isolates America. Many countries now refuse to import American beef. And well they might. American cows are injected repeatedly with antibiotics and other drugs, while conditions in American slaughterhouses have been allowed to deteriorate (at great risk to the beef-consuming public) since the deregulation of the meat industry, begun under Ronald Reagan. That deregulation has been followed, perhaps not coincidentally, by outbreaks of E.coli and other food-borne illnesses that have taken a tragic toll.

A shocking expose of the meat industry is provided by Gail Eisnitz in the book *Slaughterhouse*. Eisnitz is an investigator with the Humane Farming Association who carried out a ten-year study of the nation's largest meat-packing plants.

Centuries ago, when Native Americans killed an animal for food, they said a prayer for its departing spirit. They were in harmony with nature. Needless to say, that is not the case today in the slaughterhouses of the Death Culture.

One thing that can be said for America's death penalty is that at least humans—with the possible exception of Medina in Florida—are dispatched in a more humane manner than are animals. In her gut-wrenching expose, Eisnitz reveals a meat industry seemingly willing to do anything, no matter how abominably cruel, to enhance profits. It is an industry in which workers' safety matters little, and simple, basic humanity toward animals accounts for even less. It is also an industry in which the term "USDA Inspected" has become a meaningless joke with frightening and sometimes deadly consequences for consumers. Increases in outbreaks of E.coli over the past decade are no coincidence, says Eisnitz. They have followed closely on the heels of meat industry deregulation, begun under Reagan and carried on through the Bush and Clinton years.

"We used to trim the shit off the meat. Then we washed the shit off the meat. Now the consumer eats the shit off the meat," one Department of Agriculture (USDA) meat inspector told Eisnitz during the course of her investigation. [11]

Deregulation has brought about an on-the-job environment in which workers are forced to slaughter and dismember animals at ever-increasing speeds. Government inspectors, present in the plants but maintaining only a symbolic oversight, are intimidated when they try to do their jobs, threatened and coerced not only by plant management but by higher-ups in the USDA bureaucracy.

The result has come to be shocking, horrible conditions on the "killing floors" of the nation's packing houses. Under such conditions violations of the federal Humane Slaughter Act have become rampant. In fact, Eisnitz discovered, many workers are unaware of even the existence of such an act, or that its enforcement is charged to the USDA.

Due to management demands for increasing production speeds, animals routinely remain alive after leaving the "knocker" or "stunner"—the worker at the head of the line whose job it is to humanely slaughter the animal. The killing of the animal is usually accomplished by shooting a retractable steel bolt into the head, or by delivering an electrical charge.

Often, however, the knocker is unable to keep up with the pace, or sometimes the electrical charges are set too low so as to avoid "damaging" the meat. [12] In such an event, living, fully conscious animals will be shackled and chained, hung upside down, stuck in the throat, bled, and, in the case of pigs, dipped into tanks of scalding water (for hair removal). Even then, following this blistering deluge, animals sometimes remain alive and can occasionally, most horrific of all, begin the process of skinning and evisceration while still conscious. Yet due to the desire to maintain a profitable operation, no stoppage or slowing down of the line is tolerated. As one slaughterhouse worker related to Eisnitz:

> "A lot of times the skinner finds out an animal is still conscious when he slices the side of its head and it starts kicking wildly. If that happens, or if a cow is already kicking when it arrives at their station, the skinners shove a knife into the back of its head to cut the spinal cord."

This practice paralyzes the cow from the neck down but doesn't deaden the pain of head skinning or render the animal unconscious; it simply allows the workers to skin or dismember the animal without getting kicked. [13]

Other workers described for Eisnitz the practice of "piping," the beating into submission of struggling animals with lead pipes.

"I can remember conscious hogs blowing bubbles in the blood collection tank—it was just sickening." [14]

Yet it would not be uncommon for such inhumane practices to produce in workers a "desensitization." As one veteran slaughterhouse worker at the John Morrell packing plant in Sioux City, Iowa, explained to Eisnitz:

"...The worst thing, worse than the physical danger, is the emotional toll. If you work in that stick pit for any period of time, you develop an attitude that lets you kill things but doesn't let you care. You may look a hog in the eye that's walking around in the blood pit with you and think, God, that really isn't a bad looking animal. You may want to pet it. Pigs down in the kill floor have come up and nuzzled me like a puppy. Two minutes later I had to kill them—beat them to death with a pipe. I can't care.

"When I worked upstairs taking hogs' guts out I could cop an attitude that I was working on a production line, helping to feed people. But down in the stick pit I wasn't feeding people. I was killing things. My attitude was, it's only an animal. Kill it.

"Sometimes I looked at people that way too," he said. "I've had ideas of hanging my foreman upside down on the line and sticking him. I remember going into the office and telling the personnel man that I have no problem pulling the trigger on a person—if you get in my face I'll blow you away.

"Every sticker I know carries a gun, and every one of them would shoot you. Most stickers I know have been arrested for assault. A lot of them have problems with alcohol. They *have* to drink, they have no other way of dealing with killing live, kicking animals all day long. If you stop and think about it, you're killing several thousand beings a day. [15]

Eisnitz says that she discovered, while investigating the meat industry, a "debased side of human nature." That discovery taught her "how easy it is for some people to ride roughshod over the basic rights of others when greed and profit are their only motivating factors."

She makes it clear, however, that in her use of the word "debased," it is not the workers to whom she refers—this despite the harsh brutality of the kill floor. On the contrary, the workers she found to be "forthright to the point where they implicated themselves in their own affidavits." In Eisnitz's view the *real* "debased humans I'm talking about" are the

> corporate managers who never get blood on their shoes but who set line speeds so outlandishly high that employees can barely keep up. It's these greedy supervisors who not only drill into their foremen that production takes precedence over all else, but who demand that their employees disrespect life—their own, their co-workers', consumers', and, of course, the animals—if they wish to keep their jobs. [16]

Interestingly, the meat industry has, in terms of consolidation of ownership, followed a trajectory which has strangely paralleled that of the broadcast industry. Eisnitz discovered that in 1980, two-thirds of the nation's cattle were slaughtered by the fifty largest beef packing companies in 103 individual plants. By 1992 the same percentage were slaughtered by just three companies in 29 plants.

"In 1996 more than 40 percent of the nation's cattle were killed in a mere 11 plants that slaughter more than one million animals each year." [17]

The government agency in charge of regulating the meat industry is the U.S. Department of Agriculture. But just like the Federal Communications Commission over much of its history, the USDA has been undermined and usurped by the industry it purports to regulate. Eisnitz traced the meat industry's steps down the primrose path of deregulation.

> Prior to 1978, USDA inspectors had to condemn any bird with fecal contamination inside its body cavity. It 1978, citing the problem with the automatic eviscerators, the poultry industry convinced the USDA to reclassify feces from a dangerous contaminant to a "cosmetic blemish" and allow workers to simply rinse it off. The result: inspectors began condemning half as many birds. Consumers ate the rest. [18]

The USDA's approval of washing, rather than trimming, away of contaminants "would prove to open the floodgates to a sea of contamination." In the 1980s the Reagan administration implemented

"Streamlined Inspection," turning contamination control over to the companies themselves while allowing increased "defects," including feces, inflammations, bruises and blisters, "to pass freely into food channels." By this time "450 fewer USDA poultry inspectors were examining a billion and a half more birds than ten years earlier," theoretically inspecting for diseases at speeds of up to thirty five birds per minute. [19]

Just as relaxation of controls over the broadcast industry has had a negative impact on the public, so too has the deregulation of the meat industry—though in the latter case the consequences, as one might expect, have been somewhat more severe than a mere erosion of free speech.

Eisnitz documents dramatic increases in incidents of meat-borne illnesses such as E.coli, salmonella, and campylobacter. Of special concern to health authorities has been the rapid rise of a deadly new strain of E.coli known as E.coli 0157:H7—a "once-rare bacterium that wasn't even identified until 1982," but which has since "left a trail of sickness and death across the United States."

"This disease is so destructive and ugly," commented one mother, whose child was stricken by the pathogen after accidentally ingesting a small amount of raw hamburger. [20]

Indeed, E.coli 0157 can cause hemolytic uremic syndrome, an affliction carrying a shocking array of symptoms, including hallucinations, kidney failure, and swelling and perforation of internal organs. Victims can be left brain damaged.

The watershed year for E.coli 0157—when the disease began to make headlines nationally—was 1993. That year more than 700 people got sick after eating undercooked hamburgers at a Seattle Jack-In-The-Box restaurant. Scores of people were hospitalized, "fifty-six developed HUS (hemolytic uremic syndrome), and three young children died."

Another 106 Jack-In-The-Box customers contracted symptoms in Idaho, California, and Nevada, and one died. Incidents of E.coli poisoning continued to increase: sixty five outbreaks in 1994 and 1995. More in 1996. Finally, in '97, "in just one of many outbreaks, Hudson Foods meat processing plant in Nebraska was forced to recall 25 million pounds of potentially contaminated ground beef—the biggest meat recall in history"—after seventeen Colorado residents became infected with the bacterium.

In especially compelling reading, Eisnitz relates several case studies of E.coli 0157 poisoning, including that of ten-year-old Brianne Kiner, who had "beaten the odds," but had been left with brain damage, diabetes, a seriously-scarred stomach and lungs, and only one-third of her liver.

"Once a talkative child, Brianne no longer had much to say. She was so weak she could attend her fourth grade class for only one hour every other school day."[21]

If Newt Gingrich "loves our children" so much he's willing to introduce the death penalty for drug smugglers, perhaps he, or his successors in Congress, might also consider calling for tough, new regulations upon the meat industry. Yet that has not been the response of government leaders to date. Rather than tighten up on conditions in slaughterhouses, says Eisnitz, the "primary response" by the USDA to the Jack-in-the-Box tragedies was, incredibly, to advise consumers to cook their meat more!

"Twenty years ago," one public interest advocate commented to Eisnitz, "it wasn't a reckless, foolhardy act for a family to eat medium-rare hamburgers or steak for Sunday dinner. Something has drastically changed if the USDA is warning people that federally approved beef has to be cooked to a crisp in order to avoid food poisoning tragedies. So what's changed?...Obviously the meat's a lot dirtier."

Predictably, Eisnitz had trouble getting the corporate media interested in her findings. The story was rejected outright by the executive producer of "60 Minutes," who found it "too disgusting."[22]   "Too graphic" was the excuse given by "20/20."[23]

Said Eisnitz, "PrimeTime, meanwhile, was working on a related story which ended up running instead of mine. It concentrated on the increasingly serious problem of meat contamination. It was an important, effective show and used some of the material I'd sent the producer, but it didn't touch on the subject of animal abuse."

Thus one television newsmagazine—"PrimeTime Live"—was finally prodded into airing a show on *consumer hazards*, "while I'd been focused on the welfare of animals and workers," writes Eisnitz.

***

Yet even when the public health is at stake, the media of the Death Culture cannot always be relied upon to air an important story—at least that has been the experience of two veteran TV reporters in Florida whose station management refused to air their series on Bovine Growth Hormone (BGH) in the public's milk supply.

In 1996 Steve Wilson and Jane Akre, a veteran husband and wife reporting team, began work on the BGH story for their employer. Wilson and Akre were reporters for WTVT Channel 13, in Tampa—where the FCC carried out armed raids against three micro stations during the same year, almost at the same time Wilson and Akre were working on their story.

BGH, developed by Monsanto, was approved by the Federal Food and Drug Administration in 1993. It is a genetically engineered hormone which, when injected into dairy cows, can increase milk yields by as much as 30 percent. Yet from the start there has been concern among consumers about human health risks associated with BGH-treated milk.

Wilson's and Akre's report elaborating on these concerns was not merely killed by WTVT. In a lawsuit against the station the couple charged that station officials ordered them to *change* their report after receiving a threatening letter from Monsanto officials. When Wilson and Akre refused to report false information to the public, they were fired, according to the suit.

"We paid $3 billion for these television stations," station manager David Boylan is alleged to have told the pair. "We will decide what the news is. The news is what we tell you it is." [24]

Rather than being figments of George Orwell's imagination, people who hold views similar to those attributed to Boylan, are real-life people managing real-life newsrooms in America.

If the experiences of Wilson and Akre, as well as Eisnitz, are any indication, then, the major media simply cannot be counted upon as reliable purveyors of vital news and information. Besides these two individual cases, there are countless other examples as well of the suppression, or "underreporting," of vital, important information. Each year Project Censored at Sonoma State University in Northern California publishes a list of what it regards as the most censored news stories of the previous year. For the year 1998, the top 10 censored stories were:

1. Secret international trade agreement undermines the sovereignty of nations.
2. Chemical corporations profit off breast cancer.
3. Monsanto's genetically modified seed threatens world production.
4. Recycled radioactive metals may be in your home.
5. U.S. weapons of mass destruction linked to the deaths of half a million children.
6. U.S. nuclear program subverts UN's comprehensive test ban treaty.
7. Gene transfers linked to dangerous new diseases.
8. No mercy for women in Catholic hospital mergers.
9. U.S. tax dollars support death squads in Chiapas.
10. Environmental student activists gunned down on Chevron oil facility in Nigeria.

Where have the major media been on these stories? Instead of the above, the media have served up huge, steamy casseroles of the trite and irrelevant. Meanwhile, as all this fiddling takes place, Rome continues to burn, and the Death Culture, which is corporate culture, casts its shadow as far and wide as the BGH in the milk and the E.coli in the meat.

In deciding whether or not to legalize micro radio in any sort of meaningful manner, this is what the FCC must begin to take into consideration. If Americans are going to find a way out of this morass, they must be able to talk to each other, to communicate neighbor to neighbor, and community to community.

***

No discussion of the Death Culture would, of course, be complete without mentioning the phenomenon of "emerging new diseases," starting with AIDS.

Looking back over the past 20 years of my life, it is amazing to me when I stop and think that there is now a whole generation of young people who have never known what it was like to live in a world without AIDS—without the notion that sex with another human being might mean a potential death sentence. AIDS changed all that, as well as irrevocably changing life as a human being on this planet. Even if a cure is found tomorrow, the scars left on the collective human psyche will be permanent and deep—though, of course, no cure, at present, is in sight.

When AIDS first exploded into the homosexual populations of New York and San Francisco, many people began to refer to it as a "gay disease." This deadly new killer was blamed on the "sexual perversions" of the "gay lifestyle." Gay people themselves wondered why this had happened to them.

With the exception of New York and Los Angeles—which have far greater populations—no city in America has been harder hit by AIDS than San Francisco. As of the end of August 1998, 17,637 people had died of AIDS in this city. Why did all these people die? Gay people are some of the kindest, gentlest people I have ever known. Why did this disease strike so hard, in this country, only at them? Is it because, as has been asserted by the Christian Right, they incurred God's wrath? Or is there possibly a more earthly explanation?

Where did AIDS come from? Have the media been completely forthright and honest in presenting before the public all the available evidence about its possible origins?

While it may come as a shock to most Americans—who tend by and large to believe AIDS came from monkeys out of Africa—there is a sizeable body of evidence—admittedly only circumstantial, but a sizeable body nonetheless—to indicate that AIDS was created in a U.S. government biological warfare lab. Much of what is known about this subject is contained in two books: *Emerging Viruses: AIDS and Ebola: Nature, Accident or Intentional* by Dr. Leonard Horowitz; and *Queer Blood: The Secret AIDS Genocide Plot* by Dr. Alan Cantwell.

Both authors are medical professionals. Horowitz is a Harvard trained dentist. Cantwell, author of four books on AIDS and cancer, and more than 30 published papers, has more than 30 years experience as a dermatologist in Los Angeles. The information contained in the two books is the stuff of nightmares. Among the key points of evidence presented:

- In 1969—ten years before the onset of AIDS—a high level Pentagon official testified before a congressional committee that scientists were then at work on a "new infective microorganism" which would destroy the human immune system.
- The Pentagon official requested $10 million for the project.
- Congress approved the funding.
- The medical literature published at the time would tend to confirm the official's testimony—that medical science was in search of cancer-causing viruses.
- That among those conducting such research was the man who would later become renowned as the nation's leading AIDS researcher—Dr. Robert Gallo.
- That among the work Gallo and his associates were doing was genetically recombining RNA strands from animal viruses with human viruses, creating in the process mutant and deadly new superviruses.
- That among Gallo's collaborators at various times were Drs. Robert Ting and Stringer Yang, of Bionetics Research Laboratories of Bethesda, Maryland.
- Bionetics Research Laboratories, a subsidiary of Litton Industries, Inc., was one of the nation's leading biological warfare defense contractors.
- That Gallo and associates, perhaps most incredibly, published details of their work in top medical/scientific journals.
- In one such article, published in 1971 in *Nature New Biology* (vol. 232, p.140-142) Gallo and co-authors Sarin, Allen, Newton, Priori, Bowen, and

Dmochowski discuss adding a feline leukemia virus "template" to a human "type C" virus associated with lymphoma. (Feline leukemia has been called "AIDS in cats.") The combination reportedly increased by 30 times the rate of DNA production. This type of virus may cause many types of cancers, besides leukemias and lymphomas, including sarcomas (HIV causes Kaposi's sarcoma), the report stated.

- Gallo continued publishing such articles in 1972, 1973, and 1974, detailing his experiments with viruses from cats, monkeys, chickens and mice.

- Gallo, in the 1960s and 1970s was the top virologist at the National Cancer Institute in Bethesda, Maryland, and in 1972 was appointed as the NCI's Chief of Lab Tumor Cell Biology.

- In 1971, the year following the $10 million congressional appropriation for the development of AIDS-like viruses, the NCI acquired facilities at Fort Detrick, the U.S. Army's chemical-biological warfare (CBW) research center in Frederick, Maryland.

- The NCI was the principal beneficiary of the $10 million appropriation.

- In addition to these activities, Gallo, according to the government's Special Virus Cancer Program Report, also served as a "project officer" overseeing several Bionetics contracts.

- In the mid-1970s Public Health officials began testing an experimental hepatitis B vaccine which eventually led to the inoculation of 10,000 gay men in New York City during the years 1978 and 1979.

- Hepatitis B was a disease said by Health officials to be inordinately affecting the gay community. The trials were overseen by Dr. Wolf Szmuness, of the New York City Blood Center, who specified that subjects of the vaccine experiments had to be gay—and had to be sexually active.

- Vaccines used in the experiment were furnished by the National Institute of Health, which administrates the NCI, and by Merck, Sharp and Dohme pharmaceutical company.

- Merck's founder, George Merck, ran the U.S. Army's CBW program during World War II.

- After the war, Hitler's top scientists were recruited by the CIA in "Project Paper Clip." Among these were Erich Traub, head of biological warfare at the Reich Research Institute at Riems. Traub and assistant Anne Burger ended up, in 1951, assigned to the Naval Medical Research Institute in Bethesda, where their work included animal research into infectious viruses.

- Following the inoculation of gay men in New York, the first cases of AIDS began to appear in Manhattan, in 1979.

- In March of 1980, the Centers for Disease Control (CDC) supervised identical hepatitis B trials in San Francisco—followed by other U.S. cities, including Los Angeles.

- The hepatitis B trials, like Gallo's work mutating animal viruses, can be read about in the medical literature published at the time, including Szmuness' own article in the *New England Journal of Medicine* in 1980 (vol. 303, no. 15, p. 833-841).

- From the mid sixties through 1977 the World Health Organization (WHO) carried out a massive smallpox vaccination campaign in Africa.

- On May 11, 1987, *The London Times* published a front page story linking the WHO smallpox program to the outbreak of AIDS in Africa. Asked by the *Times* for his comments, Gallo said, "The link between the WHO program and the epidemic is an interesting and important hypothesis. I cannot say that it actually happened, but I have been saying for some years that the use of live vaccines such as that used for smallpox can activate a dormant infection such as HIV." The U.S. media never picked up on the *Times* story and Gallo never again raised the smallpox issue in public.

- In the fall of 1986 the Soviet Union proclaimed that AIDS was the result of the U.S. government's biological warfare program. *Time* magazine (Nov. 17, 1986) labeled the charge as "infectious propaganda."

The items listed in evidence above total 26—one for each letter of the alphabet. Enough additional evidence exists to run through the alphabet again. Suffice to say, people have been sent to Death Row and executed in this country on evidence far flimsier than that which presently exists to indict the U.S. government for creating AIDS.

***

Perhaps the most explosively controversial show ever to air on San Francisco Liberation Radio was a weekly program called "AIDS Biowarfare Update." It was hosted by yours truly. Both Cantwell and Horowitz were my guests at different times. The show was dedicated to a weekly exploration of the evidence, such as that above, linking AIDS to the government's chemical/biological warfare (CBW) program. This evidence has never been reported much in the major media. This is not surprising given the major media's predominantly held view that, "The news is what we tell you it is."

The problem, naturally, with such total, unbending media silence on an issue of such profound ineffability and magnitude, is that it makes the issue all the more unbelievable when somebody *does* bring it up and talk about it. You have to have documentation in hand. This is what Cantwell and Horowitz bring to the discussion—yet such people as Cantwell and Horowitz, to the extent that the media even deign to take notice of them, are routinely dismissed as "conspiracy theorists," and are hinted at being more than only slightly delusional.

A "conspiracy theorist" does, however, have his antithesis. In the event that you may consider the above 26 points of evidence as nothing more than mere coincidences, you, perhaps, then, are what Earth First! activist Judi Bari once refered to as a "coincidence theorist."

The fact is that the AIDS-biowarfare issue is the most heavily censored story in America. Even the so-called "alternative media" have stayed away from it in droves. There has never been an article about it, for instance, in the left-leaning *San Francisco Bay Guardian. Covert Action Quarterly* reported on the CBW theory in 1987—but then renounced it in a second article nine years later, in the Fall of 1996 issue.

Even left wing thinkers and luminaries, people such as Parenti, and Noam Chomsky—who have been known to draw standing-room only crowds—have left the subject wholly alone. You could say, of course, this is because they place no credence in the idea. That may well be the case. But I think also there is a feeling that many people have when approaching this subject that a) it's too horrifying with which to deal; and b) in any event it's something of a bottomless pit, a mystery that can never be solved.

"We could spend all day arguing over who started AIDS and in the meantime no work would get done toward bringing about progressive social change," the feeling seems to go.

Then, too, there is reluctance on the part of the Left to bad-mouth the government in too egregious a manner. Right-wing critics of government habitually berate the government for its sins while ignoring the sins of corporations. The Left, on the other hand, feels that while the government is bad, corporations are even worse. The Left is absolutely correct. The government, as Chomsky has noted, is, at least theoretically, somewhat subject to democratic rule with the proper amount of prodding—while corporations are but "pure tyrannies."

And finally there is that reputation-discrediting, bugaboo term, "conspiracy theorist." Coined by the corporate media, the label has been used almost as a sledgehammer to bash anyone who might challenge the establishment-sanctioned version of reality. To be called a conspiracy theorist today *is at least as bad as being called a "communist" was in the 1950s.* There are few labels which can so damage an academic or journalistic reputation.

Compounding the problem (and the confusion) is the fact that there are many, many people out there with theories about government plots who truly *are* wacky. Perhaps this is no accident. How convenient for anyone wishing to cover-up a crime of genocide to have a whole category of certifiable nut cases into which to lump serious researchers such as Horowitz and Cantwell (though, of course, the mere act of pointing this out, I realize, leaves me open to the "wacko" label myself).

In any event being branded a conspiracy theorist is a career-buster, a reputation-ruiner. Few people are willing to run the risk. Two people who have, and have paid for it, are Horowitz and Cantwell.

The threat of labels, corporate tyrannies, unsolved mysteries, bottomless pits, and neglected progressive agendas are all valid concerns. Are they valid enough to remain silent in the face of what could potentially be genocide? And if we remain silent are we allowing some gay people to go on thinking that this epidemic was somehow caused by them?

These are perhaps hard calls to make. I decided finally that someone on the Left had to start talking about this—and I resolved that someone would be me, that I would do this once a week on San Francisco Liberation Radio. Do it I did, each Wednesday night from 8 to 9, taking one angle of the story or another, and dissecting it, reviewing everything that was known about it.

***

"And don't forget that in the mid seventies the gay community was becoming a tremendous threat to many people," Cantwell told me when I first interviewed him in 1994. "There were those who felt that, 'My God, these people are coming out of the closet, and they want rights,' and basically some people felt that they should all be dead."

Cantwell may have a point. Is it simply coincidence that AIDS appeared when gays and lesbians were first coming "out of the closet" and demanding their civil rights?

If one of the monster new designer viruses created by science in the early 1970s ended up contaminating the vaccines given to gay men in America—and to blacks in central Africa—the question must be asked: was it an accident, or was it done deliberately? Cantwell, who is gay, believes it was deliberate. Horowitz, who is not, prefers to leave the question unanswered.

"What does my intuition say? My intuition says that it was most likely intentional—for population control," Horowitz told me after I had pinned him down on the subject, during a live in-studio interview in 1997. "Even though the mass of scientific evidence that I have—republished, reprinted, documented in the book—is that it was an accident waiting to happen. The biohazard and containment...(precautions taken by) these people were abysmal."

What could Congress possibly have been thinking of in 1969 when it appropriated $10 million for the development of a virus that would break down the immune system? The answer is the Cold War.

The testimony of Dr. Donald MacArthur, deputy director of the Pentagon under Richard Nixon, is recorded in *Department of Defense Appropriations for 1970*, and is reproduced by both Horowitz and Cantwell in their respective books. The testimony was given on July 1, 1969 before a subcommittee of the House Committee on Appropriations during a hearing on CBW. Members of the committee included Rep. Robert Sikes of Florida.

> Dr. MacArthur: There are two things about the biological agent field I would like to mention. One is the possibility of technological surprise. Molecular biology is a field that is advancing very rapidly and eminent biologists believe that within a period of 5 to 10 years it would be possible to produce a synthetic biological agent, an agent that does not naturally exist and for which no natural immunity could have been acquired.

Mr. Sikes: Are we doing any work in that field?

Dr. MacArthur: We are not.

Mr. Sikes: Why not? Lack of money or lack of interest?

Dr. MacArthur: Certainly not lack of interest.

Mr. Sikes: Would you provide for our records information on what would be required, what the advantages of such a program would be, the time and cost involved?

Dr. MacArthur: We will be very happy to.

(The information follows:)

The dramatic progress being made in the field of molecular biology led us to investigate the relevance of this field of science to biological warfare. A small group of experts considered this matter and provided the following observations:

1. All biological agents up to the present time are representatives of naturally occurring disease, and are thus known by scientists throughout the world. They are easily available to qualified scientists for research, either for offensive or defensive purposes.

2. Within the next 5 to 10 years it would probably be possible to make a new infective microorganism which could differ in certain important aspects from any known disease causing organism. Most important of these is that it might be refractory to the immunological and therapeutic processes upon which we depend to maintain our relative freedom from infections disease.

3. A new research program to explore the feasibility of this could be completed in approximately 5 years at a total cost of $10 million.

4. It would be very difficult to establish such a program. Molecular biology is a relatively new science. There are not many highly competent scientists in the field, almost all are in university laboratories, and they are generally adequately supported from sources other than DOD (Department of Defense). However, it was considered possible to initiate an adequate program through the National Academy of Sciences-National Research Council (NAS-NRC).

5. The matter was discussed with the NAS-NRC and tentative plans were made to initiate the program. However, decreasing funds in CB (chemical/biological), growing criticism of the CB program, and our reluctance to involve the NAS-NRC in such a controversial endeavor have lead us to postpone it for the past 2 years.

It is a highly controversial issue and there are many who believe such research should not be undertaken lest it lead to yet another method of massive killing of large populations. On the other hand, without the sure scientific knowledge that such a weapon is possible, and an understanding of the ways it could be done, there is little that can be done to devise defensive measures. Should an enemy develop it there is little doubt that this is an important area of potential military technological inferiority in which there is no adequate research program. [25]

In 1995 I interviewed for my AIDS program Eric Taylor, a Pennsylvania gay man who was initiating a class action suit on behalf of people with AIDS, charging the U.S. government with creating the virus. We joked about how we both, after reading MacArthur's testimony, had had to go to the dictionary to look up the word "refractory."

Taylor told me pretty much what by then I already knew about the AIDS story. Additionally, Taylor said, he had learned that MacArthur was dead. Taylor, who is not an attorney, was in the process of gathering signatures from every state—necessary, he said, in order to get his case into court. The Pennsylvania man pursued these efforts over the next two years, dropping them finally out of exhaustion.

Dr. Robert Gallo has been a figure of controversy since the beginning of the AIDS epidemic. He was portrayed as having a football-field-sized ego in the book, *And the Band Played On*, written by Randy Shilts, an openly-gay San Francisco newspaper reporter who later died of AIDS. Gallo's incredible paper trail through the medical literature led Horowitz to believe that Gallo "may have created the AIDS virus about a decade before he allegedly discovered it."

Perhaps what the public remembers most when Gallo's name comes to mind is his dispute, in 1984, with French scientists over who first "discovered" the AIDS virus. The dispute was finally settled at the highest levels of government with both Gallo and Luc Montagnier of the Pasteur Institute in Paris sharing equal credit. Much about the dispute—and the settlement—were apparently left undisclosed to the public.

> Between 1978 and 1983, Gallo's lab continued to pay little attention to AIDS at the "lethargic NCI." In those days the NCI's chief retrovirologist allegedly perceived the cause to be more frustrating and distracting than legitimate.
>
> During this period of AIDS research Gallo's behavior appeared at best erratic and at worst contemptuous. Shilts recorded a series of suspicious interactions in which Gallo all but sabotaged international research efforts to isolate the AIDS retrovirus. [26]

Why would Gallo do such a thing, given that his work at the NCI involved leukemia research, and that he was "among the world's champions at quickly identifying reverse transcriptase enzyme and RNA retroviruses?" How was it that Gallo was unable to isolate the AIDS virus until 1984 when the "methods and materials" necessary to do so were "researched in depth in the early 1970s?" [27] As Horowitz noted:

> It was highly suspicious then that following a decade of successfully doing so, he (Gallo) was suddenly unable to keep RNA retrovirus-infected lymphocytes alive...
>
> As "most CDC researchers privately believed," Shilts wrote, it is inconceivable that Gallo would not have readily isolated the "true" AIDS virus well before 1982 given his formidable background and resources.

"What delayed the NCI, therefore, was not the difficulty in finding the virus but their reluctance to even look."

With all the glory attached to the earliest discovery of the AIDS virus, what powerful force could have moved the world's citadel of retrovirus research—Gallo and the NCI—away from the challenge that could have been met so handily?

There were few plausible explanations—only more horrifying questions. Had Gallo been ashamed of creating the virus years earlier, so he tried to block its discovery, terrified it might be traced to BW (biological warfare) research? [28]

The New York City Blood Center's hepatitis B vaccine trials, another major part of the equation, are most vividly and shockingly described in the Cantwell book. The trials were supervised by Dr. Wolf Szmuness and involved innoculating thousands of gay men with an experimental hepatitis B vaccine.

In the late 1970s a bloodmobile began canvassing the gay neighborhood in the Greenwich Village section of Manhattan, looking for homosexual volunteers. Over ten thousand men signed up and donated blood samples for Szmuness' upcoming experiment. [29]

Szmuness first tested his vaccine on chimpanzees, then on two hundred human volunteers. By the fall of 1978 he was ready to begin large-scale innoculations of thousands of volunteers in an "experiment which would decimate the gay community in New York City."

In January 1979, purple skin lesions began to appear on the bodies of young white gay men in the Village. The doctors were not sure exactly what was wrong with these men. During the next thirty months Manhattan physicians encountered dozens of cases of a new disease characterized by immunodeficiency, Kaposi's sarcoma, and a rapidly fatal lung disease, known as *Pneumocystis carinii* pneumonia. All the men were young and gay and promiscuous. Almost all were white. All died horribly. [30]

In *Emerging Viruses*, Horowitz supplies us with the additional information that small numbers of gay men were injected as early as 1976 in a separate hepatitis B study conducted by Dr. Saul Krugman of the New York University Medical Center. (NYUMC is another documented biological warfare defense contractor.) [31]

***

Around 1994 I discovered that another micro radio station—Black Liberation Radio (BLR) in Springfield, Illinois, was also hitting hard at the AIDS-CBW story. (Having dropped the name Black Liberation Radio, BLR today broadcasts as Human Rights Radio.)

The work at getting the story out in Springfield was being done by none other than micro radio pioneer Mbanna Kantako. Kantako and I began to share tapes with each other. I sent him my interviews with Cantwell, Horowitz and Taylor, while he sent me his interviews with political researchers Bryan Harris, Zears Miles, and others.

Among the vast amount of evidence the BLR researchers had come up with was the May 11, 1987 *London Times* article linking AIDS in Africa to the WHO's smallpox vaccination program. One thing Harris and Miles—as well as Cantwell and Horowitz—were all agreed upon was the possible motive behind the "seeding" of AIDS onto the African continent: population control.

Controlling population in the Third World has in fact been a "national security" concern of the U.S. government since at least the 1960s. It was in 1968 that Paul Ehrlich published his book, *The Population Bomb*, warning that the "population explosion" was bound to bring about a future of hunger, poverty, disease, and environmental degradation if something were not done soon to curb it. There is evidence that Ehrlich's book was highly influential in shaping U.S. policy. A decade after its appearance, the U.S. government issued its "Global 2000 Report." The report is a massive volume which was prepared for President Jimmy Carter by a group of researchers from various U.S. government agencies.

What would the world be like by the year 2000 if population growth were to continue unchecked? This is the question the report sought to answer as it projected the impact soaring birth rates would have upon agriculture, water resources, forests, top soil loss, desertification, atmosphere and climate, fisheries, and species extinction. "Already the populations in sub-Saharan Africa and in the Himalaya hills of Asia have exceeded the carrying capacity of the immediate area, triggering an erosion of the land's capacity to support life," the report's preface tells us. By the year 2000, overpopulation would make the world "more vulnerable to disruption." [32]

Additionally, according to the report,

> Vigorous, determined new initiatives are needed if worsening poverty and human suffering, environmental degradation, and internal tension and conflicts are to be prevented. There are no quick fixes. The only solution to the problems of population, resources, and environment are complex and long-term. These problems are inextricably linked to some of the most perplexing and persistent problems in the world—poverty, injustice, and social conflict. New and imaginative ideas—and a willingness to act on them—are essential. [33]

The report is accompanied by a cover letter from the State Department's Thomas R. Pickering. Pickering and co-writer Gus Speth, of the Council on Environmental Quality, report that "already" the "stresses" on the Earth's "carrying capacity" are "severe enough to deny many millions of people basic needs for food, shelter, health, and jobs, or any hope for betterment." Additionally, they share the information that the study was prepared with the assistance of the CIA, Federal Emergency Management Agency, NASA, and other federal agencies. [34]

***

In 1990 Ehrlich, along with wife and co-author Anne Ehrlich, revisited the population issue with the publication of a second book. In *The Population Explosion* the Ehrlichs write,

> In 1968, *The Population Bomb* warned of impending disaster if the population explosion was not brought under control. Then the fuse was burning; now the population bomb has detonated. Since 1968 at least 200 million people—mostly children—have perished needlessly of hunger and hunger-related diseases, despite "crash programs to 'stretch' the carrying capacity of Earth by increasing food production." The population problem is no longer primarily a threat for the future as it was when the *Bomb* was written and there were only 3.5 billion human beings.[35]

Interestingly, the manner in which the media have covered world population has changed radically over the years—from widespread coverage given to the issue in the 1960s, to virtually none today. This is due perhaps in part to the Reagan administration's policy of de-emphasizing the issue while catering to the anti-abortion Right.

In truth, however, "Malthusianism"—the doctrine that population must be reduced—has never strayed very far as a central component of U.S. foreign policy. While both Horowitz and Cantwell discuss U.S.-sponsored population control efforts in the Third World, perhaps the best work on this subject has been done by Betsy Hartman.

In her book *Reproductive Rights and Wrongs*, Hartman documents population control measures carried out principally by the U.S. Agency for International Development, though with assistance from The World Bank, the New York-based Population Council, the International Planned Parenthood Federation, Ford Foundation, the UN Fund for Population Activities, and a number of smaller agencies and organizations.

As Hartman reports, among the more controversial programs implemented are various "incentive schemes" in which Third World women have received material benefits in exchange for undergoing sterilization—as well as the setting of monthly "sterilization quotas" for Third World family planning counselors. Also employed are "disincentives" in which material or monetary benefits are taken away.

Such programs may look on the surface to be "voluntary," but, says Hartman, they essentially amount to coercion in Third World countries where hunger and poverty are a daily fact of life. In addition, "community incentives" have been offered, in which whole villages have been rewarded in exchange for a high contraceptive acceptance rate, while "a study of mass vasectomy camps in India's Gujarat State found, for example, that the 'most influential' motivators were members of the local revenue department and the police." [36]

The attitudes of some members of the "population establishment" are sometimes quite openly and chillingly expressed, as Hartman reports:

> Some top policy makers openly counsel the use of coercion. In a deeply disturbing article, Bernard Berelson, the late president emeritus of the Population Council, and Jonathan Lieberson argue for the "stepladder" approach to population policy: start off with soft measures, such as voluntary family planning services, and proceed if necessary to harsher measures, such as disincentives,

sanctions, and even violence. "The degree of coercive policy brought into play should be proportional to the degree of seriousness of the present problem, and should be introduced only after less coercive means have been exhausted," they write. "Thus, overt violence or other potentially injurious coercion is not to be used before noninjurious coercion has been exhausted."

They are able to condone coercion so easily because they believe there is no such thing as a "correct" ethical system or universally "approved" ranking of human rights. In their ethically neutral, morally relative universe one thing is clear, however: They rank themselves above others. And it is their responsibility, they say, to make their "best information and policies" known to the "dominant powers" of other societies. [37]

How far would such people go, to what lengths would they resort, to stem population growth—and at whose expense?

All of this is not to say that overpopulation is not a serious world problem. According to the U.S. Census Bureau's World Population Clock, the population of the world stood at just over 6 billion by the end of 1999. Current projections, despite stabilization in some countries, are for it to increase to 9.3 billion by 2050.

In contrast, the total population of the world in 1950 was just 2.5 billion. If the "carrying capacity" of the Earth was already strained when the figure stood at 4.3 billion—at the time of the Global 2000 Report's release—think what it must be now, and what it will be like by the year 2050.

Today the U.S. government is the largest single donor to world population control, though, "it generally prefers to play its role behind the scenes." [38] Nonetheless, substantial sums are appropriated and distributed largely through USAID and the World Bank. This international funding network, involving also "Third World elites," has created a "new class of world managers, which has begun to transcend differences in culture," says Hartman.

They define most issues as "management problems" rather than as moral dilemmas, failing to question their own values and assumptions and to confront the frequent incompatibility between population control and respect for human rights. And for them, bringing the birth rate down is an enterprise that befits their managerial talents, whereas attacking poverty and inequality head-on would jeopardize their privileged position in the hierarchy of politics and power.

Today the population establishment is truly international—among a small circle of friends. [39]

It is a well-established fact that population growth is highest in areas of the world which also contain the highest rates of poverty. The general assumption—that the poor know no better and are simply incapable of practicing self control—is a mistaken one, says Hartman. In fact, "in many Third World societies, having a large family is an eminently rational strategy of survival." [40]

Children help in the fields, tend animals, fetch wood and water, look after younger siblings, or earn income as servants, etc. In the absence of social safety nets, a large family is also security for parents in old age. High infant mortality rates, too, contribute to the problem—people have more children to ensure that at least some will survive to adulthood. In fact, elevated population growth is irretrievably linked to a general lack of social and economic justice. High birth rates are often a "distress signal that people's survival is in danger."

There are, however, Third World countries where people's basic needs have been met, says Hartman. One of these is Cuba. In the latter, health care and education are free. While Cuba's infant mortality rates are among the lowest in the Third World, so too are its birth rates. This is no accident, she says.

Elsewhere in the Third World, though, the story is quite different. Having lived for a time in Bangladesh, Hartman draws frequently upon that country as an example.

Because of inadequate nutrition and health care, one out of every four Bangladeshi children dies before the age of five. Thus families had to produce many children in order to ensure that a few would survive. My neighbor's first five children had all died in infancy—she bore six more and the youngest daughter died too.

Yet once villagers had enough children to meet their needs, they often wanted to limit family size. [41]

Male dominance and the subordination of women, too, are a major cause of high birth rates, yet rather than address these social and economic issues—the root causes of world overpopulation—the "population establishment" has employed the bulk of its resources toward combating high fertility, which is but the *symptom*, says Hartman. Blaming environmental degradation on overpopulation, moreover, has been a convenient way for the rich to avoid responsibility for their own part in creating the ecological crisis now facing the planet.

The tendency, she says, has been to talk about environmental problems, while de-emphasizing the activities of corporations as the cause of those problems. Likewise, it is usually argued, Third World poverty is the direct result—not of corporate rape of the Third World's wealth and natural resources, but of the procreation of its inhabitants.

> Thus recent writers on U.S. foreign policy, such as General Maxwell Taylor and Robert McNamara (a former head of the World Bank), believe the civil war in El Salvador results in part, if not in full, from population pressure, ignoring the extreme disparities of wealth in that country and the violent suppression of any peaceful attempts at social reform. Central America's problem in general is portrayed as too many underemployed young males, who, according to Leon Bouvier of the Population Reference Bureau, increase "the availability of people for revolutionary activity." In this way Malthusianism directly serves to legitimize the status quo: if poor people are rising up it is only because their numbers are rising too fast. [42]

Also omitting any analysis of corporate responsibility are the Ehrlichs. While the pair are not reticent about laying the blame for overpopulation upon certain perceived failings of governments—including the government of the United States—one would be hard-pressed to find, in their book, *The Population Explosion*, the word "corporation" even mentioned.

Conversely, the Ehrlichs do, however, in a discussion on population and public health, offer some thoughts regarding the origins of AIDS—namely that "assigning blame" for the disease is "wrong and unfair," and that it "makes dealing with this massive public health problem much more difficult." [43]

This sentiment is echoed by David Gilbert in his attempt at debunking the AIDS-CBW connection in the left-wing journal *Covert Action Quarterly*. Though conceding that AIDS "has an uncanny knack for attacking people the dominant society considers 'undesirables'," Gilbert nonetheless denounces the AIDS-CBW link as a "false conspiracy theory" which diverts attention from the "*real* genocide"—poverty, lack of proper health care and high infant mortality rates in poor and minority communities. Furthermore, the publicizing of such theories has been harmful, Gilbert asserts, inducing people to share dirty needles, forego vaccinations and avoid safe sex.

"What's the use, believers ask, of making all the hard choices to avoid spreading or contracting the disease if the government is going to find a way to infect people anyway?" he writes. [44]

Gilbert quotes medical experts who dismiss as "scientifically impossible" the notion that HIV could have been created through the recombination of animal viruses; and he presents the AIDS-CBW connection as a right-wing-spawned conspiracy theory—sure to discredit it in the eyes of readers of a left-wing periodical.

Omitting any mention of the works of Horowitz or Cantwell, Gilbert devotes several columns of print, nonetheless, to discussing the admittedly zany theories of William Campbell Douglass, M.D., who, among other things, has suggested that warnings concerning the spread of HIV through intravenous drug use may be no more than "government propaganda." [45] Understandably angry at seeing such assertions in print, Gilbert traces Douglass' history back to alleged involvement in the John Birch Society, and attributes to him numerous racist and homophobic statements.

"What we don't need are the fundamentally right-wing conspiracy theories of Dr. Douglass and the like that lead us on a wild goose chase for the little men in white coats in a secret lab," he says. [46]

Thus Gilbert belittles the whole idea of a man-made theory of AIDS. While Douglass no doubt makes an easy target, nowhere in Gilbert's article does there appear any mention, either of the MacArthur testimony, nor of the paper trail blazed by Gallo through the medical literature of the early 1970s—apparently both undebunkable. With regard to paper trails, in fact, Gilbert finds it highly unlikely that conspirators would "publish their evil plans." [47]

Ironically, the same government around which so many suspicions abound regarding AIDS, now rejects one of the most important, scientifically proven methods for slowing its spread: needle exchange. On April 20, 1998, Health and Human Services Secretary Donna Shalala announced that the Clinton administration would not lift a nine-year-old federal ban on needle exchange programs—this despite openly acknowledging the validity of scientific evidence indicating that such programs halt the spread of HIV!

"At best this is hypocrisy. At worst it's a lie. And no matter what, it's immoral," said Dr. R. Scott Hitt, chairman of Clinton's own Advisory Council on HIV and AIDS, of the decision. [48]

At the time of the announcement, IV drug use was said by the *New York Times* to be "responsible for most of the growth in the spread of AIDS, particularly among the poor and minorities," while one AIDS researcher estimated that had the government allocated federal funding for needle exchange programs, 17,000 lives—roughly the number of people who have died of AIDS in San Francisco since the epidemic began—could have been saved during Clinton's terms in office. [49]

The decision was viewed as being simply another in a long line of Clinton capitulations to the far right. Conservative members of Congress expressed concern that funding of needle exchange programs would send the "wrong message."

Was obsession over beaming the right message the only thing on the minds of these politicians? Or were perhaps at least some of them thinking it might also be convenient to reduce certain unwanted segments of the American population? Given rising joblessness coupled with cutbacks in welfare and expansion of the U.S. prison system—given the expressed views of some members of the "population establishment" that world population must be reduced by whatever means may prove necessary—given also the rather remarkable mountain of evidence linking the biowarfare industry to the creation of AIDS—the notion is perhaps not as farfetched as it may seem.

Perhaps Loretta Dolphus, a former drug addict and sex worker now working in a Harlem recovery program, expressed it best. Of the Washington politicians who had quashed needle exchange, Dolphus commented, "They're not looking at us as people." [50]

***

In doing the AIDS show on SFLR it was always my policy, as the host, to never express an opinion of my own as to whether the U.S. government did—or did not—create AIDS. This I tried to adhere to conscientiously. Simply having the show at all was enough of an editorial expression in and of itself. My job, I strongly believed, was merely to lay the evidence out on the table and let the public decide for itself. Even this much had rarely if ever been done over a radio station.

What was the public reaction? One listener reduced it all down to basics. "You know, if what you're saying about AIDS is true, there's no longer any reason to salute the flag." Another suggested, perhaps only partly in jest, that we should do a Jolly Roger skit about an underground lab where revolutionary forces working to overthrow the government produce a virus that only attacks corporate CEOs.

Though public reaction was slow in coming in (due either to low listenership, mass denial, or plain, simple disinterest), I continued to pound away on the AIDS/CBW story.

"We know that in Africa AIDS is a basically heterosexual epidemic that is spread evenly between men and women," Cantwell said on the show one night. "Then how in God's name can you take a black heterosexual epidemic and turn it into what was originally a white homosexual epidemic?"

One theory regarding AIDS—the theory propounded by the media, the government, and the scientific establishment—is that the disease came from a monkey. The other theory—put forth by Cantwell, Horowitz, and other "conspiracy theorists"—is that it came from a lab and was introduced into the population—either deliberately or by accident (or corporate negligence)—through vaccines. Of the two theories, you might consider asking yourself, which seems the more plausible?

Despite the abundant evidence indicating there could very well be a biological holocaust in progress, still the media of the Death Culture remain silent on this issue. And not only do they not report on it, but they get extremely skittish and nervous when the subject even comes up. A prime example of this skittishness occurred in Springfield, Illinois, when BLR organized and held a public forum entitled "AIDS, the Mass Media, and Genocide." The forum took place on February 23, 1995. Special guest speaker was John Fisk, a white University of Wisconsin professor of Communications who had devoted a whole chapter of his book, *Media Matters*, to BLR's coverage of the AIDS-biowarfare story.

Fisk's credentials were rather impressive. A distinguished academic and author of numerous books, Fisk had even given presentations before the United Nations. Obviously the Springfield corporate-owned media wanted nothing to do with even hinting at or alluding to any connection between AIDS and biowarfare—yet to wholly ignore Fisk's visit to the city would have been difficult due to his stature and prestige.

The solution that was arrived at was adopted uniformly by all the white-owned media of Springfield: in reporting advance notices of the event, the word "genocide" was omitted from the title, the media merely announcing the forum as a conference on "AIDS and the Mass Media." On the night of the event, Kantako commented on the peculiar omission. Pretending not to understand why the media had dropped the word "genocide," Kantako adlibbed humorously:

I guess the word that's hardest to say in this town in
the local press this week seems to be *genocide*, don't it?

You pick up the announcements for this presentation tonight and everybody had the first two parts of announcement, but the third part they left out. You know it was entitled, "AIDS, the Mass Media, and Genocide"—but they left out "genocide."

Why'd they leave out genocide?

Let's see—is it longer than "mass media?"—no, it's shorter than mass media. Well, it's a little longer than "AIDS"—but not much...

Here Kantako dropped the pretense and continued on a far more serious note:

Maybe it's the *definition* of the word genocide. You see, some things, if they never come up—they will never be dealt with. But Malcolm X said it—Malcolm said that if you and I come into a room and we sit down at a table, and let's say your father is underneath the table and he's dead—heaven forbid—but let's say that.

And we've agreed that when we sit down at this table, we are not going to talk about this corpse under the table. After a while we won't be able to talk about nothing—because of the smell of the corpse.

***

If Kantako is correct and such a campaign of genocide really *does* exist, there are, one might expect, many different ways of waging it. Overt and outright murder by police of citizens of this country is the focus of research conducted by the Stolen Lives Project.

In April 2000, Karen Saari, head researcher for the project, guested on San Francisco Liberation Radio. Saari had compiled into a book the names and stories of 2000 people who had been killed by the police in the United States since the year 1990.

One of the case studies cited in the book is that of Aaron Williams. The latter was a 35-year-old African American who was beaten and pepper sprayed to death by San Francisco Police on June 4, 1995. At 10 p.m. that night, 12 police officers came to his home, rang the bell, and demanded that he come out into the street, where they proceeded to kill him. Aaron's brutal police-gang-murder was observed by dozens of neighborhood witnesses. The officers said they suspected he had been involved in burglary at a business earlier in the evening, though that involvement was never proven.

Much to do *was* made, however, about the fact that Williams was a "parolee." Police claimed they had had to use force because he had resisted arrest. Witness statements were conflicting on this point. One thing witnesses agreed on, however, was the incredible torrent of violence which had rained down upon Williams' body. The "parolee" was repeatedly clubbed, kicked and pepper sprayed in the face. Later, when the officers placed Williams handcuffed into a police van, he was allegedly still breathing; when the van doors were opened at the police station, however, he was found to have expired.

The brutal murder of Williams was covered extensively on SFLR. Our response even included organizing a "Community Forum on Police Violence," which took place July 10, 1995. One of the speakers was Andrea Pritchard of Berkeley Copwatch. Copwatch at that time hosted a weekly program on Free Radio Berkeley. Said Pritchard that night:

> This system is a closed system. You know, we go to the DA and say, "Look! The cop killed somebody!" But DAs don't prosecute cops. We go to a civilian review agency and say, "Oh, the cops did this, and that!" And they say, "Well, we don't have—look we're underfunded, we're understaffed, we don't have any teeth. Even if we *did* have appropriate staff, we're totally disempowered." You know, we go through—there's nothing but *dead ends*!
>
> You know, I don't *care* about *misconduct*! I'm trying to stop police *crime*! It's gotten to that level. I don't care, you know, what you *call* me—I mean, *verbal* abuse *is* abuse, and all. And "we got rights!" etc. etc. But we're just worried about them not killing people at this point!

Pritchard's fears proved to be well-founded. On September 6, less than two months after our forum, San Francisco Police blew a hole in the back of the head of William Hankston, another black youth, as he was riding his bicycle. Hankston had committed the crime of ignoring police orders to halt, continuing to peddle away as those orders were given. Hankston was unarmed.

But there was more:

- Edwin Sheehan—shot to death by SF police on November 1 as he sat behind the wheel of his car. Sheehan was unarmed.
- Anthony Wingate—collapsed and died during a struggle with police on January 24. Wingate was unarmed.
- Mark Garcia—beaten and pepper sprayed by police on April 6. Garcia was not only unarmed, but was nearly naked. Having apparently been robbed, he was wandering Cesar Chavez Street, bare from the waist down and evidently deranged.
- Sheila Detoy—shot to death when police fired into a car occupied by herself and two male companions on May 13, 1998. All three occupants of the car were unarmed. A witness later disputed police claims that the car had been moving toward them as if to run them over. Detoy, who was just 17 years old, worked as a waitress in a beach cafe.
- John M. Smart Jr.—shot to death by police on October 6, 1998. Smart, who was unarmed perished after police fired at least 13 rounds into his Mercedes convertible.

The above, though probably not a complete list, accounts for police killings occurring only within the city of San Francisco, and only during the '95-'98 time frame. Deaths occurring in the immediate surrounding area at the same time included:

- Kuan Chung Kao—shot to death on April 29, 1997, in Rohnert Park
- Brian J. Prosser—succumbed to pepper spray in Novato on October 20, 1997.

In addition to these there were, in other areas of California, incidents of police brutality which did not result in death but which were spectacularly notable for their cruelty. These included:

- the beating of two Mexican immigrants by Riverside County Sheriff's deputies on April 1, 1996. Especially savage in nature, the beating was captured on video tape, which was televised nationally, prompting a protest from the Mexican government.

- the pepper spraying of protestors in Humbolt County on September 25, October 3, and October 16, 1997. In each of these incidents police took cotton swabs soaked in pepper spray and dabbed them onto the eyelids of protestors engaged in sit-ins to stop the logging of Headwaters Forest. [51]

In her interview with us, Saari disclosed a sobering statistic. Her research, she said, had led her to conclude that in the state of California alone, one person is killed by police on average of every other day.

"I include people who die of medical neglect in the jail, abuse in the jail, as well as police killings in that figure—but in any event, every other day one person dies at the hands of law enforcement in California," Saari said.

As apropos as may have been Kantako's mix of the words "AIDS," "mass media," and "genocide" into one event title, well may have the Springfield micro broadcaster held a program on "Police Brutality, the Mass Media, and Genocide"—with special emphasis on the mass media part. Playing a huge role in justifying Williams' murder to the public was San Francisco's corporate-owned media, which regularly referred to Williams as a "parolee" while quoting police and government officials as if their statements were unquestioned fact.

One such official often quoted was Dr. Boyd Stephens, San Francisco's chief medical examine. The latter "all but eliminated" brutality or the use of excessive force as being a cause of death in the Williams case, the *San Francisco Chronicle* reported on June 17.

"I don't want to even prejudge whether police did something properly," Stephens told the newspaper. "I want to determine how he died, and that will help determine the truthfulness of witnesses statements." [52]

Better might it have been to conduct the investigation from the opposite point of view: i.e., using the witnesses statements as a barometer to determine the truthfulness of Stephens' autopsy findings. Stephens told the press on June 16 that Williams had in all probability died of "excited delirium," the coroner claiming that he had "pretty well ruled out beating because of the absence of major trauma to the body." [53] The *Chronicle* described "excited delirium" as "an agitated mental disorder that can cause a heart attack," and termed Stephens' findings "a crucial element in the controversy about whether the police acted with excessive force" in the case.
54

On June 21 Stephens allowed to the press that maybe a shoe worn by one of the 12 officers possibly contained a "pattern that could have caused" an abrasion on the deceased man's cheek. Again, however, he affirmed his belief that "excited delirium" was the probable cause of death, possibly complicated by the manner in which Williams had been placed in the back of the van—hog-tied and face down. [55]

On July 20, the medical examiner made it official: Williams had definitely died of excited delirium, Stephens informing the press additionally that the condition had been brought on by "accute cocaine toxicity."

Neither pepper spray nor the violent beating undergone by Williams (witnesses claimed that the assault had been so savage that Williams had at one point begun crying for his mother) had contributed to his death, according to the coroner. "Excited delirium is a serious complication of cocaine abuse," Stephens said. [56]

The Williams family denounced the investigation as a "whitewash". Family members who had viewed the body disputed the coroner's claims of an "absence of major trauma to the body," while an independent autopsy, conducted by Dr. Robert D. Lawrence of Stockton, California, listed multiple causes of death, including the beating, the pepper spraying, cocaine use, and Williams' having been hog-tied after the attack. [57]

On April 6, a second man, Mark Garcia, died under circumstances similar to Williams. In the wake of this attack, Stephens, perhaps finding "excited delirium" insufficient to explain away the rash of pepper spray deaths, suggested another possible medical cause: "Custody Death Syndrome."

In reporting on this strange, new "phenomenon," the *Chronicle* supplied corroborating statements as to its existence—from officials with the Los Angeles Sheriff's Department, the California Department of Corrections, and the Seattle/King County Medical Examiner's Office. The onset of the affliction is often preceded by a struggle with police, said the *Chronicle*. [58]

> The struggle typically ends with the suspect pepper sprayed, tackled and shackled—yet just when the situation seems to be under control, the suspect abruptly stops breathing and dies. Attempts to resuscitate the victim fail, even when begun immediately. [59]

Drug use was identified as a possible contributing factor, causing many sufferers to appear "medically older than their stated age." According to one official, Law Enforcement had determined that perhaps officers "should no longer use restraint methods developed when police mostly encountered young, healthy men." [60]

The *Chronicle* reported Custody Death Syndrome as having been around since at least 1989, though curiously it's not listed among the "emerging new viruses" discussed by Horowitz and Cantwell.

One of the unfortunate aspects of being killed by the police (aside from losing your life) is that your character undergoes a posthumous defamation in the media. Immediately after Williams' death, the media, assuming the basic correctness of police statements, labeled Williams as "delirious," and "aggressive."[61] Little consideration seems to have been given that it may have been the police who were "aggressive."

Perhaps one of the worst offenders in this regard was the *Chronicle*. On June 17, the newspaper, relying on information supplied by the police, described Williams as "a heavy cocaine user." On June 22 Williams became a "cocaine-using, violent parole," while "burglary suspect" was another term frequently inserted into articles.

Much of the public were not fooled by this. Community protests erupted and continued to grow over the next two years, finally forcing the firing of the ranking officer on the scene at the time Williams was murdered. Be that as it may, none of the officers who participated in the attack were ever prosecuted for their crimes.

***

The manner in which the city handled the Aaron Williams case was, from start to finish, a complete fiasco. Much of the responsibility for that fiasco rests with Mayor Willie Brown.

In 1995 the voters of San Francisco dumped Mayor and former Police Chief Frank Jordan in favor of Brown, who became the city's first African-American mayor. In campaigning, Brown, a famous state power broker and former speaker of the California Assembly, presented himself as a harbinger of great and momentous change. The voters, despite ample evidence of Brown's corporate backing, bought it. Indeed as the new mayor assumed office in early 1996, the arrests of Food Not Bombs, which had by now become an embarrassing legacy, ground to a halt.

But in virtually all other areas—from taxation to the homeless—Brown essentially continued the policies of Frank Jordan. It was Brown's irresponsible appointments to the police commission which set the stage for the travesty of justice which became the Aaron Williams case.

With Willie Brown as mayor, the corporations were still firmly in control of San Francisco.

One thing in particular Brown campaigned as an opponent of was the Matrix Program—Jordan's grand plan for getting homeless people off the streets and "into the system." Yet after Brown took office, the only thing that changed was that the word "Matrix" disappeared from the vocabulary of city officials. The Program's major components—the citations, arrests, and property confiscations—continued as before.

"The only thing that's gone about Matrix is the name," Paul Boden, of the Coalition on Homelessness, told me in an interview in 1997.

According to Boden, the premise behind Matrix had been all along "to make San Francisco a less homeless-friendly town."

What about the program's reputed social service aspects?

"Straight up dog and pony," Boden replied.

He added:

> They (the social workers assigned by Jordan to the Matrix patrols) didn't have anywhere to send anybody except for these set-aside beds that would be for one night. They would go up to a group of people in a camp and say, 'Well, we can get you one night at a shelter down south of Market, but you gotta turn in all your stuff. You gotta destroy your camp and leave here.'...And people said, 'Fuck you,' and the social workers would walk on to the next group. And then the cops would come in right behind them."

Under Brown, said Boden, "the social workers don't come in first and try to get rid of (homeless people). That's the only difference."

In late 1997, as if the climate against homeless people were not hostile enough already, there appeared a report in the *Chronicle*—largely false and hysterical—warning of "a new wave of junkies and parolees invading sections of" Golden Gate Park. The article triggered yet another frenzied round of anti-homeless reporting by the corporate media as a whole, prompting Brown to order a major *new* crackdown—above and beyond what was already happening on a normal, everyday basis!

"I couldn't even give you an estimate because there are so many people who live in this park, but I mean there is so many people that have lost a lot of their stuff," one homeless man told us in our own report on the Brown-ordered police sweeps of the park.

Another park resident told us, "On the first night they came through with a row of cops 10 feet apart, just swarming through the park kicking everyone out. They confiscated everyone's blankets, everyone's backpacks, and they threw them all away...They took all these blankets, all these people's belongings, threw them into a huge dump truck, and drove away without any regard for what these people are gonna do. You know, I mean, it's raining now—it's really cruel in the end. That's all it is."

One elderly homeless woman estimated that over 100 "children"—meaning "people as young as 20"—had had their belongings taken, while a homeless man said, "If somebody had a shopping cart full of belongings, they wouldn't even bother to take their belongings out, they would just grab the whole shopping cart, and the people would have to fight them back for their personal stuff...and people lost a lot of their personal stuff."

Were city officials once again attempting to make San Francisco less "homeless-friendly?"

In 1998 Amnesty International released a comprehensive report on human rights violations in the United States. The report documents a "persistent and widespread pattern" of abuses in areas of police brutality and the treatment of prisoners. Among Amnesty's conclusions: "that police officers, prison guards, immigration and other officials in the USA are regularly breaching their own laws and guidelines as well as international standards," and that "authorities have failed to take the necessary action to punish and prevent abuses." [62]

***

Given all the evidence, poor people and people of color need to come seriously to terms with the possibility that the corporate/government forces in control of our lives are in no way benign at heart—that they are in fact malevolent in the extreme. This is something that those who occupy America's Death Row prisons cells know instinctively.

The rest of us have a hard time being convinced, however. It's more comforting to hang on to our illusions. We need to educate ourselves—and to educate, we need control of the airwaves. We live in a nation, Death Row inmate Mumia Abu Jamal wrote in September 1998, "that condones and ignores wide-ranging 'structural' violence of a kind that destroys human life with a breathtaking ruthlessness." What is meant by "structural violence?" By way of answer, Abu Jamal offers us the thoughts of Dr. James Gilligan, a former Massachusetts prison official, from the latter's book, *Violence: Reflections on a National Epidemic*:

> By "structural violence" I mean the increased rates of
> death and disability suffered by those who occupy the

bottom rungs of society, as contrasted by those who are above them. Those excess deaths (or at least a demonstrably large proportion of them) are a function of the class structure; and that structure is itself a product of society's collective human choices, concerning how to distribute the collective wealth of society. These are not acts of God. I am contrasting "structural" with "behavioral violence" by which I mean the non-natural deaths and injuries that are caused by specific behavioral actions of individuals against individuals, such as the deaths we attribute to homicide, suicide, soldiers in warfare, capital punishment and so on. [63]

Abu Jamal comments that this structural violence, "not covered by any of the majoritarian, corporate, ruling-class protected media, is invisible to us, and, because of its invisibility, all the more insidious." Granted that this "quiet and deadly violence" goes on, as the writer says, but how numerous, really, are its casualties? Again Abu Jamal offers us the insights of Dr. Gilligan:

Every fifteen years, on the average, as many people die because of relative poverty as would be killed in a nuclear war that caused 232 million deaths; and every single year two to three times as many people die from poverty throughout the world as were killed by the Nazi genocide of the Jews over a six-year period. This is, in effect, the equivalent of an ongoing, unending, in fact accelerating, thermonuclear war, or genocide on the weak and poor every year of every decade, throughout the world. [64]

To these words of former prison official Gilligan, Abu Jamal adds his own:

Worse still, in a thoroughly capitalist society, much of that violence became internalized, turned back on the Self, because, in a society based on the priority of wealth, those who own nothing are taught to loathe themselves, as if something is inherently wrong with themselves, instead of the social order that promotes this self-loathing. This intense self-hatred was often manifested in familial violence as when the husband beats the wife, the wife smacks the son, the kids fight each other.

This vicious, circular and invisible violence, unacknowledged by the corporate media, uncriticized in substandard educational systems, and un-understood by the very folks who suffer in its grips, feeds on the spectacular and more common forms of violence that the system makes damn sure—that we can recognize and must react to it.

This fatal and systematic violence may be called The War on the Poor. [65]

The tragedy is that many in the ranks of the poor don't even know there is a war being fought against them. It is, as Abu Jamal points out, "invisible," due to the silence of the media.

Suppose the media were equally as silent in regard to other wars? Suppose the Japanese had attacked Pearl Harbor and the only people in the entire country who knew about it were the people of Hawaii who had actually seen the Japanese planes with their own eyes? Imagine the frustration and futility that would be felt by those people in their hopelessly inadequate attempts to "get the word out." Yet those who owned the presses and controlled the airwaves refused to hear the cries of these Hawaiians, and dismissed them as kooks and conspiracy theorists.

As absurd as the scenario may seem, that is what is happening today in the War on the Poor. It is a war being fought behind curtains, a genocide taking place in silence, in which bombs explode and kill people but make no sound.

"Genocide?" It is perhaps an overused word. But does that mean it's not occurring? One perhaps obvious thing was pointed out by Mbanna Kantako in 1995 during BLR's forum on "AIDS, the Mass Media, and Genocide." The Springfield free radio standard bearer stated it simply and eloquently, as is his wont to do. Commenting on the historical handing out of smallpox blankets to Native Americans, Kantako intoned, "It ain't no new thing, biological warfare. It ain't no new thing, genocide. Our ability to see it when it's in front of us—*that* will be new."

Chapter 9
Beyond the Millenium

In the summer of 1995 the city of San Francisco erected an obelisk in UN Plaza. On this obelisk was carved the preamble to the Universal Declaration of Human Rights. The occasion was the fiftieth anniversary of the founding of the United Nations. Though presently headquartered in New York, the origins of the UN can be traced back to the Conference on International Organization, convened in San Francisco in April of 1945. The 50 nations represented unanimously adopted the Charter of the United Nations—signed on June 26, 1945.

Exactly 50 years later to the day, the city's long, pointy new obelisk with the Human Rights preamble was commemorated—in the presence of a new generation of UN dignitaries—in ceremonies presided over by Frank Jordan—the same mayor who had ordered more than a thousand arrests of Food Not Bombs (FNB) for serving food to the homeless. The obelisk bears the date June 26, 1995.

More resembling an erect penis than a monument to human rights, the obelisk stood in a UN Plaza, which Jordan had ordered swept clean of homeless people. For the duration of the UN festivities those who made their hard beds in the open air were expected, essentially, not to exist.

One article, in particular, of the Universal Declaration—article 25—bears repeating here: "Everyone has the right to a standard of living adequate for the health and well-being of himself and his family, including food, clothing, housing, medical care and necessary social services, and the right to security in the event of unemployment, sickness, disability, widowhood, old age or other lack of livelihood in circumstances beyond his control." In addition, provision number 2 of article 17 states: "No one shall be arbitrarily deprived of his property."

***

Paying tribute to the Universal Declaration of Human Rights while standing in clear violation of at least two of the Declaration's articles was not an unusual level of hypocrisy for San Francisco officialdom. City leaders had risen to that level, and more, on numerous occasions. At SFLR that hypocrisy was grist for our mill.

One of our own contributions to the UN festivities was the airing of a program purporting to show how the city of San Francisco—and "by extension its accomplices in crime, the state of California and the US government"—stand in clear violation of "not one, not two, but all 30 articles" of the Declaration. The program, though humorous, was intended to be only partly tongue-in-cheek.

"The Universal Declaration of Human Rights expresses the highest ideals of the human spirit," we praised, but added somberly: "The homage paid to it by San Francisco officialdom, on whose streets reside festering Third World poverty and despair, will be remembered as one of the great ironies of 1995."

Those self-same "festering" streets became the scene of tense confrontations between FNB and the police that summer. Running concurrent to the UN-50 celebration, and designedly so, was the Food Not Bombs International Gathering. The Gathering drew some 300 people from FNB chapters across North America, and from as far away as Europe.

San Francisco's reputation for arresting food servers had far exceeded its boundaries. Word of what was going on here had spread to FNB chapters around the world. Many who came to the Gathering were drawn, in part, out of a curiosity to witness for themselves the Police State in action. They were not disappointed. Approximately 200 food-serving arrests took place during the 11 days of the Gathering, as the summer of 1995 in San Francisco became, as someone termed it, the "Summer of Love and Rage."

Some of the visiting FNB activists were as young as their teens. Many had never before witnessed the level of police repression as seen during those 11 days. The Oklahoma City bombing earlier that year had put the fear of "homegrown terrorism" into local governments across the land. In San Francisco, however, the hosting of an international spectacle appeared to have driven city leaders to the brink of paranoia.

Police were on building tops, lining sidewalks, stationed at building entrances—even riding around in city transit buses. Whole buses could be seen driving about filled with nothing but uniformed police. Police numbers at a pavilion where South African Archbishop Desmond Tutu was scheduled to speak appeared to almost exceed the numbers of ordinary people gathered to hear the Nobel laureate speak.

***

The Food Not Bombs 1995 International Gathering was remarkable in terms of what it revealed about people's ability to nonviolently resist police power and government repression in the United States. The *Summer of Love and Rage* was sandwiched on either end by police murders—Aaron Williams on June 4, and William Hankston on September 6. What took place in between, however, was an uprising—not, perhaps in the traditional sense of the word, such as the Rodney King rebellion might be viewed. But an uprising in terms of people—independent of the government, and regardless of government attempts at intervention—creating their own communities and their own systems of community infrastructure.

Certainly the micro radio stations then on the air in the Bay Area were one example of this. But it was Food Not Bombs' successful attempts to keep its food serving operation going throughout the Gathering and the UN-50 celebration—despite all efforts by Jordan and the SFPD to stop it—which perhaps most excited a sense of wonder and triumph.

"They (the police) don't realize it, but they have now trained a whole new generation of activists in how to resist police power," Keith McHenry commented in the wake of it all.

McHenry wasn't just putting a positive spin on things. Getting the food past the police and out to the hungry masses was no small task. The courage and resourcefulness employed in this endeavor by these visitors were at times amazing to behold. For the beleaguered San Francisco chapter of FNB, weary after 7 long years of police attacks, the arrival of these out-of-towners was welcomed indeed.

For his own part, Jordan poured on police in huge, heaping bucketfuls—first in an effort to make the homeless disappear, then in an effort to halt all serving of food. Yet FNB had determined that homeless people should not become invisible merely for Jordan's convenience, nor that they should have to eat their meals hidden behind bushes or concealed in back alleyways. The young visitors who had arrived from points all over the North American continent, and from the world beyond, rolled up their sleeves and pitched in with a fresh enthusiasm and determination.

While Jordan had the power of the police on his side, we, on the other hand, had the energy and idealism of youth on ours. Youthful energy should never be dismissed as insignificant, for it became a potent force by the Gathering's end.

***

The general marshaling the troops for Jordan was the ubiquitous Commander Dennis Martel—the same Martel who had once expressed delight that homeless people were being driven from San Francisco by the Matrix Program, and who, on another occasion, had said of FNB, "They obviously don't want to feed the hungry, they just want to make an anarchist-type statement, and we're not gonna allow it."

By the summer of 1995 Martel seemed finally to have learned to keep his mouth shut around the media. No inflammatory quotes from him came out during the UN celebration. However, this didn't stop Martel's underlings from pontificating generously on the prospects for terrorism from FNB. Lt. Larry Barsetti offered his views on the matter to the *Examiner*.

> "The one group that has been causing the most trouble this weekend is Food Not Bombs and, in my opinion, they would be the likeliest source of a problem," said Barsetti, third in command of the long-planned special police operation. [1]

One "source of a problem" for the "long-planned special police operation" came early on in the Gathering when FNB erected a "shantytown" in UN Plaza comprised of a number of wood and cardboard buildings which had been hammered together in an afternoon. The buildings were designated "school," "library," "clinic," and so on. Some were painted with such slogans as "Human needs not corporate greed."

Upon completion, the would-be dwellers of this shantytown surveyed their work with a feeling of satisfaction. Though intended to call attention to poverty and homelessness in the United States, the shantytown also, strangely, became a symbol of freedom—a vision in which homeless and poor people would be free to run their own affairs.

This township was short-lived, however. One super, colossal "source of a problem" for its builders, founders, and commemorators took shape in the form of the police who arrived quickly to destroy it. KTVU Channel 2 News footage of the destruction shows police demolishing the makeshift structures literally around the heads of young people crouched inside of them.

Throughout the UN-50 celebrations, FNB attempted to meet with Archbishop Tutu to discuss human rights violations in San Francisco. However, either Tutu didn't have the time or inclination, or never received word of our invitations. The meeting never took place.

Tutu did participate, however, in a panel discussion with other Nobel laureates on Sunday, June 25, and the following day there appeared in the *Chronicle* a collective statement from the illustrious group. Signed by 11 Nobel Peace laureates, the statement labeled human rights "the birthright of all people," as well as the "cornerstone of world peace," and it called upon the UN and its member states to make the protection of such rights their "utmost priority."

> Peace…will ultimately require more than the mere absence of armed conflict. As long as poverty and hunger prevail in all corners of our globe there will be no peace. Nearly 1 billion people worldwide lack access to safe water and 1.6 billion have no sanitary waste facilities. Hunger and malnourishment affects greater than 700 million people. Indeed in many developing countries the average person has but one-third the caloric intake of the average person in the industrialized countries. This stark global reality is not just an affront to human dignity, it is a clear violation of human rights and international obligations recognized by the community of nations over the last 50 years. [2]

Much in the above statement could apply equally to homeless people in this country. The homeless in America often are calorically malnourished, have no sanitary waste facilities, and lack access to safe water. In fact, American homelessness is perhaps an even *greater* "affront to human dignity" than that in the Third World, for in a country reputed to be the wealthiest on Earth, there is no reason for anyone to *be* homeless—no reason, that is, other than the insatiable and unceasing greed of those who hold that wealth.

Each day of the Gathering consisted of workshops—designed to teach poor people basic survival skills in an America which no longer needed or wanted them—as well as two meal servings in UN Plaza—at noon and six. With police determined to stop the servings, creative strategies had to be employed to ensure that the public feedings happened. Much of the credit for keeping the food serving operational goes to the folks visiting from out of town. Not only did they pitch in with the cooking and serving, but they also joined in the strategizing of ways to get the prepared food past the police.

Early in the Gathering, Martel and his forces began arresting FNB members on their way to UN Plaza, not even allowing them to reach the serving site with the food. Customarily the food was walked over from an office space a short distance away which FNB had rented for the duration of the Gathering. Police quickly learned the location of the office, however, and it became a simple matter for them to pick off anybody seen walking with food between the office and the Plaza.

In response to this move by the police, FNB began sending out decoys—people with empty buckets, whose job it was to *pretend* to be carrying food. This allowed some of the *real* food carriers to make it on into the Plaza. However, the SFPD have never been shy about arresting people without cause. Angered at being tricked, police began simply arresting the decoys.

While this demonstration of police lawlessness came as a surprise to the newcomers, for the members of San Francisco FNB, who were familiar with the SFPD's modus operandi, the response was not unanticipated. The strategy next devised was to send food into UN Plaza concealed in backpacks, tote bags, and purses.

Martel's response was to deploy forces heavily around the periphery of the Plaza. These police appeared to have no other job than to wait for FNB to show up and then spring into action at the first sign of food distribution. Yet even to this, FNB was able to devise counter strategies that proved effective. These came in the form of: a) alternating teams of food servers, one of which would invariably offer itself up publicly for arrest in order to clear the plaza of police; and, b) a "bait and switch" operation which consisted of dropping a bag of bagels in UN Plaza as a diversion while the real food serving line was set up in Civic Center Plaza a short distance away.

Such antics were reported mirthfully over SFLR.

"Now did you plan this all along—to set up here in secret?" Jo and I asked after the group had successfully employed a bait and switch maneuver which had completely fooled the police.

The food server to whom we had directed this question was a youth of no more than 18 or 19.

"You mean," the boy replied, "did we plan to dupe the idiot cops? Yes, it *was* planned and yes we *did* dupe the idiot cops. Because they're still hanging around squealing like the pigs that they are!"

This statement the youth punctuated at the end with the rendering of a pig squeal.

Earlier in the evening the police had arrested an elderly man in a wheel chair who had been carrying a bag of groceries in his lap—this under the mistaken belief that the man had been delivering food for FNB. The arrest had sparked outrage and disbelief among the crowd of young people in the plaza. These had immediately swarmed around arresting officers, remonstrating, "He's not even a member of Food Not Bombs!" The old man was wheeled out of the plaza and presumably taken off to jail nonetheless.

***

At one point during the Gathering, FNB prisoners in San Francisco County Jail announced a hunger strike. There were 27 members locked up at the time. Due to the presence of pay phones in the cells, the prisoners were able to call out and give interviews. Several called SFLR, where we put the hunger strikers on the air live.

"A couple of people had started the hunger strike last night," one man informed us. "And then by this morning all the groups of people were game for the idea."

"We're all on hunger strike," said another prisoner, one of the two who had initiated the strike. "Me and another guy—we've been on since yesterday, and then everyone else started this morning. So I haven't had anything to eat in a day and a half. And I'm not gonna eat while I'm in jail, cause if they're gonna take our right away to give food to people, then I ain't gonna eat their food either."

Shortly after we aired the interviews, all 27 prisoners were released. Apparently having hotels filled with Nobel laureates speaking about human rights; a jail filled with human rights protestors refusing to take food; plus a radio station airing live interviews with the hunger strikers—was too much for the Jordan administration to handle all at once.

The subject of human rights, in fact, seemed to be a touchy one for Jordan. On June 26, during dedication ceremonies for the obelisk, the mayor seemed determined to steer clear of the topic altogether, referring to the obelisk as a monument "dedicated exclusively to the celebration of peace among nations."

Within hours of being released from jail, the FNB prisoners were back in UN Plaza serving food.

***

After seven long years of arbitrary arrests, detentions, and property confiscations, FNB clearly triumphed over the San Francisco Police during the '95 Gathering. Significantly, the Gathering had no leaders. Keith McHenry did not direct the rotating food serving teams or order the bait-and-switch operation. In these instances, and many others throughout the Gathering, it was the people cooking and serving for that day who strategized on how to get the food past the police, and agreed on a plan of action.

Throughout the Gathering, consensus decision-making reigned. No leaders attempted to impose their will on the group. This made the 1995 Food Not Bombs International Gathering an example of anarchy in its purest form—*anarchy* in its definition as a political system—as democracy taken to the nth degree. The fact that each person participated equally in the decision making, and therefore had a stake in the outcome, lent the Gathering a strength, cohesiveness and unity it would not have otherwise had. Had leaders attempted to issue edicts, or impose "presidential orders," the Gathering would have collapsed. People would simply have left, withdrawn, or gone home. We would have seen in microcosm what we are today witnessing in the U.S. as a whole: a splintering of society.

Why didn't the San Francisco Police simply raid the FNB office and either murder or "disappear" all of us? In a more advanced police state this certainly would have been the response to our persistent protests, organizing, and food serving. But in 1995 such a drastic act would have been reported by the major news media. This is still the case today, but at the rate media ownership is being consolidated in this country, clearly there are no guarantees about the future.

As one FNB protestor stated during the Gathering, "America has two ways to go. She can either stop this nonsense (arresting people for serving food) with the kind of money she has, the kind of power she has, or she can become very much another Nazi Germany."

America's propensity toward becoming "another Nazi Germany" is indeed a focus of concern at SFLR. To that end, we have aired Martin Lee, author of *The Beast Reawakens*; Tom Burghardt, editor of the *Antifa Info Bulletin*; and radio broadcaster Dave Emory. All three "anti-fascist researchers" have documented extensively ties between neo-nazi groups in the United States with those in Europe. Lee's book especially provides an illuminating look at the evolution of American fascism—from the importing (by the U.S. government through its "Project Paper Clip") of Nazis following World War II, to the bombing of the Oklahoma City federal building in 1995.

However, of the three, it is Emory whose prognosis for the future is the gloomiest. Emory, whose home base is KFJC, a small college station in the South San Francisco Bay Area, believes that fascism is, in a word, "inevitable."

In a program produced in October 1999, Emory documents the extensive control of a German corporation, Bertelsmann, over the U.S. publishing industry. Bertelsmann, says Emory, has acquired Bantam, Doubleday, Dell and Random House, and is presently the third largest media corporation in the world, with extensive holdings in the music industry as well. Emory adds:

> As I've said so many times on so many programs,
> whenever one is looking at a major German corporation,

one should never forget about the deadly Bormann flight capital organization, that is literally the economic component of the Third Reich gone underground. And as one banker described it in correspondence with Paul Manning, the author of the definitive text about the Bormann group, it is the most important concentration of money and power under a single control in history. [3]

Martin Bormann, says Emory, was "the genius behind Adolph Hitler," who saw the defeat of the Third Reich coming and set up corporations in neutral countries using Nazi capital.

Then when the Federal Republic of Germany was incorporated in 1955, that money—again all the liquid capital of Europe looted during the second World War—that money flowed back into the Federal Republic of Germany and was used to effect the quote, German economic miracle, unquote of the post World War II years. [4]

***

Is fascism "inevitable," as Emory projects? One thing is for sure: avoidance of total domination of the planet by a few large corporations will require active, organized resistance on the part of a population now largely placid and factionalized. Perhaps most crucial of all in determining the future will be whether or not democratic groups are able to win *meaningful* access to the airwaves. Democratization of the airwaves is a battle the people of this country cannot afford to lose.

On January 28, 1999, the FCC, under new Chairman William E. Kennard, announced a Notice of Proposed Rule Making (NPRM) regarding micro radio. It was a significant turning point. The NPRM meant the FCC had gone from opposing micro radio, or being merely neutral on it, to actively considering its legalization in some form.

But what form would that legalization take? And would it afford the people of this country the truly *meaningful* access to the airwaves that is so desperately needed? And would Kennard be able to get his legalization plan through the full five-member Commission? And, finally, would the legalization plan, even if adopted by the full Commission, survive the likely court challenge from the National Association of Broadcasters (NAB)? There were a lot of uncertainties—more than you could shake a stick at.

The NPRM threw the micro radio movement into a state of confusion. Debate erupted between the "radical" and the more conservative wings of the movement over the issue of continued civil disobedience, with some favoring a halt to unlicensed broadcasting in order to give the FCC a chance to rule on the issue and to make a show of good faith. Others, Stephen Dunifer among them, opposed any such "going silent," believing that it was the thousands of acts of electronic civil disobedience nationwide which had pushed the FCC into taking the action it had taken.

For Jo and I, the NPRM came at a time of personal tragedy. Elsa, our beautiful German Shepherd, had been diagnosed with Cushings Disease the previous year, and in late January she became gravely ill from anemia. The vet was unable to offer any hope. She refused to eat. Jo and I had to hold her up in order for her to urinate. Otherwise she would pee right where she lay on the floor. The last few days of her life I spent trying to hand-feed her baby food. It was no use. Finally on Saturday, January 30—two days after the FCC issued the NPRM—Jo and I took Elsa to the vet's and had her put to sleep. We spent the night crying.

Elsa had been our beloved child. She had been with us during our highway crash returning from Death Valley seven years earlier; she had been there when we had founded SFLR six years earlier; and she had been with us every step of the way since, greeting our in-studio guests, presiding serenely from her resting place on the couch. We had lost the radio station when we went off the air the previous summer (in the wake of the Wilken decision), and now we had lost Elsa. It was a bitter blow.

The irony was that the radio station was about to make a roaring comeback.

* * *

While it was encouraging that the FCC had taken the step of issuing the NPRM, my own view was that that, in and of itself, was no reason for micro stations across the country to go silent. Most of the DJs at SFLR agreed with that assessment. The NPRM, keep in mind, was nothing more than an "indication" that the FCC was considering making micro radio legal. Nothing concrete had as yet been offered to the thousands of people nationwide who wanted to reclaim their own airwaves. Why abandon civil disobedience when it had played such a large role in getting us to where we were?

Yet civil disobedience wasn't the only tool upon which we were relying at SFLR; we were also working the system.

The previous year, following our shut-down of the station, Jo and I, with the help of SFLR DJs Kiilu Nyasha, Herb Mintz, Jackie Dove, and Harry Ashton—began drawing up the papers necessary for filing a formal broadcast license application. This turned out to be a mammoth undertaking; the FCC's form 340 is a formidable document. We completed all of it except for the engineering section. We did not have the $3,000 necessary to contract the engineering study required; we thus asked for a waiver on the study.

We had no realistic expectation the FCC would grant us a license. Our main reason for going to all the trouble of filing an application was to reap the public relations advantages that such a move would offer, for we had every intention of going back on the air—with or without a license. *With* the application on file, however, we would at least be able to say to the public, "See? We *tried* to play the game their way."

On February 12, with still no answer from the FCC on our license application, we held a press conference and announced our return to the air.

"In order that democracy may be safeguarded and preserved, it is imperative that all economic stratums of society, as well as all races and genders, have equal access to the airwaves," we asserted in a written statement handed out to the media.

The FCC noticed our return to the air almost immediately and came calling. On February 24 two FCC agents arrived at our door. We were playing Bruce Springsteen at the time. "The Ghost of Tom Joad." The FCC agents had no warrants and were refused permission to enter. On March 15, I received a notice by registered mail threatening me with dire consequences should I not cease operations.

"You are hereby warned that operation of radio transmitting equipment without a valid radio station authorization and your failure to allow an inspection of the radio station constitute violations of the Federal laws cited above and could subject the owner of this illegal operation to the severe penalties provided, including, but not limited to, a maximum criminal fine of $100,000 and/or one year imprisonment or arrest of the equipment for the first offense," the letter stated.

A hundred thousand dollars and a year in prison. They were upping the ante. The last time I had been threatened by the FCC it had been with only a $10,000 fine and no mention of prison.

In February, Luke Hiken, who had been my attorney since 1993, asked to be let off my case in order that he could devote full time to a client who was facing execution in less than a month. Dennis Cunningham, who for a decade had been FNB's lawyer, became my new attorney of record.

In his response to the new FCC threats against me, Dennis pointed out that the Commission had so far to date "failed even to acknowledge receipt" of our application submitted the previous fall. Additionally, our response stated:

> We understand the agency is considering whether to revise its rules, so as to begin to permit low-power broadcasting, although apparently on terms which will ensure that the big-power firms are enabled to gobble up the spectrum spots preemptively leaving independent voices like Richard Edmondson still out in the cold. We urge you to consider more deeply the constitutional and other consequences of such an ongoing, gross prohibition on free speech, and the total hogging of the air by commercial powers, in a general way and in the particulars of this case. Many hundreds of micro stations are now in operation around the country, as you know, with more coming on the air all the time; the rightness of allowing the LPFM (low-power FM) movement to flourish is unmistakable.

***

There was reason to believe that the new FCC rules, should they be adopted, might still leave the giant, corporate broadcasters free "to gobble up the spectrum spots pre-emptively," as Dennis had stated.

A major cause of concern to micro broadcasters was a proposal contained within the NPRM to designate LPFM stations of 100 watts or less with a "secondary" status. Such a status would require the operators of such stations to vacate their frequencies in the event that larger "primary" broadcasters wanted to raise their power levels or relocate antenna sites.

The FCC justified this provision, in part, by stating that such a measure would make it possible, in the long-run, to license *more* "LP100" stations (low power stations of 100 watts or less) than it otherwise could.

"By proposing secondary status for LP100 stations, we believe we could authorize more of these stations with less impact on primary broadcast services," the NPRM says.

Yet such a secondary status would, in effect, designate micro broadcasters as second class citizens of the airwaves, requiring them to give way to the whims and prerogatives of the wealthy.

Of even more concern than the secondary-status designation, however, was, and is, the problem of spectrum scarcity. This is most acute, of course, in urban areas of the country, where the radio dial is more crowded. Even under the most liberal legalization plan up for consideration—involving a relaxation of both second and third-adjacent frequency spacing regulations—the number of micro stations which could be licensed would be severely limited due to the scarcity of vacant frequencies in urban areas.

Current FCC rules require minimum distance separations between stations operating on the same frequency. Similar (but successively less) distance separations are also required for stations operating on first-adjacent, second-adjacent, and third-adjacent channels from each other.

The NPRM states:

> Commenters supporting LPFM services generally oppose any requirements for 2nd- or 3rd-adjacent channel protections, contending such interference from low power stations would be, at most, minimal. Some commenters, including the NAB, NPR (National Public Radio), and New Jersey Broadcasting, Inc., believe these protections should be retained to prevent interference and/or protect future digital terrestrial radio service. As noted below, these protections would limit substantially the number of channels available for low power radio generally and could preclude altogether the introduction of LPFM service in mid-sized and large cities. Therefore, to the extent possible, we are inclined to authorize low power service without any 2nd- and 3rd-adjacent channel protection standards. [5]

Were the FCC's current spacing regulations obsolete and in need of revision in light of changing technology? As attorney Luke Hiken had pointed out in the *Dunifer* case, "The FCC is relying upon regulations which were promulgated long before the advent of the technology that makes possible micro radio; indeed, even before the advent of FM broadcasting."

The fact that SFLR had been able to broadcast for six years without causing interference to our second-adjacent neighbors (broadcasting in the same metropolitan area) on the dial, was a strong argument in favor of eliminating *both* third *and* second-adjacent protections—the more liberal plan that the FCC now had up for consideration in the NPRM. The FCC itself (in the NPRM) stated that "a strong case can be made" for eliminating at least the third-adjacent protection.

Yet even if both second *and* third were dropped, the result would not be anything approaching a "tide" of new micro stations taking to the air—certainly not in urban areas at any rate. At most the difference would be between allowing a *few* micro stations—to *none* at all. The NPRM even stated this rather clearly:

> In San Francisco, no LP100 station could be located with a 2nd-adjacent standard, but two such stations would fit if there were no need for 2nd- and 3rd-adjacent channel protection standards; at least one LP1000 station could be authorized in Los Angeles and Pittsburgh, but only without 2nd- and 3rd-adjacent channel protection standards. [6]

***

In considering all of the above, the really pertinent question is this: Why is there no room on either the AM or FM bands for micro stations? The answer, of course, is that it's due to six and a half decades of mismanagement by the FCC—six and a half decades of granting broadcast licenses *only* to the rich. The existence of so many monster, megawatt stations that we now have to quibble over relaxing this or that standard just in order to fit in a few 100 watt stations is profound testimony to that mismanagement.

In every major city in this country the airwaves are filled with radio stations owned by giant corporations whose boards of directors often don't even live in the communities to which they broadcast. And because of the 1996 Telecommunications Act, the number of corporations controlling these stations has grown ever smaller. These consequences which we are facing now are essentially the result of allowing the NAB and its cronies to set national broadcast regulatory policy.

The NPRM opens the door a small crack for the people of this country to gain some access to their own airwaves, however, it does absolutely nothing to rectify the gross imbalance which has come about over the past six and a half decades and especially over the last four years. To do that the FCC would need to either, a) de-license large, corporate-owned broadcast outlets to make room on the current bands for community-run low power stations, or, b) open new spectrum for these stations. Assuming the corporations would fight tooth and nail to avoid being stripped of valuable broadcast properties, that would seem to leave us only with option (b). Yet the NPRM, issued by the FCC on January 28, 1999, envisions an ultimate rejection of this option.

> As an initial matter, we do not intend to create a low power radio service on any spectrum beyond that which is currently allocated for FM use and, as described below, we do not propose to use the AM band. To allocate spectrum not currently used for broadcasting would force consumers to purchase new equipment to gain the benefits of the new service, which would likely have a substantial dampening effect on its success. [7]

The option of taking the spectrum now designated for TV channel 6 and reassigning it to the FM band would appear to be shot down by the above passage. A window of opportunity for such a spectrum reassignment will, as discussed in Chapter 7, open in the next few years as TV stations across the country make the conversion to digital broadcasting.

Certainly the FCC and the broadcast industry are banking on consumers' willingness to purchase new equipment as the nation "goes digital." Why is such a measure rejected out of hand for LPFM? If the FCC persists in its intention of opening no new spectrum beyond that which is already "currently allocated for FM use," then micro radio—LPFM—may well end up becoming a largely rural phenomenon.

***

As modest (and, from the point of view of micro broadcasters, wholly inadequate) as the FCC proposals were regarding micro radio, the NAB opposed even this small measure of airwave democratization. Denouncing the NPRM from the very first day of its issue on January 28, NAB President Edward O. Fritts warned that micro radio legalization would "likely cause devastating interference to existing broadcasters." [8]

To this, FCC Chairman Kennard responded that the industry should not "use interference concerns as a smokescreen for other matters." [9] The implication of Kennard's words was that the real concern of broadcasters was increased competition from the new stations.

Nonetheless, the NAB continued to rail against legalization on the grounds of interference, holding a Washington press conference on August 2 to denounce the plan.

"The laws of science and physics do not lie," said Fritts. "Low-power radio would result in a significant increase in interference for a large number of radio listeners." He estimated the number of people who would experience such interference would reach well into the millions. [10]

Fritts was joined at the press conference by Bruce Reese, CEO of Bonneville International Corp., which owned, among others, station KOIT in San Francisco.

"I cannot believe the FCC will ignore what every respectable broadcast engineer knows instinctively: that when more stations are shoved onto a congested radio dial, the result will be more interference for the listener," said Reese, who had been tapped to chair the NAB's "Radio Spectrum Integrity Task Force."

"With all due respect," Reese asked, "how does extra static on the radio dial translate into 'voices for the voiceless'?" [11]

Voices of the voiceless were assuredly not the daily fare heard on KOIT in San Francisco.

Fritts and Reese unveiled a NAB-commissioned study which purported to show that "millions of Americans would suffer new interference to their existing radio service" if LPFM was legalized and second and third-adjacent channel protections were dropped. However, the study contradicted the FCC's own findings, released just two weeks earlier. It also contradicted a separate, independent study commissioned by the National Lawyers Guild Committee on Democratic Communications.

***

The FCC extended the period allowed for public commentary on the NPRM throughout much of the year 1999, closing it finally on November 15. While filing its own comments at the August 2 press conference, the NAB did not spend the rest of the year idle, however. It was busily at work behind the scenes. Two days after the commentary was closed, a bill, entitled "The Radio Broadcasting Preservation Act," was introduced in Congress with the aim of doing an end run around the FCC and halting micro radio legalization dead in its tracks.

Calling the Commission's proposals "ill-advised and unnecessary," Rep. Michael Oxley (R-Ohio), the NAB's champion in the House of Representatives, introduced the "Radio Broadcasting Preservation Act" on November 17.

"Establishing a low power radio service would require the Commission to dramatically weaken current interference standards, resulting in increased interference with existing radio services and devaluing the investment of current license holders," Oxley said. [12]

Oxley is vice-chairman of the House Subcommittee on Telecommunications, having oversight over the FCC. A former FBI agent, Oxley had also opposed efforts aimed at keeping it legal for Americans to send encrypted messages over the Internet. In his anti-micro radio legislation, he was joined by six other members of Congress—three of them members of the Telecommunications Subcommittee—as co-sponsors of the bill. If there was any doubt before about how serious the NAB was about stopping micro radio, those doubts were now erased.

The NAB immediately cranked up its powerful lobbying machine in support of Oxley and his bill, sending out a letter to all of its member stations on December 23, 1999, urging action. Warning that "this is the biggest issue facing radio," the letter called upon station owners to immediately begin arranging meetings with local Congressional representatives.

"Your message is simple: CO-SPONSOR THE OXLEY BILL," said the letter. (Emphasis not added.)

A copy of the NAB letter was obtained and posted on the Web by a micro station in Minneapolis, Beat Radio, which had been raided and shut down by the FCC three years earlier. [13]

The letter further stated:

> Our goal is simple, but it will require all of you to help us. We need to get more than half of the house (218+ members) to agree to co-sponsor the Oxley bill. If we do that we can show that there is strong opposition to LPFM, and we will have the support we need to pass the legislation, if necessary. [14]

The letter further urged station owners to "include other radio broadcasters in your market" in their meetings with Congress members. This, reasoned the NAB, would offer the benefit of "showing a united front" so as to "impress upon your House members the importance this issue has with all of us."

Would the NAB, one of the most powerful lobbies in Washington, and which had already won passage of the Telecommunications Act of 1996, be able to purchase the requisite 218 members of Congress to pass the Oxley bill?

As the year 2000 came in the issue remained undecided.

***

If the NAB has major influence in Congress, the micro radio movement has not been without some lobbying successes of its own. Working especially hard on this issue has been a group of Michigan micro radio supporters led by Tom Ness of Jam Rag Press. The group was instrumental in obtaining the support of Congressman David Bonior, among many others.

In late 1999 Ness, along with help from the Media Access Project, compiled a list of organizations and individuals that have endorsed micro radio. The list is extremely lengthy and includes 29 members of Congress, more than 40 local governments, the AFL-CIO, the Communications Workers of America, and the following prominent academics and entertainers: Jackson Browne, the Indigo Girls, Noam Chomsky, Barbara Ehrenreich, Elaine Bernard, David Barsamian, Archbishop Thomas Gumbleton, Edward Herman, Ralph Nader, Herbert Schiller, Kurt Vonnegut, Gloria Steinem, Howard Zinn, Ellis Marsalis, Bonnie Raitt, Jenny Toomey, and many others.

Another whose lobbying efforts deserve mention are those of Peter Franck of the National Lawyers Guild Committee on Democratic Communications. In an essay entitled "The Fight for Micro Radio Enters the Home Stretch: Paradise or Paradise Lost?", Franck, who has made numerous trips to Washington on behalf of the micro radio movement, discusses the effects of the Telecommunications Act of 1996.

> For example, a few years ago twenty-three different companies owned the thirty commercial radio stations in the San Francisco bay area. Today, they are owned by ten companies and 11 of the top twenty stations are owned by just two: Chancellor Media Corporation and CBS Radio. Thus, today a few large corporations have the legal right to use the public airwaves and 99.99% of US Citizens are legally barred from using this major communications medium.[15]

Continuing the FCC's ban on stations of 100 watts or less made little sense under such circumstances. Of that 20-year-old ban, Franck commented:

> It was as if a Federal Newspaper Commission in the name of efficiency, decreed that to save paper and ink only newspapers of at least 1,000,000 circulation would be allowed. All local papers, church newspapers, PTA bulletins, and community weeklies were outlawed. The situation in broadcasting is quite analogous. [16]

As desirable as micro radio legalization may be, the key question, though, was what *form* that legalization would take. It is not inconceivable that micro radio "legalization" might leave micro broadcasters in even worse shape than they had been before the whole process had begun.

Before the process began—back in the days when the FCC was completely intransigent on the issue of LPFM and vowing to never to allow it—micro broadcasters had at least stood in a favorable position to challenge the constitutionality of the ban. One side effect of embarking upon the legalization process is that the FCC had effectively undermined our standing in the courts. Thus the question might be asked: Was Chairman Kennard our friend—or was he a very clever foe?

Legalizing micro radio—but under terms which gave all preferences and advantages to those with the most money—could neutralize the whole movement as a force for change. The crossroads at which we found ourselves at the close of 1999 was very much, as Franck termed it, one of "Paradise or Paradise Lost." As he put it:

> We have come much further than we would have dared to hope ten, or even five years ago. But as the Micro radio movement seems headed for victory at the FCC, it could equally well be headed for defeat at the hands of the FCC. Whether we are about to see the glorious addition of a new democratic grass roots community radio to the FM band, or whether we will look back at the period of micro radio civil disobedience (roughly 1989-1998) as the golden age of Micro radio, is very much up for grabs as this is being written. [17]

***

Yet micro radio is only one small part of a flowering and unfolding movement of resistance. Despite the futile sense of "inevitability" fascism engenders, people continue to struggle for freedom, and the closing years of the 1990s saw some amazing acts of resistance.

In 1998 the Kensington Welfare Rights Union, based in Philadelphia, organized an *Economic Human Rights* bus tour of the United States, followed by a Poor People's Summit, while in a forest in Northern California a young woman named Julia Butterfly Hill spent more than two years perched 180 feet off the ground in a redwood tree. The goal of the tree sit, the longest on record: to preserve the remnants of California's majestic Headwaters Forest.

In Chiapas, Mexico, the Zapatistas continued to hold out against the combined efforts of the Mexican and U.S. governments, and as the year 1999 was waning to a close, people from all over the world converged upon the city of Seattle for five days of organized, sustained protest against the World Trade Organization. Clearly the population, not only of the United States but of the world, is becoming more galvanized.

The Kensington Welfare Rights Union (KWRU) has especially adopted a strategy of taking its protests international, partly in an effort to shame the U.S. government before international forums. In 1997 the KWRU held a 125-mile "March for Our Lives" from the Liberty Bell in Philadelphia, to the United Nations Building in New York—and on November 3, 1998, KWRU Director Cheri Honkala was given leave to address the United Nations.

"I bring you greetings from poor and homeless families from around the United States of America, the ranks from which I come," Honkala opened. She added:

> ...We are watching a growing polarization of the rich and poor on a global level making it difficult for much of the world's population to secure housing, employment, food or healthcare or any kind of education. Recent figures from the United Nations showed that more than half of humanity exists on less than $2.00 a day, that 1.3 billion people are so poor that they live in shantytowns and garbage dumps, and that 40,000 people die every day from preventable diseases and malnutrition.
>
> These garbage dumps, shantytowns and preventable diseases exist in my country too. As a matter of fact after the dismantling of the welfare system began we began to see things we never dreamed of seeing in our country. And this is why in June of this year we...poor and homeless people, began our Economic Human Rights Campaign. We toured the country in a new freedom bus going to over 34 cities and towns calling for freedom from unemployment, hunger and homelessness. We turned ourselves into human rights monitors and began to document our hidden stories of economic human rights violations. We began to understand that "welfare reform," the new law passed in our country, was in itself a violation of our human rights. As we traveled this country we demanded a right to a job

at a living wage. All people wanted was an ability to
provide for their families.

That ability is decreasing daily... [18]

The story of Julia Butterfly Hill's tree-sit even captured the jaded attention of the corporate-owned media. The *New York Times, London Times, L.A. Times,* ABC News and others all featured interviews with her, while Hill appeared as a guest, via her treetop cell phone, on numerous radio talk shows.

"Butterfly stands barefoot at the very top of the tree," one reporter for a San Francisco newspaper noted in print. "The wind blows her long hair, and the first sight of her seems surreal and dream-like, like an animated character from a Disney film poised on a cliff, or the two lovers on the bow of the *Titanic.*" [19]

How did a 24-year-old woman manage to charm even the corporate media out of their usual oblivious silence to environmental destruction? How did a welfare recipient from Philadelphia end up speaking before the United Nations? How have poor people all over the country managed, with essentially no resources, to put their own radio stations on the air? And how is it that FNB continues to hand out food to the hungry in San Francisco, despite having come through nearly a decade of hostile government attacks, and despite a new round of arrests in late 1999?

Did all these things—and many others as well—come about merely through the indomitability of the human spirit? Or is there, as one guest on SFLR, Ramona Africa of the MOVE organization, phrased it, "a force, a power, greater than any and all of us" that has played a hand in these things? If fascism is to be defeated, will it be done through human power alone? Or will some measure of "divine intervention" be required? The question becomes especially pertinent if one considers—as I do—that the struggle between freedom and fascism is but a new phase of the ancient struggle between good and evil.

Is some supernatural force for good "shining through" Julia Butterfly Hill? Or is Hill merely a "chirpy New Ager," as one reporter labeled her? [20] What are the metaphysical implications, if any, of the U.S. government's actions? Are we witnessing a new battle in an age-old war?

One who has pondered such questions is the author of *Emerging Viruses: AIDS and Ebola: Nature, Accident, or Intentional?* On June 19, 1997, Dr. Len Horowitz visited SFLR and spent nearly two hours with us. During that time he discussed not only his book, but his belief that "a play is being unraveled here."

"It says in Chinese proverbs, you know, 'we should be blessed to live in interesting times.' I can't think of more interesting times to live in, number one," said Len. "But also, when you think about the big picture. When you think about what motivates these people (the ruling oligarchy): it's not money or power—they have all the money and power in the world—but *evil*.

" So you have to begin to think about the great war between God and Satan. And when you begin to think about that great war—I know who wins in the end. I know who will survive because it's been prophesized—by not just Christians, it's been prophesized by Hopi Indians, it's been prophesized by Edgar Cayce, it's been prophesized by virtually every prophet who's ever walked this planet."

"And those who win in the end are the forces of truth and light and love, not darkness."

***

"We are living in a time," resumed Horowitz, "when we are being attacked on so many different fronts by so many different risks—toxins, chemicals, biologicals, economic, education, disinformation—I mean you name it, we are being hit with it. And I think that that's not by accident. As a result, the groups, the citizens groups that in the sixties were able to combine their efforts in protest of the Vietnam war, racism and civil rights issues…(have been) politically destabilized and undermined."

Several days before my interview with Horowitz, I had read a story in the news about some Japanese scientists who had genetically engineered a laboratory mouse which glowed green in the dark. This they had done by combining a gene from an ordinary mouse with that of a luminous jellyfish—ostensibly in the interest of cancer research. In *Emerging Viruses*, of course, Horowitz had documented the early work of Dr. Robert Gallo and others in recombining various animal viruses, creating monster, new superviruses—also ostensibly in the interest of cancer research.

"I can only wonder what sort of virulent life forms may be released on this planet if this keeps going," I commented now, inquiring of Horowitz whether he thought there should be a ban on further such genetic experimentation.

It's a "very, very sincere argument," he replied, that it's not the technology *itself* which poses the greatest potential for harm, but rather the manner in which humans make *use* of it.

"It's not the fact that we can clone things, but what will some people do with that technology that is gonna determine the outcome. Given the fact that we have lived through and are still paying for and suffering, even horrifyingly, today from cancers related to nuclear waste and environmental contaminants—all of this, by the way, which the bankers and the military-industrial complex have created—you see, these people that created this technology, and have control over it, don't *think* like normal human beings.

"They don't have the ethics and morals and values and love and belonging types of motivations. Their motivation—well first of all they have all the money. They own the money of the planet. I'm sure you're well aware, you've probably interviewed people who'll tell you, that the United States government is bankrupt, and all the other countries are bankrupt, and it's just the international banking community that are keeping things going...

"And so to put cloning in these people's hands, regardless of whether you could create wonderful things with cloning or not—you see that these people are not going to create things for the benefit of humanity, because if they were then we would be able to have no pollution in California. We would have been already, for two decades at least, driving electrical cars that are very low cost and utilizable. We would have tires that would last forever, because they've had that technology since World War II. Everything, instead of being designed for obsolescence, would be designed to serve humanity. And we don't have that.

"And so for me, to be asked, 'Would you prefer to just not have cloning go on at all?' I'd have to say, 'You know, given the fact that we're dealing with these people, and who they are, and what their history is—I'd prefer not to have it...

"This thing called the New World Order is here. It's now the very beginning of it. It's been evolving for centuries, of course. But ultimately it was the contemporary evolution I point out to, in the book *Emerging Viruses: AIDS and Ebola*, (that includes) Henry Kissinger's 1950s Harvard Ph.D. thesis wherein he lays it out saying, 'We not only need to have population control, but we need to have ongoing small wars around the planet on a continuing basis to maintain the economic alignment of the superpowers.'

"And because this is the Rockefeller-led military-medical-industrial complex, it's not just military wars that they're talking about today. They can kill just as many people and make even more money off of biological wars—like 'the war on cancer,' 'the war on infectious diseases,' 'the war against AIDS,' 'the war on drugs,'"—useless wars, he added, which serve only to fund the "coffers of the oligarchy, the shadow governors."

Horowitz, was dressed in jeans and a t-shirt as we spoke. The t-shirt plugged the title of his book, *Emerging Viruses*. He is trim, fit, fortyish, with an almost boyish grin. Occasionally when the grin relaxed, however, I thought I detected a note of bitterness in his tone. His book had been out for a year. Yet the facts surrounding the U.S. government's probable involvement in creating AIDS remained largely hidden from the public.

Ironically, there was at that time—summer of 1997—a billboard advertising campaign that was much in evidence throughout the city of San Francisco. The billboards urged people to "get hip" and be tested and vaccinated for hepatitis B. This was almost grotesquely ironic given the documentation in *Emerging Viruses* linking hepatitis B vaccine trials to the outbreak of AIDS in the gay community in the late 1970s.

"It's like *Village of the Damned*," he quipped of the models pictured in the billboards, who stared out at the passing traffic with eyes of jaundiced yellow.

While Horowitz thus far had managed to escape being called a "chirpy New Ager," he had, nonetheless, endured his share of being ridiculed in the corporate media. One TV newsmagazine in particular "claimed I was the 'new cult leader.' You know when the folks in San Diego allegedly committed suicide—there was a 'cult madness' which struck the American news media for over a week and a half, two weeks," said Horowitz.

"All of a sudden now (on this program) what did you see? You saw my name associated with the 'looney conspiracy theory,' that the AIDS virus was man made, and they showed my name as being kind of like the 'new cult leader' of all the lunatics who believe the AIDS virus and Ebola viruses were man made."

We laughed about that for a while. Horowitz was to deliver a talk that night at San Francisco's Fort Mason Center. He was scheduled to go straight to the talk immediately upon leaving SFLR, with scarcely even time for dinner in between.

"Time and time again, night after night," he said, "when I present programs like I'm gonna present tonight...I ask the same question: 'How many of you in this audience know people in your immediate or extended circle of friends or family, who over the past several years have developed strange, immune-system-related disorders, or bizarre cancers with no family history?' And you know what, Richard? Every night between 40 and 60 percent of the audience have their hands raised. And if you think this is not the time that's described, that's prophesized, by virtually every prophet that has walked this planet, as the time when the plagues come—this conversation most people could never imagine, and would never want to contemplate.

"But I have a tremendous spiritual faith. And when I go back and I read the Book of Revelation, what do I see who wins in the end? I *know* who wins in the end. And it is those who have eyes to see, ears to hear what we are talking about today—*those* are the people who tune themselves to a spiritual faith, and will be receiving the guidance that is necessary to move through this very, very dark.

"Because that is another incredible thing I ask my audience, and did so again last night: 'How many of you out there over the past year have experienced absolutely, totally strange, but wonderful, serendipitous, experiences, and intuitive growth and capabilities, that now (you feel) you are being somewhat guided by higher powers—spiritual forces—angels—maybe God—to make the connections, to learn the risks, to understand what you need to do next to safeguard yourself and your family?' It is astonishing. I see, again, 40-50 percent of the hands in the audience go up. And I say, 'Praise God! Because this is unbelievable!

"Think about it—what is the New World Order? Right now it's evolving because of fascists who would like to let you think they are 'socialists.' That's who's running this, and that's clearly Satan, in my opinion...If you were God and you wanted to create what's called 'Yisrael'—that means peace on Earth, when the lion lies down with the lamb—how would you go about doing that when you see humanity that ultimately only learns through pain and suffering?

"First of all, as a good God, you probably wouldn't go inflict infectious diseases and inoculate people with viruses that cause epidemics of cancer. But—you also created Satan. And you also have a plan laid out. You would have Satan do it. And that's exactly what Satan and his forces are doing—these things. Ultimately in the New World Order agenda what are they talking about? One world government, one world economy, one world religion, no more international boundaries—now that, to me, sounds wonderful! It sounds like what Christ would have wanted—love, peace on Earth. Okay?"

"Except," I replied, "they're setting up a system wherein a few people will be in control of it all."

"Yes! That's what I'm talking about. That's where it's twisted. That's Satan's work. But, you see, here's my hope, and this is why I'm celebrating—and I *am* celebrating—because I know that Satan has low self-esteem. I know that Satan is a fallen angel. I know that Satan hates himself. I know that Satan's followers are the same way.

"I know one of the reasons why I'm still alive speaking to you right now is because the Rothschilds are at war with the Rockefellers. These people can't get along. What makes you think those thirteen families who are controlling everything are gonna have peace on Earth at the very end? They're gonna be cutting each other's throats, cause that's what they'r already starting to do. I know at the very end when they have their New World Order agenda and all this comes to pass—guess what? They're gonna self-destruct. Cause that's their nature!

"And I know—and this is what I expect—I don't have all the answers, but I trust that this is what is going to happen: at some point, and it's probably going to be sooner than later, God will come—the 'forces of light,' if you will, if you're a New Ager—the 'Messiah,' if you're a Christian or a Jew or a Muslim—will come during these end times, and he will pull the rug out from under Satan, and what is going on, and what is past, will ultimately be turned right into what God has planned.

"I'm celebrating folks!" he exclaimed. "To me this is a magnificent time to live in history, and I am extremely optimistic!"

"Suppose divine intervention *doesn't* come?" I asked. "Do you think there will ever be a cure for these 'Emerging new viruses'?"

"I believe there already *is* a cure. There's numerous cures. Look at what the cures are! Whoever the FDA (Federal Food and Drug Administration) is targeting—is what the cures are!" he said.

"They're targeting the oxygenation therapists. They're targeting the electromagnetic therapists. They're targeting the botanicals. They're targeting the vitamins," Horowitz said. "All of these people are the ones that they're targeting. Why would they (the government) do that? Why not leave well enough alone? These people are doing wonderful things, if somebody wants freedom of choice, if we're living in a democratic society, and you wanna take an herb or a vitamin. It's an absolute *insult to the intelligence*, when you read in *USA Today*, that they're all up in arms about one or two cases of deaths associated with a toxic overdose. You can overdose with water. You can kill yourself by drinking three, four, five gallons of water...

"Again, I have firm faith, and I look in the Book of Revelation, and I read and it says right in there, at the very end of times when we are saved—whether you wanna be saved by the light in the New Age sense, or saved by Jesus in the Christian sense. The fact of the matter is, again, people have been divided and conquered.

"The only reason we can't see each other as brothers and sisters, various races and religions, is because the same disinformation barons have divided and conquered us. But ultimately you see what it says (in the Book of Revelation) is that once again the crystal clear waters will flow through our rivers and streams whose banks will be lined by the trees, whose *leaves* bring about the healing of the nations. You see?"

A colleague, said Horowitz, had phoned him "several weeks ago," and said, "'You know what we found? We have excellent results using olive leaf extracts on HIV/AIDS patients.'

"And then," he continued, "there's Alim Muhammad (Dr. Abdul Alim Muhammad, minister of health of the Nation of Islam) doing alpha-interferon studies, another natural botanical treatment. And there are studies all over the world ongoing."

While the "time of the plagues" may have arrived, he added, so had hope for healing.

"It's in the botanicals. It's in our leaves," he said.

***

With our interview at an end, Horowitz left me pondering "the great war" he had talked about. There was a lot about his particular version of theology that made a whole lot of sense to me—despite its similarities to Christian fundamentalism. Maybe, in fact, that was where the Christian fundamentalists had gone wrong in some respects—they had simply "gotten it twisted."

Many times over the years, of course, I had thought of the fight between Food Not Bombs and the city government in San Francisco as essentially a struggle between good and evil—and throughout much of that struggle (with the exception of the '95 Gathering) evil seemed always to be winning. What can you make of the confiscation of food and blankets from poor people, other than to say it's just evil?

But it wasn't just the evil of San Francisco's corrupt politicians. They were just small, two-bit players on the chessboard. And if the fight between Food Not Bombs and the city of San Francisco was a struggle between good and evil, so too, I would assert, is the struggle for the airwaves. Will the airwaves remain the sole property of a small number of "fascists who would like to let you think they are socialists," as Horowitz phrased it? If so, the future will be forever in doubt. Democratization of the airwaves is the crucial battlefield, is the key to winning all the other struggles.

Think about what has been allowed to happen while the airwaves have been under the control of a tiny few: the bombs falling on Iraq and, in 1999, Yugoslavia; the death squads in Central America; the genocide in East Timor; and then there was the evil of the death penalty; the imprisonment of innocent people; the destruction of the rainforests; the countless slaughters and massacres occurring wherever and whenever somebody thought they could turn a profit or win favor from a global superpower.

Yes, there was all that. But my weekly program on AIDS—and in particular my interviews with Horowitz and Cantwell—had given me something else to think about as well, something more personal: Was I, as a poor and/or homeless person in America, a member of a population group which had been targeted for genocide? The thought does not exactly fill one with a sense of peace or contentment.

With all this evil in the world, there must be some sort of evil "force," some kind of Grand Imperial Wizard from which all this evil energy emanates—otherwise, why would so many people, including, perhaps, those who control the airwaves, be in service to it? And if there were such a force for evil, did it not also stand to reason (call it a desperate hope) that there was also a countervailing force for good?

I had been an agnostic most of my life, but at some point during my long struggles with Food Not Bombs, I had—I'm not sure when, but somewhere along the way—begun to believe in God—not the white, male, patriarchal God of Christianity, but just a force of life, a "power greater than any and all of us," as MOVE's Ramona Africa put it—a Creator, if you will.

Many other things Ramona Africa had said had stayed in my mind as well, and a lot of them jibed with what Horowitz had said regarding the attacks on anyone choosing to practice medicine or live their lives in a manner not prescribed by the system. Ramona was interviewed by SFLR DJ Kiilu Nyasha. During that interview she discussed the founding of MOVE in the early 1970s, and how much of what the group did was seen as "crazy" at the time.

But today—everything that MOVE was talking about and doing has now become accepted and, you know, the thing to be involved in. For example, MOVE had demonstrations—long sustained demonstrations—in support of animal life and animal rights. We demonstrated at the zoo, at the circus, against the enslavement and abuse of animals. Today, animal rights is a very popular issue...we also composted, or what *today* they call composting. We did that back in 1970, and people thought we were nasty and throwing garbage in the back yard...

It was such things as that, and our long demonstrations that we did, that caused the police, caused the system, to start attacking us. What happened is the *information* that MOVE was putting out, to let people know what this system was doing to them, and not only to humans, but to *all* life—we talked to people about the importance of health, and what this government was allowing industry to do to our water, our soil, our air. We were talking about how our youth were being misdirected and why we were determined to keep our young people at home with us and to teach them ourselves, rather than turn them over to our enemy—whether they be called a teacher in the school system, or whatever—the system is our enemy and we were not gonna charge them with educating our children...

We were healthy. We did not believe in hospitals and going to hospitals unless, you know, it was a life-threatening situation. MOVE women had babies naturally, at home, without doctors, medicine, midwives—any of that. It set an example for people—an example that the system could not afford to have set in people's minds.

Eleven MOVE members were killed on May 13, 1985, when the city of Philadelphia dropped a bomb on the group's house. The death toll included five children as well as MOVE founder John Africa. Ramona and a small child she was able to carry to safety were the only survivors of the bombing. The explosion set off a fire, which turned an entire Philadelphia neighborhood into a raging inferno, destroying 61 homes. Predictably, not a single Philadelphia official was ever charged with a crime. In 1996—11 years after the fact—Ramona Africa was awarded one million dollars by a court. Given the suffering through which she had been, and the burn scars on her body, the amount was paltry

Ramona believes the city of Philadelphia was deliberately trying to murder MOVE members. She describes her survival of the bombing as "miraculous," and she adds that she "can't even explain it to this day except to say there is a force, a power greater than any and all of us, that wanted myself alive."

***

The MOVE bombing has been compared with the government attack on the Branch Davidians in Waco, Texas in 1993. Both were examples of brute military force run amok. Yet some folks have questioned why the militias and other "patriot" groups didn't become as outraged over the burning alive of black people in Philadelphia, as they apparently did over the incineration of white people in Waco.

Leaving aside issues of race and racism for a moment, it is abundantly clear that rich people in this country are never—*ever*—treated in the manner in which MOVE and the Branch Davidians were treated. If, as the saying goes, "we're all in the same boat," white "separatist" organizations (which the Branch Davidians assuredly were *not*—the group, in addition to whites, also had black, Hispanic and Filipino members [21]), as well as black "nationalist" ones, ought to look around and check out who else is occupying seats on that lifeboat: while there may be faces of many different colors, one thing we all share in common is we are all poor. The MOVE bombing becomes doubly ironic considering that the city of Philadelphia at the time was under an African-American mayor, Wilson Goode. Goode's ordering of the bombing is a profound indication that the *real* issue, the more salient factor, dividing Americans these days is that of class, not race.

Given the fact that there are only a relatively small number of extremely wealthy people on the planet, and that they are hogging up just about all the wealth and natural resources for themselves, *class* solidarity makes a whole lot more sense in the 21st century than *racial* solidarity. This is something which the rich have always known instinctively, yet which the poor forever have difficulty learning. However, the case of Goode can perhaps offer us a lesson. In the end it was his *class*—and not his *race*—to whom Goode remained loyal.

***

During her visit with us, Ramona Africa also talked about the MOVE organization's friendship with Pennsylvania death row journalist Mumia Abu Jamal. The latter's writings, in fact, are filled with frequent references to MOVE, and to the 1985 bombing, while Abu Jamal has upon numerous occasions professed himself an adherent to the religious teachings of MOVE founder John Africa.

While the state of Pennsylvania has confined Abu Jamal's body to a cell, it has not succeeded in caging his mind or his spirit. The power of his writings and spoken commentaries, plus the story of his struggle, have deeply and profoundly affected millions. That such a man should be awaiting execution in America has been taken by people throughout Europe and much of the rest of the world as proof of the corruption of our judicial system. Corporate-owned media outlets such as the *Philadelphia Inquirer* have attempted to explain away this global outpouring of support by attributing it to "the near fanatical drive by the radicals of MOVE" as well as to the "energy" springing from "opponents of the death penalty who have sought an appealing symbol." [22] The truth, of course, is far different, for it goes much deeper.

Abu Jamal, indeed, has become a symbol, but to far more than just death penalty opponents. As the "voice of the voiceless," he has become a symbol for the very voiceless and oppressed themselves, for all who fear tyranny and hate injustice, and who must claw for their daily survival, and fight for a blanket or a piece of concrete on which to sleep at night in peace.

Perhaps more so than anything else, have people the world over marveled at Abu Jamal's willingness to continue speaking out against the system—even while the system holds his fate in its hands. Such is a courage seldom matched in contemporary society, and which has only surfaced at rare moments in the course of human history.

As this is being written, Abu Jamal continues to await execution by the State of Pennsylvania.

Religion, as Mumia Abu Jamal writes, "has often been less a force for liberation than a tool of oppression," while God equally "has been utilized to justify more human evil than has Satan." Nonetheless, Abu Jamal, in his book, *Death Blossoms*, calls for a "religion of Life" for a world "sliding down the slope of death." He says:

> Wherever one stands on the religion divide, it seems clear that a new, Life-affirming spirit needs expression as we end a century of carnage and move into a new millenium...
>
> If religion has had no impact on the shedding of...blood (has it done anything other than aid and abet it?) then why the need for it? How is it we have become so numbed, that we can pretend our faith is one of resurrection and life, when in reality it serves as one of the worst flash points of conflict in our culture of death?
>
> We live in a world of megadeath, on lands reddened by its original peoples, and saddened with the tears of unwilling captives. We missionize and maim, westernize and rob, torture and starve the same fellow humans around the globe. We kill each other, but not only that, we abuse the Earth, our common mother.
>
> We kill animals so as to be able to eat the dead. We make of our rivers, lakes and seas, cesspools of leaden lifelessness. We pillage and burn our forests, then seek to determine why the raped earth beneath them dries into desert. We violate the mountains and line our pocketbooks with the sum of their gleaming ore. We poison our air...
>
> Is our "God" the god of man alone? Can a Creator-God really bring into being creatures whose sole function is to serve the interests of themselves? Or is such belief really a smokescreen for our narrow schizophrenia, for the unholy greed that has brought our environment to the brink of destruction on which it now teeters? Put quite another

way, do alligators live solely to be skinned for expensive shoes and luggage? Don't they—doesn't every life form—have an intrinsic right to exist?

It is time to recognize, as do increasing awakened numbers, that the old split-brain approach that perceives man's existence in a vacuum dooms humankind, and species uncounted, to oblivion.

We are in need of a religion of Life that sees the world in more than merely utilitarian terms. A religion that reveres all life as valuable in itself; that sees Earth as an extension of self, and if wounded, as an injury to self. [23]

Out of death, it is said, comes rebirth and life—and out of the media of the Death Culture comes the micro radio movement. Perhaps the best thing I, as a broadcaster on a free radio station in America, can do, is to offer people, if they choose to take it, such a "religion of Life." Doubtless this might be a better use of the airwaves than to merely sell people things—and the alternative could well be a continued roll down that steep slope—downward, ever downward...into a planet-wide abyss of misery, death, homelessness and genocide.

Free the people; free the animals; free the Earth; free the airwaves.

Afterword

O n January 20, 2000, the Federal Communications Commission announced its long-awaited decision on micro radio. Citing the need to "provide opportunities for new voices to be heard," the FCC opened the door a small crack for some democratization of the airwaves. Under the new rules, the Commission would begin accepting license applications for stations of up to 100 watts in power. However, the number of licenses which could be granted—particularly in urban areas of the country—would be small.

While loosening third-adjacent channel protections, the FCC left second-adjacent standards in place (see Chapter 7). It further envisioned no expansion of the FM band such as that described in Chapter 7. The upshot of the ruling was that in most large cities the number of low-power stations granted licenses would be no more than a few—while in a small number of especially crowded urban centers there existed no hope for even one.

The ruling fell considerably short of heralding the sort of "golden age" of free speech for which micro radio advocates had hoped. It was also a far cry from the dream of former Rep. Lionell Van Deerlin, who had envisioned hundreds of new low-power stations per metropolitan area under the right regulatory structure. The problem, Van Deerlin had noted 23 years earlier, was not a technical problem, but a political one. Largely the same political obstacles remain today.

While the FCC had handed the micro radio movement but a pathetically small crumb, the National Association of Broadcasters, predictably, opposed even giving away this much. In this staunch opposition, the NAB was joined—again predictably—by National Public Radio (NPR). The lobbying effort which had begun the previous year with the introduction (discussed in Chapter 9) of the Oxley "Radio Broadcasting Preservation Act," intensified—and on April 13, 2000, the bill passed the House by a staggering 274-110.

FCC Chairman William Kennard estimated that the "Radio Broadcasting Preservation Act" would reduce by as much as 80 percent the number of stations which would otherwise be licensed under his new rules—that number of stations, as noted above, being miniscule to begin with.

Kennard also sharply upbraided the NAB in a manner reminiscent of his predecessor, Newton Minow, 39 years earlier.

"Why, amidst all this opportunity for broadcasters, have you chosen to muster your considerable resources to deny churches and schools and community-based organizations just a little piece of the broadcast pie?" the FCC chairman queried rhetorically in a speech at the NAB convention in April 2000.

Also taken to task was NPR. In a Washington statement issued shortly after passage of the Oxley Bill, Kennard said, "Special interests triumphed over community interests today. While the National Association of Broadcasters frequently opposes new competitive services, I'm particularly disappointed that National Public Radio joined with commercial interests to stifle greater diversity of voices on the airwaves."

Politics, it is often said, makes for strange bedfellows. If the match-up between the NAB and NPR was an unlikely one, the alliance developing on the other side was an even stranger one: for the first time in the micro radio movement's history, the chairman of the Federal Communications Commission and the nation's "pirates" were on the same side of an issue. Yet if it was a truce which had developed between these two warring factions, the truce was a shaky one at best.

Specifically, the FCC's micro radio "legalization" plan excludes "pirates"—those who "once violated or who are still violating Commission rules"—from obtaining licenses. Such people, Kennard and his fellow commissioners believed, had "character" problems.

Nonetheless America's "pirates" went to bat to save Kennard's plan to open up the airwaves—for all that plan's irrelevancies and inadequacies.

In late March 2000, San Francisco Liberation Radio DJs launched a two-week over-the-air campaign to defeat the Oxley Bill, urging listeners to phone local representatives in Congress. Though not enough ultimately to stop the bill's passage, San Francisco's two congressional representatives, Nancy Pelosi and Tom Lantos, *did*, nonetheless, join the minority of House members who voted against.

What will happen in the Senate remains unclear as of this writing. Even if Kennard's plan survives this and other likely challenges brought by corporate media barons—a rather large "if"—the nation will be a long way from broadcast utopia. The Kennard plan, as noted above, is wholly inadequate in terms of bringing anything even remotely resembling democracy of the airwaves.

An astute assessment of the whole situation was offered by by Tom Ness of Jam Rag Press.

"The (corporate) broadcasters have been very clever to ensure that the debate over community radio is about interference exclusively," said Ness, who was instrumental in winning support for micro radio from Congressman David Bonior and other politicians from the state of Michigan.

Ness added:

> But we express concern for fundamental issues of fairness regarding the allocation of public resources. Who has the right to use the public highways, sidewalks, parks, libraries—or airwaves? The FCC is obligated to institute a system of license allocation where the rights of one are not held superior to the rights of others, and where those rights are not held in perpetuity such that the rights of others are never recognized. Is there a problem with interference? I don't think so. But if the corporations really believe it, then fine—go off the air. Turn in your license, and make room for someone else. Why isn't *anyone* suggesting that the fellow who has made a killing off the public airwaves for the last 70 years *give someone else a turn?*

Ness' next words were perhaps especially salient.

> I cannot reserve a campground in the public parks for the rest of my life, nor can I reserve a lane on the highway exclusively for myself forever, nor can I take a book out of the library and keep it. So why should anyone expect a permanent spot on the dial? Thirteen thousand Americans asked for a broadcasting license in 1998, but were told there is no room.

Of all the many shortcomings of the FCC's new rules, perhaps one of the worst was the Commission's decision to give priority to implementation of digital broadcasting under the IBOC (In-Band-On-Channel) model. That plan, as discussed previously in Chapter 7, will result in the already-overcrowded FM dial becoming packed and crowded even further. This, as one may imagine, even further reduces the possibilities for new low-power stations to go on the air.

With all these many qualifications and restrictions, the noose around the neck of micro radio appeared to be growing tighter rather than looser under this new era of "legalization." And what was shaping up in Congress? Was it a "veto-proof" majority in favor of eliminating by 80 percent the number of low-power stations that might be licensed? Well, certainly the picture didn't look good. Said Ness, who in the year 2000 launched a Green Party bid for the U.S. Senate seat from Michigan:

> It (the FCC decision) requires that community radio be given second priority to IBOC digital radio. This could very well mean the elimination of the other 20 percent of potential stations...The question is not interference. The question is, *when will it ever be our turn*?

For all its failings, the FCC's "Report and Order" on micro radio is a remarkable document. At more than 70 pages in length, it encompasses an exhaustive, highly technical and detailed analysis of the interference issues. Its importance is that its engineering studies belied the interference objections raised by the NAB. It was important for another reason as well: for the first time it placed an agency of the federal government on record as recognizing the need for greater diversity on the airwaves.

Yet the NAB seemed determined, by hook or by crook, to kill it—and the NAB seemed to own the Congress. The latter had the authority to take the matter completely out of the FCC's hands. It could even disband the FCC if it chose to do so (a threat which had been made on at least one occasion).

In May 2000, Free Radio Berkeley founder Stephen Dunifer called for a micro radio "war council." The council, said Dunifer, would formulate a response to what essentially amounted to "an open declaration of war" by the NAB.

The battle, it would seem, was just beginning.

Notes on Preface

[1] Sanchez, Rene, "City of Tolerance Tires of Homeless," *Washington Post*, Nov. 28, 1998, p. A3

[2] Van Derbeken, Jaxon, "S.F. Throat-Slasher Stalking Homeless," *San Francisco Chronicle*, Nov. 7, 1998, p. 1

[3] Van Derbeken, Jaxon, "Slasher Suspect Arrested, Tells Cops He's Vampire," *San Francisco Chronicle*, Nov. 11, 1998, p. A17.

[4] Constantinou, Marianne, and Zamora, Jim Herron, "Police search for City slasher," *San Francisco Examiner*, Nov. 7, 1998, p. A1.

[5] Zamora, Jim Herron, and Fries, Jacob H., "Murder charge filed; police say man made series of bizarre claims," *San Francisco Examiner*, Nov. 11, 1998, p. A1.

[6] Constantinou and Zamora.

[7] "Car 54 Where Were You?" *Street Sheet*, a publication of the Coalition on Homelessness, San Francisco, Dec. 1998, p. 1

[8] Ibid.

[9] Ibid.

[10] Ibid.

[11] Revelation, chapter 18, verse 11 (King James Version). Interestingly, ancient Babylon was sacked by the Persians some 630 years *before* the Book of Revelation was written. Modern-day mainstream theologians argue that in prophesying the destruction of a "Babylon," the author of Revelation—John—was in reality referring to Rome, the dominant power on Earth during John's time. By Babylon, John *really* meant Rome. So today's mainstream Christians believe. Be that as it may, nowhere in the entire Book of Revelation is Rome mentioned by name. Moreover, the Roman empire did not fall in the space of "one hour."

[12] Matier & Ross, "Heaping Helping of Politics in Decision to go Easy on Pie Tossers," *San Francisco Chronicle,* Nov. 11, 1998, p. A17.

Notes on Chapter 1

[1] Clark, Ramsey, *The Fire This Time*, Thunder's Mouth Press, 1992, p. 135.

[2] Ibid.

[3] Ibid, p. 138.

[4] Ibid, p. 136-137.

[5] Sward, Susan and Sandelow, Mark, "Policing Protests is Costly, Agnos Says," *San Francisco Chronicle*, January 19, 1991, p.1.

[6] Brazil, Eric, "Biggest peace rally since '71," *San FranciscoExaminer*, Jan. 20, 1991, p. 1.

[7] *San Francisco Examiner*, Jan. 20, 1991, p. A-6.

[8] *San Francisco Bay Guardian*, editorial, p. 8, Nov. 27, 1996.

[9] Abu Jamal, Mumia, "Just Doing My Job," Nov. 18, 1996, <mumia@aol.com>

[10] *San Francisco Bay Guardian*, editorial, p. 17, Oct. 23, 1991.

[11] Baca, Kathleen, "Hongisto: Knock it off, folks," *San* Francisco Bay Guardian, May 6, 1992.

[12] *San Francisco Examiner*, "Soup in the Civic Center," May 10, 1991, p. A-20.

Notes on Chapter 2

[1] . Gould, Jay M. and Goldman, Benjamin A., *Deadly Deceit: Low Radiation, High Level Cover-up*, Four Walls Eight Windows press, New York, 1990, p. 146. Gould and Goldman also discuss the Chernobyl disaster and its deleterious effects on human and animal life even as far away as the United States.

[2] Gilardin, Maria, TUC Radio, Radio Democracy series, featuring Michael Parenti, pt. 5, "Lazy Law and Social Control."

[3] Barsamian, David, Alternative Radio, featuring Ward Churchill, "Fascism, the FBI and Native Americans: Historical and Current Perspectives."

[4] Alden, John R., *George Washington: A Biography*, Wings Books, 1995, New York, p. 48, 1984, Louisiana State University Press

[5] Simon, Harry, "Towns Without Pity: A Constitutional and Historical Analysis of Official Efforts to Drive Homeless Persons from American Cities," *Tulane Law Review*, vol. 66, no. 4, March 1992, p. 632-33

[6] Ibid, p. 676

[7] Casteneda, Ruben and Melillo, Wendy, "White House Shooting Proves Fatal," *Washington Post*, Dec. 22, 1994, p. C6

[8] Food Not Bombs Radio Network

[9] Casteneda and Melillo, p. C6

[10] Quoted in *Homelessness: A Sourcebook*, Fantasia, Rick, and Isserman, Maurice, Facts on File, p. 22

[11] Ibid, p. 2

[12] Ibid, p. 20

[13] Ibid, p. 22

[14] Ibid, p. 22

[15] Ibid, p. 23

[16] Ibid

[17] UN Development Program, Human Development Report," reported by Reuter Information Service, *Nando Times,* July 15, 1996

[18] Barnet, Richard J., and Cavanagh, John, *Global Dreams,*Simon and Schuster, 1994, p. 179

[19] Thurow, Lester, "How Much Inequality can a Democracy Take?" *New York Times Magazine*, Nov. 19, 1995, p. 78

[20] Ibid

[21] Ibid

[22] Gordon, Bill, "Volunteers Arrested at S.F. Food Giveaway," *San Francisco Chronicle*, Aug. 16, 1988, p. A3

[23] Gordon, Bill, "29 Arrested at Food Giveaway in the Haight," San Francisco Chronicle, Aug. 30, 1988

[24] "Unacceptable Behavior," *Haight Ashbury Newspaper*, Sept. 1988

[25] Halstuk, Martin, "Cease-Fire Declared in Free Food War,"
San Francisco Chronicle, Sept. 10, 1988

[26] Gordon, Bill, "Legal Puzzle in Food Giveaway," *San Francisco Chronicle,* Sept 7, 1988, p. A5.

[27] Ibid

Notes on Chapter 3

[1] Hyde, Henry, *Forfeiting Our Property Rights*, Cato Institute, 1995, p. 77

[2] Ibid, p. 36

[3] Webb, Gary, "The Forfeiture Racket," *The San Jose Mercury News*, Aug. 29, 1993, p. 1

[4] Following a deluge of criticism at the national level, the "Dark Alliance" series was later denounced in a column by *Mercury News* executive editor Jerry Ceppos. Webb stuck by his story.

[5] Webb, "A Cop's Eye-View," *San Jose Mercury News*, Aug. 30, 1993, p. 8a

[6] Ibid

[7] Parenti, Christian, "Street Combat," *The San Francisco Bay Guardian,* April 9, 1997, p. 24

[8] Parenti, "Less than lethal weapons or nightmares from Marvel Comics?" *San Francisco Bay Guardian,* April 9, 1997, p.27.

[9] Ginsburg, Marsha, Marine, Craig, "Many S.F. looters got caught in feeding frenzy," *San Francisco Examiner*, May 10, 1992, p.A-11

[10] Jacot, B.L., and Collier, D.M.B., *Marconi—Master of Space*, Hutchinson & Co., London, 1935, p. 148

Notes on Chapter 4

[1] The views of Matrix held by Bay Area religious leaders were largely summed up in an op-ed piece by the Rev. Phil Lawson, president of the Northern California Ecumenical Council. The piece appeared in the *San Francisco Chronicle* (see "Drop Matrix Program and Help Homeless," *San Francisco Chronicle*, Jan. 4, 1994, p. A17). In the arena of city politics, the chief opponent of Matrix was Supervisor Angela Alioto, who initiated resolutions within the Board of Supervisors condemning the program and granting amnesty to thousands of homeless people issued citations under it (see "Mayor Appeals to Matrix Backers," *San Francisco Chronicle*, Dec. 6, 1993, p. A17, and Saunders, Debra J., "Civility Not Crime," *San Francisco Chronicle*, Sept. 10, 1993, p. B8).

[2] "Homeless: SF Mayor Says Roundups Will Be Expanded," *San Francisco Chronicle*, Oct. 7, 1993, p. A15.

[3] See Saunders, *San Francisco Chronicle*, columns for Sept. 10, Nov. 17 and Dec. 27, 1993.

[4] Saunders, Debra J., "Continuum of Cadging," *San Francisco Chronicle*, Dec. 27, 1993, p. A18.

[5] Saunders, "Civility Not Crime," *San Francisco Chronicle*, Sept. 10, 1993, p. B8.

[6] Dann, Jonathan, and Lyon, Greg, "The Truth About the City's Homeless," *San Francisco Chronicle*, June 24, 1993, p. A23.

[7] Salter, Stephanie, "A desperate need for public toilets in San Francisco," *San Francisco Examiner*, Sept. 5, 1993, p. A19.

[8] Ibid.

[9] Lynch, April, and King, John, "How Homeless Avoid the Long Arm of the Law, *San Francisco Chronicle*, Sept. 24, 1993, p. A4.

[10] Saunders, Debra J., "Civility Not Crime," *San Francisco Chronicle*, Sept. 10, 1993, p. B8.

[11] "Homeless: More Street People in Berkeley," *San Francisco Chronicle*, Sept. 10, 1993, p. A17.

[12] Lynch, April, and King, John, "How Homeless Avoid Long Arm of the Law," Ibid.

[13] Lynch, April, and Johnson, Clarence, "S.F. Police Confiscate Homeless People's Carts," *San Francisco Chronicle*, Nov. 13, 1993, p. A17.

[14] Ibid.

[15] Saunders, Debra J. "Matrix A La Cart," *San Francisco Chronicle*, Sept. 24, 1993, p. A24.

[16] Lynch and Johnson.

[17] "Homeless: Jordan Extends Crackdown," *San Francisco Chronicle,* Sept. 1, 1993, p. 13.

[18] Ibid.

[19] Morse, Rob, "San Francisco, the city that knows chow lines," *San Francisco Examiner,* Aug. 31, 1988, p. A-3.

[20] Saunders, "Civility Not Crime."

[21] Ibid.

[22] Ibid.

[23] Ibid.

[24] "Police Commission Hears ACLU Complaint," *San Francisco Chronicle,* Oct. 21, 1993, p. A20.

[25] Ibid.

[26] Zane, Maitland, "Sleeping Homeless Man Set Ablaze on S.F. Sidewalk," *San Francisco Chronicle,* Nov. 17, 1993, p. A1.

[27] Ibid.

[28] Ibid.

[29] Morse, Rob, "The burning of a man," *San Francisco Examiner,* Nov. 18, 1993, p.A3.

[30] Ibid.

[31] For information on the Folsom Street Hotel fire, hotel owner Chhotubhai B. Patel, and a history of the code violations cited against Patel's hotels, see: Hatfield, Larry D., and Glover, Malcom, "S.F. hotel fire kills 1; cops call it homicide," *San Francisco Examiner*, Sept. 8, 1993, p. A1; Gordon, Rachel, and Zamora, Jim Herron, "S.F. had cited hotel where fire killed man," *San Francisco Examiner*, Sept. 9, 1993, p. A1; Carlsen, William, "Jordan's Homeless Plan Questioned," *San Francisco Chronicle,* Sept. 9, 1993, p. A15; Wallace, Bill, and Walker, Thaai, "Owner of hotel that burned often cited," *San Francisco Chronicle,* Sept. 10, 1993, p. A1; and Wallace, Bill, "S.F. Housing for Homeless Violates Codes," *San Francisco Chronicle*, Sept. 16, 1993, p. A1.

[32] Hatfield and Glover.

[33] Ibid.

[34] Wallace and Walker.

[35] Wallace, Bill, *San Francisco Chronicle,* Sept. 16, 1993, p. A1.

[36] Gordon and Zamora, p. A16.

Notes on Chapter 5

[1] Weiner, Allan H., with McCormick, Anita Louise, *Access to the Airwaves*, Loompanics Unlimited, 1997, Port Townsend, WA., p. 154.

[2] Ibid, p. 156.

[3] Ibid, p. 158.

Notes on Chapter 6

Where not footnoted, the comments of Dennis Cunningham, Vincent Giacomini, Catherine Marsh, Francis Pinnock, Sarge Holtzman, Andrew Rose, Hugh Mejia, Jess Mejia and Brian Wickenheiser were gleaned from personal interviews with the author. Interviews with Marsh and Jones were also conducted in the studio of San Francisco Liberation Radio in 1994 by Jo Swanson.

[1] *Keith McHenry and Andrea McHenry v. Mayor Art Agnos et. al.* 927377, San Francisco Superior Court, "Fourth Amended Complaint for Damages and Injunctive Relief..." Cunningham, Dennis, Holtzman, Sarge, Baker, Randy; Jan. 20, 1992, p. 12.

[2] Ibid, p. 13.

[3] Ibid, p. 14.

[4] Ibid, p. 16

[5] *People of the State of California ex rel...v. Food Not Bombs, 908-581,* San Francisco Superior Court, "Reporter's transcript of proceedings, July 21, 1989, p. 16

[6] Annual Report, 1996, Office of the City Attorney, City and County of San Francisco, p. 8.

[7] Keith McHenry.

[8] Case 927377, "Memorandum of points and authorities in support of defendants' demurrer to plaintiff's third amended complaint," p. 1, Nov. 18, 1991

[9] "Renne Bungles a Big One," *San Francisco Bay Guardian,* Nov. 27, 1996, p. 8.

[10] "The Latest PG&E Stonewall," *San Francisco Bay Guardian,* Jan 31, 1996, p. 6.

[11] Ibid.

[12] Ibid.

[13] "Renne Bungles a Big One."

[14] Blackwell, Savannah, "Lights Out: City Takes a Dive in Multi-million-dollar Suit to Keep PG&E Out of Presidio," *San Francisco Bay Guardian,* Nov. 27, 1996, p. 10.

[15] "Renne Bungles a Big One."

[16] Blackwell, p.10.

[17] "Renne Bungles a Big One," p. 8.

[18] *People of the State of California ex rel v. Food Not Bombs*, San Francisco Superior Court, 908581, "Complaint for Permanent Injunction, Preliminary Injunction, and Temporary Restraining Order," July 14, 1989, p. 6 & 7.

[19] Case 908581, "Memorandum of points and authorities in support of application for temporary restraining order to show cause re. preliminary injunction," p. 5 & 6.

[20] Case 908581, "Memorandum of points and authorities in opposition to motion for temporary restraining order and order to show cause re. preliminary injunction," July 21, 1989, p. 2.

[21] Ibid, p. 3.

[22] Ibid, p. 3.

[23] Ibid, p. 3 & 4.

[24] Ibid, p. 4 & 5.

[25] Ibid, p. 5 & 6

[26] Ibid, p. 8

[27] Case 908581, San Francisco Superior Court, "Reporter's transcript of proceedings," July 21, 1989, p. 1.

[28] Ibid, p. 2.

[29] Ibid, p. 13

[30] Ibid, p. 14

[31] Ibid, p. 16

[32] Ibid, p. 18.

[33] Ibid, p. 19

[34] 2533*McHenry v. Agnos*, U.S. Dist. Ct., N. California, C-89-2655 VRW, "Transcript of Proceedings," Aug. 7, 1990, p. 17.

[35] Ibid, p. 25.

[36] Ibid, p. 26.

[37] Ibid, p. 26.

[38] Ibid, p. 15.

[39] Case 927377, "Reply memorandum of points and authorities in support of defendants' demurrer to plaintiffs' third amended complaint and motion to strike portions of complaint," Nov. 25, 1991, p. 5.

[40] Case 927377, "Memorandum of points and authorities in support of defendants' demurrer to plaintiffs' third amended complaint," Nov. 18, 1991, p. 8.

[41] *McHenry v. Renne*, U.S. Dist. Ct., N. Cal., C-92-1154 VRW, "Memorandum of Points and Authorities in Reply to Plaintiffs' Opposition to Defendants' motion to dismiss," feb. 12, 1993, p. 2, 8.

[42] Case 927377, "Reply memorandum of points and authorities," Nov. 25, 1991, p. 6.

[43] Case C-92-1154 VRW, "Order," Oct. 8, 1992, p. 7.

[44] *McHenry v. Agnos*, 92-15123, U.S. Ct. of Appeals, 9th Cir., Jan 19, 1993, p. 6.

[45] Ibid, p. 6.

[46] *People v. Wickenheirser,* 1471594, San Francisco Municipal Ct. "Supplemental declaration of Frances Pinnock," May 2, 1994, p. 1

[47] Ibid, exhibit B, see also "Rear Window: Does Franks with Frank Break the Law?" *SF Weekly,* Dec. 4, 1991, p. 8.

[48] WTVU, Channel 2, Oakland, September , 1993, Channel 2 reporter Rita Williams.

[49] Sward, Susan, "S.F. Police Investigating One of their Own," *San Francsisco Chronicle,* Nov. 24, 1993, p. A15.

[50] Ibid.

[51] Ibid.

[52] *Marsh v. Johnson,* 958298, "Petition Prohibiting Harassment," San Francsiico Superior Court, Feb. 2, 1994.

[53] *Price v. Lindo,* 958293, *Marsh v. Johnson,* 958298, "Orders to Show Cause," San Francisco Superior Court, Arata.

[54] Roemer, John, "Eccentric Jordan Aide Stalked Homeless Activist for Months," *SF Weekly,* Jan. 12, 1994, p. 7.

[55] Ibid.

[56] Ibid.

[57] Ibid.

[58] Incident Report Form, San Francisco Police Department, 940634404, May 13, 1994.

[59] Ibid, p. 5. For a review of Frank Jordan's remarks on KSFO see chapter 4.

[60] Nadel was later murdered in his own night club. No arrest was ever made in the case.

[61] Psalms, chapter 10, verses 2 & 3.

[62] Cockburn, Alexander, "Beat the Devil," *The Nation,* July 4, 1994, p. 7.

[63] Roemer, John, "Bizarre Court Record of Keith McHenry's Accuser," *SF Weekly,* Aug. 3, 1994.

Notes on Chapter 7

[1] Ballinger's speech was recorded by Free Radio Berkeley. It is also printed in its entirety in *Seizing the Airwaves*, Stephen Dunifer, Ron Sakolsky, AK Press, 1998, p. 25

[2] *United States of America vs. Stephen Dunifer*, C-94-3542-CW, U.S. Dist. Ct., N. Cal. "Memorandum of Amici Curiae in support of Plaintiff's motion for summary judgement," Dec. 6, 1995, p. 1.

[3] Barnouw, Erik, *A History of Broadcasting in the United States-Volume 1*," Oxford University Press, 1966, p. 120

[4] Kendrick, Alexander, *Prime Time: The Life of Edward R. Murrow*, Little Brown, 1969, p. 180.

[5] "The New Code for the Broadcasting Industry," *New York Times*, July 12, 1939, p. 7.

[6] Kendrick, p. 153, 155.

[7] Wyman, David S., *The Abandonment of the Jews: America and the Holocaust 1941-1945*, Pantheon Books, 1984, p. 322.

[8] "Excerpts from Speech by Minow," *New York Times*, May 10, 1961, p. 91.

[9] Ibid.

[10] Ibid.

[11] "Minow's Criticism of TV Scored by Stanton and Robert Sarnoff," *New York Times*, Dec. 8, 1961, p. 1.

[12] Ibid.

[13] Ibid.

[14] Ibid.

[15] Wicker, Tom, "Lobbies Defeat Reform for the FCC," *New York Times*, June 18, 1961, p. 6E.

[16] Ibid.

[17] Ibid.

[18] Kendrick, p. 453.

[19] Ibid, p. 453-454

[20] Spector, Bert, "A Clash of Cultures: The Smothers Brothers vs. CBS Television," from *American History/American Television: Interpreting the Video Past*, O'Connor, John E., Frederick Ungar Publishing, New York, 1983, p. 161.

[21] Ibid, p. 167.

[22] Ibid, p. 165.

[23] Ibid, p. 163.

[24] Ibid, p. 178.

[25] Ibid

[26] Ibid, p. 180.

[27] Ibid.

[28] Ibid, p. 181

[29] Ibid, p. 166

[30] Ibid, p. 165

[31] William Paley's rather sybaritic surroundings at the top of the CBS skyscraper at 51 W. 52 St., New York, were described in detail by his former news director, Fred W. Friendly in *Due to Circumstances Beyond Our*

Control: "Paley's suite, facing east and north on the thirty-fifth floor, is furnished with antiques and Picasso, Dubuffet and Rouault originals. The central piece of furniture is a round leather-topped desk which was once a Paris gaming table. On one wall hang the microphones of all the original CBS radio stations, and an authentic cigar-store Indian (a gift of Mrs. Paley) stands in a corner as a nostalgic reminder of Paley's early days with La Palina cigars. Paley is a gourmet who often stops at The Ground Floor, a restaurant in the CBS lobby, to sample a dish before ascending to his private dining room, where the poulet au pot and lamb stew are specialties of the house." Friendly also informs us that Paley's wartime occupations had included assisting the U.S. military in "psychological warfare." Vintage Books, 1967, p. xvii, xxiii.

[32] Fishbein, Leslie, "Roots: Docudrama and the Interpretation of History," from *American History/American Television: Interpreting the Video Past*, O'Connor, John E., Frederick Ungar Publishing, New York, 1983, p. 280.

[33] Ibid, p. 281.

[34] Ibid.

[35] Brown, Les, "New Band for Radio Proposed," *New York Times*, March 31, 1977, p. C-28.

[36] Ibid.

[37] Stuart, Reginald, "Fairness Doctrine Assailed by FCC," *New York Times*, Aug. 8, 1985, p. 1.

[38] Ibid.

[39] Safire, William, "Stop the Giveaway," *New York Times,* Jan. 4, 1996, p. A21.

[40] Ibid.

[41] Wexler, Celia Viggo, "Channeling Influence: The Broadcast Lobby and the $70 Billion Free Ride," prepared for Common Cause. Available from: Common Cause, 1250 Connecticut Ave. N.W., Washington D.C. 20036.

[42] Safire.

[43] Wexler.

[44] Reply comments in the matter of micro station Radio Broadcast Service petition for rule-making, RM-9208, RM-9242, RM-9246, Before the Federal Communications Commission, National Lawyers Guild Committee on Democratic Communications.

[45] A-Infos Radio Project/Radio 4 All, http://www.radio4all.org

[46] Wexler.

[47] Ibid.

[48] NAB web page, www.nab.org/STATEMENTS/s2497.htm

[49] C-94-3542 CW, National Association of Broadcasters, "Memorandum of Amici Curiae in support of Plaintiff's motion for summary judgement," p. 2.

[50] Barnouw, vol. 1, p. 218.

[51] C-94-3542-CW, Affidavit of Robert McChesney.

[52] C-94-3542 CW, NAB amicus brief.

[53] Ibid.

[54] Reply comments, RM-9208, RM-9242, RM-9246, Harold Hallikainen, Before the Federal Communications Commission, July 22, 1998.

[55] Ibid.

[56] Ibid

[57] C-94-3542 CW NAB amicus brief.

[58] Hiken, Louis, "In the matter of Stephen Dunifer; NAL/Acct. No. 315SF0050; SF-93-1355," Before the Federal Communications Commission, June 28, 1993.

[59] Ibid.

[60] Hiken, Louis, "Application for Review," Before the Federal Communications Commission in the matter of Stephen Dunifer, NAL/Acct. No. 315SF0050.

[61] C-94-3542 CW NAB amicus brief.

[62] C-94-3542 CW, "Transcript of Proceedings," Jan. 20, 1995, p. 6.

[63] Ibid, p. 11.

[64] Ibid, p. 19.

[65] Ibid, p. 21.

[66] Ibid, p. 23.

[67] Ibid, p. 27.

[68] Reply comments, National Lawyers Guild Committee on Democratic Communications, RM-9208, RM-9242, RM-9246, Before the Federal Communications Commission.

[69] Statement of National Public Radio in the matter of RM-9208 and RM-9242, before the Federal Communications Commission, April 27, 1998.

[70] Comments of Harold Hallikainen, before the Federal Communications Commission, RM-9208, RM-9242, April 22, 1998.

[71] Dunifer, Stephen, Sakolsky, Ron, *Seizing the Airwaves*, AK Press, 1998, p. 27.

[72] Barnouw, vol. 2, p. 44.

Notes on Chapter 8

[1] "The Death Penalty in 1997: Year End Report," Death Penalty Information Center, 1320 18th St., NW, Washington DC, 20036

[2] Ibid.

[3] Deiter, Richard C., "Killing for Votes: The Dangers of Politicizing the Death Penalty Process," Death Penalty Information Center, p. 1.

[4] Ibid, p. 2-3.

[5] Ibid, p. 4.

[6] Ibid.

[7] Ibid, p. 13.

[8] Ibid, p. 20.

[9] Ibid, p. 23.

[10] Ibid.

[11] Eisnitz, Gail, *Slaughterhouse: The Shocking Story of Greed, Neglect, and Inhumane Treatment Inside the U.S. Meat Industry*, Prometheus Books, 1997, Amherst, New York, p. 155.

[12] Ibid, p. 20.

[13] Ibid, p. 29.

[14] Ibid, p. 84.

[15] Ibid, p. 87.

[16] Ibid, p. 291.

[17] Ibid, p. 62.

[18] Ibid, p. 167.

[19] Ibid, p. 170.

[20] Ibid, p. 39.

[21] Ibid, p. 52.

[22] Ibid, p. 213.

[23] Ibid, p. 214.

[24] "In the Circuit for the Thirteenth Judicial Circuit, in and for Hillsborough County, Florida, General Civil Division," Fox BGH suit Website, http://www.foxBGHsuit.com/complaint.htm, (10-27-98).

[25] Horowitz, Leonard, *Emerging Viruses: AIDS and Ebola: Nature, Accident or Intentional*, Tetrahedron Publishing Group, Rockport, MA, 1996, p. 6-7. From *Department of Defense Appropriations for 1970*, hearings before a Subcommittee of the Committee on Appropriations, House of Representatives, 91st Congress, part 5 research, Development, Test, and Evaluation, Dept. of the Army, Tuesday July 1, 1969, U.S. Government Printing Office, p. 79, 129. See also Cantwell, Alan, *Queer Blood: The Secret AIDS Genocide Plot*, Aires Rising Press, Los Angeles, 1993, p. 32-33.

[26] Horowitz, p. 62.

[27] Ibid, p. 63.

[28] Ibid, p. 64.

[29] Cantwell, Alan, *Queer Blood: The Secret AIDS Genocide Plot*, Aires Rising Press, Los Angeles, 1993, p. 17.

[30] Ibid, p. 18.

[31] Horowitz, p. 244. For information on New York University Medical Center as a biological warfare defense contractor, see p. 78.

[32] Barney, Gerald O. et al., *Global 2000 Report to the President,* a report prepared by the Council on Environmental Quality and the Department of State, Penguin Books, vol I, p. 3, p. 1.

[33] Ibid, p. 4.

[34] Ibid, letter of transmittal.

[35] Ehrlich, Paul R., Erlich, Anne H., *The Population Explosion*, Simon and Schuster, 1990, p. 9.

[36] Hartman, Betsy, *Reproductive Rights and Wrongs*, Harper and Row, 1987, p. 67.

[37] Ibid, p. 122.

[38] Ibid, p. 111.

[39] Ibid, p. 120.

[40] Ibid.

[41] Ibid, p. x.

[42] Ibid, p. 27.

[43] Ehrlich, Paul, and Ehrlich, Anne, p. 147.

[44] Gilbert, David, "Tracking the *Real* Genocide," *Covert Action Quarterly,* fall 1996, p. 57.

[45] Ibid, p. 60.

[46] Ibid, p. 64.

[47] Ibid, p. 60.

[48] Stolberg, Sheryl Gay, "Clinton Decides Not to Finance Needle Exchange Program," *New York Times*, April 21, 1998, p. A-1.

[49] Ibid.

[50] Ibid.

[51] The forest protestors brought suit against Humbolt County law enforcement officials who dabbed pepper spray into their eyes. Unfortunately for the protestors, they drew as judge in their case Vaughn Walker, who seized the opportunity to enhance his notorious reputation. Walker threw the forest protestors' case out of court after a jury had deadlocked on the issue.

[52] Sward, Susan, "Coroner Doubts Brutality in Suspect's Death," *San Francisco Chronicle*, June 17, 1995, p. A1.

[53] Ibid.

[54] Ibid.

[55] Sward, "Cop Shoe Could Have Bruised Man Who Died in Custody," *San Francisco Chronicle*, June 22, 1995, p. A17.

[56] Sward, "S.F. Coroner Blames Drug, Not Cops In Custody Death," *San Francisco Chronicle*, June 30, 1995, p. A20.

[57] Sward, "Police Probe of Suspect's Death Called a Cover-Up," *San Francisco Chronicle*, June 30, 1995, p. A25.

[58] Gaura, Marcia Alicia, "Clues to Police Custody Deaths," *San Francisco Chronicle*, April 8, 1996, p. A1.

[59] Ibid.

[60] Ibid.

[61] Sward, "Coroner Doubts Brutality..."

[62] "Rights for All--USA Report," Amnesty International's campaign on the USA, Amnesty International
Website: http://www.rightsforall-usa.org/info/report/index.htm.

[63] Abu Jamal, Mumia, "A Quiet and Deadly Violence," Antifa Info Bulletin, Oct. 15, 1998. The quote is taken from *Violence: Reflections on a National Epidemic*, by Dr. James Gilligan, New York, Vintage, 1996, p. 192.

[64] Ibid.

[65] Ibid.

Notes on Chapter 9

The quotes in this chapter from Ramona Africa, Dr. Len Horowitz, and the Food Not Bombs 1995 International Gathering, come from SFLR interview tapes.

[1] Delgado, Ray, et. al., "S.F. cops put on alert for UN protests," *San Francisco Examiner*, June 26, 1995, p. A8.

[2] "A Statement by Nobel Peace Laureates," *San Francisco Chronicle*, June 26, 1995, p. A19.

[3] *For the Record*, program number 177, "Update on German Control of American Publishing," by Dave Emory. Dave Emory tapes are available from Spitfire, Box 1179 Ben Lomand, CA 95005. See also, Paul Manning, *Martin Borman: Nazi in Exile*, Lyles-Stuart, 1981

[4] Dave Emory's *For the Record*, program number 145, "Paul Manning's Correspondence with Other Journalists."

[5] "Notice of Proposed Rule Making" Federal Communications Commission, MM Docket No. 99-25, Creation of a Low Power Radio Service, http://www.fcc.gov/Bureaus/Mass_Media/Notices/1999/fcc99006.txt

[6] Ibid.

[7] Ibid.

[8] Labaton, Stephen, "FCC Offers Low Power FM Stations, *New York Times*, Jan. 29, 1999, p. C1.

[9] Ibid.

[10]   NAB   press   release,   NAB   Website: http://www.nab.org/PressRel/Releases/4499.ASP , downloaded 12-30-99

[11] Ibid

[12] Oxley Website: http://www.house.gov/oxley/s9911f.htm, dowloaded on 12-30-99.

[13] Beat Radio Website: http://www.beatworld.com/,

[14] Ibid

[15] Franck, Peter, "The Fight For Micro Radio Enters the Home Stretch: Paradise or Paradise Lost?", Committee on Democratic Communications Website, http://www.nlgcdc.org/articles/paradise_lost.html, .

[16] Ibid

[17] Ibid.

[18] From the web page of the Kensington Welfare Rights Union, <http://www/libertynet.org/KWRU> dec. 15, 1998.

[19] Boulware, Jack, "Up a Tree Still?" *SF Weekly*, Nov. 11—17, 1998, p. 18.

[20] Ibid, p. 18, quoting from *Time* magazine, May 11, 1998.

[21] See *Why Waco*, by James Tabor and Eugene Gallegher, University of California Press, 1995.

[22] Kaufman, Marc, et. al., "Abu—Jamal's long climb to a world stage," *Philadelphia Inquirer*, from web site of Philadelphia Online, <http://interactive.phillynews.com/talk—show/mumia> Dec. 9, 1998.

[23] Abu Jamal, Mumia, *Death Blossoms*, Plough Publishing House, Farmington, PA, p. 35—37.

Index

San Francisco Liberation Radio T-Shirts

San Francisco Liberation Radio
93.7 FM

$20
Small, Medium, Large, or X-tra Large
In Black or Red

Order Form

Name: _____

Address:_____

_____

Phone: _____

Email:_____

Size _____ Color _____

Shipping and Handling
First shirt...$4.50
Each additional shirt.................................. 2.25

Send me _____ shirt (s)   Amount enclosed:_____

Make checks payable to: **Friends of San Francisco Liberation Radio**

Visit the San Francisco Liberation Radio Website at
liberationradio.org